THE POLITICS OF KNOWLEDGE IN INCLUSIVE DEVELOPMENT AND INNOVATION

This book develops an integrated perspective on the practices and politics of making knowledge work in inclusive development and innovation.

While debates about development and innovation commonly appeal to the authority of academic researchers, many current approaches emphasise the plurality of actors with relevant expertise for addressing livelihood challenges. Adopting an action-oriented and reflexive approach, this volume explores the variety of ways in which knowledge works, paying particular attention to dilemmas and controversies. The six parts of the book address the complex interplay of knowledge and politics, starting with the need for knowledge integration in the first part and decolonial perspectives on the politics of knowledge integration in the second part. The following three parts focus on the practices of inclusive development and innovation through three major themes of learning for transformative change, evidence, and digitisation. The final part of the book addresses the governance of knowledge and innovation in the light of political struggles about inclusivity.

Exploring conceptual and practical themes through case studies from the Global North and South, this book will be of great interest to students, scholars, and practitioners researching and working in development studies, epistemology, innovation studies, science and technology studies, and sustainability studies more broadly.

David Ludwig is associate professor in the Knowledge, Technology and Innovation (KTI) group at Wageningen University and the principal investigator of the 'Global Epistemologies and Ontologies' (GEOS) project. He works at the intersection of philosophy and social studies of science with a focus on global negotiations of knowledge diversity.

Birgit Boogaard is postdoc in the Knowledge, Technology and Innovation (KTI) group at Wageningen University, where she teaches courses on African philosophy as well as on social justice, technology, and development. She has an interdisciplinary PhD in Rural Sociology and Animal Science from Wageningen University.

Phil Macnaghten is professor in the Knowledge, Technology and Innovation (KTI) group at Wageningen University. His PhD is from Exeter and he has held appointments at Lancaster, Durham and Campinas before joining Wageningen in 2015. His research background is in science and technology studies (STS) and sociology.

Cees Leeuwis is professor in the Knowledge, Technology and Innovation (KTI) group at Wageningen University. He studies processes of socio-technical innovation and transformation, inter- and transdisciplinary collaboration, research for development policy, the functioning of innovation support systems, and the role of communication, extension, and brokers therein.

Pathways to Sustainability Series

This book series addresses core challenges around linking science and technology and environmental sustainability with poverty reduction and social justice. It is based on the work of the Social, Technological and Environmental Pathways to Sustainability (STEPS) Centre, a major investment of the UK Economic and Social Research Council (ESRC). The STEPS Centre brings together researchers at the Institute of Development Studies (IDS) and SPRU (Science Policy Research Unit) at the University of Sussex with a set of partner institutions in Africa, Asia and Latin America.

Series Editors:
Ian Scoones and Andy Stirling
STEPS Centre at the University of Sussex

Editorial Advisory Board:
Steve Bass, Wiebe E. Bijker, Victor Galaz, Wenzel Geissler, Katherine Homewood, Sheila Jasanoff, Melissa Leach, Colin McInnes, Suman Sahai, Andrew Scott

Titles in this series include:

Transformative Pathways to Sustainability
Learning Across Disciplines, Cultures and Contexts
The Pathways Network

The Politics of Knowledge in Inclusive Development and Innovation
Edited by David Ludwig, Birgit Boogaard, Phil Macnaghten and Cees Leeuwis

Building Innovation Capabilities for Sustainable Industrialisation
Renewable Electrification in Developing Economies
Edited by Rasmus Lema, Margrethe Holm Andersen, Rebecca Hanlin and Charles Nzila

For more information about this series, please visit: www.routledge.com/Pathways-to-Sustainability/book-series/ECPSS

THE POLITICS
OF KNOWLEDGE
IN INCLUSIVE
DEVELOPMENT AND
INNOVATION

Edited by David Ludwig, Birgit Boogaard,
Phil Macnaghten, and Cees Leeuwis

Routledge
Taylor & Francis Group

LONDON AND NEW YORK

from Routledge

First published 2022
by Routledge
2 Park Square, Milton Park, Abingdon, Oxon OX14 4RN

and by Routledge
605 Third Avenue, New York, NY 10158

Routledge is an imprint of the Taylor & Francis Group, an informa business

British Library Cataloguing-in-Publication Data
A catalogue record for this book is available from the British Library

Library of Congress Cataloging-in-Publication Data
A catalog record has been requested for this book

ISBN: 978-0-367-63229-8 (hbk)
ISBN: 978-0-367-63225-0 (pbk)
ISBN: 978-1-003-11252-5 (ebk)

DOI: 10.4324/9781003112525

Typeset in Bembo
by Deanta Global Publishing Services, Chennai, India

The ebook and paperback cover image and the illustrations with each chapter were created by Birgit Boogaard, and appear with her permission.
© Birgit Boogaard

CONTENTS

ILLUSTRATIONS

Figures

Tables

CONTRIBUTORS

Conny Almekinders is Associate Professor at the Knowledge, Technology and Innovation group, Department of Social Sciences of Wageningen University. She obtained a PhD from the same university, based on her potato crop physiology research. She has been working for many years on issues related to seed systems and farmers' management of plant genetic resources, including participatory plant breeding and in situ conservation. A major topic in her current research work is the social differentiated use and adoption of agricultural technologies. Currently she collaborates with CGIAR Research Programs and enjoys an NWO grant to support this work.

Christine Alokit is a communication and extension scientist who coordinates Plantwise and other CABI activities in Uganda. She has worked with a wide range of stakeholders across the East African community on projects including working directly with smallholder farmers; institutional capacity building; commercialisation of agricultural technologies; and market development for smallholder farmers. She holds an MSc in agricultural development economics from the University of Reading, UK.

Andy Bonaventure Nyamekye is a Digital Capacity Development Specialist at the CSI Division of the United Nations Food and Agriculture Organization, Rome, Italy. His research borders on technology, innovation, and sustainability governance. Andy is interested in investigating how developing countries can leverage technology and innovation in solving societal problems. As a multi-disciplinary researcher, his recent works employ multiple lenses such as responsible innovation, adaptive decision-making, adaptive governance, and informational governance.

Birgit Boogaard is a lecturer at the Knowledge, Technology and Innovation Group at Wageningen University, where she teaches courses on African philosophy as well as on social justice, technology, and development. She has an interdisciplinary PhD in Rural Sociology and Animal Science from Wageningen University. As postdoctoral researcher at the International Livestock Research Institute she lived two years in Mozambique. Her interests include African philosophy, agricultural development, food system transformation, international development, epistemic justice, indigenous knowledge, and transformative dialogues.

Margreet van der Burg is a senior scholar in gender studies/history, since 2002 mandated to teach and research gender in food, agricultural, and rural research and development at Wageningen University; since 2019 attached to KTI. From her early work she became known as the Dutch pioneer in agriculture-related history from a women's and gender perspective. Her recent work aims at better understanding and tackling of international gender issues and approaches, both from an intersectional perspective as well as by interconnecting them with their often hidden or forgotten historical roots.

Katarzyna Cieslik is a research associate at the Department of Geography, University of Cambridge, specialising in Development Studies. Her work focuses on the interaction among livelihoods, environment, and technology, and their implications for sustainable development. Her most recent research examines the role of information and communication technology (ICT) in facilitating collective management of public bads in subsistence contexts. Katarzyna pursues an actively international and interdisciplinary research agenda: she has been a visiting researcher at Yale's Agrarian Studies Center, USA, and a postdoctoral fellow at the University of Wageningen, the Netherlands. She has conducted multi-disciplinary research in Ethiopia, Nepal, Kyrgyzstan, Peru, Colombia, Nigeria, and Burundi.

Sarah Cummings is a researcher at the Knowledge, Technology and Innovation (KTI) group, Wageningen University & Research, with the NWO-WOTRO NL-CGIAR project 'Improving the effectiveness of public-private partnerships within the CGIAR: knowledge sharing for learning and impact.' With a background in development practice and consultancy related to knowledge management, Sarah's research focuses on the private sector and knowledge inequalities in global development. An active member of the Knowledge Management for Development (KM4dev) community, she founded with colleagues the community-led, open access Knowledge Management for Development Journal in 2005.

Elias Damtew obtained a PhD from the Knowledge, Technology and Innovation (KTI) group, Wageningen University, Netherlands. His research interest lies in understanding innovation and social-technological change processes in agri-food, socio-ecological systems. He previously worked as a Research Associate at the International Livestock Research Institute, Ethiopia. He had also been a PhD fellow at the International Potato Center and a visiting scholar at the School of Integrative Plant Sciences of Cornell University, USA. Elias is currently working as an external researcher at KTI studying theory and practices of scaling of agri-food innovations in CGIAR-RTB funded projects in Africa and Latin America.

Art Dewulf (1975) obtained a PhD in Organisational Psychology (Leuven, 2006) and is Personal Professor of 'Sensemaking and decision-making in policy processes' at the Public Administration and Policy group (Wageningen University). He studies complex problems of natural resource governance with a focus on interactive processes of sensemaking and decision-making in water and climate governance.

Šarūnas Jomantas has recently concluded Development and Rural Innovation (MSc) studies at the University of Wageningen. Next to a long-standing career in Information and Communication Technologies, his academic interests range from Tropical Ecosystems and Anthropology of lowland South America to Lacanian Psychoanalysis. Sarunas's multi-disciplinary interests have led him to north-eastern Brazil where he studied and learned from native societies seeking to comprehend the best means of solving some of the locally pertinent natural resource management issues.

Laurens Klerkx is Professor of Agrifood Innovation and Transition at the Knowledge, Technology and Innovation Group of Wageningen University, The Netherlands, of which he has been part since 2002. He works on various topics such as implementation of transdisciplinary science and co-innovation approaches, digital agriculture innovation, transformative innovation in agri-food systems, and innovation system development and innovation policy. He is editor-in-chief of the *Journal of Agricultural Education and Extension*, editor of *Agricultural Systems* and associate editor of *Agronomy for Sustainable Development*.

Cees Leeuwis is professor of Knowledge, Technology and Innovation at Wageningen University. He studies processes of socio-technical innovation and transformation, inter- and transdisciplinary collaboration, research for development policy, the functioning of innovation support systems and the role of communication, extension, and brokers therein. Eventually, these efforts are geared towards making processes of technical and social innovation more responsible, responsive, and democratic. He has published widely about these themes in the context of societal domains such as sustainable agriculture, natural resources management, and poverty related diseases.

Rico Lie (PhD 2000, Catholic University of Brussels) is a social anthropologist working at the research group Knowledge, Technology and Innovation, Wageningen University, The Netherlands. He previously worked at the University of Brussels in Belgium and the Universities of Nijmegen and Leiden in The Netherlands. At Wageningen University he is an assistant professor in international communication with an interest in the areas of development communication and intercultural communication.

Diana E. Lopez is a Doctoral Fellow at the Knowledge, Technology & Innovation Group, Wageningen University. Her research interests include gender, knowledge diversity, multispecies engagements, sustainable livelihoods and responsible business, innovation & research. She has worked on these issues particularly in Mexico, Brazil, Sweden, Egypt, Ethiopia, and the Philippines. Diana's current research embraces a feminist ethos of care that seeks to advance propositive ideas and practices towards a genuine commitment to gender equality in the agricultural development sector.

David Ludwig is an associate professor in Knowledge, Technology, and Innovation (KTI) Group of Wageningen University and the principal investigator of the 'Global Epistemologies and Ontologies' (GEOS) project. He works at the intersection of philosophy and social studies of science with a focus on global negotiations of knowledge diversity. Recent publications have focused on local biological knowledge of indigenous and peasant communities, on contested categories such as 'race' in scientific practice, and on questions of global justice in science policy.

Harro Maat studies technological practices and social dynamics in agriculture, food, and health. His research is on the History of Technology, Science and Technology Studies (STS) and Political Agronomy. He has studied past and contemporary farmers' practices in a variety of Asian and African countries. One focus of his recent work is the circulation of food crops and crop varieties within and between continents. Through a combination of historical reconstruction and analysis of current farming practices, new insights, and perspectives are developed on the agency of farmers in the global circulation of crop innovations.

Phil Macnaghten is a Professor in the Knowledge, Technology and Innovation (KTI) group at Wageningen University. His PhD is from Exeter and he has held appointments at Lancaster, Durham, and Campinas before joining Wageningen in 2015. His research background is in science and technology studies (STS) and sociology. He is author of *Contested Natures* and one of the leading scholars on responsible innovation and the governance of techno-visionary science. He has developed in-depth qualitative methodologies for researching controversial technologies which, in turn, have informed policy approaches to dialogue and public engagement. His current research focus is on responsible innovation, gene editing, and the politics of anticipation.

Mariette McCampbell is a PhD candidate at Wageningen University's Knowledge, Technology and Innovation group. She has a background in development and rural innovation, and participatory design and research processes. Previously, Mariette worked for the International Institute of Tropical Agriculture (IITA) and Bioversity International in Uganda and Rwanda. Her research interests are socio-technical interactions, and technology development and adoption processes. Mariette's PhD project studies the design, deployment, and consequences of digital technologies that promise to address complex problems in smallholder agriculture, especially in Africa.

Senna Middelveld is a postdoctoral researcher in the Just Editing? NWO project. Her PhD is from the University of Aberdeen, and her research background is in sociology and in science and technology studies. Her key research interests are in human-animal-nature-technology relations and in responsible research and innovation. Whose knowledge counts, when, where, how, and why is central in her work. Her current work focuses on the responsible use of gene-editing technology in livestock breeding.

Barbara van Mierlo is an associate professor, working as a sociologist in the Knowledge, Technology and Innovation Group of Wageningen University. Her research focuses on processes of transformative, systemic change towards sustainability and their intersection with everyday social practices. Being actively engaged in these processes, special interests include the significance and features of interactive learning and discursive strategies, the value of change-oriented evaluation, emergence of reflexivity, responsible innovation, and transdisciplinary collaboration. She developed the methodology of Reflexive Monitoring in Action (RMA), which has a wide international uptake in diverse domains.

Nyamwaya Munthali (PhD) is a postgraduate thesis supervisor at University of Lusaka. Her research interests that involve field work in Zambia, Tanzania, India, and Ghana relate to the social situatedness of (information and communication) technology, and the potential and role of strategic (digital) communication mechanisms to foster development as well as the pervasive effects of these innovations. She also has over eight years' experience working in the Zambian agriculture sector on mobile innovation, livelihood enhancing, and business and social enterprise development projects, specifically contributing as a project manager and contributing to the development and implementation of monitoring, evaluation, and communication systems.

Dorine E. van Norren is a diplomat, scientist, and artist. She is an associate researcher at Leiden University. She holds a master in international and Dutch law (1995) and a PhD in law and development studies (2017, Tilburg University and university of Amsterdam), titled 'Development as Service: A Happiness, Ubuntu and Buen Vivir interdisciplinary view of the Sustainable Development Goals.' She worked as a diplomat in Sri Lanka (Colombo, 1998–2001) and Turkey (Ankara, 2001–2005) and held several positions at the ministry of foreign affairs (Southern Africa, '96–'98, North America, 2005–2009, European Integration, 2013–2014, desks). She was seconded to the Ministry of Education, Culture and Science, as a coordinator for UNESCO (2016–2020). She is currently strategic advisor North and South America and the Caribbean at the Ministry of Foreign Affairs.

Faustina Obeng Adomaa is a PhD candidate at the Knowledge, Technology and Innovation group, Wageningen University, and a graduate research fellow at the International Institute of Tropical Agriculture (IITA), Ghana. She has a background in economic geography and rural development. Her research focuses on sustainability, governance mechanisms, and inclusiveness of global commodity chains. Faustina's current research is on public and private service delivery models in the global cocoa chain. She combines institutional theory and practice lens to understand institutional arrangements that enable or constraint inclusive service delivery fitting the complexities of the global cocoa commodity chain.

Willis Ochilo is the Plantwise regional coordinator for Africa, coordinating programme implementation in nine countries across sub-Saharan Africa. He previously led the roll-out of e-plant clinics. He has a PhD in entomology from the University of Nairobi, Kenya; and before joining CABI, he worked in agricultural research and mass rearing of beneficial insects and mites for biological control of crop pests.

Birgitta Oppong-Mensah coordinates Plantwise activities across West Africa, as well as the PRISE project in Ghana. She has worked extensively in rural communities, including training farmers in good agricultural practice and certification standards, and supporting farmer-based organisations through technical assistance and technology transfer. She also has experience in plant health extension planning and delivery. She holds an MSA in international development administration from Andrews University, USA.

Annemarie van Paassen is an associate professor at the Knowledge, Technology and Innovation group of Wageningen University. After a decade of practical work in gender, community development, and agricultural advisory projects in Africa, her academic research first focused on transdisciplinary research, (ict) tools and methods for social learning in natural resource management & agricultural innovation. Recent work aims more at understanding the institutional logics of actors, and how this influences the brokerage and partner collaboration for innovation and transformation; what it requires to make these processes more responsible and inclusive, ensuring resilient rural livelihoods and sustainable food systems.

Kelly Rijswijk has a background in rural innovation and innovation systems research. Currently, she is a researcher and a PhD candidate for the Knowledge, Technology and Innovation group at Wageningen University. Her PhD research focuses on the perceptions and understanding of various agricultural knowledge and innovation system actors of digital transformation, and their abilities to undertake such a process. Additionally Kelly is involved in various EU projects, studying the social and economic impact of digital transformation on agriculture and rural areas, as well as achieving gender equality and diversity in agricultural science organisations.

Dannie Romney is CABI's global director for Development, Communication and Extension (DCE). The DCE theme focuses on activities to facilitate or support 'research into use' and building capacity in countries to address key issues related to plant health, in some cases through training, but more often by addressing the way that different stakeholders interact. Her role is to provide strategic and technical leadership in this thematic area. She also worked at International Livestock Research Institute, including as acting theme leader for a research program in innovation systems. She has more than 30 years' experience in designing, implementing, and managing research and development projects.

Mirjam Schoonhoven-Speijer is finishing her PhD project at the Knowledge, Technology and Innovation (KTI) group of Wageningen University. The PhD is entitled 'Food security, governance and embedded coordination in value chains: understanding what makes market institutions in the Ugandan oilseed sector viable.' Her research focuses on making food available for consumers, including trade, wholesale, cooperatives, processors, and services such as finance, extension, transport, and storage. How are the institutions governing these practices reinforced by actors, within a certain context? She studies these subjects interdisciplinary, with a background in development studies, cultural anthropology, and sociology, using both qualitative and quantitative methods.

Esha Shah is a feminist scholar who believes that 'structures don't march in the streets' (slogan of the 1968 French student protests) only ideas do. Currently, she is interested in understanding (through research and teaching) how subjectivity (including emotions and affects) shapes modes of rationality, normativity, and objectivity in the making of knowledge. She employs anthropological and historical methods in all her research and increasingly uses sources from popular and oral culture and (auto)/biographical life-writings. She has recently published a monograph on *Affective History of the Gene* (Routledge, 2018) in which she has argued that intellectual paradigms 'affect' worlds.

Peter Shapland is a mid-career agricultural development advisor in the Sahel and a PhD candidate in the Knowledge, Technology, and Innovation Group at Wageningen University. He researches Community-Driven Development and participatory development approaches. Peter is interested in investigating how collective and individual aspirations are negotiated, brought to fruition, and evaluated within community development projects in rural Mali.

Sietze Vellema is an associate professor at the Knowledge, Technology and Innovation group, Wageningen University, and senior researcher at the Partnerships Resource Centre, Rotterdam School of Management. His interest is to understand why and how different actors collaborate in solving organisational, managerial, and technical problems related to inclusive development and sustainable food provision. He researches partnerships, certification, and institutional arrangements in global commodity chains and leads action-oriented research in the field of food and nutrition security, inclusive agribusiness and partnerships in Africa. With the Centre for Frugal Innovation in Africa he develops research on scarcity and resilience in food provisioning.

Hannah Wilson is finishing her master degree in Climate Studies, after completing her bachelors in Communication and Life Sciences at Wageningen University and Research. Her research focuses on the human-environment interactions, highlighting the importance of the social sciences within the natural domain. Currently she is working on her master thesis, which looks at the interactions and feedbacks within a social–ecological system in the Netherlands. This is linked to sustainable water management and enhancing the resilience of ecosystems in the face of climate change.

Margit van Wessel is an assistant professor at the Strategic Communication Chair Group at Wageningen University & Research, Netherlands. Her research focuses on communicative dimensions of governance, zooming in on questions of voice, representation, inclusion, and power. She has published on civil society advocacy and advocacy evaluation in the context of international development, relations, and interactions between government and citizens; policy processes and intra-organisational communication. Recent key publications have been in Development Policy Review, Evaluation, VOLUNTAS, World Development, and Journal of Environment and Development.

Loes Witteveen leads the research group Communication, Participation and Social Ecological Learning at Van Hall Larenstein University of Applied Sciences and also works with Knowledge, Technology, and Innovation (KTI) and Environmental Policy (ENP) of Wageningen University, the Netherlands. Her work relates to themes such as visual strategies and community art for social change, participatory and deliberative governance and is situated at interfaces of environmental and sustainable development, social sciences, and the arts. Current research links to social imaginaries and sustainable water management, access, inclusion, and affordance in emic approaches to user experience and user interface design and visual research methods.

Anna Wood is a crop health advisor at CABI's Swiss centre, working with farmers and partner organisations to develop and implement sustainable agricultural practices. Her background is in agriculture, integrated pest management, food security, and rural livelihoods programming. She holds an MSc in sustainable agriculture and rural development from the University of London and a PhD in insect physiology from the University of Bangor, Wales.

PREFACE

In 2012, I became chair of a newly formed 'Knowledge, Technology and Innovation' group in which scholars with diverse disciplinary backgrounds and historical roots joined forces. Members of the group originated from agricultural extension studies, communication and innovation sciences, and studies on technology and agrarian development. Together we set out to study, support, and intervene in processes of socio-technical innovation and transformation, with special attention to understanding the dynamics involved in the production, integration, and use of scientific and other knowledge in such processes. By tradition, the group has an international orientation, works together with practitioners, and is home to many PhD candidates from across the globe.

As a relatively new unit with a diverse composition, we had to do some soul searching to find and present our common identity to the outside world. In 2015, I initiated the development of a new MSc-level course for students of International Development, and—in hindsight—this served as a catalyst to discovering what we had in common. As a title for the course we chose 'Politics of Knowledge and Inclusive Innovation.' Over the years it became clear that a large variety of staff, postdocs, and PhD candidates felt comfortable presenting their work under this banner as guest lecturers in the course, and that it offered opportunities to discuss a richness of themes. Subsequently, the course experiences became the inspiration for initiating this book. As is further explained in the introductory chapter to this edited volume, we share the idea that knowledge is not a neutral phenomenon, but that it has a performative character, and is intricately intertwined with the pursuit of societal values and objectives. We recognise that there is always a variety of bodies of knowledge that can be deemed relevant to a situation, and that the knowledge which is eventually developed and used tends to be tied to strategic consideration and objectives. This implies that we cannot understand the role of knowledge in society (including academia) without paying attention to political dimensions, and that it is often pertinent to ask questions like 'what and whose knowledge counts and why?'

Clearly, such questions also apply to our own work. This book is written to inspire our current and future students, professional audiences, and academic peers. But whose knowledge and understanding is presented? Who has determined the language and terminology, and in whose discourse to we position ourselves? Admittedly, all permanent staff in the Knowledge, Technology and Innovation group have a European academic background, and despite a sensitivity to knowledge politics, it is likely that our perspectives are biased and affected by blind spots and privileges. In order to somehow anticipate and correct for these, we have applied a couple of strategies. We have deliberately invited our collaborators and current and former PhD candidates from across the world to become involved as author, co-author, and reviewer for the chapters in this book. Thus, we have secured diverse input and perspectives in its making. In the workshops that went along with the preparation of the book, we have also created spaces to discuss matters related to terminology and discourse. This because language and words—like knowledge—are performative, value-laden, and potentially political. Hence it is pertinent to reflect on questions like: What is it that terms like 'development,' 'donors,' or 'knowledge from below' may signify or perform? Is it legitimate to use such terms in our writings? Why and when? While we have thus organised a degree of reflexivity, we as editors have decided not to impose specific languages or theoretical perspectives, but, instead, allow for diversity in perspectives and terminology among authors. Undoubtedly, certain biases and blind spots will remain present in what the authors have written, and we are looking forward to learn about these through further discussion and interaction with students and scholars across the globe. In all, we hope this book serves the purpose of inspiring further dialogue and discussion on 'the politics of knowledge in inclusive development and innovation' in both science and practice.

Cees Leeuwis
Professor of Knowledge, Technology and Innovation
Wageningen University

MAKING KNOWLEDGE WORK DIFFERENTLY

The politics of knowledge in inclusive development and innovation

David Ludwig, Cees Leeuwis, Birgit K. Boogaard, and Phil Macnaghten

While knowledge has a privileged and even definitive role in addressing societal challenges and in realising sustainable development goals (SDGs), there is less clarity pertaining to 'what knowledge?', 'whose knowledge?', 'knowledge in what form?', and even 'why knowledge?'. This book invites students, scholars, and professionals to engage critically with such questions. Our starting point is the observation that 'knowledge for development' is a concept embraced by a plethora of actors and institutions ranging from United Nations organisations and global research establishments, to national governments and local non-governmental organisations. Similarly, critical perspectives on development also commonly emphasise the importance of knowledge by highlighting indigenous and local knowledge and epistemologies that have remained marginalised in dominant institutional discourses of knowledge for development.

Why is the concept of knowledge such a central issue in debates on development and change? And is all this attention justified? One could argue that there are other issues and concepts that merit more attention than knowledge when the goal is to foster sustainable development. What about creating a 'level playing field' in international relations and politics? What about preventing 'negative externalities' by establishing a fairer way of organising and regulating local and global markets? What about addressing the 'underlying causes' of violent conflict and abject poverty? While these issues are indeed of major concern, they are intertwined with the contested role of knowledge in development. First, there are questions about how and by whom concepts like 'sustainable development,' 'underlying causes,' 'negative externalities,' or 'abject poverty' are defined and given meaning in specific settings. Scientists from different disciplines approach such concepts differently, and, in addition, societal stakeholders and local communities think differently about such matters as well. For example, while a sociologist might argue that 'assimilation into market economies' constitutes the

DOI: 10.4324/9781003112525-101

root problem of a development project, an economist might regard 'insufficient liberalisation of markets' as the key obstacle, while a local community might propose the main constraining factor as a 'lack of political autonomy.' Second, it clearly matters which of these differential bodies of knowledge and understanding is used to guide the development of solutions and underpin development interventions. After all, interventions aimed at 'bypassing capitalism' are likely to be highly different from those aimed at 'liberalising markets' or 'fostering autonomy.'

The brief example above makes clear that knowledge is not a neutral phenomenon, but that it has a performative character (Richards, 1989; Leeuwis, 2013). In other words: the concepts and understandings we have about the world around us orient and allow us to discuss, negotiate, and work towards particular courses of action (or 'performances') that make a difference and that have 'positive' or 'negative' consequences, depending on what, and whose values and standards one considers. This performativity is not only inherent to the practical application of knowledge (e.g. the design of a technology or intervention to address a certain challenge), but also to the creation and production of knowledge. When researchers, for example, set out to develop knowledge about the management of agricultural pests and diseases, it makes a difference whether they ask: 'what chemical agent is most effective for killing a newly emerging harmful insect'? or 'what natural enemies and inter-cropping systems are most effective for controlling a newly emerging harmful insect'? While such research questions may be addressed empirically, the questions themselves are not neutral as they allow the development of very different future pathways of action (e.g. large agrochemical companies promoting chemical pesticides versus extension organisations promoting biological pest-control). Similarly, locations where such research are conducted (laboratory or field, large or small farms, highlands or lowlands) are likely to influence the answers and their relevance for particular segments in society. Even the methods used to collect data may have important implications: when data on crop damage are collected and analysed by farmers during field inspections as part of a citizen science project this is likely to give rise to different discussions and impacts in society than when data are collected by means of a drone equipped with sensors that can detect specific types of crop damage. This example demonstrates that the generation of knowledge too has performative implications, and thus that we cannot make a strict separation between the 'production' and the 'application' of knowledge. The type of knowledge generated and the process of knowledge production can have immediate societal consequences, and hence already includes forms of 'application' to and in society. This performativity not only applies—as the example illustrates—to research and knowledge production, but clearly also to processes that are linked more directly to making knowledge count in society, such as knowledge exchange, education, technology design, and efforts to integrate or bridge knowledge from different communities of actors.

The performative character of knowledge makes clear that knowledge is intricately intertwined with the politics and dynamics of inclusion and exclusion: which outcomes and values are being pursued wittingly or unwittingly through the generation, exchange, and application of knowledge, and which not? The phrase '*making knowledge work*' in the title of this chapter refers to this performative character and reflects that 'making knowledge' and 'putting knowledge to work' are two sides of the same coin. The addition '*differently*' suggests that there may be good reasons to alter and redirect the ways in which knowledge is made and put to work in the context of inclusive development, a view to which many of the authors in this book subscribe.

While questions about the production and application of knowledge are deeply entangled, they have often been separated into expert-driven approaches that employ linear and top-down models of development and innovation. According to such models, the production of knowledge falls primarily in the domain of science in the sense that academic experts produce knowledge that is later applied by innovators who take scientific insights into development practice. While such a simple division of labour between the production and the application of knowledge has been widely criticised in development and innovation studies (Briggs, 2005, Mawdsley et al., 2002, Sillitoe, 2007), it remains often implicitly assumed in the organisation of development projects that, we argue, are in need of novel perspectives on the dynamic interactions between the production and use of knowledge.

By integrating insights from epistemology and development practice, we highlight three dimensions that require reconsideration in the debate about knowledge for development. First, there is the domain of formalised knowledge production in academic research. Research for development is too often misunderstood through outdated clichés of value-freedom and context-independence. Rather, what needs to be analysed is its constant interaction with the performativity of knowledge, from the formulation of questions to the negotiation of research methods to the choice of field sites. A second dimension for reconsideration is the diversity of different forms of experiential, indigenous, local, and traditional knowledge, all beyond institutionalised academic knowledge, and all too often marginalised in the top-down organisation of development projects that appeal exclusively to the epistemic authority of academic research. Local communities are not only experts about local ecological and social dynamics, but their knowledge is also intertwined with practices, values, and worldviews that often articulate different perspectives on the co-production of knowledge and social orders. A third dimension of reconsideration is the interaction between different knowledge systems that requires methodological reflection about the opportunities of inclusive knowledge production as well as a political epistemology for the negotiation of knowledge and practice in the light of power differentials and colonial legacies.

These three dimensions of epistemological reflection interact in various ways with practices of development and innovation. Different epistemic resources shape the formulation of problems and research questions as discussed in Chapter 17 on demand articulation and Chapter 1 on transdisciplinarity. They also affect the use of concepts and framings as discussed in relation to notion of 'elite capture' in Chapter 5 and contestations of the very concept of 'development' as outlined in Chapter 6. Negotiations of knowledge shape methods of intervention and standards for evaluation as reflected in Chapter 10 on theories of change and Chapter 11 on evidence-based advocacy. Furthermore, the performative character of knowledge also creates heterogeneous spaces for intervention by pointing to different technologies (Chapters 12, 13, and 14), by creating novel spaces for dialogues (Chapters 3, 6, and 15), and by affecting styles of governing knowledge (Chapters 10, 11, 15, 16, and 17). In addition, a focus on the epistemological dimension in development and innovation requires reflexivity of involved actors as addressed by many chapters (Chapters 1, 2, 4, 5, 7, 8, and 9).

This landscape of different ecologies of knowledge demonstrates that knowledge is intricately intertwined with dynamics of inclusion and exclusion in development and innovation. Much has been written on the shortcomings of top-down and expert-driven approaches that marginalise the standpoints of local stakeholders in the negotiation of social-environment change and its global contestations (Boogaard, 2019, Leeuwis, 2004, Ludwig, 2016, Macnaghten, 2020). For example, a corpus of work has been led out of the UK STEPS (Social, Technological and Environmental Pathways to Sustainability) Centre that has argued for 'a more deliberate, equitable and accountable politics around progress towards sustainability' (Stirling, 2009: 9), that has developed a 'pathways approach' that embraces the dynamic interactions between social, technological, and ecological processes in pursuit of a more inclusive politics of sustainability (Leach, Scoones, and Stirling, 2010; Leach et al., 2012), including the role for grassroots innovation (Smith and Stirling, 2016, 2018), and that has analysed how innovation interacts with social, technological, and ecological systems to contribute to transitions at multiple levels (Ely et al., 2013).

While such critical interventions have contributed significantly to academic and policy debates on inclusive development and innovation as responses to these shortcomings (see also Gupta et al., 2015, Opola et al., 2020), this book focuses more explicitly on the applied and political epistemology that inclusivity demands and that is needed to make knowledge work *differently*. In developing such an approach towards the politics of knowledge, the chapters of this volume articulate an integrated research vision of 'doing and studying' that is equally reflexive about epistemological challenges and action-oriented in focusing on practices of making knowledge work. Parts I and II of the volume address fundamental methodological questions about epistemic diversity, the integration of different knowledge systems, and the tensions between them. Parts III to VI explore these issues through four core challenges for inclusive development and innovation in terms of transformative learning and dialogue (III), evidence in development (IV), technological change and digitalisation (V), and the governance of knowledge and innovation (VI). The six sections and 17 chapters are visualised in the illustration at the end of this chapter. In addition, each chapter includes one illustration with the main concepts or case studies of the chapter. The illustrations aim to enhance understanding of the themes and topics throughout the book and are especially suitable for educational purposes. All illustrations are brought together in Appendix I, which provides a visual summary of the entire book.

Knowledge integration: crossing epistemic boundaries

Inclusive development and innovation require an equally inclusive epistemology that recognises the standpoint diversity of stakeholders (Chapter 1) and their various forms of situated knowledge about local environments and practices. Middelveld, Maat, and Macnaghten (Chapter 2) highlight the diversity of local knowledge systems through three case studies of resistance against Caribbean slave-based plantation economies, sheep farming in Scotland, and public responses to genetically modified foods. While the cases draw from vastly different geographic, historical, and disciplinary contexts, they share a political positioning of 'knowledge from below' that challenges the domination of institutionalised forms of scientific knowledge in practice. Middelveld, Maat, and Macnaghten conclude by highlighting the need to configure knowledge as a plural concept that incorporates heterogeneous academic and non-academic practices and in which knowledges from below can resist dominant epistemologies and governance regimes.

Recognition of 'knowledge from below' raises complex epistemological questions about the relations between academic and non-academic knowledge systems and their prospects for integration. As Ludwig and Boogaard (Chapter 1) point out, knowledge integration has become widely endorsed and articulated through integrative frameworks that appeal to 'collaboration,' 'co-creation,' 'citizen science,' 'intercultural dialogue,' 'interdisciplinarity,' 'multi-stakeholder platforms,' 'participatory design,' 'participatory action research,' 'science society dialogue,' 'transdisciplinarity,' 'public engagement,' and 'open science' (p. 20). The burgeoning literature on knowledge integration reflects intertwined epistemological and social promises for development and innovation (Byskov, 2020, Ludwig and El Hani, 2020). Epistemologically, knowledge integration contributes to a diversified knowledge base that is sensitive to local contexts and mitigates blindspots and biases of an exclusive reliance on academic—and often Global North—expertise. Furthermore, knowledge integration also contributes to more equitable knowledge production that mitigates the marginalisation of stakeholders whose knowledge often remains excluded in development and innovation processes.

Many chapters of this book demonstrate how knowledge integration can simultaneously contribute to more effective and equitable development and innovation processes. For example, Jomantas et al. (Chapter 14) draw insights from the 'Plantwise' programme that supports smallholder farmers in addressing plant health issues. By embracing online chats as knowledge sharing platforms, the programme gathered diverse expertise and experiences while also bridging social gaps between stakeholders with otherwise isolated bodies of knowledge about plant diseases and pests. Lopez and Ludwig (Chapter 3) argue that criticism of narrow Eurocentric approaches to gender mainstreaming in development requires a transdisciplinary approach that brings together different sites of knowledge production about gender. Building on insights from feminist epistemology, Lopez and Ludwig examine three sites of knowledge production (institutional documents, gender specialists, and rural communities) about 'gender equality' in the CGIAR, an international agricultural development organisation. Their analysis suggests that engagement with different forms of situated knowledge creates opportunities for a transdisciplinary approach beyond narrow framings of gender mainstreaming that are commonly employed in the development industry.

Decolonising knowledge integration

Knowledge integration constitutes an important starting point for inclusive approaches in development and innovation that reflect on standpoint diversity in complex social-environmental contexts. However, knowledge integration does not provide a simple cure to the pathologies of expert-driven top-down approaches. As Ludwig and Boogaard (Chapter 1) point out, knowledge integration raises challenging questions: What kind of knowledge is integrated? For what purposes? Through what kind of frameworks? Without critical reflexivity about these issues, integration projects can reproduce hierarchies between stakeholders by treating local knowledge as an additional data source in frameworks that are already defined by the interests and methods of external researchers. These challenges motivate Ludwig and Boogaard's case for critical transdisciplinarity that reflects about the political structure of epistemic 'trading zones' and approaches them through intercultural and transformative dialogues.

Cummings, Munthali, and Shapland (Chapter 4) complement this critical perspective by turning to epistemic decolonisation both as a challenge and as an opportunity for the negotiation of knowledge in development projects. On the one hand, epistemic decolonisation challenges established practices of knowledge production to critically reflect on the reproduction of colonial hierarchies through institutional factors such as the organisation of the academic publishing system, disconnects between the ambitions of researchers and communities, the dominance of English as the language of academic exchange, unequal attributions of testimonial credibility, and the application of categories of difference such as ethnicity, gender, and race. Shapland, van Paassen, and Almekinders (Chapter 5) focus on 'elite capture' as a more detailed case study of how colonial legacies and hierarchies are reproduced in development projects. 'Elite capture' refers to an increasingly prominent concern in decentralised development projects about the roles of local elites in usurping benefits of development interventions. Using Bourdieu's concepts of reflexivity and symbolic power, the authors address the contested development of the notion of elite capture. They argue that dominant framings identify 'elite capture' exclusively as a problem of local elites while ignoring equally severe concerns about capture by NGOs and donors. As a result, appeals to 'elite capture' commonly legitimise top-down control of development resources and arbitrary power relations between international development institutions and rural communities in the Global South.

While epistemic decolonisation challenges simple narratives of harmonious knowledge integration, it also creates new opportunities for rethinking the relations between stakeholders and their standpoints. For example, Boogaard and van Norren (Chapter 6) focus on contested understandings of 'development' and their entanglements with underlying philosophies and practices. Focusing on *Buen Vivir* and *Ubuntu* as two prominent indigenous philosophies in the Global South, the authors show how heterogeneous epistemologies and ontologies can contribute to the articulation of alternative perspectives on inclusive development that can reimagine relations between humans and with nature beyond frameworks that are currently dominant in development projects. Rather than thinking of knowledge integration as the incorporation of easily digestible pieces of local knowledge, the cases of *Buen Vivir* and *Ubuntu* emphasise the need for deeper intercultural dialogues about different ways of relating knowledge and practice in the negotiation of development and innovation.

Learning for transformative change: creating space for diversity and dialogues

Inclusive knowledge production has the potential to transform development and innovation processes through the concerns and perspectives of stakeholders who commonly remain marginalised in narrow appeals to technological and scientific expertise. At the same time, knowledge integration is not a smooth process but creates tension between different standpoints in different positions of power. Successfully crossing epistemic boundaries therefore requires learning for transformative change which creates space for diversity and dialogue. This challenge is addressed by several chapters of this book (van Mierlo et al.; Lie, Boogaard, and Witteveen; van der Burg).

While these three chapters are rather different in their approach—from a systems approach in Chapter 7, to an educational approach in Chapter 8, and a historical approach in Chapter 9—the authors all argue for transformative change through learning processes. Lie, Boogaard, and Witteveen's chapter identifies design principles for diversity sensitive learning based on a study of three university courses: Intercultural Communication, African Philosophy, and Visual Research Methods. The authors argue that diversity sensitive learning can be fostered by designing courses through three principles of (1) situating knowledges, (2) enabling dialogical encounters, and (3) integrating experience and reflection. Van Mierlo et al. discuss how action-oriented research stimulates learning for transformative change through a discussion of three methodologies of Companion Modelling, Visual Problem Appraisal, and Reflexive Monitoring in Action. Van der Burg's chapter adopts a historical approach in discussing social segregation of agricultural education along gender and race in Ghana, the Netherlands, and the United States. Her discussion shows how 'adapted' agricultural education for marginalised groups often functioned to reinforce this marginalisation and argues for a transformative approach beyond segregated agricultural education.

Rather than being a smooth and straightforward process, all three chapters demonstrate that learning for transformative change is full of challenges. Many of these challenges emerge because the political dimension of knowledge in such learning processes is essential: knowledge and learning are not neutral or objective, but—as Paulo Freire already wrote many years ago—knowledge is political (1970). Learning for transformative change occurs when people learn about and from different or new perspectives and knowledge than their own. As such, learning processes recognises diversity in terms of people, content, and process (Chapter 8). This means that existing biases and 'blind spots' in learning processes—such as those that reinforce 'othering' (Chapter 8) or maintain structurally built-in gender and racial inequalities (Chapter 9)—should be made explicit and overcome. As such, reflection and learning are deeply interwoven, and learning processes for transformative change require critical reflection at an institutional as well as a personal level.

In this regard, Chapter 8 identifies critical reflection as one of the three design principles in diversity sensitive learning at Higher Education, while Chapter 7 emphasises the importance of reflexivity in action-oriented research, in other words, the ability to interact with and affect the institutional setting in which actors operate (Van Mierlo et al.). Dialogues are particularly suitable to reflect on one's thinking and acting, to learn from each other, and to open up for different perspectives and knowledges (Bohm, 2004, Kimmerle, 2012). As such, dialogues are essential to create space for diversity where transformative change can occur. Chapter 7 therefore endorses dialogues as requirement for good facilitation in action-oriented research, and Chapter 8 identifies dialogues as one of the three design principles for diversity sensitive learning.

Rethinking evidence in development

The notion of evidence is at the centre of many debates in the development sector that are driven by donor demands to use resources more effectively (McMichael et al., 2005, Storeng and Béhague, 2014). The imperative to provide evidence for effectiveness creates an important site for the negotiation of knowledge by raising questions about the nature of evidence and about development goals for which this evidence is produced. The chapters by Cieslik and Leeuwis (Chapter 10) and by Van Wessel (Chapter 11) discuss such questions in connection with the ex-ante and/or ex-post assessment of development interventions, with emphasis on relevant sources and methods for constructing evidence. Cieslik and Leeuwis discuss the widespread use of 'Theories of Change' (ToC), a development tool that many projects and programmes (have to) use in order to make plausible that and how proposed interventions will yield desired effects in a given context. While such ToC are typically formulated at the outset of a project, Cieslik and Leeuwis signal that, in the era of 'evidence-based policy,' there is an increasing trend, and even pressure, to demonstrate the validity of ToCs through Randomised Controlled Trials (RCT), and to use ex-post 'validated' ToCs as an underpinning for interventions in other time and space settings. Cieslik and Leeuwis discuss why the use of RCT is methodologically unsound for such purposes. They make a plea for including other sources of knowledge in the design of ToCs, notably locally contextual stakeholder knowledge and forms of historical and/or social science evidence that has been created through other methods and forms of analysis.

Van Wessel (Chapter 11) seamlessly connects to this discussion. On the one hand she broadens the debate by pointing to the relational, dynamic, and political dimensions of evidence in the everyday reality of Civil Society Organisations (CSO), and at the same time she zooms in on a particular type of intervention (evidence-based advocacy) and points to specific qualitative strategies and sources for gathering local stakeholder evidence, including testimonies, visuals, case studies, and storytelling. Van Wessel demonstrates how CSOs are tapping into the language of 'evidence-based' intervention and using multiple communicative strategies and roles to influence various stages of policy-making, whereby scientific evidence is only one of the sources used to build credibility. In doing so, she argues that the role of evidence is only relative in efforts to build legitimacy, exert influence, and attract resources. Importantly, Van Wessel makes clear there are large differences between Northern CSOs and Southern CSOs in their capacity to engage with evidence, voice concerns, and make these count in policy and/or resource mobilisation. Thus, evidence-based advocacy does not take place in a level playing field of CSOs, so that the creation, interpretation, and use of evidence is intricately intertwined with political processes, the exertion of power, and the privileging of certain types of evidence over others, which may lead to the exclusion of less powerful groups and marginalised interests. In order to make evidence-based advocacy more inclusive, Van Wessel argues, we need to consider altering the structural conditions under which CSOs operate, including reform in the way development funds are controlled.

In all, the two chapters highlight several forms and mechanisms of exclusion in relation to both the production of evidence and its use in the arena of development intervention, and emphasise complementary strategies for 'making evidence differently' (through different methods), 'making different evidence count' (from different sources), and 'making evidence count differently' (through different strategies).

Negotiating technological change and digitisation

Several chapters in the book engage with the widespread expectation and optimism that new digital technologies will transform and improve interaction in innovation systems (Klerkx et al., 2019) and yield considerable benefits for users. In relation to this, the chapter by Jomantas et al. (Chapter 14) discusses the role of social media in enhancing knowledge exchange in and around agricultural advisory organisations, while Nyamekye et al. (Chapter 13) examine efforts of a social enterprise to deliver information on market conditions, weather, and best agricultural practices to farmers through a digital platform. Preceding these chapters is a critical problematisation by McCampbell et al. on forms of inclusion and exclusion that may occur in relation to the digitisation of African agriculture (Chapter 12).

McCampbell et al. draw lessons from experiences in the Global North and South, and argue that we need to move beyond simplistic frameworks of thinking about inclusion and exclusion in digital settings. They argue that we must abandon the binary distinction of inclusion and exclusion; being excluded from something can at the same time imply inclusion in something else. Similarly, they point out that, over time, inclusion may not always yield favourable consequences, while forms of exclusion can eventually become advantageous. They apply this refined understanding to several levels and spheres in which inclusion and exclusion in relation to digitisation may happen, ranging from differential access conditions to specific technologies (such as with digital divides), to design choices made in the development trajectories of digital platforms (such as with privileging certain logics or actors in intended or unintended ways), to system level complexities (such as with unequal control over data or vulnerability to cybercrime and digital traps). McCampbell et al. assess that the latter levels receive relatively little attention in debates on digitisation, even though they can become powerful determinants of who is included or excluded and whether inclusion and exclusion is beneficial or harmful. Thus, they make a plea for more careful consideration of trade-offs and unintended consequences in digitisation processes.

This challenge is taken up by Nyamekye al. (Chapter 13) who look at the development of digital information services in Ghana through the lens of the Responsible Research and Innovation (RRI) framework (see also Chapter 15 Macnaghten, Shah, and Ludwig). This approach is directed at making innovation trajectories more inclusive and responsive to societal demands and values, and also invites greater reflexivity and anticipation of possible negative consequences and trade-offs. However, Nyamekye et al. suggest that applying RRI principles to the development of digital information services in Ghana is hampered by strategic, institutional, and substantive uncertainties. As a response, they suggest several mechanisms to address such challenges, including greater integration of scientific and indigenous knowledge (see also Chapter 1 Ludwig and Boogaard) and the development of a tailored and culturally sensitive RRI rubric for digital agriculture.

While Nyamekye et al. examine a route to making digital technologies that are deliberately designed by relative outsiders more inclusive and responsible, Jomantas et al. (Chapter 14) report on a trajectory where users themselves initiated the use of digital platforms in their professional work. The chapter discusses and compares two experiences where agricultural advisers started to informally use social media chat groups. The authors make a plausible case that these chat groups have complemented face-to-face communication in useful ways, and have played a significant role in knowledge sharing and problem solving when a crisis (the rapid spread of a new pest, the fall armyworm) emerged. At the same, they point to interesting differences between the platforms in terms of their composition (homogeneous versus heterogeneous), size (small versus large number of participants), scope (local versus national), and the patterns of interaction that evolve (more and less egalitarian). The chapter shows how these differences are interrelated, and also signals that they are affected by a process whereby one of the initially self-organised platforms became more formalised, regulated, and integrated into organisational policy. While the chapter demonstrates the strength of self-organised digital initiatives, it also signals that interaction on social media platforms is shaped by social, institutional, and political processes, and it raises pertinent issues on whether and how bottom-up initiatives may be 'professionalised.'

In all, the chapters in this cluster help us to rethink inclusion and exclusion in digital agriculture, and examine the complexities involved in 'making knowledge work' through digital platforms. Moreover, they all offer food for thought on pathways and processes through which the design and 'making' of digital technologies may become more responsible and effective. In doing so they call into question the naive and sometimes strategic technological optimism that surrounds investment in digital agriculture.

Governing knowledge and innovation

The goal of inclusive innovation is not simply the procedural challenge of including a broad range of societal stakeholders in innovation processes, including in sites and processes of knowledge production and application, but also in ensuring that innovation works for and with society and local communities. Since we know that science and innovation wield unfathomable power in the shaping of social life and the environment it becomes necessary to shape such processes to help ensure they contribute to the common good. This is what we mean by governance. Such a goal fits loosely under the concept of responsible innovation and in its constitutive frameworks that have been developed to align innovation with societal and democratic values. One such model is the AIRR framework (Stilgoe, Owen, and Macnaghten, 2013) that has been configured to help innovators to anticipate (A) future impacts on the basis of inclusive (I) deliberation that fosters reflexivity (R) about background assumptions and that responds (R) to concerns, interests, and values of diverse stakeholders. Yet, as we show in Part VI, the appeal to democratise and align knowledge with and for society is far from straightforward.

In Chapter 15, Macnaghten, Shah, and Ludwig analyse the complexities associated with making societal dialogues work in practice. While it has become commonplace that there should be inclusive and early dialogue in the development of emerging science and technology, not least to improve science and society relations and ensure socially robust innovations, it is not at all clear that inclusive dialogues in themselves will lead to effective democratisation of knowledge. Using the case of gene editing, the chapter analyses the dialogue that took place at the 2019 Wageningen CRISPRcon forum, highlighting how the forms of dialogue acted primarily to legitimate existing relations of professional power, reinforcing a quintessentially positive view of the technology and its promises of societal benefit. Subsequently, the chapter set out design principles that mitigate against the use of dialogue to legitimate dominant perspectives, and how these were put to use in a particular public engagement research aimed at identifying public concerns to the application of gene editing in livestock.

This line of argument is extended by Leeuwis (Chapter 17) in a wide-ranging and critical engagement with attempts to better align knowledge with the needs, values, and demands of societal user groups. Again, this process of alignment is seen as far from straightforward. Engaging with five case studies that have taken place over a period of more than two decades, each set up to include citizens in agenda setting for research, Leeuwis shows the multiple reasons why such initiatives so commonly disappoint. Largely, these failures are due to questionable and even naive assumptions about the nature and structure of societal demands and in the incapacity of (participatory) methods to accommodate these. Leeuwis concludes the chapter through an imaginative attempt to integrate a more dynamic, iterative, interactional, and cross-disciplinary account of change into demand articulation processes.

This need for what we might term a 'second order' critique is developed once more by Vellema, Adomaa, and Schoonhoven-Speijer (Chapter 16), in their engagement with the domain of practice. Just as Leeuwis seeks to problematise a naive account of demand articulation, Vellema et al. focus on the highly contextual and situated domain of everyday practice in their investigation of how users make knowledge work in daily life. Taking two diverse case studies—pruning in the global commodity chain of cocoa in Ghana and the practice of aggregating volumes in local food markets for oilseed and edible oil in Uganda—the aim of the chapter is to open up innovations in methodology at the interface of situated practices, coordination practices, and knowledge-based interventions. Drawing on literatures from organisation studies, technology studies, and learning studies, the chapter demonstrates the value of a practice-based account on localised attempts to repair errors, improvise workable action, and navigate unanticipated problems.

Conclusion

Debates about development and innovation are situated at the intersection of research and intervention that is addressed by traditions such as 'action research,' 'participatory research,' and 'research for development.' This book reflects these action-oriented traditions that aim to 'make knowledge work' at the intersection of research and intervention. At the same time, it aims for critical reflexivity by asking how to make knowledge work *differently*. Inclusive development and innovation require an applied and political epistemology that addresses the complex challenges of integrating different forms of knowledge, negotiating different standpoints, relating knowledge to contested social and technological change, and governing practices of knowledge production.

The goal of 'making knowledge work differently' should not be misunderstood as providing one unified framework for inclusive knowledge production. Plurality is a core message of this book and undermines the prospects of one universally applicable framework for integrating heterogeneous knowledge systems for development and innovation. Instead, the chapters of this book relate through a shared commitment to both critical reflexivity and practical intervention. On the one hand, the book discusses knowledge production as a site of exclusion that reproduces deeply entrenched and often colonial hierarchies through narrow notions of expertise and reliance on epistemological framings of dominant stakeholders. Furthermore, generic appeals to inclusivity are not sufficient but can reproduce these hierarchies in how local knowledge is integrated and assimilated into dominant frameworks. On the other hand, this book is not merely an exercise in critique but explores avenues for inclusive knowledge production and epistemological negotiation. Again, these avenues are heterogeneous and require engagement with a wide range of domains from intercultural education and dialogue to inclusive uses of digital technologies, to responsible governance of research and innovation.

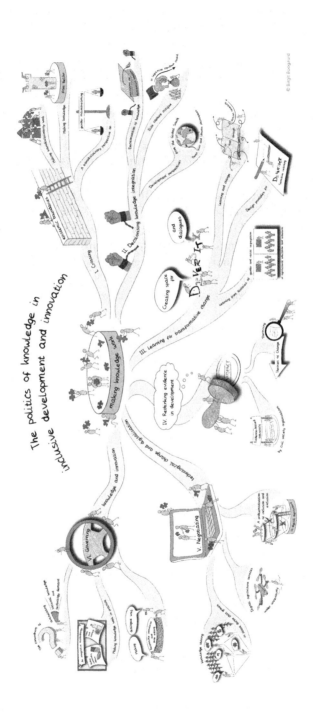

References

Bohm, D. (2004). *On dialogue.* London: Routledge.

Boogaard, B. K. (2019). The relevance of connecting sustainable agricultural development with African philosophy. *South African Journal of Philosophy*, 38(3), 273–286.

Briggs, J. (2005). The use of indigenous knowledge in development: Problems and challenges. *Progress in Development Studies*, 5(2), 99–114.

Byskov, M. F. (2020). Four challenges to knowledge integration for development and the role of philosophy in addressing them. *Journal of Global Ethics*, 16(3), 262–282.

Ely, A., Smith, A., Stirling, A., Leach, M., & Scoones, I. (2013). Innovation politics post-Rio+20: Hybrid pathways to sustainability? *Environment and Planning C: Government and Policy* 31(6), 1063–1081.

Freire, P. (1970). *Pedagogy of the Oppressed. 30th Anniversary Edition (2005).* London: Continuum International Publishing Group.

Gupta, J., Pouw, N. R., & Ros-Tonen, M. A. (2015). Towards an elaborated theory of inclusive development. *The European Journal of Development Research*, 27(4), 541–559.

Kimmerle, H. (2012). Dialogues as form of intercultural philosophy. Irian Society of Intercultural Philosophy. http://isiph.ir/en/?p=27

Klerkx, L., Jakku, E., & Labarthe, P. (2019). A review of social science on digital agriculture, smart farming and agriculture 4.0: New contributions and a future research agenda. *NJAS - Wageningen Journal of Life Sciences*, 90-91, 100315.

Leach, M., Scoones, I., & Stirling, A. (2010). *Dynamic sustainabilities: Technology, environment, social justice.* London: Earthscan.

Leach, M., Rockström, J., Raskin, P., Stirling, A., Smith, A. et al. (2012). Transforming innovation for sustainability. *Ecology and Society*, 17(2), 11.

Leeuwis, C. (2004). *Communication for rural innovation: Rethinking agricultural extension.* Oxford: Blackwell Science.

Leeuwis, C. (2013). *Coupled performance and change in the making*, Inaugural lecture. Wageningen: Wageningen University.

Ludwig, D. (2016). Overlapping ontologies and Indigenous knowledge. From integration to ontological self-determination. *Studies in History and Philosophy of Science*, 59, 36–45.

Ludwig, D., & El-Hani, C. N. (2020). Philosophy of ethnobiology: Understanding knowledge integration and its limitations. *Journal of Ethnobiology*, 40(1), 3–20.

McMichael, C., Waters, E., & Volmink, J. (2005). Evidence-based public health: What does it offer developing countries? *Journal of Public Health*, 27(2), 215–221.

Macnaghten, P. (2020). *The making of responsible innovation.* Cambridge: Cambridge University Press.

Mawdsley, E., Townsend, J. G., Porter, G., & Oakley, P. (2002). *Knowledge, power and development agendas: NGOs North and South.* INTRAC NGO Management and Policy Series.

Opola, F. O., Klerkx, L., Leeuwis, C., & Kilelu, C. W. (2020). The hybridity of inclusive innovation narratives between theory and practice: A framing analysis. *The European Journal of Development Research*, 33, 626–648.

Richards, P. (1989). Agriculture as a performance. In R. Chambers, A. Pacey, & L. A. Thrupp (eds.), *Farmer first: Farmer innovation and agricultural research* (pp. 39–43). London: Intermediate Technology Publications.

Sillitoe, P. (ed.) (2007). Local science vs. global science: Approaches to indigenous knowledge in international development. New York: Berghahn Books.

Smith, A., & Stirling, A. (2016). *Grassroots innovation and innovation democracy.* STEPS Working Paper 89, Brighton: STEPS Centre.

Smith, A., & Stirling, A. (2018). Innovation, sustainability and democracy: An analysis of grassroots contributions. *Journal of Self-Governance and Management Economics,* 6(1), 64–97.

Stilgoe, J., Owen, R., & Macnaghten, P. (2013). Developing a framework for responsible innovation. *Research Policy,* 42(9), 1568–1580.

Stirling, A. (2009). *Direction, distribution and diversity! Pluralising progress in innovation, sustainability and development,* STEPS Working Paper 32. Brighton: STEPS Centre.

Storeng, K. T., & Béhague, D. P. (2014). "Playing the numbers game": Evidence-based advocacy and the technocratic narrowing of the safe motherhood initiative. *Medical Anthropology Quarterly,* 28(2), 260–279.

PART I

Crossing epistemic boundaries

1

MAKING TRANSDISCIPLINARITY WORK

An epistemology of inclusive development and innovation

David Ludwig and Birgit K. Boogaard

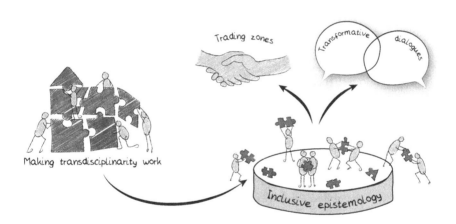

Introduction

'Development' and 'innovation' are concepts in perpetual crisis. After almost 30 years of post-development discourse (Asher and Wainwright, 2019; Escobar, 1991; Sachs, 1992), there is little shock value in challenging development as a concept that has contributed to global inequality and environmental destruction by pushing agendas of economic growth and modernisation onto the Global South. The concept of innovation has also long lost its innocence. While innovation narratives often appeal to depoliticised and supposedly neutral notions of progress, it has been widely argued that innovation discourses strategically highlight certain practices and technologies that reinforce growth- and

DOI: 10.4324/9781003112525-1

modernisation-oriented development agendas (Blok and Lemmens, 2015; Ludwig and Macnaghten, 2020).

There is no shortage of attempts to reimagine both development and innovation by making them more inclusive, responsible, participatory, social, and sustainable (Heeks, Foster, and Nugroho, 2014; Pansera and Owen, 2018; Siddiqi and Collins, 2017; Stilgoe, Owen, and Macnaghten, 2013). Despite this diversity of frameworks, development and innovation scholars commonly emphasise the need to shift target outcomes from an exclusive focus on economic growth to the inclusion of societal and environmental concerns (Chataway, Hanlin, and Kaplinsky, 2014; Gupta and Vegelin, 2016). At the same time, it is not sufficient to swap target outcomes in a top-down process that fails to include affected stakeholders in the negotiations of these targets and the pathways of achieving them. This chapter focuses on the epistemic conditions of this process of reimagination by addressing different forms of knowledge and their interactions in transdisciplinary approaches to development and innovation.

Attempts to reimagine development and innovation have become closely connected to wider debates about inclusive strategies for knowledge production that are framed through 'collaboration,' 'co-creation,' 'citizen science,' 'intercultural dialogue,' 'interdisciplinarity,' 'multi-stakeholder platforms,' 'participatory design,' 'participatory action research,' 'science society dialogue,' 'transdisciplinarity,' 'public engagement,' and 'open science.' While all of these notions have different genealogies, they are connected through an overall concern with opening up knowledge production and research processes for input from heterogeneous actors. This chapter focuses on transdisciplinarity as arguably the most developed framework for reimagining the epistemology of inclusive development and innovation beyond a mere change of target outcomes.

The need for transdisciplinary approaches has been widely emphasised in the development domain and is commonly motivated by social-environmental challenges that are not suited for narrow disciplinary solutions but require negotiation and heterogeneous forms of situated knowledge (Brown, Harris, and Russel, 2010; OECD, 2020; Pohl, Truffer, and Hadorn, 2017). The following section motivates this move towards transdisciplinarity by interpreting two case studies of agricultural development projects as studies of epistemic failures. The section thereafter builds on this analysis through introducing transdisciplinarity as an inclusive epistemology that has the potential to integrate heterogeneous forms of situated knowledge in the negotiation of social-environmental change. While transdisciplinarity takes knowledge diversity seriously, we argue that its integrationist agenda has been limited by both methodological, political, and historical factors, in which there continues to be a hegemony of Global North epistemologies over Indigenous and local epistemologies on account of a complex fusion of colonial legacy, scientism, and unequal power relations. For decades 'decolonisation' of knowledge has been addressed by post-development scholars (amongst many, see Escobar, 1991) and African philosophers (amongst many, see Wiredu, 1995), and over the past years is gaining increased attention by a wider audience in academia and beyond (see, for example, Brahma et al., 2018). However, the underlying questions of how to bring a diversity of epistemologies, ontologies, and values together are far from straightforward. Making transdisciplinarity work requires moving beyond an integrationist agenda that recognises knowledge diversity only insofar as it can be accommodated in a shared academic framework. Knowledge integration matters, but a critical transdisciplinarity also needs to engage with its limitations through transformative dialogues about epistemology, ontology, and values.

Epistemic failures in agricultural development projects

The agricultural modernisation paradigm in which 'traditional' ways of farming are viewed as in need of transformation to more 'modern' ways of farming—with improved productivity, increased specialisation, at larger scale, leading to increased farmer incomes—has been imposed on smallholder farmers across the globe. This paradigm has been widely criticised, because the arsenal of agricultural modernisation innovations—machines, fertilisers, pesticides, seed varieties—often opened countries to a global agri-food industry that left environments degraded, traditional agricultural practices eroded, and smallholder farmers dispossessed (Van der Ploeg et al., 2000; McMichael, 2015). These critiques led to the desire to move away from the agricultural modernisation paradigm, and instead focus on community-led rural development (Van der Ploeg et al., 2000). In this line, there have been numerous approaches to make agricultural development more inclusive—ranging from participatory action research (PAR) to the formation of multi-stakeholder platforms—focused on agriculture's contributions to ensuring food security and improving livelihoods. However, the ideal of agricultural modernisation has not disappeared from the stage entirely and is still reflected in present-day agricultural development approaches and programmes, ranging from large-scale industrial agriculture initiatives to 'sustainable intensification' by smallholders. The aim of this section is not to provide an in-depth analysis of all critiques on agricultural modernisation, but rather to focus on the epistemic dimension of it, while recognising that this is but one mode of analysis and critique.

The wider characterisation of the agricultural modernisation paradigm as a neo-liberal perspective on development dominated by market institutions and formal market logic (van der Ploeg, 2009) interacts with a more specific assumption of an epistemic hierarchy between academic researchers and local communities. The 'firm belief in technological solutions and economic progress' (Boogaard, 2019, p. 275) in the agricultural modernisation paradigm often remained unquestioned because modern science and technology were positioned as the only valid source of knowledge for improving livelihoods, while at the same characterising local communities in terms of a knowledge deficit. This section will focus on how this assumption of an epistemic hierarchy created and reinforced epistemic failures by marginalising local forms of knowledge that are of crucial importance for responding to social-environmental challenges and for developing innovations that reflect the needs and perspectives of local communities. Epistemic failures can therefore be understood as symptoms of an underlying hierarchical epistemology that is inadequate for recognising and integrating a diversity of knowledges. In this sense, agricultural modernisation can be interpreted as producing: (1) epistemic failures that over-focus on academic knowledge while excluding the knowledge of local communities; and (2) a hierarchical epistemology that generates these failures through an assumption of the superiority of Global North epistemologies that structurally excludes Indigenous and local epistemologies. Two case studies are used to underpin these arguments: Lansing's (2009) study of rice farming in Bali, and Boogaard's (2021) study on epistemic injustice in a livestock development project in Mozambique.

Lasing's case study of agricultural modernisation discusses the effects of the so-called 'Green Revolution' on rice farming in Bali that was organised around water temples that would regulate the flow of water to *subaks*, systems of terraced paddy fields, through religious rituals. Green Revolution engineers, guided by a narrow focus on scientific knowledge, not only failed to recognise the functions of these religious practices but also dismissed the system as a whole as inefficient and in need of modernisation through agricultural innovations ranging from novel rice varieties to externally introduced pesticides to more efficiently organised irrigation schedules. Lansing (2009, p. 115) summarises this attitude by quoting a 'frustrated American irrigation engineer' claiming that 'these people don't need a high priest, they need a hydrologist!'

The narrow focus on externally produced scientific knowledge and the exclusion of local epistemic resources motivated a modernisation programme that turned into an ecological and social disaster. As Lansing (2015, p. 114) puts it,

> The threat of legal penalties against anyone failing to grow the new rice led to continuous cropping of Green Revolution rice. Religious rituals continued in the temples, but field rituals no longer matched the actual stages of rice growth. As soon as one crop was harvested, another was planted, and cropping cycles began to drift apart. During [...] the dry season, the supply of irrigation water became unpredictable. Soon, district agricultural offices began to report 'chaos in the water scheduling' and 'explosions of pest populations.'

Lansing's computational modelling of water flows highlights two crucial functions of water temples. First, the rituals distributed water as a scarce resource by ensuring that *subaks* downstream would still receive sufficient water during the dry season. Second, the rituals coordinated the water temples, which controlled pest populations through synchronised watering and cropping schedules over hundreds of hectares. While Lansing's model suggests that the religious rituals led to an optimal balance of these two factors, the enforcement of an agricultural modernisation paradigm led to the breakdown of this system with the consequence of water shortages and pest outbreaks.

These above epistemic failures are not unique to rice farming in Bali, but are mirrored by agricultural development projects until today. The following case study is an ex-post analysis of a livestock development project in Mozambique (2011–2013) that aimed to improve goat keeping and marketing in the Inhassoro district in Mozambique. The project brought different stakeholders of the 'goat value chain' together in an innovation platform with the aim to jointly identify problems, search for solutions, and arrive at collective action. The case study did not evaluate the effectiveness of the project, but in retrospect looked at epistemic injustices, in the sense of the systematic and structural exclusion of Indigenous ways of knowing and doing. The study identified various ways in which epistemic injustice was maintained or reinforced (Boogaard, 2021); below we will mention three epistemic failures in this agricultural development project.

To begin, the project provided training on 'improved' goat keeping practices and marketing, based mainly on the transfer of academic knowledge. Indigenous knowledge, including of goat husbandry, was not considered as relevant by the project team. Through the framing of terms such as 'improved,' academic scientific knowledge and practices were (implicitly) regarded as superior to Indigenous knowledge (Van der Ploeg, 2016). Secondly, the case study reveals that epistemic injustice was produced not only directly through training and instruction, but also in more 'subtle' ways that included the ways in which the project imposed goals of commercialisation and modernisation onto rural goat keepers, in this case without recognising or addressing residual tensions between market-led thinking and Indigenous values and practice such as mutual assistance.

The one-sided focus of the project on the commercialisation of goat keeping reflects the underlying Global North development ideology of agricultural modernisation and commercialisation. This constitutes a form of epistemic paternalism in which Global North-led project organisations assume to know what is 'best' for the rural goat keepers: that in order to improve their livelihoods, they needed to commercialise goat keeping. In such ways, the project disregarded existing social structures and practices including the value of life as embedded in relationships of mutual assistance and aid that is commonplace in African philosophies (Wiredu, 2003; see also Boogaard and Van Norren, this volume). Thirdly, while rural goat keepers were included in the project through an innovation platform, the Global North-led project organisations had set the vision, conditions, definitions, borders, and some of the interventions at the start of the project, and these were not open for change or negotiation throughout the project. In that sense, the project was entrenched in Eurocentric thinking and doing, which had the effect of reinforcing unequal epistemological hierarchies in which Global North knowledge remained dominant over other types of knowledge. Overall, it can be concluded that the innovation platform included people but excluded their epistemology. Thus while in theory, 'inclusive innovation' and 'inclusive development' can offer space for 'knowledge co-creation' or 'knowledge diversity,' in practice such platforms can become a vehicle that in fact reinforces dominant Global North epistemologies.

The cases of water temples in Bali and goat production in Mozambique provide complementary lessons about epistemic failures in development projects. Both programmes of agricultural modernisation were deeply steeped in *epistemic paternalism* in the sense that they recognised mainly the expertise of agricultural engineers and scientists while casually dismissing any epistemic resources of the affected communities. Local communities were recognised as beneficiaries of development interventions but not as epistemic actors with relevant knowledge of their own. In both cases, epistemic paternalism produced *epistemic injustices* in the sense of epistemology viewed as a social achievement (Kidd, Medina, Pohlhaus, 2017). Fricker (2007) distinguishes between testimonial and hermeneutic injustice, where the former refers to an unfair attribution of credibility and the latter refers to injustices in the epistemic resources in interpreting experiences and livelihoods. Epistemic paternalism produces widespread testimonial injustices as reflected in the lack of consideration of Indigenous knowledge about goat keeping and rice farming in Mozambique and Bali, respectively. Furthermore, both cases illustrate how development projects produce hermeneutic injustices by imposing concepts and frameworks that exclude local perspectives and practices, such as those on irrigation as practised through rituals in water temples in Bali and the entangled social and spiritual perspectives on mutual help that are commonplace among goat keepers in Mozambique.

Transdisciplinarity as an inclusive epistemology

The previous section highlighted problems of epistemic paternalism and epistemic injustice and how these were prevalent in development projects even in those that sought to include local communities in the formulation of target outcomes (for example, on 'improved' rice farming and goat keeping) but which at the same time excluded local knowledge and expertise. Transdisciplinarity has emerged as a widely embraced approach that promises to overcome these epistemic challenges by including heterogeneous stakeholders in the process of knowledge production (Lawrence, 2015; Scholz and Steiner, 2015). For example, a recent policy report from the OECD calls for a 'paradigm shift in research practice' and hails transdisciplinarity as a new mode of research 'that integrates both academic researchers from unrelated disciplines—including natural sciences and SSH—and non-academic participants to achieve a common goal, involving the creation of new knowledge and theory' (OECD, 2020, p. 9). The OECD report converges with the wider transdisciplinary literature (Cole, 2017; Schmidt and Pröpper, 2017) in highlighting the need to rethink knowledge production for development and innovation agendas. As we examine below, much of this transdisciplinary literature can be described as combining: (1) an ontological claim about the multi-dimensional and multi-scale nature of social-environmental problems; (2) an epistemological claim about the broad distribution of expertise about social-environmental problems; and (3) a methodological agenda of integrating diverse forms of expertise in addressing them.

First, transdisciplinarity is commonly motivated by pointing to the multi-dimensional nature of global challenges in the sense that they involve the interaction of a wide range of factors that have been traditionally studied by separate disciplines. For example, the challenge of global food production encompasses a wide range of heterogeneous factors that include the genetics of new crop varieties, the division of labour in agrarian communities, carbon emissions of livestock, profit margins of agricultural producers, soil erosion, food security and sovereignty of smallholder farmers, local culinary traditions, and deforestation and spiritual practices. Beyond this general observation that points to the need for multi-dimensional approaches in the sense of a large diversity of interacting factors, global challenges also exhibit a multi-scale character in the sense that they take different shapes at different local, regional, national, and global levels. The global challenge of 'feeding the world' materialises in very different ways for different actors (such as smallholder farmers, workers in a food processing plant, end consumers in a supermarket) and in different geographic contexts (for example, for farmers in Bali as compared to, say, Kansas). The multi-scale character of global challenges limits the usefulness of generic accounts of global challenges such as 'feeding the world' and rather challenges researchers to address a large variety of contextually variable and interacting factors.

Second, the multi-dimensional and multi-scale character of global challenges justifies an epistemology that emphasises the diversity of relevant epistemic actors. Multi-dimensionality requires interdisciplinary approaches that bring together epistemic resources from a wide range of disciplines. Agricultural development, for example, relates to the technical expertise of various disciplinary fields from plant breeding to water management to cultural anthropology to political economy. In the Balinese case study, for example, technical agricultural expertise was in dire need of interdisciplinary interaction with the social sciences and humanities to understand social practices and their interactions with local religious traditions. Furthermore, the multi-scale character of global challenges demonstrates the crucial role of non-academic actors and their situated knowledge about environmental and social contexts. For example, Mozambique and Bali do not exhibit identical dynamics in the interaction of environmental and social factors. As debates about Indigenous and local knowledge have highlighted (Berkes, 2018; Ludwig and Poliseli, 2018), local communities tend to be experts about the specificities of local social and environmental systems. Many relevant factors from local soil conditions to social division of labour are best understood by local community members while external researchers tend to struggle to grasp the nuances of local dynamics.

Third, this acknowledgement of distributed expertise leads to an integrationist methodology of bringing relevant actors together in transdisciplinary processes. In this sense, Scholz and Steiner (2015, p. 532) describe 'knowledge integration as the core of transdisciplinarity' and argue that the 'main added value of transdisciplinarity [...] is the integration or relationship of different forms of epistemics (i.e., ways of knowing). Whereas disciplines are brilliant at explaining specific aspects in a theoretical form, the major asset of transdisciplinarity is the merging and relating of different types of perception, knowledge, and valuations in an integrated manner.' In both the cases of Bali and Mozambique, such a process of integration would promise not only a more nuanced understanding of complex social-environmental dynamics, but also contribute to better development interventions that are responsive to cultural, economic, environmental, and social contexts.

Transdisciplinary promises and transdisciplinary failures

The transdisciplinary push for an inclusive epistemology can contribute to reimagining development and innovation through the recognition of diverse knowledge of heterogeneous actors, from laboratory scientists to farmers. Rather than thinking of 'inclusion' as a simple expansion or reconfiguration of target goals towards societal and environmental concerns, transdisciplinary frameworks allow a (re)conceptualisation of 'inclusion' at the deeper level of negotiating concerns and the process of how to achieve them.

Beyond such programmatic statements, however, it remains important to tell a more cautionary tale about transdisciplinarity in practice. It has been 50 years since the OECD put transdisciplinary on the agenda at its 1970 *International Conference on Interdisciplinary Research and Education*, and many promises of inclusive knowledge production remain mostly programmatic declarations. In fact, the implementation of transdisciplinary processes comes with challenges, as it is often 'difficult to reconcile the idea of knowledge co-production with research realities' (Schmidt and Pröpper, 2017, p. 365). Of course, there are many technical and organisational barriers in bringing together heterogeneous actors with limited funding, time frames, language barriers, lack of interest, and so on. However, the challenges of transdisciplinarity are not merely pragmatic and point towards two more fundamental shortcomings that arise from a simple integrationist agenda of transdisciplinarity. First, knowledge integration is only one aspect of a wider negotiation process, and an exclusive focus on integration runs the risk of obscuring epistemological and ontological tensions. Second, transdisciplinary models tend to incorporate idealised assumptions about the equality of actors and therefore run the risk of producing depoliticised frameworks that fail to address that integration often amounts to selective use and appropriation of knowledge between actors in vastly different positions of power (Healy, 2019).

There is no doubt that knowledge integration matters and can contribute to more just and inclusive development and innovation processes. In the case of Bali, the incorporation of Indigenous knowledge about irrigation schedules could have avoided water shortages and pest-spread that were managed through rituals in water temples. In the case of Mozambique, the inclusion of Indigenous knowledge of goat keepers could have led to a better understanding of goats as supporting mutual aid in communities rather than only focussing on commercialisation. Both cases provide clear examples of Indigenous knowledge that could have improved development interventions but which remained marginalised through the epistemic paternalism of expert-driven development projects. A transdisciplinary process that challenges these epistemic injustices through the recognition of distributed expertise could have detected these issues early on and avoided interventions that further harmed local communities.

While development practice illustrates the potential of knowledge integration, it provides at least as many cases of integration failures (Byskov, 2020). Reflective transdisciplinary practices need to avoid a simple additive model of knowledge integration. For example, Klein et al. (2001, p. 7) present transdisciplinarity through the idea that 'knowledge of all participants is enhanced, including local knowledge, scientific knowledge, and the knowledges of concerned industries, businesses, and non-governmental organisations (NGOs). The sum of this knowledge will be greater than the knowledge of any single partner.' However, knowledge often does not stack up like this and there is not an obvious 'sum of knowledge' that guides better development interventions. Instead, the knowledge of heterogeneous actors often creates tensions as it is embedded in different epistemic traditions, ontological assumptions, and value systems (Ludwig and El-Hani, 2020). Not everything that counts as knowledge from the perspective of one actor will be recognised as knowledge from the perspective of another actor. Transdisciplinarity is full of intellectual contestation, equivocation, misunderstanding, and tension.

Simple transdisciplinary agendas that employ an additive model of knowledge integration therefore run the risk of 'knowledge mining' (Kimmerer, 2012) in the sense of recognising non-academic knowledge only as far as it fits into the intellectual frameworks of academic researchers. In Lansing's case of water temples, local knowledge is validated through computational modelling according to which ritual practices established an optimal balance between concerns about water shortage and pest-spread. However, such an academic justification and validation will not always be feasible when engaging with religious and other local practices that are deeply embedded in Indigenous worldviews and ways of relating to environments. Even if academic researchers struggle to understand Indigenous knowledge due to this embedding of different worldviews, this knowledge is often crucial for local practices and sustainable relations to environments (Boogaard et al., forthcoming).

Demanding scientific validation in analogy to the Bali case therefore runs the risk of excluding large parts of Indigenous and local knowledge that does not easily integrate into academic frameworks due to its embedding in different epistemological, ontological, and value standpoints. A demand for validation also runs the risk of reproducing the basic asymmetry of epistemic paternalism as characterised in the last section. Often, the legitimacy of Indigenous and local knowledge is treated as dependent on its academic validation while the legitimacy of academic knowledge does not have to be proven in the light of Indigenous and local standards.

Deep differences between epistemological, ontological, and value standpoints limit simple integrationist agendas that appeal to Indigenous and local knowledge if it fits into frameworks of academic researchers. These complex relations beyond integration become especially pressing from the perspective of the 'politics of knowledge' that address the question of what knowledge is considered, what knowledge is seen as in need of validation, and in whose frameworks knowledge becomes integrated. Knowledge integration matters but needs to be positioned in a framework of critical transdisciplinarity that is reflexive about tensions and limits of integration in the negotiation of knowledge.

Making transdisciplinarity work: the need for knowledge negotiation and transformative dialogues

The limitations of a simple integrationism point towards two core challenges for 'making transdisciplinarity work' in the context of inclusive development and innovation. First, transdisciplinary processes need to move beyond an additive model of knowledge integration and address tensions that arise from diverging epistemologies, ontologies, and values (Ludwig and El-Hani, 2020). Second, critical transdisciplinarity requires a positive approach to knowledge negotiation that can respond to these limitations of integration and to power differentials between heterogeneous actors in transdisciplinary processes. Below, we will draw on two philosophical resources to address these challenges: philosophy of science and intercultural philosophy.

In developing an account of knowledge negotiation beyond a simple additive model of knowledge integration, it is helpful to start with the notion of 'trading zones' that has been introduced to the history and philosophy of science through Galison's (1997) *Image and logic: A material culture of microphysics*. Studying the development of high energy physics in the second half of the 20th century, Galison focused on laboratories as transdisciplinary negotiation spaces that involved scientists from a wide range of fields such as 'engineers, physicists, chemists, and metallurgists' (1997, p. 46), but that also included a wider range of actors, from public regulators to laboratory technicians. While Galison's context of modern physics contrasts with debates about inclusive development in the Global South, his analysis of the relation between knowledge and practice provides wider lessons for modelling transdisciplinary processes. Galison's analysis differs from simple integrationist narratives in characterising laboratories as transdisciplinary meeting grounds without assuming that underlying epistemological and ontological tensions were resolved through integration and consensus. In this sense, trading zones appear as 'an intermediate domain in which procedures could be coordinated locally even where broader meanings clashed' (1997, p. 46). In contrast to additive models of knowledge integration, Galison's trading zones are epistemically productive despite and sometimes because of unresolved tensions, by allowing actors to 'hammer out a local coordination, despite vast global differences [and] establish; contact languages, systems of discourse' (Galison, 1997, p. 783).

Framing transdisciplinary research in terms of trading zones helps to shift the focus from an additive model of knowledge integration to a focus on complex processes of knowledge negotiation. Of course, knowledge negotiation in development projects is very different from laboratories in high energy physics. One difference is the depth of epistemological and ontological tensions. In Galison's study, laboratory actors tend to share more background assumptions than in development contexts that bring up additional challenges of intercultural communication. In addition, many development projects operate in a (at least politically) post-colonial environment, which is another important reason why Galison's work on laboratories is so different from transdisciplinary development projects. Transdisciplinary development projects are full of unequal power relations that have their roots in colonial history, which makes the situation even more complex. Diverse ontologies and epistemologies in development projects do not meet by coincidence or in a vacuum, but the unequal relation between these ontologies is based on historical oppression by the Global North. In African philosophy it has been made clear that the false idea of ontological hierarchy between Africans and their former colonisers continues to influence Africa's international relations and the ongoing struggle for reason in Africa (Ramose, 2003).

In this line, the case study from Mozambique showed that despite 'good intentions' to make development and innovation processes more inclusive, epistemic paternalism and epistemic injustice remained persistent in practice. In an attempt to overcome this persistence of colonial legacies, we can learn from insights and approaches in intercultural philosophy as a way to move towards more equal epistemic relations. As mentioned before, the integrationist frame assumes knowledge exchange between equals, while knowledge negotiation emphasises that this process is always politically structured. In intercultural philosophy the importance of negotiation is also recognised as a way to create a proper place at the table (see Roothaan, 2019); in this case to have access to and participate in the trading zone. In addition, there is a need to bring diverse epistemologies, ontologies, and values into dialogue with each other. Thus, dialogues are an important approach in intercultural philosophy (Kimmerle, 2012).

There are at least three insights from intercultural dialogues that are relevant for transdisciplinarity. To start with, 'intercultural philosophical dialogues presuppose that the philosophies of all cultures are equivalent in rank and different in style as well as in content' (Kimmerle, 2011, p. 137). This does not mean there are no power differences between dialogue partners, but there is no pre-assumed ontological and epistemological hierarchy between them. Second, although intercultural dialogues can lead to mutual understanding, this may not always be reached (Kimmerle, 2011). Instead, '"Erratic blocs" of misunderstanding will remain so that the method of these dialogues only partly can be a hermeneutical one' (Kimmerle, 2011, p. 139). This means that the question of to what extent it is possible to truly understand 'the other' requires attention, and there may be partial incommensurability between epistemologies, ontologies, and values. Third, intercultural dialogues require an open attitude which assumes that 'the others tell me something, which I could not have told me myself by any means' (Kimmerle, 2012). Thus, through intercultural dialogues, actors reflect on their own thinking, learn from others, and simultaneously influence others. In doing so, the involved actors as well as their philosophies are transformed. As such, intercultural dialogues are *transformative* dialogues. This means that engagement in transdisciplinary projects is not non-committal, but requires an openness and willingness of involved actors to be influenced and transformed by others.

Addressing transdisciplinary processes through trading zones and transformative dialogues allows the formulation of a descriptively and normatively more adequate approach. First, it is descriptively more accurate by locating successful cases of knowledge integration in a wider context of knowledge negotiation that also involves countless cases of partial understanding, misunderstanding, and tension. Second, such an account of complex knowledge negotiation is also normatively more adequate by highlighting contested processes of mutual interpretation and misinterpretation. Transdisciplinary research is not a neutral process of knowledge aggregation but raises normative questions about which interpretations prevail and how trading zones are institutionally structured. Third, transdisciplinarity processes are transformative processes in which all involved actors and their philosophies are transformed through intercultural dialogues.

Conclusion

The aim of this chapter has been to address the epistemological conditions of reimaging development and innovation. Rather than merely shifting targets towards societal and environmental goals, we have argued that inclusive development and innovation require an inclusive epistemology that is responsive to the knowledge diversity of heterogeneous actors. Transdisciplinarity promises such an inclusive epistemology; one that integrates diverse sources of academic and non-academic knowledge. Making transdisciplinarity work, however, is far from trivial. Most importantly, transdisciplinary research tends to emphasise an integrationist agenda that runs the risk of recognising the knowledge of non-academic actors only insofar as it fits into frameworks of academic researchers. Overcoming the limitations of a simple integrationism requires recognition of the complexity of knowledge negotiation: we argue that a more realistic approach will have to address partly incommensurable epistemologies, ontologies, and values. Making transdisciplinarity work requires practices that create openings for knowledge integration as much as procedures for negotiating difference and engaging in transformative dialogues.

References

Asher, K. and Wainwright, J. (2019). After post-development: On capitalism, difference, and representation. *Antipode*. Wiley Online Library, 51(1), 25–44.

Berkes, F. (2018). *Sacred ecology: Traditional ecological knowledge and resource management*. New York: Routledge.

Boogaard, B. K. (2019). The relevance of connecting sustainable agricultural development with African philosophy. *South African Journal of Philosophy*, 38(3), 273–286.

Boogaard, B. K. (2021). Epistemic injustice in agricultural development: Critical reflections on a livestock development project in rural Mozambique. *Knowledge Management for Development Journal*. 16(1), 28–54.

Boogaard, B. K., Ludwig, D., Guri, B. Y. and Banuoku, D. (forthcoming). A reconsideration of African spirituality in agricultural development projects: Traditional ecological knowledge from Dagara elders in Koro, Ghana. In: Roothaan, A., Bateye, B., Masaeli, M. and Müller, L. (eds.). *Beauty in African thought: Critique of the Western idea of development*. Washington: Lexington Books.

Blok, V. and Lemmens, P. (2015). The emerging concept of responsible innovation. Three reasons why it is questionable and calls for a radical transformation of the concept of innovation. In: Koops, B. J., Oosterlaken, I., Romijn, H., Swierstra, T. and Van den Hoven, J. (eds.). *Responsible Innovation 2*. Springer, 19–35.

Bhambra, G. K., Gebrial, D. and Nişancıoğlu, K. (2018). *Decolonising the university*. London: Pluto Press.

Brown, V. A., Harris, J. A. and Russell, J. Y. (2010). *Tackling wicked problems through the transdisciplinary imagination*. London: Earthscan.

Byskov, M. F. (2020). Four challenges to knowledge integration for development and the role of philosophy in addressing them. *Journal of Global Ethics*, 16(3), 1–21.

Chataway, J., Hanlin, R. and Kaplinsky, R. (2014). Inclusive innovation: An architecture for policy development. *Innovation and Development*, 4(1), 33–54.

Cole, A. (2017). Towards an indigenous transdisciplinarity. *Transdisciplinary Journal of Engineering & Science*, 8, 127–150.

Diao, X., Headey, D. and Johnson, M. (2008). Toward a green revolution in Africa: What would it achieve, and what would it require? *Agricultural Economics*, 39(supplement), 539–555.

Escobar, A. (1991). Anthropology and the development encounter: The making and marketing of development anthropology. *American Ethnologist*, 18(4), 658–682.

Fricker, M. (2007). *Epistemic injustice: Power and the ethics of knowing*. Oxford: Oxford University Press.

Galison, P. (1997). *Image and logic: A material culture of microphysics*. Chicago: University of Chicago Press.

Gupta, J. and Vegelin, C. (2016). Sustainable development goals and inclusive development. *International Environmental Agreements: Politics, Law and Economics*. Springer, 16(3), 433–448.

Healy, H. (2019). A political ecology of transdisciplinary research. *Journal of Political Ecology*, 26(1), 500–528.

Heeks, R., Foster, C. and Nugroho, Y. (2014). *New models of inclusive innovation for development*. Milton Park: Taylor & Francis.

Kidd, I. J., Medina, J. and Pohlhaus Jr, G. (2017). *The Routledge handbook of epistemic injustice*. Milton Park: Taylor & Francis.

Kimmerle, H. (2011). Respect for the other and the refounding of society: Practical aspects of intercultural philosophy. In: Oosterling, H. and Ziarek, E.

P. (eds.). *Intermedialities: philosophy, arts, politics.* Washington: Lexington Books, 137–152.

Kimmerle, H. (2012). Dialogues as Form of Intercultural Philosophy. *Iranian Society of Intercultural Philosophy.* http://isiph.ir/en/?p=27.

Klein, J. T., Grossenbacher-Mansuy, W., Häberli, R., Bill, A., Scholz, R. W. and Welti, M. (eds.) (2001). *Transdisciplinarity: Joint problem solving among science, technology, and society: An effective way for managing complexity.* Dordrecht: Springer Science & Business Media.

Lansing, J. S. (2009). *Priests and programmers: Technologies of power in the engineered landscape of Bali.* Princeton: Princeton University Press.

Lawrence, R. J. (2015). *Advances in transdisciplinarity: Epistemologies, methodologies and processes.* Amsterdam: Elsevier.

Ludwig, D. and El-Hani, C. N. (2020). Philosophy of ethnobiology: Understanding knowledge integration and its limitations. *Journal of Ethnobiology,* 40(1), 3–20.

Ludwig, D. and Macnaghten, P. (2020). Traditional ecological knowledge in innovation governance: A framework for responsible and just innovation. *Journal of Responsible Innovation,* 7(1), 26–44.

Ludwig, D. and Poliseli, L. (2018). Relating traditional and academic ecological knowledge: mechanistic and holistic epistemologies across cultures. *Biology & Philosophy,* 33(5–6), 43.

McMichael, P. (2015). *Food regimes and agrarian questions. Agrarian change and peasant studies.* Rugby: Practical Action Publishing.

OECD (2020). *Addressing societal challenges using transdisciplinary research.* Paris: OECD. https://doi.org/10.1787/0ca0ca45-en.

Pansera, M. and Owen, R. (2018). Framing inclusive innovation within the discourse of development: Insights from case studies in India. *Research Policy,* 47(1), 23–34.

Pohl, C., Truffer, B. and Hirsch Hadorn, G. (2017). Addressing wicked problems through transdisciplinary research. In: Frodeman, R., Klein, J. T. and Pacheco, R. C. D. S. (eds.). *The Oxford handbook of interdisciplinarity,* 319–331, Oxford: Oxford University Press.

Ramose, M. (2003). Introduction. The struggle for reason in Africa. In: Coetzee, P. H. and Roux, A. P. J. (eds.). *The African philosophy reader.* Second edition. Oxford: Oxford University Press, 1–9.

Roothaan, A. (2019). *Indigenous, modern and postcolonial relations to Nature: Negotiating the environment.* New York: Routledge.

Sachs, W. (1992). *The development dictionary: A guide to knowledge as power.* Hyderabad: Orient Blackswan.

Schmidt, L. and Pröpper, M. (2017). Transdisciplinarity as a real-world challenge: A case study on a North–South collaboration. *Sustainability Science,* 12(3), 365–379.

Scholz, R. W. and Steiner, G. (2015). Transdisciplinarity at the crossroads. *Sustainability Science,* 10(4), 521–526.

Siddiqi, A. and Collins, R. D. (2017). Sociotechnical systems and sustainability: current and future perspectives for inclusive development. *Current Opinion in Environmental Sustainability,* 24, 7–13.

Stilgoe, J., Owen, R. and Macnaghten, P. (2013). Developing a framework for responsible innovation. *Research Policy,* 42(9), 1568–1580.

Van der Ploeg, J. D., Renting, H., Brunori, G., Knickel, K., Mannion, J., Marsden, T., ... and Ventura, F. (2000). Rural development: From practices and policies towards theory. *Sociologia Ruralis,* 40(4), 391–408.

Van der Ploeg, J. D. (2009). *The new peasantries. Struggles for autonomy and sustainability in an era of empire and globalization.* London: Earthscan.

Van der Ploeg, J. D. (2016). Theorizing agri-food economies. *Agriculture*, 6(30), 1–12.

Wiredu, K. (1995). *Conceptual decolonization in African philosophy.* Ibadan: Hope Publications.

Wiredu, K. (2003). The moral foundations of an African culture. In: Coetzee, P. H. and Roux, A. P. J. (eds.) (2015). *The African philosophy reader.* London: Routledge, 287–296.

2

MAKING KNOWLEDGE FROM BELOW

Senna Middelveld, Harro Maat, and Phil Macnaghten

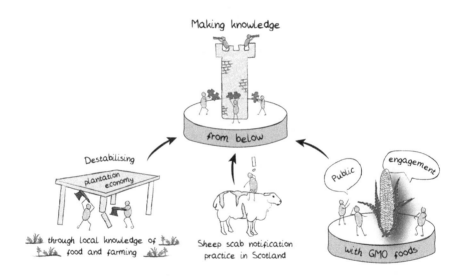

Making knowledge

from below

Destabilising plantation economy

through local knowledge of food and farming

Sheep scab notification practice in Scotland

Public engagement with GMO foods

Introduction

Several established scholarly domains and academic disciplines originate from practices in which locally vernacular knowledge and established techniques once prevailed. Known examples are medicine and agricultural science. Since at least the dawn of the Modern age, institutional scientific knowledge making practices have become the dominant source for practical application. Yet far from being a value free enterprise, practices of scientific knowledge making have contributed to thin simplifications of nature and society, conducive to prevailing and utilitarian models of social order. The domination of institutionalised scientific

DOI: 10.4324/9781003112525-2

knowledge over other forms of knowledge implies not only that formal scientific knowledge is considered somehow superior to local vernacular knowledge, but also that its application through science-led innovation conjoined with rational planning is the motor of prosperity and social progress. Perhaps not surprisingly, this domination by science has been resisted by civil society and critical social scientists who have sought recognition and engagement with local and indigenous perspectives.

In this chapter we contribute to an appraisal of institutionalised scientific knowledge making practices through an assessment of what we call 'knowledge from below' and its potential for social innovation (see also Carenzo, 2020 for a wider theorisation of initiatives that usually remain below the radar). The 'below' refers to people's daily practices and experiences in a broad sense, and as such a prominent domain for the 'life sciences' both as a source of empirical data and as an 'application environment' for science-based interventions. However, in normal scientific procedures information from below is often stripped from its social and epistemological situatedness. For example, what people prefer to eat, what crops and animals farmers hold on their fields or the birds we see when looking at our backdoor gardens all end up as data points in spreadsheets and computer files, processed and interpreted from the scientific models about human behaviour, farming systems, or ecology. Knowledge 'from below' is therefore not used to indicate that local knowledge or the people having it *are* below. Instead, we use it to emphasise that these knowledges come *from* below, illustrating a resistance from below against institutionally embedded knowledge 'from above.'

More than arguing for the need to critique scientific knowledge, this chapter highlights ways in which novel forms of productive engagement with local, plural, and deliberative ways of knowing opens up new and potentially more inclusive forms of knowledge production. The argument of the chapter is inspired by a co-production model and approach in which the spheres of science and social order are viewed as mutually constitutive. Developed by Sheila Jasanoff and colleagues and building on science and technology studies (STS) scholarship, the co-production concept has proven very helpful to unveil how the incontrovertible facts produced by science 'are designed to persuade publics [in ways that] are co-produced along with the forms of politics that people desire and practice' (Jasanoff and Simmet, 2017, p. 752). There are two broad implications that derive from this approach.

First, if science and social order are co-produced, then it becomes incumbent to examine precisely the relationship in practice between scientific knowledge production and social order as evinced in particular sites. STS scholars have taken up this task for a wide variety of cases, identifying both the values out of which science is conducted—including the interests it serves—as well as the ways in which these configurations can, over time, contribute to the formation of new meanings of life, citizenship, and politics, or what can more generally be dubbed 'social ordering' (Jasanoff, 2004; Rose, 2006). Second, if it is acknowledged that science and social order are co-produced, the question arises what values underpin the scientific knowledge production system (and its associated cultures), and to what extent these align with articulations of broader societal values and visions of the social good. Indeed, to what extent have the values and priorities tacitly embedded in scientific innovation been subjected to democratic negotiation and reflection? Or, perhaps more worryingly, to what extent are dominant scientific values reflective of those of incumbent interests that may be, perhaps unwittingly, closing down possibilities for different scientific pathways linked to alternative visions of the social good (Stirling, 2008)?

This chapter takes up the challenging insights and questions raised by the co-production concept by exploring novel forms of productive engagement with local, plural, and deliberative ways of knowing, Moreover, we introduce additional concepts, endorsing and extending the co-production argument, and furthering a critical examination of the way 'knowledge from below' contributes to alternative social orderings.

In the first case, we offer a historical perspective by reassessing forms of resistance against Caribbean slave-based plantation economies with productivist social organisation. For plantation owners and estate managers, nature and slaves were subjects for exploitation, and both served to extract financial profit. Resistance and *maronnage* contested the plantation order successfully because subsistence farming was a viable alternative reflecting a counter understanding and ordering of nature and human relations. Theoretically, and drawing on the writings of Durkheim and Mauss, we view knowledge from below as embodied interaction with natural environments from which particular social orderings emerge.

The second case draws on ethnographic fieldwork conducted in Scotland with sheep farmers and veterinarians. We analyse how the Scottish government's decision to remake sheep scab a notifiable disease, based on expert scientific knowledge, led to resistance and alternative ways of knowing and practising the disease. In this case, knowledge from below is embodied and located in Scottish farmers' and veterinarians' knowledge practices and experience with sheep and sheep scab. From an STS tradition, we draw on the ideas of Haraway (1988) about situated knowledges and on skilled visions, a notion developed by Grasseni (2007) as a way of attending to local knowledge practices at the level of epistemology and ontology.

In the third case, we show how a public engagement research project on public responses to genetically modified foods was used to contest a dominant science policy framing that had viewed negative public attitudes as based on emotion and dogma. Designing and developing a new kind of collective—using deliberative focus groups (Macnaghten, 2021; see also Chapter 12 in this volume) in which lay publics are empowered to negotiate the meanings of issues endogenously—the research brought to the fore questions of trust, agency, the 'reasonableness' of public concerns, and the need for new policy architectures that embrace 'beyond risk' dimensions. In this case, knowledge from below emerges from lay publics during focus group discussions. Their knowledge about emerging technologies is often marginalised and overlooked, especially when compared with knowledge and knowledge frames produced by the scientific community developing the technology, knowledge that is institutionally legitimated by regulators and industry.

Case 1. Destabilising the plantation economy through local knowledge of food and farming

The colonisation of territories in Asia, Africa, and the Americas involved the forceful imposition of the European social order on other societies. Centuries of colonisation, competition, and maritime warfare made armed force the central means by which access to natural resources and produce was secured. The ferocious commodification extended to human beings, most prevalent and systematic in the transatlantic slave trade (Eltis and Richardson, 2010). The majority of the slaves were sold to European plantation owners on the Caribbean islands and on mainland South America. Science was called in to justify the plantation system as an 'efficient' agricultural system, most prominently towards the end of the 19th century, when agricultural research explored new technologies to further increase the productivity of soils, crops, and plantation workers (Ross, 2014). During the same period, slave-based labour on plantations in the Caribbean came to be replaced by contract labour, recruited primarily from India and other Asian countries. Despite European dominance, the social order of the plantation system was continuously challenged by revolts, resistance, and escape by the resident labour force. The various forms of resistance, it is argued here, were rooted in the co-production of knowledge from below and a social order based on subsistence farming.

Two notions from the work of Marcel Mauss are helpful to understand the ways in which knowledge from below sustains an alternative model of social order that underpins the practices of resistance of plantation workers. Mauss used the method of his uncle Emile Durkheim to investigate how social structures and moral order emerge through specific and formational social phenomena. One such phenomenon is the human capacity to use technology.[1] Mauss's interpretation of technology is well summarised by the title of his best-known essay on the topic: *Techniques of the Body*. He observed substantial variation in the way people from different societies employ and develop bodily techniques for numerous simple tasks. This variation, Mauss argued, is cultural in that it is transferred from parent to child over many generations, resulting in traditions and routines. The principle—that knowledge transfer takes place through bodily techniques in social interaction—can be extended to the use of tools, machines, and technical systems as societies connect, expand, and innovate. Exchange of techniques and knowledge about techniques between cultures are key drivers of social innovation, to the effect that 'societies, like techniques and like the [person] who practices them, are made out of synthesis rather than distillation, that their lack of "purity" is their source of strength, that *métissage* or *créolisation* is not their worst nightmare but their salutary fate' (Schlanger, 2006, p. 28; see also Tsing, 2015).

A second insight from Mauss is from his influential essay on *The Gift*, where he theorises on principles of exchange based on a study of symbolic items circulating within and between communities. These practices, Mauss argued, reveal that reciprocity and moral obligation are essential mechanisms in any society. Variations of the phenomenon across different cultural contexts reveal that exchange and service performed out of obligation are not diametrically opposed to exchange for money out of economic self-interest. Rather, these co-exist in different configurations and with fluid boundaries between them (Hart, 2014). Mauss's notion of reciprocity is taken up by James C. Scott (1976) in his book on the 'moral economy' of peasant societies. Scott (1976, p. 167) argued that the norms of reciprocity and the right to subsistence are fundamental to communities of smallholder farmers: 'The right to subsistence, in effect, defines the minimal needs that must be met for members of the community within the context of reciprocity.' In other words, what counts as an acceptable quality and quantity of (food) items necessary for survival is premised on the perceived legitimacy of the social interactions and transactions underlying subsistence.

We can deploy what, according to Mauss, are two constitutive elements of social formation—bodily techniques in social interaction, and exchange relations based on reciprocity—to develop a novel analysis of practices of resistance against the slavery system in the Americas. We can examine bodily social practices, other than plantation agriculture, through which social interaction became a source of revolt, escape, and resistance contesting the illegitimacy of the suppressive plantation regime. One option is to assume the alternative must be stored in the minds of the enslaved Africans as memories from the communities they once lived in. However, the nature of historical sources makes it impossible to provide evidence in favour (or against) this assumption. More likely, and supported by recent historiography, the alternative practices existed within and alongside the plantation system. The predominant activity of the slave-based plantation system in the Americas was the production of crops and products made from these crops for export to Europe. Cane fields and sugar factories dominated in most places, next to cotton, coffee, cocoa, and other products. Besides the export crop, plantations also had fields reserved for growing food. What crops were grown on these provision grounds was partly determined by plantation managers but with considerable options for slaves to add crops.

Some plantations differentiated between fields for provisions and fields for the slaves, the latter often containing a larger variety of food crops and medicinal plants. There were more spaces within and around the plantation that slaves used to provide for their food. These spaces enabled slaves to employ and cultivate their own techniques of farming, hunting, and fishing, following traditional practices from Africa or learned in social interaction in the plantation context. The same techniques also formed the basis of maroon communities (Van Andel et al., 2016). *Marronage*—forms of deflection varying from secretive escape to flight after revolt—became a viable option due to the knowledge and techniques of subsistence that slaves were able to develop in combination with working on the fields and in the factories of the plantations. Marronage was common in most New World areas where European colonisers set up slave-based plantation agriculture.

The options for slaves to spend time on provision grounds and other subsistence activities depended on the characteristics of the plantation, such as the ecology and landscape, the crop, the tasks, and the strictness of the regime. The shelter of swamps, hills, and dense forest made a move away from the plantation a worthwhile alternative and subsistence farming was the technique by which enslaved groups re-established a moral economy that changed the nature of plantation-based societies. In the Pará region of Brazil, this resulted in a parallel economy that occasionally dominated the plantation economy (De la Torre, 2018). In Haiti, subsistence farming and marronage formed a launchpad for the slave revolt of 1791 and continued as a source for resistance, a reason why subsequent governments of the free nation failed to sustain former estate models of agriculture (Gonzalez, 2019). In Suriname and most British plantation economies in the Caribbean, Asian contract labourers, like the enslaved Africans before them, also opted for subsistence. In many of these areas the smallholders of Asian origin became successful rice farmers and collectively transformed the rural economies (Maat and Van Andel, 2018).

Case 2. Situated knowledges and skilled visions: Sheep scab notification practices in Scotland

Sheep scab has a long history in Scotland, and until the late 1980s sheep scab numbers had been very low due to compulsory bi-yearly treatments observed by the local police, and notification legislation. However, when sheep scab was nearly eradicated the UK government decided that full eradication was not feasible or cost effective, and the policy of compulsory treatment changed in 1989, with the removal of sheep scab from the list of notifiable diseases in 1990. This led to major scab outbreaks in the early 1990s, with more than 3,000 sheep farms affected in the UK year-on-year (ADAS, 2008). The Scottish government decided to reissue sheep scab as a notifiable disease under the 2010 Sheep Scab Scotland Order and its 2011 amendments. This order means that in case of sheep scab suspicion, the disease has to be notified to the animal health authorities. In practice, however, notification is often avoided, or only done when sheep scab has become clearly visible. To understand why the renewed notification legislation for sheep scab is not being taken up by sheep farmers in the way envisioned by the Scottish government, we need to follow their local knowledge of sheep scab from below, and how this is premised on a social order based on 'preventing' disease outbreaks.

The concepts of situated knowledges and skilled visions are particularly helpful for understanding the practices of sheep farmers and veterinarians (not) to notify sheep scab at an early clinical stage. Donna Haraway (1988) coined the term 'situated knowledges' as an attempt towards 'a more adequate, richer, better account of a world, in order to live in it well and in critical, reflexive relation to our own as well as others' practices of domination and the unequal parts of privilege and oppression that make up all positions' (p. 579). For Haraway, rejecting the notion of objectivity as a 'view from nowhere, from above' (p. 589), knowledge is inevitably situated in time and space (also see Mol, 2002) and thus is inherently partial and never fully visible. The concept of skilled visions extends the concept to emphasise how visions and detached observation are not necessarily identifiable and should therefore not be opposed to other senses. Thus, skilled visions are 'embedded in multi-sensory practices' (Grasseni, 2007, p. 4). Methodologically, this means that in order to understand how farmers tackle sheep scab we need to attend closely to the diverse practices through which they recognise and act upon it, where seeing 'involves an on-going combination of recognising, acknowledging and acting upon' (Cohn, 2007, p. 94). Seeing, knowing, and practising are co-joined, and one cannot pre-empt the other. The practices performed in recognising and suspecting sheep scab combines multiple—though not only human—senses.

The social order of preventing sheep scab is rooted in the skilled visions of farmers to recognise and treat sheep scab at an early stage and in its situated knowledges that include a former history of near eradication through preventive bi-yearly treatments. First, to suspect sheep scab at an early stage is skilled work, because it is caused by scab mites that are invisible to the naked human eye. Their invisibility, and the possibility of having other ectoparasites that cause itchy sheep (such as lice, ticks, maggots, or keds) makes it skilled work to recognise sheep scab early on (Van den Broek and Huntley, 2003). Many farmers mentioned sweaty wool, hypersensitivity (biting or spasm when being touched), itchiness on their backs and sides (dirty scratch marks from hooves, clean marks from licking/biting the fleece), and crusty skin as early signs of sheep scab (Middelveld, 2019). These clinical signs clearly are about more than looking at sheep alone, including touching sheep (the texture of their skin), as well as about the sheep's response to being touched. Recognising sheep scab at an early stage is therefore an embodied practice, based on skilled visions and situated knowledges. Furthermore, sheep scab suspicion grows stronger when visible and tangible clinical signs add up (Mol, 2002).

Once sheep scab is suspected, many farmers and veterinarians prefer to treat scab as soon as possible to prevent it from spreading, instead of notifying the authorities (Middelveld, 2019). The focus on 'preventive' treatments at an early stage of the disease is rooted in its history of near eradication before the regulations changed. Many farmers and veterinarians mentioned that scab is easily prevented (Middelveld, 2019). Furthermore, the absence of sheep scab on a farm strengthens the good reputation of the farmer (Burton, 2004), because it indicates that their biosecurity practices are effective, whereas the (known) presence of sheep scab results in reputation damage to the farm, resulting in low prices for their sheep. For these reasons, Patrick, a veterinarian, mentioned he prefers not to notify sheep scab when he encounters it:

> [W]e don't want to make it a notifiable outbreak. We want the farmer to be able to treat it, and [to] be on top of it before anybody realises that he's got

scab [...] Because of that quite often we diagnose what would be, it *may* be scab rather than it *is* scab. And treat *in case of*, rather than *because of* [...] It's because the farmers feel that it's an awful stigma to actually have them report it to the government because they have scab [...] If you can step in quickly it means that it's contained within one farm rather than spread to neighbours.

Notification is also not preferred because of the paperwork hassle, and to avoid government interference at the farm (Middelveld, 2019). The visit of ministry veterinarians at the farm also alerts neighbours that there is a problem with live-stock from the visited farm. Notification is thus considered necessary only in case of a clearly visible outbreak of sheep scab, whereas sheep scab in an early stage should be treated as soon as possible. Mark, a farmer, explained that he would only notify clinically visible sheep scab as follows: 'Well, we've never actually experienced it, because we've never got to that stage. We recognised it and cured it before we needed the Department.' Thus, a notification is issued only when sheep scab is identified at a late clinically visible stage. If it is recognised and treated before that stage, it is not considered an outbreak in need of notifica-tion, but a disease that warrants preventive treatment instead. This means that identification practices at the clinical stage of sheep scab shapes the boundaries for notification.

This case clearly shows that farmers' and veterinarians' situated knowledges and skilled visions of sheep scab are based on their experience with and know-how of the disease, which is embedded in recognition and notification prac-tices. These local knowledges and practices conflict with assumptions embedded in legislation which not only have reissued sheep scab as a notifiable disease but which rely on farmers and veterinarians notifying authorities of sheep scab suspicion at an early stage of the disease, which are then used by the Scottish government to monitor the disease. However, it is clear that these numbers are inherently flawed, because the notification of the disease by local farmers and veterinarians is often only executed at a late clinical stage of the disease and only when early-stage treatment has been unsuccessful. The mismatch between notification practices based on skilled visions of sheep scab 'from below' and the vision of the government to use notification numbers to monitor the disease 'from above' is paramount and has an important implication for sheep scab gov-ernance. By not taking sheep scab knowledges and practices 'from below' seri-ously (English et al., 1992; Lavau, 2017), policymakers are overlooking valuable alternative ways of coping with sheep scab in practice (Hinchliffe et al., 2017).

Case 3. Public engagement with GM foods

Agricultural biotechnology is commonly presented as part of the solution to the grand challenge of global food security. With rising world populations, persistent hunger, and a growing demand for food globally, it is unsurprising that food security is one of this century's most critical challenges for global policymaking. A current and dominant policy narrative is the 'sustainable intensification of global agriculture' frame (Royal Society, 2009), which presents novel science and technology as having a primary role to play in meeting these challenges. Without radical advances, particularly at the molecular level—the argument runs—it is hard to imagine how yields can be increased without adverse environmental impact or the cultivation of new land. Novel science and technology have, at least within this epistemic framework, the potential to contribute to food production through forms of genetic improvement, including genetically modified (GM) crops that have been altered to introduce new and desirable traits.

While the global imperative for the genetic modification of crops and foods is often made by policymakers and establishment scientific communities, it is less clear how dominant science policy framings map onto public opinion. While institutions such as the Royal Society (2015, p. 1) may feel entitled to say that 'the science demonstrates that these [GM] techniques are not inherently any more risky than conventional breeding approaches used to produce crops,' that 'robust regulatory processes [are] in place to assess the safety of GM crops and approve those that can be used for cultivation, food and feed,' and that by implication the key task for policymakers and science policy organisations is to ensure that 'the science around the production of GM food and feed needs to be better communicated so that people are able to feel informed,' this does not exhaust the science policy framing. What if there are alternative ways to frame the science policy debate that speak more directly to the ways that people feel and think about GMOs from the bottom up; or that address actual and latent public concerns and that recognise the 'reasonableness' of public apprehension and ambivalence? Such a frame contrasts starkly to the still prominent policy narrative where public opinion (typically viewed as overly negative) is represented as a problem that needs to be addressed, classically through the provision of one-way communication flows rather than as the holders of legitimate views and concerns that need to be engaged with through dialogue.

It was this ambition to scrutinise and hold to account this dominant science policy configuration that structured an early piece of public engagement research conducted in 1996/1997 in the UK, the Uncertain World study (Grove-White et al., 1997). Importantly, this study pre-dated the public controversy over GM crops and foods that came to prominence in the UK and mainland Europe in 1998/1999. The study sought to cast light on how people feel about agricultural genetic modification technology in the UK, to explore possible future public reactions and responses, and to offer suggestions for improved institutional handling of the technology. The study rested on the interpretation of nine focus group discussions, involving a selection of population groups in the north and south of England, covering a spectrum of social classes and age groups, with a bias towards women. The research was designed to develop clues about factors shaping public attitudes and likely responses in a field where few at the time could be claimed to have 'informed' or 'settled' views.

Given this unfamiliarity, the discussions began with a contextual discussion (see Chapter 12, this volume, on the importance of context in public deliberations on emerging technology) on what had changed in the world of food over the last five to ten years or so, exploring with participants what had been lost and gained. How people will respond to genetically modified (GM) foods, the argument went, depends on how they think about food in general and what they consider to be the issues surrounding the role and application of technology in food production. The discussions themselves were illuminating, as participants spoke of their ambivalence towards the use of advanced technology in food: while technology had enabled people to lead busy and convenient lives, it had also generated concerns about food processing, the use of artificial preservatives, and the apparent increase in food health scares. Drawing on the then proximate 'mad cow' disease controversy, participants expressed unease about the integrity and adequacy of government regulations, about official 'scientific' assurances of safety, about the benign intentions of food producers and processors, and about the increasing perceived 'unnaturalness' of food. Such early discussions provided clues to the ways in which public responses to GM foods would later be configured, highlighting the salience of concepts of trust, naturalness, justification, and perceived agency in moderating public responses. Subsequently, different frames on GMOs were introduced, making clear distinctions between current and proposed uses of genetic modification techniques, highlighting the potential for the transgenesis of different genes (both plant and animal) in different contexts of application, from food production to animal rearing to medical uses.

The study produced a distinctive set of findings. It reported people's considerable ambivalence towards the prospect of GM foods, a profound sense of inevitability and fatalism that the technology would become pervasive in food production despite public concern, and the apparent paradox that while people may purchase GM foods they may also harbour significant unease about the technology as a whole and about the potential implications of its trajectories. In addition, the study found that people had concerns about the integrity and adequacy of present patterns of government regulation, and in particular about official 'scientific' assurances of safety that reflected at the time wider issues of trust in UK political institutions. While these findings were not wholly novel at the time—other public opinion research had similarly identified latent public concern—what was novel was the interpretation of these findings as offering a critique to established GMO policy and regulatory frameworks which had tended to view public concerns as irrational and as best ameliorated through scientifically robust information (e.g. on harms). This 'deficit' understanding of the public had been critiqued in previous scholarship by one of the authors of the study, Brian Wynne, and this critique underpinned both the conceptual frame of the research and the interpretation of its findings (Wynne, 1992).

In the Uncertain World report, the authors sought to articulate the sense of open-ended uncertainty evoked by public deliberation on the technology, and the strong feelings of impotence and fatalism this seemed to engender. In such circumstances, unambiguous unilateral assertions by industry and government spokesmen that the technology can and should be managed safely on a 'case-by-case' basis was presented as likely to have the effect of compounding, rather than assuaging, the mistrust felt by individuals across all population groups. Thus, notwithstanding differences in participants' responses, it was the convergences in public talk and their contrast with official discourses and understandings that drove the analysis of the data and their interpretation. Indeed, when the GM food and crop controversy unfolded in the UK and Europe in 1998/1999, and when the then UK government chief scientific adviser (GCSA) was exposed to the Uncertain World study, he responded in a personal communication as follows, speaking to the potential political salience of this anticipatory mode of focus group research on public perceptions:

> I now have had a chance to read 'Uncertain World,' which I wish I had indeed read earlier. It is in many ways a remarkably prescient document. (May 1999)

Conclusion

What lessons can we draw from the three cases above? A key lesson from the first case—involving the history of slave revolt and *marronage* as rooted in alternative agricultural practices—lies in the persistence and recurrence of similar forms of challenge and contestation to the predominant social order of plantation economies. The long-lasting suppression by subsequent colonial regimes aimed at exploitation of labourers was continuously challenged by the moral economy of subsistence out of which alternative social orderings emerged. The enslaved Africans, Maroons, and, after abolition, many Asian contract labourers all cherished the limited options to grow their own food and spend time in the fields the way they wanted. Escape, through *marronage* and illicit networks within and between plantations, allowed a gradual expansion of these practices to the extent to which they gradually overturned the plantation system. The specific historical setting of a ruling colonial class versus an exploited and suppressed labour force that nevertheless persisted in pursuing an alternative social order may suggest that knowledge from below flourishes under conditions of extreme adversity, or may require antagonistic divides between minority elites and an impoverished rural population. The second case challenges such interpretations.

In this case, we see how the sheep scab outbreaks triggered the Scottish government to devise policy measures and regulations that not only ignored the knowledge of sheep farmers, but also existing ways of incorporating official health requirements within their practices through collaboration with local veterinarians. Local sheep farmers and veterinarians joined hands in early treatment of sheep scab to prevent it from spreading, but also to prevent government authorities from taking over, thereby losing control over their herds and farms. The case thus highlights the role of proactive intervention as a significant mechanism and feature of knowledge from below. The case also makes clear that knowledge from below and 'action from below' are mutually reinforcing. The values that triggered the need for early treatment enhanced local knowledge of sheep bodies and sheep behaviour, as much as the other way around.

Finally, in the third case it is the anticipation and probing of future consequences that is central, and how such anticipation can be produced through deliberation. The case of introducing genetically modified (GM) crops revealed the partiality of institutional views on what constitutes desirable innovation, including assumptions about how the general public would perceive such innovations in real world circumstances. The limitations of in-built norms and assumptions came to light after engaging with the wider public through a series of focus group meetings. What stands out from the case is that the complexity of the advanced scientific and regulatory knowledge that underpins GM crops appeared not to obstruct the 'lay' public from identifying and critiquing the specific values and interests deeply embedded in the development of GM crops, including the articulation of concerns over their limitations and the sketching of alternatives. Moreover, in the public deliberation, both science-based GM applications and alternatives are projected on a (nearby) future, highlighting the potential and importance of addressing such issues in an anticipatory manner before applications are realised.

In assorted ways, summarised in Table 2.1, these contributions configure knowledge as a plural concept that is built out of scientific, institutional, practical, and local practices, and where a failure of alignment can lead to contestation. In each case the knowledges from below were resistant to, and unrecognised by, dominant epistemologies of knowledge production and their associated governing social orderings. It is important therefore to take knowledge from below seriously; both because it provides valuable alternatives and for how it opens up

TABLE 2.1 Connectivity and the making of legitimacy

Cases	Epistemic and social connections	Making knowledge from below legitimate
Destabilising the plantation economy.	Antagonistic and suppressive, leading to resistance and escape, eventually gaining recognition and rapprochement.	Through historical analysis.
Sheep scab notification practices.	Parallel and disconnected, local coalitions between lay and expert knowledge challenging 'top-down' science-based policies.	Through stakeholder analysis and participatory observation.
Public engagement with GM foods.	Multiple and disconnected, causing suspicion and alienation from formal (scientific) institutions.	Through stakeholder analysis and public engagement.

the possibility of doing things (agriculture, sheep scab, or GM) differently. These findings—both epistemic and practical—raise implications for governance and inclusive development for which this chapter provides a set of solid insights.

Note

1 This paragraph is based on Schlanger (2006).

References

ADAS (2008). *An evidence base for new legislation and guidance for implementation of a compulsory treatment period for sheep scab*. Accessed 18 June 2020. https://www.webarchive. org.uk/wayback/archive/20170701074158/http://www.gov.scot/Publications/ 2008/07/17113358/51

Burton, R. (2004). Seeing through the 'good farmer's' eyes: Towards developing an understanding of the social symbolic value of 'productivist' behaviour. *Sociologia Ruralis*, 44(2), 195–215.

Carenzo, S. (2020). Contesting informality through innovation 'from below': Epistemic and political challenges in a waste pickers cooperative from Buenos Aires (Argentina), *Tapuya: Latin American. Science, Technology and Society*, 3(1), 441–471.

Cohn, S. (2007). Seeing and drawing: The role of play in medical imaging. In: C. Grasseni (ed.). *Skilled visions: Between apprenticeship and standards*. New York: Berghahn Books, 91–105.

De la Torre, O. (2018). *The people of the river: Nature and identity in Black Amazonia, 1835–1945*. Chapel Hill: University of North Carolina Press.

Eltis, D. and Richardson, D. (2010). *Atlas of the transatlantic slave trade*. Yale: Yale University Press.

English, P., Burgess, G., Segundo, R. and Dunn, J. H. (1992). *Stockmanship: Improving the care of the pig and other livestock*. Ipswich: Farming Press.

Gonzalez, J. (2019). *Maroon nation: A history of revolutionary Haiti*. Yale: Yale University Press.

Grasseni, C. (ed.) (2007). *Skilled visions: Between apprenticeship and standards*. New York: Berghahn Books.

Grove-White, R., Macnaghten, P., Mayer, S. and Wynne, B. (1997). *Uncertain world: GMOs, food and public attitudes in Britain*. CSEC and Unilever.

Haraway, D. (1988). Situated knowledges: The science question in feminism and the privilege of partial perspective. *Feminist Studies*, 14(3), 575–599.

Hart, K. (2014). Marcel Mauss' economic vision, 1920–1925: Anthropology, politics, journalism. *Journal of Classical Sociology*, 14(1), 34–44.

Hinchliffe, S., Bingham, N., Allen, J. and Carter, S. (2017). *Pathological lives: Disease, space and biopolitics*. Chichester: Wiley Blackwell.

Jasanoff, S. (ed.) (2004). *States of knowledge: The co-production of science and the social order*. London: Routledge.

Jasanoff, S. and Simmet, H. (2017). No funeral bells: Public reason in a 'post-truth' world. *Social Studies of Science*, 47(5), 751–770.

Lavau, S. (2017). Public policy and calculative practices of risk: Making matters of concern and 'non-communicable' threats, from farm to fork. *Sociologia Ruralis*, 57(1), 23–40.

Maat, H. and van Andel, T. R. (2018). The history of the rice gene pool in Suriname: Circulations of rice and people from the eighteenth century until late twentieth century. *Historia Agraria. Revista de Agricultura e Historia Rural*, 75, 69–91.

Macnaghten, P. (2021). Towards an anticipatory public engagement methodology: deliberative experiments in the assembly of possible worlds using focus groups. *Qualitative Research*. 21(1), 3–19.

Mauss, M. (1923/2000). *The gift: forms and functions of exchange in archaic societies*. W.W. Norton.

May, R. (1999). Personal communication to Robin Grove-White. Unpublished manuscript.

Middelveld, S. (2019). *Sheep scab in Scotland: An exploration of multiple disease situations*. Unpublished PhD dissertation. University of Aberdeen.

Mol, A. (2002). *The body multiple: Ontology in medical practice*. Duke University Press.

Royal Society (2009). *Reaping the benefits: Science and the sustainable intensification of global agriculture*. Assessed 17 June 2020. https://royalsociety.org/topics-policy/publications/2009/reaping-benefits/

Royal Society (2015). *Response to the Food Standards Agency call for views on the European Commission proposal on GM food and feed*. Assessed 17 June 2020. https://royalsociety.org/~/media/policy/Publications/2015/28-10-15-food-standards-agency-GM-food-and-feed.pdf

Rose, N. (2006). *The politics of life itself: Biomedicine, power, and subjectivity in the twenty-first century*. Princeton: Princeton University Press.

Ross, C. (2014). The plantation paradigm: Colonial agronomy, African farmers, and the global cocoa boom, 1870s–1940s. *Journal of Global History*, 9(1), 49–71.

Schlanger, N. (2006). *Marcel Mauss; Techniques, technology and civilisation*. New York: Durkheim Press/Berghahn Books.

Scott, J. (1976). *The moral economy of the peasant: Rebellion and subsistence in Southeast Asia*. Yale: Yale University Press.

Stirling, A. (2008). 'Opening up' and 'closing down': Power, participation, and pluralism in the social appraisal of technology. *Science Technology & Human Values*, 33(2), 262–294.

Tsing, A. (2015). *The mushrooom at the end of the world: On the possibility of life in capitalist ruins*. Princeton: Princeton University Press.

Van Andel, T., Meyer, R., Aflitos, S. et al. (2016). Tracing ancestor rice of Suriname Maroons back to its African origin. *Nature Plants*, 2(10), 16149.

Van den Broek, A. and Huntley, J. (2003). Sheep scab: The disease, pathogenesis and control. *Journal of Comparative Pathology*, 128(2/3), 79–91.

Wynne, B. (1992). Misunderstood misunderstanding: Social identities and the public uptake of science. *Public Understanding of Science*, 1(3), 281–304.

3

A TRANSDISCIPLINARY PERSPECTIVE ON GENDER MAINSTREAMING IN INTERNATIONAL DEVELOPMENT: THE CASE OF THE CGIAR

Diana E. Lopez and David Ludwig

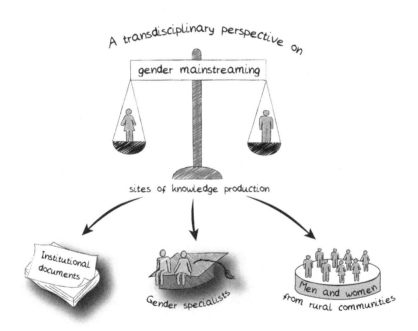

Introduction

Gender mainstreaming constitutes the dominant policy approach to gender in international development (Beck, 2017; Lyons et al., 2004; Verma, 2014). First promoted at the 1995 World Conference on Women in Beijing, the strategy seeks to integrate women's and men's concerns and experiences across all aspects

DOI: 10.4324/9781003112525-3

of development programmes—from conceptualisation to evaluation (Tegbaru et al., 2010). Endorsed by donors and high-level decision makers, it has become integrated across development programmes. However, its efficacy to achieve gender equality is widely questioned (Charlesworth, 2005; Palmary & Nunez, 2009). Feminist scholars are especially critical of the way gender has been mainstreamed across organisations. For them, mainstreaming has led to a depoliticisation of gender—a concept that is essentially political (Baden & Goetz, 1998; Hawthorne, 2004).

At the heart of the critique lies the perception that gender issues in development organisations are often sidelined or implemented in a truncated form (Palmary & Nunez 2009; Sohal, 2005); for example, by prioritising short-term targeted measures to the detriment of long-term gender-transformative goals; by an organisational preference for universalism which fails to account for context-specific gendered experiences and practices; and by reducing gender complexities into ready-to-apply packages such as gender tools, frameworks, and guidelines. Gender mainstreaming has also been labelled as 'neo-colonial' due to its projection of a contingent perspective of gender onto the developing world without acknowledging its (European, liberal, middle-class, technocratic, white, feminist) origins (Lyons et al., 2004; Østebø, 2015). These issues of conceptualisation and institutionalisation have led many feminist and gender professionals to question the gender mainstreaming project as a whole (Cornwall et al., 2007; Lyons et al., 2004; Razavi & Miller, 1995; Sohal, 2005).

The challenges of gender mainstreaming in international development therefore benefit from a transdisciplinary perspective that highlights opportunities for mutual learning about gender by incorporating different sites of knowledge production. Building on insights from feminist epistemology (Anderson, 2000; Longino, 2017), this chapter develops an account of 'situated knowledge' (Haraway, 1988) that recognises diverse epistemic resources for engaging with gender in international development. Rather than interpreting gender mainstreaming through a decontextualised academic perspective, this chapter highlights different forms of situated knowledge about gender and their embedding in different sites of knowledge production. Harding's (2015) notion of 'strong objectivity' emphasises that this acknowledgement of the situated character of knowledge does not imply a cultural relativism that treats all beliefs about gender as equally valid. On the contrary, the situatedness of knowledge can strengthen objectivity by diversifying its evidence base through the inclusion of actors who often remain marginalised in international development projects. Rather than 'romanticizing and/or appropriating the vision of the less powerful while claiming to see from their positions' (Haraway, 1988, pp. 583–584), using a lens of situated knowledge enables a critically reflexive engagement with diverse epistemic resources. Situated knowledge further allows for a transdisciplinary perspective that engages with standpoints that commonly remain marginalised in dominant framings of gender mainstreaming.

This chapter examines situated knowledge about the contested notion of gender equality in the context of a major agricultural organisation, the CGIAR

(Consultative Group for International Agricultural Research), by investigating how this notion is portrayed in three sites of knowledge production. A closer examination at this organisation is pertinent given its impact in agricultural research as well as its political influence in the agricultural research and development agendas of the countries where it works. Our triangulated approach builds on (1) a literature analysis of seven CGIAR institutional documents; (2) semi-structured interviews conducted with 25 gender specialists across the CGIAR; and (3) focus group discussions about gender equality with women and men from 13 countries who participated in GENNOVATE—a CGIAR initiative focused on the interlinkages between gender norms, agency, and innovation in agriculture (Table 3.1). Informed by feminist and innovation theories, GENNOVATE features a comparative, qualitative, case study method and purposive sampling techniques to detect broad gender normative patterns while retaining their grounding in local contexts and realities (see Badstue et al., 2018). The triangulated approach guides our general proposal towards a transdisciplinary perspective for gender mainstreaming in the CGIAR and similar organisations.

Transdisciplinarity has been endorsed in development as a methodology that brings diverse forms of knowledge together. However, as discussed in Chapter 1, transdisciplinary knowledge integration is a challenging process in light of heterogenous ontologies and values that underlie situated knowledge. In the development sector, knowledge about 'gender' constitutes a prime example of these difficulties, as local perspectives frequently diverge from those of development organisations—often leading to the marginalisation of local perspectives on 'gender.' Yet, and as evidenced in Chapter 16 in this volume, significant opportunities arise from challenging the epistemic hierarchy (Table 3.1).

Three sites of knowledge production about 'gender equality'

According to CGIAR institutional documents

The CGIAR is an international non-profit organisation in agricultural research for development. It has the world's largest global agricultural innovation network, including national governments, academic institutions, global policy bodies, private companies, and non-governmental organisations (Özgediz, 2012). The CGIAR is constituted by 15 autonomous research centres[1] working in agricultural policy, commodity crops and livestock, eco-regional, and natural resource management. Originally established in 1971 with a focus on technological efficiency and productivity for agricultural transformation, the CGIAR has expanded its emphasis beyond efficiency and productivity to include other goals, from sustainability to gender equality. At present, the organisation is undergoing the 'One CGIAR' reform aimed at further unification among centres, including an improvement of the current gender mainstreaming strategy

TABLE 3.1 Sources of data

Data source	(1) CGIAR institutional documents	(2) Semi-structured interviews with gender specialists					(3) Focus Group Discussions with men and women		
No.	7	25					454		
Selection criteria	Publicly available documents from 2011–2020 focused on organizational structures and gender strategies. The documents are marked with an '*' in References.	Purposively selected based on CGIAR centre, sex, origin, experience, and academic background[1]					Purposively selected based on country, sex, and age**		
		Distribution of Gender Specialists					*Distribution of FGDs*		
		CGIAR centres	Sex	Origin[a]	Experience[b]	Academic background[c]	Country	Sex	Age
		13	21 females	HICs: 14	>5:10	LS:5	Afghanistan:16	228 with females	227 with Youth
			4 males	LMICs:11	4–3:7	SS:11	Bangladesh:24	226 with Males	227 with Adults
					3–1:8	Both:9	Ethiopia:32		
							India:18		
							Malawi:8		
							Mexico:21		
							Morocco:12		
							Nepal:24		
							Nigeria:16		
							Pakistan:48		
							Tanzania:16		
							Uzbekistan:16		
							Zimbabwe:16		

FDGs = Focus group discussions

[1] This was done as much as possible, based on availability

[a] HICs = high income countries; LMICs=low-and-middle-income countries

[b] Working years in the CGIAR

[c] LS = life sciences; SS = social sciences

**According to GENNOVATE methodology, see Badstue et al., 2018

(CGIAR, 2019). For the first time in its history, the strategy identifies gender equality as one of the five impact areas to be addressed by the reform (CGIAR, 2019).

Across the documents analysed, gender equity/equality are consistently presented as crucial for achieving development goals such as poverty reduction, improved food and nutrition security, and better natural resource systems and ecosystem services (CGIAR-IEA, 2017; CGIAR, 2016, 2019); as well as 'prerequisite for growth, prosperity and competitiveness' (CGIAR, 2020a, p. 1). The current consortium-level gender strategy further reflects this orientation by committing research programmes to developing agricultural technologies, farming systems, and policies to support women's agricultural productivity across the 70 countries where the CGIAR works (CGIAR, 2011). This is operationalised by including clearly assigned budgets, integration plans, and monitoring and evaluation mechanisms as part of the CGIAR gender mainstreaming strategy (CGIAR, 2011). Besides an emphasis in supporting rural women's agricultural productivity, the recent *Action Plan for Gender, Diversity, and Inclusion in CGIAR's Workplaces* (CGIAR, 2020b) indicates that gender equality is becoming a central component within the organisation. This is evidenced, for instance, by the CGIAR's commitment to increase women's representation across the organisational hierarchy by 35% (CGIAR, 2020b). Fostering gender equality within the organisation in this and other ways is thus expected to lead to 'significant improvements in employee engagement, ability to innovate, responsiveness to changing client needs and team collaboration [...] [which] allows to draw on different perspectives to enhance the quality of our decision making, deepen the relevance of our advice and outputs, and enhance our efficiency and effectiveness' (CGIAR, 2020a, p. 1). The documents assert that the risk of failing to attain a diverse and inclusive environment will result in the CGIAR losing its position as a front runner in agri-food systems research for development (CGIAR, 2020a).

The analysis suggests that institutional knowledge about gender is primarily produced in its relation to broader CGIAR objectives. Both in the workplace and in relation to the research and strategies developed to serve rural women, the CGIAR increasingly produces knowledge about gender but positions gender equality less as a goal in itself and more as an instrument for wider institutional goals—i.e., strengthening its strategic position as a development organisation or contributing to goals such as food security and poverty reduction.

According to gender specialists working in the CGIAR

We conducted interviews with CGIAR gender specialists from 2018 to 2020 focused on four areas: (i) institutional climate for gender work in the organisation; (ii) differences and similarities in gender research across the CGIAR; (ii) experiential learning in translating gender theory into practice; and (iv) institutional challenges and opportunities to create gender-transformative change. In this section, we examine their views about gender equality.

Overall, the interviews indicate broad agreement among gender specialists about gender equality being part of the mandate of the CGIAR (21 out of 25) and about their own work contributing to this mandate (24/25). With most of them also thinking that 'doing gender' means focusing on *both women and men* (22/25). Despite this common starting point, gender specialists highlighted different concerns and roles in their contributions to gender equality—evidencing the contested nature of this issue within the CGIAR. For example, the interviews indicate different attitudes towards gender-sensitive approaches (that aim to address gender-specific needs) and gender-transformative approaches (that aim to change gender-specific roles). Fourteen gender specialists, mostly from high-income countries, stated that the organisation needs to move from being gender-sensitive to become gender-transformative as noted by a specialist from CIMMYT,

> I firmly believe that transformative research is the only way to get closer to gender equality in the agricultural sector. But I do not believe the CGIAR has the expertise currently to do that well. Therefore, they could potentially be doing harm if they took on that particular mandate. We don't have the methods, we don't have the skills [...] So, if we suddenly move to transformative methods, they're going to mess it up and they're going to do harm.

A researcher from IWMI also emphasised that a lack of transformation perpetuates inequality and poverty:

> We [gender specialists] have inspired a whole generation of women to become researchers and scientists; that's a win, right? But we have not transformed the lives of rural women in different parts of the world [...] I think part of the development work [we do] also perpetuates poverty, because if you keep thinking of them as women who lack agency then they'll forever be poor women who lack it. If they had any [agency] we will be out of a job, so in a way is good for us [development workers] that there is inequality.

However, 11 specialists, mostly from low-and-middle-income countries (LMICs), considered that being gender-sensitive suffices in some research areas such as breeding, and that transformative ambitions do not always benefit the rural communities that are served by the CGIAR work:

> I don't think we have to transform everything. We need to find the things that work well in the communities without necessarily transforming their culture [...] so I think it's both approaches, but I mean, these white people in those senior positions, oh, they are all about 'we have to transform and to use transformative approaches.' I say that if you go to the communities and talk about

transforming structures and forget to see what is good and works there you just confuse the community members. So no, I don't think it should be fully transformative but I think we have to be strategic and know which approach to use in different cases […] Honestly, I don't think even gender people [in the CGIAR] really understand what it is that we want to transform for sure and I worry that if we try to push something that we don't know, it would just back-fire. So, is transformation the best way for the CGIAR to go? That's exactly what we should be asking ourselves now. (*Specialist from ILRI*)

These heterogeneous attitudes towards gender-transformative and gender-sensitive approaches indicate the diversity of gender specialists' perspectives across the CGIAR. On the one hand, transformative ambitions towards gender reflect that gender specialists are situated in feminist discourses that highlight systemic issues of inequality and the limitations of incremental approaches for achieving gender equality. On the other hand, endorsement of gender-sensitive perspectives reflects that gender specialists in the CGIAR often see themselves as working together with local communities in improving gender equality and people's livelihoods without necessarily striving to transform local structures.

The interviews also revealed that gender specialists do not always consider their position aligned with the institutional gender perspective of the CGIAR. For example, specialists widely agreed that they are expected to contribute, among other goals, to (a) build institutional gender awareness (25); (b) empower rural women and help them challenge unequal power structures (18); (c) empower other women researchers and staff in their centre (25); and (d) help to increase the rate of adoption of practices and/or technologies developed by their centre (22). However, 20 respondents felt that (d) was more an institutional priority than their own. Furthermore, 22 specialists noted that while (a)–(c) were only deemed as 'desirable' objectives by the organisation, they themselves considered these goals as being fundamental to their jobs.

The interviews suggest different forms of situated knowledge about gender equality influencing gender specialists' engagements with gender and agricultural innovation issues. The heterogeneous responses regarding gender-transformative and gender-sensitive approaches, for instance, reflect how specialists produce knowledge about gender equality in heterogeneous contexts and through varied standpoints that contribute to different attitudes towards development interventions. Furthermore, the situated knowledge of gender specialists partially differs from the institutional knowledge of the CGIAR, which focuses on the relation between gender equality and wider institutional goals.

According to men and women from rural communities

This section draws from two questions about gender equality asked during GENNOVATE focus group discussions (FGDs) with men and women from rural communities across 13 countries. The first question aimed to gather *descriptive* responses to the term 'gender equality'; whereas the second sought to encourage people to share *their own views*—including making individual assessments.

Almost all FGDs (445/454) had come across the concept of gender equality; with most responses to the first question (*what comes to mind when you think of the term gender equality?*) closely related to mainstream definitions of gender equality; including references to equal rights, responsibilities, and opportunities between women/girls and men/boys. People also spoke about gender equality in relation to several issues. As shown in Figure 3.1, gender equality was most frequently discussed in reference to cultural, social, and gender norms (i.e., informal institutions). For instance, seclusion norms were reported to affect women's freedom of mobility, especially in Afghanistan, Bangladesh, India, and Pakistan. Gender equality was also identified to provoke strong emotional responses—particularly stress, discomfort, and even violence.

In response to the second question (*do you think gender equality is a good or a bad thing?*), most people talked about gender equality favourably. Overall, women made more favourable assessments than men (63% compared to 52%); with young women and men making the most favourable assessments (Figure 3.2).

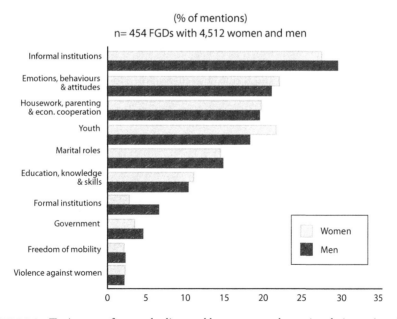

FIGURE 3.1 Topics most frequently discussed by women and men in relation to 'gender equality.'

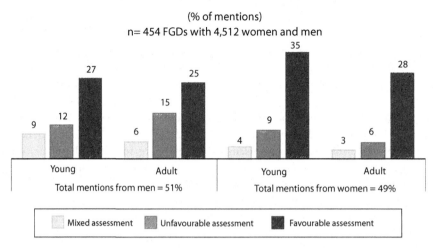

FIGURE 3.2 Normative assessments of 'gender equality' among men and women from different age groups.

However, the understanding of and knowledge about gender equality between different groups of men and women was diverse. People referenced various sources of knowledge influencing their own assessment of gender equality. These sources derived from (1) their own (bodily) experience, i.e., setting themselves as examples or by referencing other cases they had seen or heard about; (2) external conceptualisations, such as attending a training about gender equality; and (3) associations between external conceptualisations of gender equality with local notions of equality between men and women as described by religion, the Holy Scriptures, Sharia law, or cultural norms and traditions. The following quotes show how attitudes towards gender equality interact with situated knowledge about cultural, economic, and religious contexts:

Ethiopian FGDs

> We know about equality and today there are meetings to ensure women's participation. But when we go out and attend the meeting, we face problems back home and our husbands asked where we have been and would say 'go back where you have been, go ahead leave the house.' Then he will beat us when we refuse to leave the house. There are women who are not even allowed to go anywhere so they cannot participate in trainings or meetings. (*Ethiopian adult woman*)

> I know a man who sent his wife to an Arab country to work. He prepared meals including baking 'Injera' and feeding his children all the time while she was absent. Since this was not an accustomed practice in our

community we were amused by his ingenuity. This is what I call equality because we all learned from him. (*Ethiopian adult man*)

Afghan FGDs

Equality between men and women is good. Islam has shown us the rights of men and women. In Islam they are not as equal as stipulated by the human rights advocates and from what people from NGOs are talking nowadays. But their rights are clearly mentioned in the Quran. (*Adult man from Afghanistan*)

We men are responsible of all the rights that Allah has given to women. For instance, if we make dresses for ourselves but not for our wives, this is wrong. We, in accordance to the regulations of Sharia, have to meet the needs of women. A family is also responsible to provide equal education rights to their kids, both girls and boys. I would say as an example, that of two families deciding that when their kids grow-up they will marry. When the kids grow-up, if the girl doesn't like to marry the boy, the Quran has given right to the girl to decide whom to marry. So, if she is illiterate, she will not know her rights. It is then compulsory to provide education to kids in order for them to have enough knowledge. (*Adult man from Afghanistan*)

Zimbabwean FGDs

Gender equality is good only when it applies to the work place. In the past it was rare to see a woman driving a car or being a technician. Now women drive cars and have technical jobs. We [men] have no problem with that, but let it end there. If we apply gender equality in the home, we lose our cultural values and practices. (*Adult man from Zimbabwe*)

Gender equality is a bad thing because we [men] are not receiving the respect we are supposed to get from our wives. As I was passing by a certain household, I heard a woman saying to her husband, 'Can you wash these plates, please.' You hear a woman saying can you please wash these plates not acknowledging that I would have paid 15 head of cattle to her parents for her to be with me. Otherwise, this gender equality [issue] is one of the causes of poor rains because long ago we used to have enough rainfall, but when this gender equality was introduced our climate suddenly changed. (*Adult man from Zimbabwe*)

Figure 3.1 shows that people across geographical settings associate gender equality with particular sociocultural norms and gender stereotypes (e.g. around economic participation or education); the quotes showed how people's attitudes are also embedded in different forms of situated knowledge: for example, patriarchal practices of social control (Ethiopia, quote 1), changing gender roles due to migration (Ethiopia, quote 2), local religious interpretations of gender relations (Afghanistan, quote 1+2), or sociocultural conflicts arising from changing gender roles (Zimbabwe, quote 1+2). As gender permeates all dimensions of social life, everybody can be seen to have their own particular 'gender knowledge' with their 'durable gendered assumptions [...] enmeshed in local understandings of "mainstream" issues and local practices' (Cavaghan, 2017, p. 43). However, much of the situated knowledge about the contextual negotiations of gender equality is not available to external gender specialists or even present at the CGIAR's institutional level. This section highlights the opportunities of incorporating diverse forms of situated knowledge within the gender and agriculture initiatives in the CGIAR.

Reflections and conclusions

Gender mainstreaming has become increasingly challenged as an institutional strategy that often pursues short-term and technocratic goals that lack transformative capacities towards gender equality (Charlesworth, 2005; Palmary & Nunez, 2009; Verma, 2014). In the international development context, gender mainstreaming has also been criticised as relying on a narrow Western understanding of gender that is projected onto LMICs (Østebø, 2015). This chapter aims to contribute to a transdisciplinary reconfiguration of gender mainstreaming in the CGIAR and in similar organisations by expanding its treatment of gender equality into one that acknowledges its contested and context-specific nature.

As advanced here, diverse knowledge about gender equality is associated with distinct sites of knowledge production. At the *institutional level*, CGIAR knowledge about gender equality/equity primarily relates to its role in achieving development goals from reduced poverty to food security to sustainability. *Gender specialists*, however, express knowledge about gender equality in relation to systemic issues that demand transformative change, as well as about gender sensitivity, being crucial for achieving gender equality in local community structures. Whereas the *focus group discussions* denote knowledge about gender equality in relation to personal bodily experiences, external conceptualisations, and local cultural and religious norms and socio-economic realities. This heterogeneity of situated knowledges about gender equality points towards the need for a transdisciplinary perspective. Especially, as a neglect of such knowledge diversity runs the risk of reproducing a narrow perspective on gender equality that largely reflects the concerns and issue framing of dominant institutional actors. However, transdisciplinary processes that bring different sites of knowledge production together do not only come with opportunities but also with many challenges (Ludwig & El-Hani, 2020). In the three sites of knowledge production researched, many challenges for transdisciplinary knowledge integration are salient as gender equality becomes interpreted through very different (and sometimes outright contradictory) concerns, values, and worldviews.

Despite challenges in knowledge integration, engagement with different sites of knowledge production—in this case, in relation to the contested notion of gender equality—creates substantial opportunities for mutual learning. We conclude with three areas of potential contributions for adopting a transdisciplinary perspective on situated knowledges in current debates about the formulation of a CGIAR gender mainstreaming strategy.

(a) From decontextualisation to context-specific knowledge through strategic gender research: A new CGIAR strategy for gender mainstreaming could become more inclusive towards different forms of situated knowledge by strengthening 'strategic' gender research,[2] in which projects are specifically designed to engage with situated knowledge about gender and food security. For instance, the knowledge derived from rural men and women in this chapter was only possible through the support of strategic gender initiatives like GENNOVATE—which highlights the need for CGIAR research and technologies to be designed and adapted in accordance with the situated knowledge of the actors affected by CGIAR interventions. Increasing representation of local knowledge through strategic gender research would also facilitate a shift from research that identifies gender inequalities to one that seeks to address them in practice. As highlighted in the wider literature on local knowledge (Lacey, 2019), academic texts tend to produce decontextualised knowledge (e.g. general statements about the link between gender equality and food security in institutional documents) while the knowledge of rural communities tends to be more adapted to its local context (e.g. statement about how gender equality relates to social particularities in a village). This context sensitivity of local knowledge often proves indispensable for moving from the identification of inequalities towards successful interventions.

(b) Addressing gender complexities beyond ready-to-apply packages: Strategic gender research that engages with local knowledge could also help to overcome limitations of generalised 'gender packages' by contributing to tools and resources that reflect situated knowledge and are adapted to the concerns and particularities of local communities. GENNOVATE, for instance, has developed a series of evidence-based inputs and recommendations to ensure gender considerations are integrated into projects on various development, nutrition, climate-smart agriculture, conservation agriculture, mechanisation, or farmer training events.[3] These resources and tools are designed to be adapted to different contexts, with some having broad geographical relevance and others only regional, country, or community-level significance. For instance, the resource 'Gender in Agricultural Mechanization' (Kawarazuka et al., 2018) presents case studies of gender implications in mechanisation in roots, tubers, and banana crops across geographies evidencing positive and negative outcomes which could help engineers and agronomists working with these crops to ensure mechanisation does not further local inequality.

(c) Relational approaches beyond women-only measures: The CGIAR often approaches gender mainstreaming through an exclusive focus on women—both *internally* (e.g. in their aim of ensuring representation of women across the organisational hierarchy) and *externally* (e.g. in their goal of empowering rural women

to achieve CGIAR goals). However, most of the gender specialists interviewed emphasised the relational character of gender equality; with some of them recommending a family, household, or another integrative approach to advance gender equality in the geographies where the CGIAR works. Focus group discussions in rural communities also often emphasised relational dimensions of gender equality at the household and community levels. A relational gender mainstreaming strategy would help to ensure that both men and women have an equal opportunity to participate in and to overcome limitations of common practices where only men attend agricultural trainings and only women attend gender equality talks. As pointed out by an adult Ethiopian woman: 'I wish there were different programs that engaged our men on equality of men and women, to teach them to stop treating women as if they are their property.'

Our three suggestions show how a transdisciplinary perspective on situated knowledge can contribute to reflective approaches to gender in the CGIAR and beyond. The ongoing transformation of the CGIAR system reflects its embeddedness in wider shifts of the development sector—which aim to diversify its mission beyond economic growth and technological innovation via sustainable development goals (SDG) including gender equality (SDG 5). However, the power of the organisation lies in its agricultural research work rather than on its focus on gender transformation (CGIAR-IEA, 2017). This may result in a gender mainstreaming strategy with insufficient conceptual reflectivity or institutional depth. The acknowledgement of distinct forms of situated knowledge embedded in different sites of knowledge production could mitigate this risk. A transdisciplinary perspective, as the one advanced in this chapter, can therefore contribute to understanding heterogeneous (e.g. cultural, economic, environmental, religious) relations and negotiating their relevance for fostering gender equality in agricultural contexts.

Notes

1 See all centres and their locations: https://www.cgiar.org/research/research-centers/.
2 The current CGIAR Gender Strategies involve two approaches: strategic gender research to deepen understanding of how gender disparities or gender relations affect agricultural innovation, productivity, and sustainability; and gender integrated analysis into ongoing agri-food systems research: https://gender.cgiar.org/genderplatform/gender-strategies/.
3 All GENNOVATE resources are available at: https://gennovate.org/.

References

Anderson, E. (2000). Feminist epistemology and philosophy of science. *Stanford Encyclopaedia of Philosophy*.
Baden, S. and Goetz, A. M. (1998). Who needs [sex] when you can have [gender]. In: Jackson, C. and Pearson, R. (eds.). *Feminist visions of development*, London: Routledge, 19–38.

Badstue, L., Petesch, P., Feldman, S., Prain, G., Elias, M. and Kantor, P. (2018). Qualitative, comparative, and collaborative research at large scale: An introduction to GENNOVATE. *Journal of Gender, Agriculture and Food Security*, 3(1), 1–27.

Beck, E. (2017). What a feminist curiosity contributes to the study of development. *Studies in Comparative International Development*, 52(2), 139–154.

Cavaghan, R. (2017). Bridging rhetoric and practice: New perspectives on barriers to gendered change. *Journal of Women, Politics & Policy*, 38(1), 42–63.

★CGIAR (2020a). Framework for gender, diversity and inclusion in CGIAR's workplaces. https://hdl.handle.net/10568/108036

★CGIAR (2020b). Action plan for gender, diversity and inclusion in CGIAR's workplaces: Principles, key Objectives, performance benchmarks and targets. https://hdl.handle.net/10568/108037

★CGIAR Consortium Board (2011). Consortium level gender strategy. https://cgspace.cgiar.org/bitstream/handle/10947/2630/Consortium_Gender_Strategy.pdf?sequence=4

★CGIAR Consortium Office (2016). CGIAR strategy and results framework 2016–2030. https://development.science.ku.dk/development-news/news/cgiar-strategy-and-results-framework/CGIAR_Strategy_and_Results_Framework.pdf

★CGIAR-IEA (2017). CGIAR-IEA. Evaluation of gender in CGIAR, Independent Evaluation Arrangement (IEA) of CGIAR.

★CGIAR System Council (2019). One CGIAR: A bold set of recommendations to the system council. CGIAR 9th meeting in Chengdu, China (13–14 November).

Cornwall, A., Harrison, E. and Whitehead, A. (2007). Gender myths and feminist fables: The struggle for interpretive power in gender and development. *Development and Change*, 38(1), 1–20.

Charlesworth, H. (2005). Not waving but drowning: Gender Mainstreaming and Human Rights in the United Nations. *Harvard Human Rights Journal*, 18, 1–18.

Haraway, D. (1988). Situated knowledges: The science question in feminism and the privilege of partial perspective. *Feminist Studies*, 14(3), 575–599.

Harding, S. (2015). *Objectivity and diversity: Another logic of scientific research*. Chicago: University of Chicago Press.

Hawthorne, S. (2004). The political uses of obscurantism: Gender mainstreaming and intersectionality. *Development Bulletin*, 64, 87–91.

Kawarazuka, N., Prain, G., Forsythe, L., Mayanja, S., Mudege, N. N., Babini, C. and Polar, V. (2018). *Gender in agricultural mechanization: Key guiding questions*. CIP.

Lacey, H. (2019). Ciência, valores, conhecimento tradicional/indígena e diálogo de saberes. *Desenvolvimento e Meio Ambiente*, 50, 93–115.

Longino, H. E. (2017). Feminist epistemology. In: Greco, J. and Sosa, E. (ed.). *The Blackwell Guide to Epistemology*, Oxford: Blackwell, 325–353.

Ludwig, D. and El-Hani, C. N. (2020). Philosophy of ethnobiology: Understanding knowledge integration and its limitations. *Journal of Ethnobiology*, 40(1), 3–20.

Lyons, T., Curnow, J. and Mather, G. (2004). Developing gender mainstreaming and "gender respect". *Development Bulletin*, 64, 37–41.

Palmary, I. and Nunez, L. (2009). The Orthodoxy of gender mainstreaming: Reflecting on gender mainstreaming as a strategy for accomplishing the Millennium Development Goals'. *Journal of Health Management*, 11(1), 65–78.

★Özgediz, S. (2012). The CGIAR at 40: Institutional evolution of the world's premier agricultural research network. https://cgspace.cgiar.org/handle/10947/2761

Østebø, M. T. (2015). Translations of gender equality among rural Arsi Oromo in Ethiopia. *Development and Change*, 46(3), 442–463.

Tegbaru, A., Fitzsimons, J., Gurung, B. and Odame, H. H. (2010). Change in gender relations: Managerial and transformative approaches of gender mainstreaming in agriculture. *Journal of Food, Agriculture and Environment*, 8(3/4), 1025.

Razavi, S. and Miller, C. (1995). From WID to GAD: Conceptual shifts in the women and development discourse. Occasional Article 1, no. 3, UNRISD.

Sohal, R. (2005). Strategic engagements: Exploring instrumentalist approaches to engendering development. *Canadian Journal of Development Studies*, 26(1), 665–676.

Verma, R. (2014). Business as unusual: The potential for gender transformative change in development and mountain contexts. *Mountain Research and Development*, 34(3), 188–196.

PART II

Decolonising knowledge integration

4

A SYSTEMIC APPROACH TO THE DECOLONISATION OF KNOWLEDGE

Implications for scholars of development studies

Sarah Cummings, Nyamwaya Munthali, and Peter Shapland

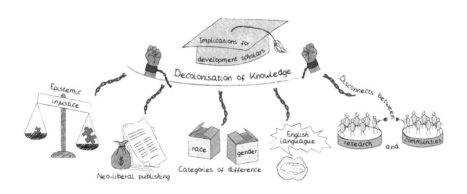

Introduction

The academic world has experienced a 'visible resurgence of decolonisation/decoloniality' evident in many recent publications (Bumpus, 2020; Demeter, 2020; Doharty et al., 2021; Istratii and Lewis, 2019; Ndlovu-Gatsheni, 2019; Pailey, 2020; Patel, 2020) that build on the work of others (Busia, 1960; Mafeje, 1978; Nkrumah, 1961; Okot p'Bitek, 1997; Said, 1979). Decolonisation of knowledge is a group of processes and actions that intentionally dismantle the entrenched, unequal patterns of knowledge creation and use that emanate from our colonial past; it is a process full of 'complexities, tensions and paradoxes' (Oliveira Andreotti et al., 2015, p. 22). Given that decolonisation of knowledge has been criticised as being 'an intellectual rather than a political project' (Broadbent, 2017), we aspire to make an important contribution to the overall decolonisation process by emphasising the importance of action, suggesting how scholars of development studies can 'walk the walk' on the decolonisation

DOI: 10.4324/9781003112525-4

of knowledge. To bring about change, we need activism and transformational knowledge which 'challenges each of us not to stop at the analysis, to oppose the status quo, to devise innovative solutions, and to include reflexivity and meta-learning.'[1]

In this chapter, we employ a systems perspective to investigate how coloniality is manifested in the current academic knowledge system and how we can make progress toward the 'decolonisation of knowledge.' We reflect on how individual scholars located in Western donor countries, who benefit from the coloniality of the current knowledge system, can undermine and contest this coloniality with their research and activism, resonating with Pailey's (2020, p. 742) statement that 'Until white development workers and scholars confront how they benefit from the racial hierarchies that underpin this field, and actively work to upend their unearned privilege, development will always suffer from a "white gaze" problem.' As we will discuss later, although we recognise that decolonisation is an ethical issue, we contend that cognitive diversity represents progress and improvements to our pool of knowledge.

Development studies and coloniality

The field of development studies focuses primarily on institutional and structural changes in formerly colonised countries, including empirical and normative concerns: how social change occurs, and what changes should occur (Kothari, 2019). Numerous scholars have shown how the international development project emerged directly out of colonialism, as a continuation of colonialist discourses (Chandra, 1992; Cooke, 2003; Goldsmith, 1997; Kothari, 2019; Miege, 1980). Although the 'good intentions' of development practitioners and researchers are an intrinsic part of development studies, these intentions tend to conceal the colonial roots of international development via the 'dichotomy between a colonialism that is "bad," exploitative, extractive and oppressive and a development that is "good," moralistic, philanthropic and humanitarian' (Kothari, 2019, p. 51). Against this background, 'coloniality' can be understood as the entrenched power dynamics and patterns of knowledge creation and use that have emerged from the accidental historical power relations of colonial domination. The term 'coloniality' was first used by Mignolo (1995) according to Torres (2007, p. 243):

> Colonialism denotes a political and economic relation in which the sovereignty of a nation or a people rests on the power of another nation, which makes such nation an empire. Coloniality, instead, refers to long-standing patterns of power that emerged as a result of colonialism, but that define culture, labour, intersubjective relations, and knowledge production well beyond the strict limits of colonial administrations. Thus, coloniality survives colonialism. It is maintained alive in books, in the criteria for academic performance, in cultural patterns, in common sense, in the self-image of peoples, in aspirations of self, and so many other aspects of our

modern experience. In a way, as modern subjects we breathe coloniality all the time and everyday.

All of us, Western scholars and marginalised groups alike, internalise or 'breathe' dominant knowledge structures via the learning and utilisation of categories that act as the elementary building blocks of cognition (Arce and Long, 1987). Some scholars argue that the categories that we currently use in development studies (such as the Global North and South, modern and traditional knowledge, formal and informal institutions, etc.) emerged from disempowering or 'othering' distinctions made by the colonial discourse (for example, McEwan, 2009).

The coloniality of knowledge is exemplified by specific knowledge being prioritised over other knowledges (Heleta, 2018). The publication and distribution of development studies research takes place in a scientific context dominated by a small group of top institutions in developed countries because of complex systemic processes which affect all academic fields (Cummings and Hoebink, 2017; Dahdouh-Gubas et al., 2003). In this respect, the domain of international development studies advances perspectives on participation and bridging inequalities while the knowledge production and use mechanisms in the domain often fail to consider and apply these perspectives in their own knowledge-related practices.

A systemic approach to the decolonisation of knowledge

Decolonisation of knowledge aims to challenge the hegemonic Eurocentric, Western knowledge system in which 'Western knowledge is considered universal and it is widely accepted that assumptions rooted in European modernity are applicable in different contexts' (Schöneberg, 2019, p. 97). According to Heleta (2018, p. 48), 'Decolonisation of knowledge implies the end of reliance on imposed knowledge, theories and interpretations, and Theorising based on one's own past and present experiences and interpretation of the world.' If the current knowledge system is fundamentally subject to coloniality, the ability to bring about systems change is limited by the way we 'breathe' coloniality—in the sense that much of it will be tacit and implicit—but also by the fact that the knowledge system itself represents a complex system, and that complex systems are characterized by many embedded interests which are not conducive to change (Leeuwis et al., 2020). As Istratii and Lewis (2019, p. 4) remark, 'colonial continuities that reflect in ways of knowing and theoretical thinking are underpinned by structural and normative factors and are perpetuated by a matrix of actors and processes simultaneously and in complex ways, not always intentional.'

In an effort to shed light on the entrenched patterns of knowledge coloniality and outline a roadmap toward more inclusive, representative, useful, and empowering constructions for development studies, we employ the multi-level perspective (MLP) to innovation systems, originating from the work of Geels (2002, 2005) and others. The MLP approach can reveal how sociotechnical

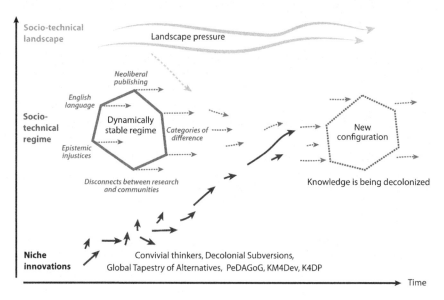

FIGURE 4.1 Multi-Level Perspective (MLP) (adapted from Schot and Geels 2008)

systems change over time by modelling the interaction of three analytical levels: first, the macro-level sociotechnical landscape which is beyond the direct influence of change agents (Grin et al., 2010), but includes societal trends that can put pressure on regimes and make them more liable to change; second, the meso-level sociotechnical regime which includes the dominant approach and is resistant to change because it is conditional on the landscape, including coloniality and the modern institutions of the university and academic publishing; and third, micro-level niches which are protected spaces where new ways of working are developed (see Figure 4.1). Within this model, system change is driven by change agents, in combination with landscape pressures, regime destabilisation processes, and 'upscaling' of innovations developed in niches (Wieczorek, 2018). This framework provides a useful perspective for efforts to understand and potentially change the current knowledge system because it recognises the power of actors to bring about change, while implicitly acknowledging the difficulties of changing this complex system.

At the sociotechnical regime level, there are enormous numbers of different, interlinked inequalities in the knowledge system, strongly linked to coloniality. We describe some of the most important of these below. There is no hierarchy in this description because they are strongly interlinked.

Neo-liberal publishing

At the landscape level, the prevailing neo-liberal economic system has an enormous impact at the regime level on university, research, and scientific publishing. As the journalist Monbiot (2011) explains, scientific publishers are 'the most ruthless capitalists in the Western world.' Given that journals are published behind paywalls that limit access, many scholars in formerly colonised countries are not able to legally access them. In addition, despite the fact that academic research could legitimately be viewed as a global public good, development practitioners are also not able to easily access these journals, leading to a situation where 'we have the development practitioners, who can't afford £2,000 for a journal [subscription] and academics, who are working separately' (Jha, 2012).

Disconnects between research and communities

The gap between development research and development practice (Edwards, 1989; Kothari, 2019, p. 4) is also amplified by disconnects between theory and communities, reflecting a 'fundamental perversity underpinning Western epistemology' (Istratii and Lewis, 2019, p. 2). Disconnects between research and communities are also evident in extractive research practices in which 'marginalised peoples frequently have no voice in the research or education that impacts them, while privileged others co-opt the right to define and describe their lives, their learning, and their identities' (Kouritzin and Nakagawa, 2018, p. 676).

English language

Some 75–90% of the research literature from the social sciences/humanities and natural sciences is published in English to the detriment of other international languages (Hamel, 2007, p. 53). Not only does this trend towards monolingualism benefit research institutions and individuals in English-speaking countries, as reflected in the authors and editorial boards in journals in the field of development studies (Cummings and Hoebink, 2017), it is also part of a process begun during colonialism in which African writers and intellectuals were also compelled to write in English. Ngũgĩ wa Thiong'o (1986, p. 286), a Kenyan thinker and writer, considers that 'language was the most important vehicle through which [colonial] power fascinated and held the soul prisoner.' This situation contributes to 'neglecting non-Western conceptual repertoires and understandings of the world and humanity' (Istratii and Lewis, 2019, p. 2) which is strongly linked to a series of epistemic injustices.

Epistemic injustices

A wide range of epistemic injustices have been identified by scholars, based on the perspective that 'far from being the apolitical study of truth, epistemology points to the ways in which power relations shape who is believed and why' (Collins, 2000, p. 252). Fricker (2007) is credited as distinguishing between two kinds of epistemic injustice: testimonial injustice and hermeneutical injustice.

Testimonial injustice comprises attributing too little or too much credibility to a testimony due to identity prejudice on the hearer's part, often related to intersectional racial, class, and gender identity; for example, testimonial injustice is a 'candidate explanation for some of the existing forms of racial disparity found in financial services' (de Bruin, 2019, p. 1). Hermeneutical injustice is 'where a socially disadvantaged group is blocked—whether intentionally or unintentionally—from access to knowledge, or access to communicating knowledge (to those in more socially privileged locations) due to a gap in hermeneutical resources, especially when these resources would help people understand the very existence and nature of the marginalisation' (McKinnon, 2016, p. 441). However, according to McKinnon (2016), attributing these concepts to Fricker also represents a form of epistemic injustice because 'in a deep irony, while Fricker's work is extremely important in detailing the concept and structure of epistemic injustice, this topic finally achieved wider uptake with Fricker's work [...] but the large body of, primarily, black feminist thought isn't acknowledged' (McKinnon, 2016, p. 439).

There are different types of ignorance or 'unknowing' associated with hermeneutical ignorance. When this unknowing is intentional, it is known as 'wilful hermeneutical ignorance' in which 'dominantly situated knowers refuse to acknowledge epistemic tools developed from the experienced world of those situated marginally. Such refusals allow dominantly situated knowers to misunderstand, misinterpret, and/or ignore whole parts of the world' (Pohlhaus Jr., 2012, p. 715).

Categories of difference

In this section, we consider two categories of difference that exist at the landscape level—namely, race and gender—while recognising the importance of intersectionality which we will discuss further below. According to Patel (2020), the issue of race has largely been ignored in development studies, despite considerable literature on its historical and contemporary effects, numerous movements to decolonise the university, and recognition that race is directly relevant to both decolonisation and development. Kothari (2006, p. 9) also considers that 'understanding development in terms of "race" can spotlight inadequacies, contradictions and misrepresentations in development ideologies, policies and practices, as well as relations of power.' Indeed, it appears that widespread calls to decolonise universities may have 'further embedded rather than dismantled whiteness' (Doharty et al., 2021, p. 1). Doherty and colleagues take a Critical Race Theory method of counter-storytelling to identify institutional racism, racial 'microaggression,' racial battle fatigue, and steadfast fugitive resistance in British higher education. Other commentators use a wider brush and argue that the development sector is 'reluctant—make that adamantly opposed—to placing a focus on race and racism in the aid sector [...] allowing larger systemic problems to go unchallenged' (Bruce-Raeburn, 2017). Race and gender as categories of difference are interlinked. For example, a study of 20 British and US public health universities demonstrated that 'clear gender and ethnic disparities remain at the most senior academic positions, despite numerous diversity policies and action plans reported' (Khan et al., 2019, p. 594).

Dominance of the English language, a variety of epistemic injustices, the neo-liberal economic system, racism, and other inequalities interact to create a knowledge system that is unequal, subject to coloniality, and resistant to change. In the next section, we consider what scholars from Western donor countries can do to 'walk the walk' and be part of the solution.

What can scholars from Western donor countries do?

'How are *you* [our emphasis] de-centring the "white gaze" of develop- ment?' (Pailey, 2020, p.742).

'I call on over-represented people in science who are expressing outrage about racism in broader society to focus the same level of energy on look- ing inwards, to wake up to how the culture in academic science is exclu- sionary' (Bumpus, 2020, p. 661).

In this final part of the chapter, we look at ways in which scholars from Western donor countries can work in niches to engage with the decolonisation of knowl- edge in order to avoid acting with 'wilful hermeneutical ignorance.' Although we recognise that the current status of the knowledge system is the result of embedded systemic issues which are subject to historical, landscape issues beyond the control of individuals, scholars represent an important group of actors in this field: together, they can make a difference. This means that academics need to become activists, so that the decolonisation of knowledge moves away from becoming a theoretical project, to becoming an activist one. This involves work- ing in transformative niches, developing new epistemologies and new ways of working.

Working in niches

'Why not also commit to speak only at scientific conferences and on pan- els that feature Black voices or those from other historically marginalized groups?' (Bumpus, 2020, p. 661).

Changes to sociotechnical regimes—such as the current colonial knowledge system—are assumed to take place in two ways: through action in niches, and through changes due to external forces. There are currently a number of niches where academics are trying to work in new ways to create decolonial narratives. These include an open group of scholars known as the Convivial Thinkers,[2] an initiative of four European women scholars with links to the European

Association for Development Research and Training Institutes (EADI), working and writing on issues related to post- and decolonial approaches. Another decolonial project comprises the new journal *Decolonial Subversions*, an open access, multilingual platform committed to decentring Western epistemology in the humanities and social sciences, based at the School of Oriental and African Studies (SOAS), University of London, UK. But there are many others, such as the Global Tapestry of Alternatives[3], which focuses on radical or transformative alternatives that are attempting to break with the dominant system and take paths towards direct and radical forms of political and economic democracy, localised self-reliance, social justice and equity, cultural and knowledge diversity, and ecological resilience. It represents a network of networks, while seeking to connect with other networks. It is also linked to PeDAGoG: the Post-Development Academic-Activist Global Group[4], a global network of academics and academic-activists interested in post-development, radical alternatives, and related themes, initiated in early 2020. Other networks, such as the Knowledge Management for Development (KM4Dev) community[5] and the Knowledge for Development Partnership (K4DP)[6], are also attempting with others to 'decolonise' knowledge management. There are many more of these sorts of spaces but decolonisation will only be achieved if these niches are activist in nature and if they work together.

Promising epistemologies

At the niche level, intersectionality is another approach to dismantle racism and other inequalities in development studies. Intersectionality is 'a critical theoretical idea and an approach to research that aims to redress inequality by revealing and responding to the oppressions and privileges that result when peoples' identities or positions intersect with each other, and with social structures' (Levac et al., 2018, p. 8). It is based on the understanding that 'categories of difference' (Sosa, 2017, p. 16) such as gender, race, class, sexual orientation, age, ableness, and location, interact and cannot be seen as single entities. For example, 'women of colour are not "doubly oppressed" based on a race-gender addition; they experience a new and different form of discrimination and are often not covered by the combination of policies and laws addressing single categories of subordination' (Sosa, 2017, p. 18). The origins of intersectionality can be found in 'black feminist scholarship, queer and postcolonial theory, Indigenous feminism, and other academic work addressing issues of race, class, gender and power' (Institute for Intersectionality Research and Policy, 2012, p. 11). Debates around intersectionality highlight 'epistemological questions about the relationship between the identity and interests of the individual knower and her contribution to scholarship at a micro-level, and how the composition of the scholarly community at a macro-level shapes which and whose questions, dimensions and contributions are prioritised' (Mügge et al., 2018, p. 18).

While the injustices of the dominant epistemic system are described above, framing this as an ethical issue potentially inadvertently reflects North–South relations of domination. Decolonisation of knowledge is not only about academics from Western donor countries realising that they *should* be more inclusive to other academics. Instead, decolonization is about *all* academics realising that knowledge production emanating from the Western donor countries rests on accidental, historical power relations of domination that legitimise themselves via unsound claims of universal reason. At the niche level, decolonisation of knowledge calls for a radical openness and vulnerability to disempowered constructions, in order to offset the 'distorting and exclusionary effects of domination' (Allen, 2016, p. 224). This change represents progress toward more inclusive, representative, useful, and empowering constructions. It is in the spirit of this progress that we

> enter into intercultural dialogue with subaltern subjects without presuming that we already know what the outcome of that dialogue should be, that is to say, with an openness to the very real possibility of unlearning. Indeed, both Foucault and Adorno see a kind of unlearning—a critical problematization of our own, historically sedimented point of view that frees us up in relation to it—as the very point of critique.
>
> *(Allen, 2016, p. 203–204)*

There is no doubt that new epistemologies are needed to replace the 'paternalistic and patronising undercurrents of an earlier period' (Melber, 2015). Based on an analysis of the debate 'Can the subaltern speak?' (Spivak, 1988), Schöneberg considers that development knowledge needs to be retheorised to involve varied epistemological frameworks and further consideration of indigenous and non-Western knowledges. There are many scholars taking up this challenge—for example, Brown's conception of multiple knowledge (Brown, 2011)—but an overview of these different approaches is probably needed in order to understand how these niche innovations can impact the sociotechnical regime.

New ways of working

New Information and Communication Technologies (ICTs) could play a role in decolonising knowledge-related practices in the development studies field. These technologies have revolutionised how people connect and interact, and therefore present opportunities to influence or improve communication aspects of service delivery (Martin and Hall, 2011). These technologies' capabilities are especially of issue in the Covid-19 era in which online engagement is taking precedence over face-to-face engagement. Mentorship and networking are knowledge-related practices that new ICTs may also impact. Through online skills development, lectures, talks, and networking events, academics from Western donor countries can connect with scholars in formerly colonised countries to provide mutual support and perspectives. Alternatively, such fora may be used by African scholars to provide their perspectives on global development issues. Furthermore, these forays can also serve as contextual review events that can also enable scholars from Western donor countries to broaden their engagement with scholars outside their context, and to identify possible partners for inclusion on editorial boards, joint publications, or to engage as guest lecturers in courses. As Acosta-Cazares et al. (2000) note, with '[t]he possibility of easier communication that the internet brings about, it would also have a favourable impact in developing countries because researchers and health care personnel could be in direct contact before and after starting a study.' At the same time, scholars in the field of development studies need to understand more of the knowledge practices which are excluding their colleagues from scientific journals, university appointments, and other academic spaces (Khan et al., 2019), and agitate for change through working with like-minded colleagues and through their own actions.

New discourses

Recent studies have also emphasised that the discourse in development studies is characterised by 'separating, distancing, dominating, extracting and hoarding riches, and justifying actions by "othering"' mindsets, influenced by a 'colonial, imperial, unequal, patriarchal' legacy (Hendrix-Jenkins 2020). In an online discussion with colleagues in the KM4Dev network, Kishor Pradhan argues that 'the discomfort with the racial and colonial supremacy of language is not about processes or results but if anything then it is about dignity and equality' (communication, 28 August 2020). Many scholars, such as Pailey (2020, p. 734), emphasise the importance of abandoning problematic binaries in development studies, such as 'developing vs developed, industrial vs agrarian, low income vs high income, Third World vs First World, Global South and Global North, core vs periphery, sub-Saharan Africa vs North Africa, etc. [...] These binaries shackle us, they do not liberate.' In this context, some commentators consider that the term 'international development,' based on the North–South binary, appears to be inappropriate for addressing the major challenges facing the world; Horner (2020) and others consider that 'global development' should be the new paradigm to replace international development, recognising that 'we are all developing countries now' (Raworth, 2018), along with the need for universal approaches to deal with, for example, climate change. Others have suggested we use 'formerly colonised countries' instead of 'the global South'[7] which could call attention to the continuous impact of colonialism, and disrupt development's effort to conceal its colonial roots. Attempting to follow this line of argumentation, and in an effort to strive for dignity and equality, in this chapter we have replaced the term 'global North' with the term 'Western donor countries' and 'global South' with the 'formerly colonised countries.' We are not sure that this has been successful but it reflects the historical nature of global development and is a work in progress.

Changing our practice

Against this background, scholars from Western donor countries need to recognise that they are implicit in this unequal knowledge system and change their own practices, particularly given new insights. For example, Michael Hutt, Professor of Nepali and Himalayan Studies, speaking at the SOAS Decolonising Research Initiative event on 18 September 2019, explained: 'I published this book on Nepal in the Nineties on political change, and all of the chapters were written by non-Nepali's and deservedly I got hammered in a review by Pratyoush Onta […] and 24 years later Praytoush and I jointly edited [Political change and public culture in post-1990 Nepal].' As researchers, writers, editorial board members, and editors, we need to oppose current knowledge practices when we feel they are unequal.

Conclusions

In this chapter, we have discussed some of the key systemic issues that are responsible for coloniality as it relates to knowledge, and highlighted some of the approaches that scholars can take to disrupt coloniality and support the decolonisation of knowledge. We recognise that other actors—both groups of individuals and institutional actors—can play an important role in decolonising knowledge but scholars themselves also need to take action and avoid the charge of willful hermeneutical ignorance. Although there are many different niche activities which are challenging current knowledge practices, their apparent focus on promising epistemologies and new ways of working can be augmented with an activist approach.

Acknowledgements

We would like to thank the editors of this book for their support in the process of formulating and writing this chapter. We would also like to thank Katarzyna Cieslik and Cees Leeuwis for their detailed feedback and discussions which have helped us to improve the chapter; the shortcomings remain our own.

Notes

1 https://drift.eur.nl/topics/transformative-knowledge/.
2 https://www.convivialthinking.org/.
3 https://globaltapestryofalternatives.org/.
4 https://globaltapestryofalternatives.org/pedagog.
5 www.km4dev.org.
6 www.k4dp.org.
7 https://gen.medium.com/i-spent-much-of-my-career-listening-to-white-folks-complain-about-africa-and-africans-88cc677f3a3.

References

Acosta-Cazares, B., Browne, E., LaPorte, R. E., Neuvians, D., de Camargo, K. R., Tapia-Conyer, R. and Ze, Y. (2000). Scientific colonialism and safari research.

Clinical Medicine and Health Research, BMJ. Accessed 5 October, 2020. https://staticw eb.bmj.com/clinmed/content/2000/200001/fulltext/2000010008v1/200001000 8v1.htslp

Allen, A. (2016). *The end of progress, decolonizing the normative foundations of critical theory.* New York: Columbia University Press.

Arce, A. and Long, N. (1987). The dynamics of knowledge interfaces between Mexican agricultural bureaucrats and peasants: A case study from Jalisco. *Boletín de Estudios Latinoamericanos y del Caribe,* 43, 5–30.

Broadbent, A. (2017). It will take critical, thorough scrutiny to truly ecolonize knowledge. *The Conversation.* https://theconversation.com/it-will-take-critical-thorough-scrutiny-to-truly-decolonise-knowledge-78477

Brown, V. A. (2011). Multiple knowledges, multiple languages: Are the limits of my language the limits of my world? *Knowledge Management for Development Journal,* 6(2), 120–131.

Bruce-Raeburn, A. (2017). Opinion: International development has a race problem. *DEVEX,* 17, May 2019. Accessed 5 August 2020. https://www.devex.com/news/opi nion-international-development-has-a-race-problem-94840

de Bruin, B. (2019). Epistemic injustice in finance. *Topoi,* 1–9. Doi:10.1007/ s11245-019-09677-y

Bumpus, N. (2020). Too many senior white academics still resist recognizing racism. *Nature,* 583(7818), 661.

Busia, K. A. (1960). *The sociology and culture of Africa: Its nature and scope.* Universitaire Pers.

Chandra, R. (1992). *Industrialisation and development in the Third World.* London: Routledge.

Collins, P. H. (2000). *Black feminist thought: Knowledge, consciousness, and the politics of empowerment.* London: Routledge.

Cooke, B. (2003). A new continuity with colonial administration: Participation in development management. *Third World Quarterly,* 24(1), 47–61.

Cummings, S. and Hoebink, P. (2017). Representation of academics from developing countries as authors and editorial board members in scientific journals: Does this matter to the field of development studies? *European Journal of Development Research,* 29(2), 369–383.

Dahdouh-Guebas, F., Ahimbisibwe, J., van Moll, R. and Koedam, N. (2003). Neo-colonial science by the most industrialised upon the least developed countries in peer-reviewed publishing. *Scientometrics,* 56(3), 329–343.

Demeter, M. (2020). *Academic knowledge production and the Global South: Questioning inequality and under-representation.* New York: Palgrave Macmillan.

Doharty, N., Madriaga, M. and Joseph-Salisbury, R. (2021). The university went to 'decolonise'and all they brought back was lousy diversity double-speak! Critical race counter-stories from faculty of colour in 'decolonial' times. *Educational Philosophy and Theory,* 53(3), 233–244.

Edwards, M. (1989). The irrelevance of development studies. *Third World Quarterly,* 11(1), 116–135.

Fricker, M. (2007). *Epistemic injustice: Power and the ethics of knowing.* Oxford: Oxford University Press.

Geels, F. (2002). Technological transitions as evolutionary reconfiguration processes: a multi-level perspective case-study. *Research Policy,* 31(8/9), 1257–1274.

Geels, F. (2005). Processes and patterns in transitions and system innovations: refining the co-evolutionary multi-level perspective. *Technological Forecasting and Social Change,* 72(6), 681–696.

Goldsmith, E. (1997). Development as colonialism. *The Ecologist*, March/April, 27(2), 69–77.

Grin, J., Rotmans, J. and Schot, J. (2010). *Transitions to sustainable development: New directions in the study of long term transformative change.* London: Routledge.

Hamel, R. E. (2007). The dominance of English in the international scientific periodical literature and the future of language use in science. *AILA Review*, 20(1), 53–71.

Heleta, S. (2018). Decolonizing knowledge in South Africa: Dismantling the 'pedagogy of big lies'. *Ufahamu: A Journal of African Studies*, 40(2), 47–65.

Hendrix-Jenkins, A. (2020). It's time to put an end to supremacy language in international development. Accessed 5 October 2020. https://www.opendemocracy.net/en/tr ansformation/its-time-to-put-an-end-to-supremacy-language-in-international-development/

Horner, R. (2020). Towards a new paradigm of global development? Beyond the limits of international development. *Progress in Human Geography*, 44(3), 415–436.

Institute for Intersectionality Research and Policy (2012). *Summary of themes: Dialogue on intersectionality and indigeneity.* Wosk Centre for Dialogue, Institute for Intersectionality Research and Policy.

Istratii, R. and Lewis, A. (2019). *Applying a decolonise lens to research structures, norms and practices in higher education institutions.* Conversation event report, SAAS University of London, Research and Enterprise Directorate.

Jha, A. (2012). UK government will enforce open access to development research. *The Guardian*, 25 July 2012. Accessed 6 April, 2016. https://www.theguardian.com/sc ience/2012/jul/25/uk-government-open-access-developmentresearch

Khan, M. S., Lakha, F., Tan, M. M. J. et al. (2019). More talk than action: Gender and ethnic diversity in leading public health universities. *The Lancet*, 393(10171), 594–600.

Kothari, U. (2006). An agenda for thinking about 'race' in development. *Progress in Development Studies*, 6(1), 9–23.

Kothari, U. (2019). *A radical history of development studies: Individuals, institutions and ideologies.* London: Zed Books.

Kouritzin, S. and Nakagawa, S. (2018). Toward a non-extractive research ethics for transcultural, translingual research: Perspectives from the coloniser and the colonised. *Journal of Multilingual and Multicultural Development*, 39(8), 675–687.

Levac, L., McMurtry, L., Stienstra, D., Baikie, G., Hanson, C. and Mucina, D. (2018). Learning across indigenous and Western knowledge systems and intersectionality. Canadian Research Institute for the Advancement of Women. Accessed 5 October 2020. https://www.criaw-icref.ca/en/product/learning-across-indigenous-and-w estern-knowledge-systems

Leeuwis, C., Boogaard, B. and Attah Krah, K. (2020) How food systems change (or not): Governance implications for system transformation processes. Draft paper, International Fund for Agricultural Development (IFAD).

Mafeje, A. (1978). *Science, ideology and development: Three essays on development theory.* Uppsala: Scandinavian Institute of African Studies. Accessed 15 September 2020. https://www.diva-portal.org/smash/get/diva2:275758/FULLTEXT02.pdf

Martin, B. L. and Hall, H. (2011). Mobile phones and rural livelihoods: Diffusion, uses, and perceived impacts among farmers in rural Uganda. *Information Technologies & International Development*, 7(4), 17–34.

McEwan, C. (2009). *Postcolonialism and development.* London: Routledge.

McKinnon, S. L. (2016). *Gendered asylum: Race and violence in U.S. law and politics.* Champaign: University of Illinois Press. Accessed 28 July 2020. http://search.ebscoh

ost.com.ezproxy.library.wur.nl/login.aspx?direct=true&db=nlebk&AN=1423207 &site=ehost-live.

Melber, H. (2015). Knowledge is power and power affects knowledge: Challenges for research collaboration in and with Africa. *Africa Development/Afrique et Développement,* 40(4), 21–42.

Miege, J. L. (1980). The colonial past in the present. In: Morris-Jones, W. H. and Fischer, G. (eds.), *Decolonisation and after: The British and French experience.* London: Frank Cass.

Mignolo, W. (1995). Decires fuera de lugar: sujetos dicentes, roles sociales y formas de inscripción. *Revista de Crítica Literaria Latinoamericana,* 11, 9–32.

Monbiot, G. (2011). Academic publishers make Murdoch look like a socialist. *The Guardian,* 29 August. Accessed 11 August 2020. https://www.theguardian.com/co mmentisfree/2011/aug/29/academic-publishers-murdoch-socialist

Mügge, L., Montoya, C., Emejulu, A. and Weldon, S. L. (2018). Intersectionality and the politics of knowledge production. *European Journal of Politics and Gender,* 1(1–2), 17–36.

Ndlovu-Gatsheni, S. J. (2019). *The struggles of epistemic freedom and decolonization of knowledge in Africa.* Webinar Lecture delivered at the Convivial Thinking Collective in Collaboration with European Association of Development Research and Training Institutes (EADI), 12 March 2019. Accessed 27 July 2020. https://www.eadi.org/ typo3/fileadmin/user_upload/Webinars/EADI_Webinar_12_-_The_Struggles_of _Epistemic_Freedom_and_Decolonization_of_Knowledge_in_Africa__2019-03 -12_.pdf

Ngũgĩ wa Thiong'o (1986). *Decolonising the mind: The politics of language in African literature.* Melton: James Currey.

Nkrumah, K. (1961). *I speak of freedom: A statement of African ideology.* Portsmouth: Heinemann.

Okot p'Bitek (1997). Indigenous ills. *Transition,* 75–76, 40–42.

Oliveira Andreotti, V., de, Stein S., Ahenakew, C. and Hunt, D. (2015). Mapping interpretations of decolonization in the context of higher education. *Decolonization: Indigeneity, Education & Society,* 4(1), 21–40.

Pailey, R. N. (2020). De-centring the 'white gaze' of development. *Development and Change* 51(3), 729–745.

Patel, K. (2020). Race and a decolonial turn in development studies. *Third World Quarterly,* 41(9), 1463–1475.

Pohlhaus Jr., G. (2012). Relational knowing and epistemic injustice: Toward a theory of willful hermeneutical ignorance. *Hypatia,* 27(4), 715–735.

Raworth, K. (2018). Doing the Doughnut at the G20?' Blog, 1 December 2018. www.k ateraworth.com/2018/12/01/doing-the-doughnut-at-the-g20/

Said, E. W. (1979). *Orientalism.* 1st edition. New York: Vintage Books.

Schöneberg, J. (2019). Imagining postcolonial-development studies: Reflections on positionalities and research practices. In: Baud, I., Basile, E., Kontinen, T. and Von Itter, S. (eds.). *Building development studies for the new millennium.* Dordrecht: Springer.

Schot, J. and Geels, F. W. (2008). Strategic niche management and sustainable innovation journeys: Theory, findings, research agenda, and policy. *Technology Analysis & Strategic Management,* 20(5), 537–554. Doi:10.1080/09537320802292651

Sosa, L. (2017). *Intersectionality in the human rights legal framework on violence against Women: At the centre or the margins?* Cambridge: Cambridge University Press.

Spivak, G. C. (1988). Can the subaltern speak? In: Nelson, C. and Grossberg, L. (Eds.). *Marxism and the interpretation of culture.* Champaign: University of Illinois Press, 271–313.

Torres, N. (2007). On the coloniality of being: Contributions to the development of a concept. *Cultural Studies*, 21(2), 240–270.

Wieczorek, A. J. (2018). Sustainability transitions in developing countries: Major insights and their implications for research and policy. *Environmental Science and Policy*, 84, 204–216.

5

HOW THE ELITE CAPTURE CRITIQUE IS USED TO LEGITIMISE TOP-DOWN CONTROL OF DEVELOPMENT RESOURCES

Peter Shapland, Annemarie van Paassen, and Conny Almekinders

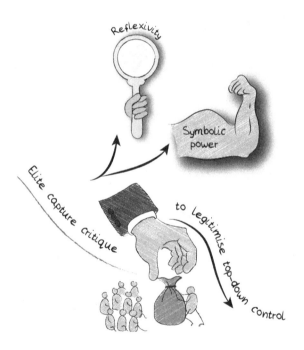

Introduction

Community-Driven Development (CDD) and other bottom–up approaches empower poor communities with control over project resources (Dongier et al., 2003), but they are criticised for their vulnerability to elite capture (Jean-Philippe Platteau, 2004). Elite capture largely refers to the phenomena of local

DOI: 10.4324/9781003112525-5

elites leveraging superior political and economic status to usurp the benefits of community development and decentralisation programmes that transfer control over public goods to lower-level governance structures (Bardhan & Mookherjee, 2006; Dasgupta & Beard, 2007; Kusumawati & Visser, 2016; J-P. Platteau & Abraham, 2002). Lower-level governance structures are widely assumed to be more susceptible to elite capture because of greater opportunities for collusion (Bardhan & Mookherjee, 2005; Dutta, 2009).

Some critical authors note, however, that development interventions can be understood in terms of political and normative struggles that determine resource flows and socially constructed notions of development (Long, 2003, p. 41). The elite capture debate is a site of one of these struggles— development institutions are reluctant to relinquish control over the conditions in which development projects are implemented (Bornstein et al., 2006, pp. 4–8; Chambers, 2010), and development researchers explicitly employ the elite capture critique to legitimise top-down control over development resources (Classen et al., 2008; D'Exelle, 2009; Fox, 2020; Kusumawati & Visser, 2016; Lawson, 2011; Mansuri & Rao, 2003; Jean-Philippe Platteau, 2004; J-P. Platteau & Abraham, 2002; Ward et al., 2018; Sam Wong, 2010).

According to Bourdieu, our worldviews emerge from historical struggles over symbolic and material power and lead us to experience arbitrary social power relations as justified and even necessary (Pierrre Bourdieu, 1977, pp. 80–82). Symbolic power imposes classification systems that legitimise structures of domination (Bourdieu & Wacquant, 1992; p. 13), and it thereby operates on our pre-reflective 'commonsense' understanding of the world: 'below the level of calculation and even consciousness' one falls into acceptance of arbitrary power relations without taking into account the coincidence between our dispositions and position (Pierre Bourdieu & Wacquant, 1992, p. 128). Bourdieu's thinking appears relevant because our *disposition* toward the elite capture critique frequently aligns with our *position* in the power struggle. Development researchers and practitioners identify elite capture as the central problem in bottom-up development approaches (Casey, 2018; Duchoslav, 2013; Fox, 2020), while the participants of development projects see many of these alleged instances of elite capture as unproblematic or even pro-social behaviour (Beath et al., 2011; Conning & Kevane, 2002; Khatun et al., 2015; Kita, 2019; Mawomo, 2019, p. 340; Jean-Philippe Platteau, 2004, 2009; Rao & Ibáñez, 2005).

In this chapter, we investigate the pertinence and use of the notion of elite capture. This is a fraught exercise because we are vulnerable to reaffirming symbols and entrenched power relations when we consider issues of empowerment and capture, as we tend to see them within frameworks that legitimise the existing relations of domination. For example, when development institutions capture development resources and decision-making powers, it's generally considered a necessity of good project management, but when local elites capture them, it's often considered to be 'pernicious' graft that aggravates oppressive social hierarchies (Andersson et al., 2018; Jean-Philippe Platteau, 2004). On the other side of the elite capture debate, the project participants' acceptance of elite capture could also emerge from the internalisation of symbolic power that legitimises arbitrary power relations within the villages. Bourdieu's reflexive approach challenges us to be aware of how symbolic power has shaped the pre-reflective framework of our thinking.

To appreciate the pertinence of the elite capture critique, we investigate the origin and form of the concept and debate in development practice and science, being cognisant of the historical struggle over material and symbolic power as elaborated by Bourdieu. Besides this general historical analysis of the elite capture critique, we also highlight issues forwarded in the literature that show flaws of the mainstream conceptualisation, which needs to be considered for a more nuanced and context-specific analysis. Our contribution to the debate is to show how the problematisation of elite capture in the mainstream development discourse is a form of symbolic power that legitimises arbitrary power relations between international development institutions and rural communities in the Global South.

How elite capture is understood and used

The emergence of the concept of elite capture

Throughout its evolution, the elite capture critique has functioned as a form of symbolic power that legitimises centralised forms of governance over rural areas. Bardhan and Mookherjee (2000) peg the origins of the elite capture critique to Federalist Paper No.10—the USA's founding fathers wrote the Federalist Papers to lobby for the adoption of a national constitution (Miller, 1988). The notion of elite capture later emerged in the Global South when the colonialists used it to justify their policies of extracting wealth from agricultural producers in the Global South (Li, 2007, p. 35; Spurr, 1993, p. 77). The centralised authority's struggle against local elites appeared again in the post-colonial states. Boone's (1998) comparative analysis of local institutions in Senegal, Cote d'Ivoire, and Ghana shows how post-colonial institutions were shaped by the national government's struggle with rural elites to capture the agricultural surplus generated by small farmers, in order to nurture the development of urban/industrial sectors of the economy. Boone (2003) and le Meur (1999) argue that for nascent central governments the underlying goal of 'rural development' was to extract agricultural surplus. The decentralisation debate (from 1985 to the present day) is also characterised by this same struggle over rural surplus between the government and local elites (Boone, 2003).

The concern about elite capture appeared in international development when Holdcroft (1978) wrote about its emergence in community development in the 1950s. The elite capture critique rose to prominence in development studies as a response to the decentralisation debate and bottom-up development approaches; see Figures 5.1 and 5.2. Argawal (2001), Guijt and Shah (1998), and Kothari (2001) laid the groundwork by criticising proponents of community

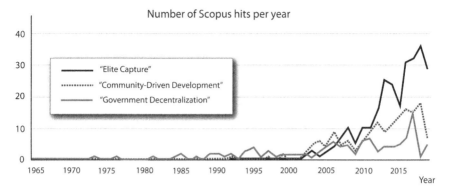

FIGURE 5.1   Scopus searches show how the term 'elite capture' rises in usage compared to 'Community-Driven Development' and 'Decentralisation,' eventually overtaking both of them

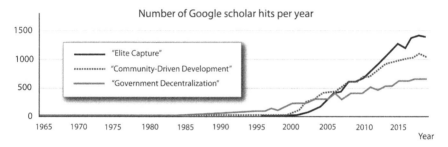

FIGURE 5.2   Google Scholar search results. Differences correspond to Google Scholar's wider (at times more eclectic) coverage than both Web of Science and Scopus. By including grey literature and technical documents, Google Scholar can be more representative of debates which involve both scientific and policy communities

empowerment for their tendency to uncritically celebrate the 'local community' without considering entrenched local power relations. Platteau 'set the tone' of the elite capture critique (Kusumawati & Visser, 2016, p. 304) when he argued that 'personalised relationships in tribal societies' lead to community imperfections, inequality, and elite capture (Jean-Philippe Platteau, 2004; J-P. Platteau & Abraham, 2002, p. 111). Numerous scholars since (D'Exelle, 2009; Iversen et al., 2006; Labonte, 2012; Ribot, 2004; Williams et al., 2003; Sam Wong, 2010) have underscored the elite capture critique. However, other research on CDD and decentralisation shows how the act of devolving power to communities can undermine elite capture (Blair, 2000; Dufhues et al., 2015; Fritzen, 2007), but it takes marginalised groups longer to mobilise and gain control over resources devolved to communities (J. F. Lund & Saito-Jensen, 2013; Manor,

1999, p. 48). Some scholars make the distinction between elite capture (elite's usurping undue portions of project benefits for personal gain) and elite control (elite's controlling decision-making processes potentially for everyone's benefit) (Dasgupta & Beard, 2007; Fritzen, 2007; Lucas, 2016; Musgrave & Wong, 2016; Rao & Ibáñez, 2005; Saguin, 2018). These studies demonstrate cases of elites controlling CDD resources in equitable and pro-poor manners. Finally, of the five existing meta-analyses of CDD programmes, four conclude that elite capture is generally not a problem (Casey, 2018; Everatt & Gwagwa, 2005; Kumar et al., 2005; Susan Wong, 2012) and the fifth finds that elite capture in CDD is context specific (Mansuri & Rao, 2003).

In the late 20th century, development theory largely characterised local elites as impediments to economic development and social change (Mitra, 1991). The elite capture critique perpetuates this ethos by focusing on the negative aspects of local elites while disregarding their pro-social functions (Kusumawati & Visser, 2016). Development professionals tell countless stories of elite capture while the research shows mixed results (Duchoslav, 2013).

A major challenge in development is the constant effort of powerful actors throughout the aid chain to capture resources that are intended for the world's poor (Wenar, 2006). Development's focus on upward accountability (Bornstein et al., 2006) has made accountability a powerful weapon that development actors strategically use to delegitimise their competitors in the struggle for resources (Thomas et al., 2008). The use of the elite capture critique emerged in mainstream development, despite more nuanced research studies and mixed results because it serves the interests of higher-level structures. Throughout its evolution—in American federalism, colonialism, post-colonial state formation, decentralisation, and now development—the elite capture critique has been inseparable from the economic and political power it serves.

The narrow framing of elite capture in the development arena

A literature review on the use of the term 'elite capture' reveals an interesting trend—the term is mostly used in reference to local elites in the Global South (see Figure 5.3). By explicitly employing the elite capture critique to legitimise top-down control over development resources, development researchers and practitioners implicitly argue that elite capture in decentralisation and CDD is worse than the capture that occurs when national elites or development institutions maintain top-down control over development resources. However, the evidence to support this claim does not exist.

Regarding national-level elites ('corruption'), Bardhan and Mookherjee (1999) developed a theoretical model to compare elite capture and national-level corruption, and found that capture is too context specific to support generalisable results. Bardhan and Mookherjee (2005, p. 40) subsequently conducted a literature review and concluded that the effects of decentralisation on elite capture and national corruption are too complex for summarisation yet 'tend to indicate

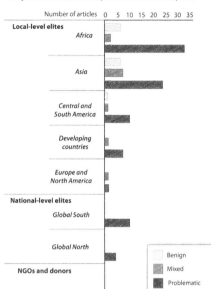

Type of conclusions about Elite Capture from the first
100 journal articles in a Scopus search of "Elite Capture"

FIGURE 5.3   A Scopus search of 'elite capture' (no time period constraints) produces articles that are largely about lower-level governance structures in the Global South.[1]

that the problems of local capture within communities have not been excessive and have been dominated by beneficial effects on targeting across communities.'

Regarding NGO and donor capture (also known as 'lodging') (Harsh et al., 2010), the elite capture critique simply ignores the capture and control of resources at these higher levels. Looking at Figure 5.3, how can we conclude that local elites in the Global South are *more* likely to control and capture resources than NGOs and donors, when they are excluded from the elite capture debate? We found only two case studies that look into the matter. Both studies show that elite capture in devolved development projects is small compared to targeting errors and misallocation in top-down projects, and neither compared elite capture to NGO/donor capture (Alatas et al., 2019; Galasso & Ravallion, 2005).

The narrow framing of elite capture in CDD evaluates it in a vacuum without taking into account higher levels of control and capture in the top-down organisation of development projects, in which the local communities are routinely excluded from control over development resources and disempowered (Khadka, 2009, p. 231; Pfeiffer, 2003; Power et al., 2002; Townsend et al., 2002). Bornstein et al. (2006, pp. 4–8) and Chambers (2010) point out that the prioritisation of upward accountability (and the concomitant use of logical frameworks, verifiable indicators, and results-based management) leads NGOs to strictly control the conditions in which projects are implemented and create a disempowering effect among the target populations. NGO projects tend to arrive at rural villages as a fixed package of activities and if-then clauses (within a Theory of Change) that claim to account for the communities' context, behaviours, and motivations. Large donors currently tend to require proposals to be organised according to an overarching Theory of Change that resource-intensive Monitoring and Evaluation (M&E) processes validate via a predictive Results Framework. These practices conceive of the farmers as deterministic 'things' that will conform to the project's predictions, rendering the farmers passive in their own development (Chambers, 2010). This mode of practice is designed to reveal rapid and easily observed results (Boulding, 2009), while the less visible, empowerment-related goals of development initiatives, like self-determination, community initiative, and a self-reliant capacity to thrive, are neglected (Power et al., 2002).

The question isn't whether community-driven approaches face challenges with elite control and capture (they do). The question is whether elite capture in community-driven approaches is more or less disempowering than the current top-down model dominating international development, but the elite capture critique ignores capture by NGOs and donors.

The elite capture critique also fails to consider global inequality. Zooming out and taking a brief look at inequality and the elite at the global level, one finds a global Gini Coefficient ranging from 0.61 to 0.71 (Hillebrand, 2009; UNDP, 2010), with eight people controlling as much wealth as half of humanity (Hardoon, 2017). Stand up from your desk and seek out both the leader and a groundskeeper at your institution and inquire into their respective renumeration—claiming that elites capture more resources than non-elites is tautological. So why is the development community so preoccupied with elite capture in rural communities in the Global South, where the intra-village Gini Coefficient can be as low as 0.14 (Arcand & Wagner, 2016)?

The elite capture critique effectively frames 'capture' on local elites in the Global South and leads us to ignore capture that occurs in NGOs/donors and also global inequality. This is how the symbolic power of the elite capture critique operates on our pre-reflective thinking—it frames the boundaries of a classification around a disempowered group. Thus, symbolic power imposes classification systems that legitimise structures of domination.

Elite capture is context specific: A review of rural West African elites and their responsibilities

The proclivity and capacity of local elites to capture resources in CDD or government decentralisation is highly dependent on the context (Bardhan & Mookherjee, 2000; Smoke, 2003). Our analysis is focused on local elite living in Labor-Constrained Agricultural Systems in West Africa (LCASWA) to demonstrate a context where the broad strokes of the elite capture critique appear less relevant.

The financial means of the village elite in LCASWA are categorically different from Western notions of the elite. Dryland agricultural production in West Africa is characterised by high levels of uncertainty and low levels of possible capital accumulation (Long, 2003, p. 102). In Sahelian West Africa, agro-pastoralists have an unpredictable and short window of time to grow as much food as possible. Based on the last 70 years of climate data, the probability of a very good year is 12%, a good year is 28%, a normal year is 43%, a mediocre year is 17%, and a catastrophic year is 14% (Aune, 2011). The agro-pastoralists' proclivity for early-maturing varieties, despite their lower yield capacity in good rainfall years, is indicative of the prevailing agricultural strategy in a harsh and unpredictable environment: they are more interested in hedging against risk than maximising production.

To cope with the unpredictable environment, the majority of rural Africans inhabit cultures that apply social pressure on anyone with a surplus (especially the local elite) to share their wealth with poor friends and family (Alby & Auriol, 2010; Bergh, 2004; Kazianga, 2006; Jean-Philippe Platteau, 2006). Bernard et al. (2008) frame this social pressure as a crucial safety net for the above-mentioned risks associated with dryland agricultural production in West Africa. Households that fall into financial crisis often sell livestock as a source of emergency cash, but for those who are too poor to own livestock, their true safety net is their participation in the extended family (Bulte et al., 2018, p. 67). As a result, economic differentiation is more focused on staving off poverty than accumulation (C. Lund & Benjaminsen, 2001, p. 300). Wealth distribution in rural West Africa is characterised by relative equality (Saul, 1983). A measure of intra-community inequality in 177 villages in Senegal revealed Gini Coefficients at a mere 0.14 to 0.18, 'indicating that at the village level the households are equally poor' (Arcand & Wagner, 2016, p. 109).

Village elite in LCASWA are less able to entrench their position of wealth because the primary constraint in agriculture is labour, not land (Bulte et al., 2018, p. 61; Hussein & Nelson, 1998). In land-constrained agricultural systems, village elites can entrench their position via the acquisition of land. Research from land-constrained systems has confirmed that unequal land holdings play an important role in the prevalence of elite capture (Bardhan & Mookherjee, 2003; Galasso & Ravallion, 2005; Pan & Christiaensen, 2012). In labour-constrained systems, however, the competition over labour has a greater impact on productivity and wealth (Binswanger & McIntire, 1987; Bulte et al., 2018, pp. 60–61; Saul, 1983). The quantity of labour a household can access is highly dynamic—households grow and contract, members shift in and out of working age, and other members emigrate to urban areas. Shifting quantities of labour, combined with low levels of possible capital accumulation in dryland agriculture, create unstable and ambiguous class structures (Berry, 1993, p. 184; Long, 2003, p. 102). Nevertheless, outsiders from the Global North have a history of projecting rigidity onto fluid class structures in traditional Sub-Saharan systems (Berry, 1993, p. 25). The under-appreciation of rural class fluidity is not endemic to LACSWA—it has been widely observed in rural India too, despite the caste system (Powis, 2007).

The elite capture critique characterises the rural non-elite in the Global South as powerless vis-à-vis the local elite (Labonte, 2012; Jean-Philippe Platteau, 2004; Williams et al., 2003; Sam Wong, 2013). However, some scholars show the various accountability mechanisms that non-elites uphold to ensure just leadership (Arnall et al., 2013; Scott, 1985), and still others argue that local elites have little room for manoeuvre in the struggle for influence and depend on the non-elites for support (C. Lund & Benjaminsen, 2001, p. 95; J. F. Lund & Saito-Jensen, 2013; Musgrave & Wong, 2016). In this same vein, Pitcher et al. (2009) point out that the stability of 'personalised leadership' depends on reciprocity and mutual respect. Thus, where Platteau (2002) sees an immediate cause of elite capture, Pitcher et al. see a functioning accountability mechanism grounded in personal interaction. 'Scholarly debates over participatory development rarely explicitly address [this] core dimension of accountability: countervailing power' (Fox, 2020, p. 2). Including countervailing power dynamics in participatory development studies would provide a more nuanced picture.

Elite capture in perspective: Including higher-level capture in the elite capture critique

The elite capture critique is not capable of processing the various ways that resources and decision-making powers in a multimillion-dollar grant are captured by numerous kinds of elites before it reaches the intended project participants.

While a thorough comparison of the disempowering effects of top-down development and elite capture is beyond the scope of this article, a brief review of resource capture by local elites and NGOs is possible. Unfortunately, detailed information of NGO capture in a typical top-down project is unavailable because NGOs routinely recategorise administrative costs as programmatic costs to hide their overheads (Walsh & Lenihan, 2006). Conversations with NGO staff reveal that staff salaries, administrative costs, equipment for the NGOs (computers, cars, etc.), and air travel typically comprise at least 50% of project budgets, and some studies show that NGO and donor capture can be as high as 60–90% (Acemoglu & Robinson, 2012, p. 452; Harsh et al., 2010), but a more concrete benchmark is necessary for our purposes. NGOs implementing CDD projects provide a straightforward means of measuring NGO capture: the NGO's total project budget minus the amount issued to the communities as block grants (*NGO budget–block grants=NGO capture*).[2]

The elite capture critique has enabled/justified NGOs to implement intensive community trainings to ensure broad participation in resource allocation (Casey, 2018; Fritzen, 2007; Lawson, 2011). This heavy-handed approach to CDD, coupled with resource-intensive M&E practices and other NGO lodging leads to high levels of capture. Casey's (2011) evaluation of the *GoBifo*, a CDD project in Liberia, showed that the implementing NGO spent 30% of the budget on social facilitation (to prevent elite capture), 23% on NGO operating costs, and 47% was devolved to the communities in the form of grants. Casey et al. (2012) showed that local elites captured minimal levels of the grants. Thus, the non-elites of the GoBifo communities gained access to almost half of the grant. *Tuungane 1*, another large-sale CDD program with heavy NGO involvement, allocated 43% of the £30 million budget to the communities in the form of block grants and 57% went to the implementing NGO's operating/facilitation costs. The project discovered only £21,251 of locally-misappropriated funds throughout the £13 million in block grants—a fraction of 1% was captured by the local elite in this heavy-handed approach to CDD (IRC & CARE, 2012). Humphreys (2012) conducted a follow-up study to the *Tuungane* project. Using a random sampling of *Tuungane* and control villages, Humphrey's research team issued $1,000 to each community for a development project of their choosing. In the follow-up study, the research team did not conduct community meetings to promote inclusivity and transparency. They found that an average of 15% of the grant (in both *Tuungane 1* and control villages) was not accounted for, thus insinuating the level of elite capture. Thus, NGO implementing *Tuungane* captured 57%, while the local elites captured 15%.

Discussion

Researchers' normativities and worldviews projected into the elite capture critique

According to Bourdieu, 'scientists exercise symbolic power by shaping the categories through which agents perceive the social world; indeed, the potential symbolic effects of scientific theories are all the greater because science claims to speak in the name of the universal (i.e. of reason) and to be neutral and impartial with respect to social struggles' (Cronin, 1996, p. 76). However, social scientists are prone to projecting their own worldview onto the social practices that they research (Pierre Bourdieu, 1980, pp. 29–41, 1989, p. 42). For example, Platteau (2004, p. 27) explains the project participants' lack of concern for elite capture by arguing that they lack the reflective capacity to see beyond 'the logic of clientelistic politics characteristic of the African continent.' However, perhaps it is development researchers who struggle to see beyond their worldview when analysing foreign groups. After all, it appears that researchers and the people living in LCASWA villages each arrive at distinct conclusions about elite capture, which align with their own experiences of social stratification and the concomitant pro- or anti-social conceptions of the elite.

While much of the elite capture research uses qualitative surveys that consider the community members' perspectives, a lot of the elite capture research still relies on quantitative proxies for capture that are devised by the researchers. These proxies typically calculate elite capture by adding up the resources that benefit the local elite versus those directly benefiting the poor, or by attempting to account for all the community's project expenditures and subtracting that from the amount of the community grant (on the assumption the elite captured the missing portion). These simple accounting exercises fail to account for the interlocking complexities of local tradition, legitimacy, and pro-social service delivery by the local leadership (Takasaki, 2011b), nor do they account for cultural norms and traditions of allocation and mutual care that could be disrupted by perfectly equal allocations (Kita, 2019). The simple accounting measures are also prone to reifying researchers' unacknowledged normative assumptions that are not necessarily shared by the people they study. For example, although some research measures elite capture via the selection of public goods that favour elites (Nath, 2014), other studies measure it by the proportion of community expenditure on private goods targeting the poorest people versus public good projects (Araujo et al., 2008; Darmawan, 2014; Darmawan & Klasen, 2013). This method subjects the target communities to the researchers' normative judgment that only the community's poorest people should benefit from development. When community leaders decide that their community would be better served by a public goods project that targets everyone, their actions were classified as elite capture. Kusumawati and Visser (2016, p. 305) argue that elite capture 'studies remain too much driven by a northern, hegemonic view and expatriate concern with the institutional norm of a Weberian transparent, democratic, and inclusive, but narrowly defined financial accountability.'

The elite capture critique requires a reflexive approach

Bourdieu's reflexive approach enabled us to look at the history and emergence of the elite capture critique, serving the interests of central authorities in American federalism, colonialism, post-colonial state formation, decentralisation, just as it now serves top-down development institutions in the struggle over development resources. In mainstream development, the elite capture critique is explicitly used (as a form of symbolic power) to legitimise top-down approaches and conceal the arbitrary relations of dominance between development institutions and local communities. This symbolic power operates on our pre-reflective understanding of top-down development by framing capture exclusively around the local elites, and researchers seem prone to easily align their research, rather than critically question this perspective. Consequently, the elite capture critique is apt to misunderstand the functions, roles, and capacities of local elite, as our LCASWA case study showed.

Notes

1 The category of Local Level refers to capture by village/community elites or local/regional government actors, and the category of National Level refers to capture by national government actors and the elites in their orbit. The Developing Countries column is not a product of our classification. The authors of these articles wrote about the placeless local elite of 'developing countries'—Escobar (1995, p. 53) argued that a

major effect of the development discourse is the erasure of the complexity and diversity of developing country populations. The Global South column includes research about 'Eastern and Southern Africa', Ghana, Cambodia, Indonesia, Bangladesh, and North Korea. Of the four articles that fell into the category of National-Level elite capture in the Global North, two were about elite capture in all countries (Morck et al., 2011; Oberlack et al., 2016), one was about 19th century Russia (Finkel, 2015), and the final one was about energy politics in New Zealand (MacArthur and Matthewman, 2018). The one article about local elite capture in Western Europe was about Swedish democracy in the early 1900s (Hinnerich and Pettersson-Lidbom, 2014). Only two articles were discarded from the review: Maryudi's (2018) article about wood furniture firms in Indonesia and Deolalikar's (2002) article about the clients of subsidised hospitals in Vietnam. These two articles did not fit into our local-national dichotomy. See the appendix for Scopus' list of the 100 most highly cited articles on 'elite capture'.

2 However, this method fails to include capture even higher up the aid chain, in (government and private) donor institutions.

Bibliography

Acemoglu, D., & Robinson, J. (2012). *Why Nations Fail The Origins of Power, Prosperity and Poverty by Daron Acemoglu, James A. Robinson (z-lib.org).pdf*. London: Profile Books.

Adhikari, K. P., & Goldey, P. (2010). Social Capital and its "Downside": The Impact on Sustainability of Induced Community-Based Organizations in Nepal. *World Development*, *38*(2), 184–194. https://doi.org/10.1016/j.worlddev.2009.10.012

Agarwal, B. (2001). Participatory Exclusions, Community Forestry, and Gender: An Analysis for South Asia and a Conceptual Framework. *World Development*, *29*(10), 1623–1648. https://doi.org/10.1016/S0305-750X(01)00066-3

Alatas, V., Banerjee, A., Hanna, R., Olken, B. A., Purnamasari, R., & Wai-Poi, M. (2019). Does Elite Capture Matter? Local Elites and Targeted Welfare Programs in Indonesia. *AEA Papers and Proceedings*, *109*, 334–339. https://doi.org/10.1257/pandp.20191047

Alatas, V., Rema, A. B., Benjamin, H., Tobias, J., & Olken, A. (2010). Targeting the Poor: Evidence From a Field Experiment in Indonesia. Working Paper 15980 Http://Www.Nber.Org/Papers/W15980. NATIONAL BUREAU OF ECONOMIC RESEARCH.

Alby, P., & Auriol, E. (2010). *Social Barriers to Entrepreneurship in Africa: The Forced Mutual Help Hypothesis. 36.*

Andersson, K. P., Smith, S. M., Alston, L. J., Duchelle, A. E., Mwangi, E., Larson, A. M., de Sassi, C., Sills, E. O., Sunderlin, W. D., & Wong, G. Y. (2018). Wealth and the Distribution of Benefits from Tropical Forests: Implications for REDD+. *Land Use Policy*, *72*, 510–522. https://doi.org/10.1016/j.landusepol.2018.01.012

Araujo, M. C., Ferreira, F. H. G., Lanjouw, P., & Özler, B. (2008). Local Inequality and Project Choice: Theory and Evidence from Ecuador. *Journal of Public Economics*, *92*(5–6), 1022–1046. https://doi.org/10.1016/j.jpubeco.2007.12.005

Arcand, J.-L., & Wagner, N. (2016). Does Community-driven Development Improve Inclusiveness in Peasant Organizations? – Evidence from Senegal. *World Development*, *78*, 105–124. https://doi.org/10.1016/j.worlddev.2015.10.016

Arnall, A., Thomas, D. S. G., Twyman, C., & Liverman, D. (2013). NGOs, Elite Capture and Community-driven Development: Perspectives in Rural Mozambique. *The Journal of Modern African Studies*, *51*(2), 305–330. https://doi.org/10.1017/S0022278X13000037

Aspinall, E. (2014). Health Care and Democratization in Indonesia. *Democratization*, *21*(5), 803–823. https://doi.org/10.1080/13510347.2013.873791

Aune, J. (2011). *Agro-Sahel—A Collection of Evidence-Based Techniques and Approaches for Agricultural Improvement in the Sahel*. Oslo, Norway: Published by the Drylands Coordination Group (DCG).

Baird, I. G. (2014). The Global Land Grab Meta-Narrative, Asian Money Laundering and Elite Capture: Reconsidering the Cambodian Context. *Geopolitics*, *19*(2), 431–453. https://doi.org/10.1080/14650045.2013.811645

Baird, S., McIntosh, C., & Özler, B. (2013). The Regressive Demands of Demand-Driven Development. *Journal of Public Economics*, *106*, 27–41. https://doi.org/10.1016/j.jpubeco.2013.07.002

Bardhan, P., & Mookherjee, D. (1999). *Relative Capture of Local and National Governments: An Essay in the Political Economy of Decentralization*. Working Paper, Institute for Economic Development, Boston University.

Bardhan, P., & Mookherjee, D. (2000). Capture and Governance at Local and National Levels. *American Economic Review*, *90*(2), 135–139. https://doi.org/10.1257/aer.90.2.135

Bardhan, P., & Mookherjee, D. (2003). Poverty Alleviation Effort of West Bengal Panchayats. *Economic and Political Weekly*, *22*.

Bardhan, P., & Mookherjee, D. (2005). Decentralization, Corruption and Government Accountability—An Overview.pdf. In S. Rose-Ackerman (Ed.), *Handbook of Economic Corruption*. Edward Elgar.

Bardhan, P., & Mookherjee, D. (2006). Decentralisation and Accountability in Infrastructure Delivery in Developing Countries. *The Economic Journal*, *116*(508), 101–127.

Beath, A., Fotini, C., & Enikolopov, R. (2011). *Elite Capture of Local Institutions: Evidence from a Field Experiment in Afghanistan*.

Bergh, S. (2004). Democratic Decentralisation and Local Participation: A Review of Recent Research. *Development in Practice*, *14*(6), 780–790. https://doi.org/10.1080/0961452042000284012

Bernard, T., Collion, M.-H., de Janvry, A., Rondot, P., & Sadoulet, E. (2008). Do Village Organizations Make a Difference in African Rural Development? A Study for Senegal and Burkina Faso. *World Development*, *36*(11), 2188–2204. https://doi.org/10.1016/j.worlddev.2007.10.010

Berry, S. (1993). *No Condition Is Permanent: The Social Dynamics of Agrarian Change in Sub-Saharan Africa*. University of Wisconsin Press.

Binswanger, H. P., & McIntire, J. (1987). Behavioral and Material Determinants of Production Relations in Land-Abundant Tropical Agriculture. *Economic Development and Cultural Change*, *36*(1), 73–99.

Blair, H. (2000). Participation and Accountability at the Periphery: Democratic Local Governance in Six Countries. *World Development*, *28*(1), 21–39. https://doi.org/10.1016/S0305-750X(99)00109-6

Bodin, Ö., & Crona, B. (2011). Barriers and Opportunities in Transforming to Sustainable Governance: The Role of Key Individuals. In O. Bodin & C. Prell (Eds.), *Social Networks and Natural Resource Management* (pp. 75–94). Cambridge: Cambridge University Press. https://doi.org/10.1017/CBO9780511894985.005

Boone, C. (1998). State building in the African countryside: Structure and Politics at the Grassroots. *Journal of Development Studies*, *34*(4), 1–31. https://doi.org/10.1080/00220389808422527

Boone, C. (2003). Decentralization as Political Strategy in West Africa. *Comparative Political Studies*, *36*(4), 355–380. https://doi.org/10.1177/0010414003251173

Bornstein, L., Wallace, T., & Chapman, J. (2006). *The Aid Chain: Coercion and Commitment in Development NGOs.* Rugby: ITDG Publishing.

Boulding, C. (2009). *Accountability in Foreign Aid Delivery: Links between Donors and NGOs. 21.*

Bourdieu, P. (1980). *The Logic of Practice.* Cambridge: Polity Press. Stanford: Stanford University Press.

Bourdieu, P. (1989). *La noblesse d'Etat. Grands corps et Grandes ecoles.* Paris: Editions de Minuit.

Bourdieu, P., & Wacquant, L. J. D. (1992). *An Invitation to Reflexive Sociology.* Cambridge: Polity Press.

Bourdieu, P. (1977). *Outline of a Theory of Practice.* Cambridge: Cambridge University Press.

Bulte, E., Richards, P., & Voors, M. (2018). *Institutions and Agrarian Development: A New Approach to West Africa.* Dordrecht: Springer. https://doi.org/10.1007/978-3-319-9 8500-8

Casey, K. (2011). *The GoBifo Project Evaluation Report*: 56.

Casey, K. (2018). Radical Decentralization: Does Community-driven Development Work? *Annual Review of Economics, 10*(1), 139–163. https://doi.org/10.1146/annurev -economics-080217-053339

Casey, K., Glennerster, R., & Miguel, E. (2012). Reshaping Institutions: Evidence on Aid Impacts Using a Preanalysis Plan★. *The Quarterly Journal of Economics, 127*(4), 1755–1812. https://doi.org/10.1093/qje/qje027

Chambers, R. (2010). Paradigms, Poverty and Adaptive Pluralism. IDS Working Papers, *2010*(344), 01–57. https://doi.org/10.1111/j.2040-0209.2010.00344_2.x

Chemouni, B. (2014). Explaining the Design of the Rwandan Decentralization: Elite Vulnerability and the Territorial Repartition of Power. *Journal of Eastern African Studies, 8*(2), 246–262. https://doi.org/10.1080/17531055.2014.891800

Chomba, S., Kariuki, J., Lund, J. F., & Sinclair, F. (2016). Roots of Inequity: How the Implementation of REDD+ Reinforces Past Injustices. *Land Use Policy, 50*, 202–213. https://doi.org/10.1016/j.landusepol.2015.09.021

Chomba, S., Treue, T., & Sinclair, F. (2015). The Political Economy of Forest Entitlements: Can Community Based Forest Management Reduce Vulnerability at the Forest Margin? *Forest Policy and Economics, 58*, 37–46. https://doi.org/10.1016/j .forpol.2014.11.011

Chome, N. (2015). 'Devolution is Only for Development'? Decentralization and Elite Vulnerability on the Kenyan Coast. *Critical African Studies, 7*(3), 299–316. https://doi .org/10.1080/21681392.2015.1075750

Classen, L., Humphries, S., FitzSimons, J., Kaaria, S., Jiménez, J., Sierra, F., & Gallardo, O. (2008). Opening Participatory Spaces for the Most Marginal: Learning from Collective Action in the Honduran Hillsides. *World Development, 36*(11), 2402–2420. https://doi.org/10.1016/j.worlddev.2008.04.007

Conning, J., & Kevane, M. (2002). Community-Based Targeting Mechanisms for Social Safety Nets: A Critical Review. *World Development, 30*(3), 375–394. https://doi.org /10.1016/S0305-750X(01)00119-X

Cooper, S. J., & Wheeler, T. (2015). Adaptive Governance: Livelihood Innovation for Climate Resilience in Uganda. *Geoforum, 65*, 96–107. https://doi.org/10.1016/j.geof orum.2015.07.015

Crespo, J., Réquier-Desjardins, D., & Vicente, J. (2014). Why Can Collective Action Fail in Local Agri-food Systems? A Social Network Analysis of Cheese Producers in Aculco, Mexico. *Food Policy, 46*, 165–177. https://doi.org/10.1016/j.foodpol.2014.03 .011

Cronin, C. (1996). Bourdieu and Foucault on Power and Modernity. *Philosophy & Social Criticism, 22*(6), 55–85. https://doi.org/10.1177/019145379602200603

Crook, R. C. (2003). Decentralisation and Poverty Reduction in Africa: The Politics of Local-Central Relations. *Public Administration and Development, 23*(1), 77–88. https://doi.org/10.1002/pad.261

Darmawan, R. (2014). *Three Essays on Indonesian Political Economy: Elite Capture, Corruption, and Female Policy Makers.* Networked Digital Library of Theses & Dissertations, *2014*, 107.

Darmawan, R., & Klasen, S. (2013). *Elite Capture in Urban Development: Evidence from Indonesia.* Göttingen: University of Göttingen.

Darrow, M., & Tomas, A. (2005). Power, Capture, and Conflict: A Call for Human Rights Accountability in Development Cooperation. *Human Rights Quarterly, 27*(2), 471–538.

Dasgupta, A., & Beard, V. A. (2007). Community Driven Development, Collective Action and Elite Capture in Indonesia. *Development and Change, 38*(2), 229–249. https://doi.org/10.1111/j.1467-7660.2007.00410.x

Daum, T., & Birner, R. (2017). The Neglected Governance Challenges Of Agricultural Mechanisation in Africa – Insights from Ghana. *Food Security, 9*(5), 959–979. https://doi.org/10.1007/s12571-017-0716-9

D'Exelle, B. (2009). Excluded Again: Village Politics at the Aid Interface. *Journal of Development Studies, 45*(9), 1453–1471. https://doi.org/10.1080/00220380902890268

Dongier, P., Domelen, J. V., Ostrom, E., Ryan, A., Wakeman, W., Bebbington, A., Alkire, S., Esmail, T., & Polski, M. (2003). Chapter 9 *Community-Driven Development.* *1*, 32.

Duchoslav, J. (2013). *Limiting Elite Capture in Community Driven Development: Evidence from a Randomized Controlled Trial in Sierra Leone.* Wageningen: Wageningen University.

Dufhues, T., Theesfeld, I., & Buchenrieder, G. (2015). The Political Economy of Decentralization in Thailand: How Past and Present Decentralization Affects Rural Actors' Participation. *The European Journal of Development Research, 27*(5), 793–810. https://doi.org/10.1057/ejdr.2014.68

Dutta, D. (2009). *Elite Capture and Corruption: Concepts and Definitions.* National Council of Applied Economic Research.

Escobar, A. (1995). El desarrollo sostenible: diálogo de discursos. *Ecología política*, (9), 7–25.

Everatt, D., & Gwagwa, L. (2005). *Community Driven Development in South Africa, 1990–2004. 109.*

Findley, M. G., Harris, A. S., Milner, H. V., & Nielson, D. L. (2017). Who Controls Foreign Aid? Elite versus Public Perceptions of Donor Influence in Aid-dependent Uganda. *International Organization, 71*(4), 633–663. https://doi.org/10.1017/S0020818317000273

Finkel, E. (2015). Does Reform Prevent Rebellion? Evidence From Russia's Emancipation of the Serfs. *Comparative Political Studies 2015, 48*(8), 984–1019.

Fox, J. (2020). Contested Terrain: International Development Projects and Countervailing Power for the Excluded. *World Development, 133*, 104978. https://doi.org/10.1016/j.worlddev.2020.104978

Fritzen, S. A. (2007). Can the Design of Community-Driven Development Reduce the Risk of Elite Capture? Evidence from Indonesia. *World Development, 35*(8), 1359–1375. https://doi.org/10.1016/j.worlddev.2007.05.001

Galasso, E., & Ravallion, M. (2005). Decentralized Targeting of an Antipoverty Program. *Journal of Public Economics*, *89*(4), 705–727. https://doi.org/10.1016/j.jpubeco.2003.01.002

García-López, G. A. (2019). Rethinking Elite Persistence in Neoliberalism: Foresters and Techno-Bureaucratic Logics in Mexico's Community Forestry. *World Development*, *120*, 169–181. https://doi.org/10.1016/j.worlddev.2018.03.018

German, L., Schoneveld, G., & Mwangi, E. (2013). Contemporary Processes of Large-Scale Land Acquisition in Sub-Saharan Africa: Legal Deficiency or Elite Capture of the Rule of Law? *World Development*, *48*, 1–18. https://doi.org/10.1016/j.worlddev.2013.03.006

Ghuman, B. S., & Singh, R. (2013). Decentralization and Delivery of Public Services in Asia. *Policy and Society*, *32*(1), 7–21. https://doi.org/10.1016/j.polsoc.2013.02.001

Grillos, T. (2017). Participatory Budgeting and the Poor: Tracing Bias in a Multi-Staged Process in Solo, Indonesia. *World Development*, *96*, 343–358. https://doi.org/10.1016/j.worlddev.2017.03.019

Guijt, I., & Shah, M. K. (Eds.). (1998). *The Myth of Community: Gender issues in participatory development*. Rugby: Practical Action Publishing. https://doi.org/10.3362/9781780440309

Gurung, A., Bista, R., Karki, R., Shrestha, S., Uprety, D., & Oh, S.-E. (2013). Community-based Forest Management and Its Role in Improving Forest Conditions in Nepal. *Small-Scale Forestry*, *12*(3), 377–388. https://doi.org/10.1007/s11842-012-9217-z

Hall, R., & Kepe, T. (2017). Elite Capture and State Neglect: New Evidence on South Africa's Land Reform. *Review of African Political Economy*, *44*(151), 122–130. https://doi.org/10.1080/03056244.2017.1288615

Hardoon, D. (2017). *Economy for the 99%*. Oxfam. https://oi-files-d8-prod.s3.eu-west-2.amazonaws.com/s3fs-public/file_attachments/bp-economy-for-99-percent-160117-summ-en.pdf

Harsh, M., Mbatia, P., & Shrum, W. (2010). Accountability and Inaction: NGOs and Resource Lodging in Development. *Development and Change*, *41*(2), 253–278. https://doi.org/10.1111/j.1467-7660.2010.01641.x

He, J. (2016). Rights to Benefit from Forest? A Case Study of the Timber Harvest Quota System in Southwest China. *Society & Natural Resources*, *29*(4), 448–461. https://doi.org/10.1080/08941920.2015.1062949

Hernández-Trillo, F., & Jarillo-Rabling, B. (2008). Is Local Beautiful? Fiscal Decentralization in Mexico. *World Development*, *36*(9), 1547–1558. https://doi.org/10.1016/j.worlddev.2007.09.008

Herrmann, R. T. (2017). Large-Scale Agricultural Investments and Smallholder Welfare: A Comparison of Wage Labor and Outgrower Channels in Tanzania. *World Development*, *90*, 294–310. https://doi.org/10.1016/j.worlddev.2016.10.007

Higgins, D., Balint, T., Liversage, H., & Winters, P. (2018). Investigating the Impacts of Increased Rural Land Tenure Security: A Systematic Review of the Evidence. *Journal of Rural Studies*, *61*, 34–62. https://doi.org/10.1016/j.jrurstud.2018.05.001

Hillebrand, E. (2009). *Poverty, Growth, and Inequality Over The Next 50 Years*. In Piero Conforti, ed., Looking Ahead in World Agriculture: Perspectives to 2050. Rome: Food and Agriculture Organization of the United Nations, 159-190.

Hinnerich, B., & Pettersson-Lidbom, P. (2014). Democracy, Redistribution, and Political Participation: Evidence From Sweden 1919–1938. *Econometrica*, *82*(3), 961–993. https://doi.org/10.3982/ECTA9607

Holdcroft, L. (1978). *The Rise and Fall of Community Development in Developing Countries, 1950–65*. Michigan State University. Rural Development. Paper No.2, 79.

Holden, S. T., & Otsuka, K. (2014). The Roles of Land Tenure Reforms and Land Markets in the Context of Population Growth and Land Use Intensification in Africa. *Food Policy, 48*, 88–97. https://doi.org/10.1016/j.foodpol.2014.03.005

Humphreys, M. (2012). *Social and Economic Impacts of Tuungane: Final Report on the Effects of a Community Driven Reconstruction Programme in the Democratic Republic of Congo.* 3ie Impact Evaluation Report 7. New Delhi: International Initiative for Impact Evaluation *(3ie).*

Hussein, K., & Nelson, J. (1998). *Sustainable Livelihoods and Livelihood Diversification.* IDS WORKING PAPER *69*, 32.

IRC & CARE. (2012). *Annual Review of Tuungane.doc.* ARIES CODE: 105862. http://iati.dfid.gov.uk/iati_documents/4131936.odt.

Iversen, V., Chhetry, B., Francis, P., Gurung, M., Kafle, G., Pain, A., & Seeley, J. (2006). High Value Forests, Hidden Economies and Elite Capture: Evidence from Forest User Groups in Nepal's Terai. *Ecological Economics, 58*(1), 93–107. https://doi.org/10.1016/j.ecolecon.2005.05.021

Jackson, P. (2011). Decentralised Power and Traditional Authorities: How Power Determines Access to Justice in Sierra Leone. *The Journal of Legal Pluralism and Unofficial Law, 43*(63), 207–230. https://doi.org/10.1080/07329113.2011.10756662

Kamoto, J., Clarkson, G., Dorward, P., & Shepherd, D. (2013). Doing More Harm Than Good? Community Based Natural Resource Management and the Neglect of Local Institutions in Policy Development. *Land Use Policy, 35*, 293–301. https://doi.org/10.1016/j.landusepol.2013.06.002

Kazianga, H. (2006). Motives for Household Private Transfers in Burkina Faso. *Journal of Development Economics, 79*(1), 73–117. https://doi.org/10.1016/j.jdeveco.2005.06.001

Khadka, M. (2009). *Why Does Exclusion Continue?: Aid, Knowledge and Power in Nepal's Community Forestry Policy Process.* Düren: Shaker Pub.

Khatun, K., Gross-Camp, N., Corbera, E., Martin, A., Ball, S., & Massao, G. (2015). When Participatory Forest Management Makes Money: Insights from Tanzania on Governance, Benefit Sharing, and Implications for REDD+. *Environment and Planning A: Economy and Space, 47*(10), 2097–2112. https://doi.org/10.1177/0308518X15595899

Kita, S. M. (2019). Barriers or Enablers? Chiefs, Elite Capture, Disasters, and Resettlement In Rural Malawi. *Disasters, 43*(1), 135–156. https://doi.org/10.1111/disa.12295

Kothari, U. (2001). Power, Knowledge and Social Control in Participatory Development. *Published in Participation: The New Tyranny?.* London: Zed Books.

Kumar, N., Vajja, A., Pozzoni, B., & Woodall, G. G. (2005). *The Effectiveness of World Bank Support for Community-Based and -Driven Development: An OED Evaluation.* The World Bank. https://doi.org/10.1596/978-0-8213-6390-4

Kundu, D. (2011). *Elite Capture in Participatory Urban Governance.* 10, 3.

Kusumawati, R., & Visser, L. (2016). Capturing the Elite in Marine Conservation in Northeast Kalimantan. *Human Ecology, 44*(3), 301–310. https://doi.org/10.1007/s10745-016-9830-0

Labonte, M. T. (2012). From Patronage to Peacebuilding? Elite Capture and Governance from below in Sierra Leone. *African Affairs, 111*(442), 90–115. https://doi.org/10.1093/afraf/adr073

Lake, M. (2017). Building the Rule of War: Postconflict Institutions and the Micro-Dynamics of Conflict in Eastern DR Congo. *International Organization, 71*(2), 281–315. https://doi.org/10.1017/S002081831700008X

Lange, S., & Kinyondo, A. (2016). Resource Nationalism and Local Content in Tanzania: Experiences from Mining and Consequences for the Petroleum Sector. *The Extractive Industries and Society, 3*(4), 1095–1104. https://doi.org/10.1016/j.exis.2016.09.006

Lawson, B. S. (2011). *Developing Stability: Community-Driven Development and Reconstruction in Conflict-Affected Settings. 306.*

le Meur, P.-Y. (1999). *Décentralisation par le bas et participation clientéliste au Benin. Published in Les Dimensions Sociales Et Economiques Du Developpement Local Et La Decentralisation En Afrique Au Sud Du Sahara.* Lit Verlag; Bilingual edition. https://journals.openedit ion.org/apad/562

Lebert, T., & Rohde, R. (2007). Land Reform and the New Elite: Exclusion of the Poor from Communal Land in Namaqualand, South Africa. *Journal of Arid Environments,* 70(4), 818–833. https://doi.org/10.1016/j.jaridenv.2006.03.023

Lee, Y. S. (2018). International Isolation and Regional Inequality: Evidence from Sanctions on North Korea. *Journal of Urban Economics, 103,* 34–51. https://doi.org/10 .1016/j.jue.2017.11.002

Lewis, B. D. (2005). Indonesian Local Government Spending, Taxing and Saving: An Explanation of Pre- and Post-decentralization Fiscal Outcomes★. *Asian Economic Journal, 19*(3), 291–317. https://doi.org/10.1111/j.1467-8381.2005.00214.x

Li, T. M. (2007). *The Will to Improve.* Durham & London: Duke University Press.

Liu, Z., Müller, M., Rommel, J., & Feng, S. (2016). Community-based Agricultural Land Consolidation and Local Elites: Survey Evidence from China. *Journal of Rural Studies, 47,* 449–458. https://doi.org/10.1016/j.jrurstud.2016.06.021

Long, N. (2003). *Development Sociology: Actor Perspectives.* London: Routledge. https://doi .org/10.4324/9780203398531

Lucas, A. (2016). Elite Capture and Corruption in Two Villages in Bengkulu Province, Sumatra. *Human Ecology, 44*(3), 287–300. https://doi.org/10.1007/s10745-016-9837-6

Lund, C., & Benjaminsen, T. A. (2001). *Politics, Property, and Production in the West African Sahel: Understanding Natural Resources Management.* Uppsala: Nordiska Afrikainstitutet.

Lund, J. F. (2015). Paradoxes of Participation: The Logic of Professionalization in Participatory Forestry. *Forest Policy and Economics, 60,* 1–6. https://doi.org/10.1016/j .forpol.2015.07.009

Lund, J. F., & Saito-Jensen, M. (2013). Revisiting the Issue of Elite Capture of Participatory Initiatives. *World Development, 46,* 104–112. https://doi.org/10.1016/j .worlddev.2013.01.028

MacArthur, J., & Matthewman, S. (2018). Populist Resistance and Alternative Transitions: Indigenous Ownership of Energy Infrastructure in Aotearoa New Zealand. *Energy Research & Social Science, 43,* 16–24. https://doi.org/10.1016/j.erss.2018.05.009

Manor, J. (1999). *The Political Economy of Democratic Decentralization.* The World Bank. https://doi.org/10.1596/0-8213-4470-6

Mansuri, G., & Rao, V. (2003). *Evaluating Community-Based and Community-Driven Development: A Critical Review of the Evidence. 54.*

Mapedza, E., & Bond, I. (2006). Political Deadlock and Devolved Wildlife Management in Zimbabwe: The Case of Nenyunga Ward. *The Journal of Environment & Development,* 15(4), 407–427. https://doi.org/10.1177/1070496506294635

Martinez-Bravo, M., Mukherjee, P., & Stegmann, A. (2017). The Non-democratic Roots of Elite Capture: Evidence From Soeharto Mayors in Indonesia. *Econometrica,* 85(6), 1991–2010. https://doi.org/10.3982/ECTA14125

Mattingly, D. C. (2016). Elite Capture: How Decentralization and Informal Institutions Weaken Property Rights in China. *World Politics, 68*(3), 383–412. https://doi.org/10 .1017/S0043887116000083

Mawomo, K. (2019). *The Dynamics of Community Participation: Evidence from Practice.* Keele University, England.

McMillan, R., Spronk, S., & Caswell, C. (2014). Popular Participation, Equity, and Co-Production of Water and Sanitation Services in Caracas, Venezuela. *Water International*, *39*(2), 201–215. https://doi.org/10.1080/02508060.2014.886844

Miller, J. (1988). The ghostly body politic: The federalist papers and popular sovereignty. *Political Theory*. 16, 99–119.

Minamoto, Y. (2010). Social Capital and Livelihood Recovery: Post-tsunami Sri Lanka as a Case. *Disaster Prevention and Management: An International Journal*, *19*(5), 548–564. https://doi.org/10.1108/09653561011091887

Mitra, S. K. (1991). Room to Maneuver in the Middle: Local Elites, Political Action, and the State in India. *World Politics*, *43*(3), 390–413. https://doi.org/10.2307/2010400

Mohammed, A. J., & Inoue, M. (2014). Linking Outputs and Outcomes from Devolved Forest Governance Using a Modified Actor-Power-Accountability Framework (MAPAF): Case Study from Chilimo Forest, Ethiopia. *Forest Policy and Economics*, *39*, 21–31. https://doi.org/10.1016/j.forpol.2013.11.005

Morck, R., Deniz Yavuz, M., & Yeung, B. (2011). Banking System Control, Capital Allocation, and Economy Performance☆. *Journal of Financial Economics*, *100*(2), 264–283. https://doi.org/10.1016/j.jfineco.2010.12.004

Musgrave, M. K., & Wong, S. (2016). Towards a More Nuanced Theory of Elite Capture in Development Projects. The Importance of Context and Theories of Power. *Journal of Sustainable Development*, *9*(3), 87. https://doi.org/10.5539/jsd.v9n3p87

Mustafa, D., Altz-Stamm, A., & Scott, L. M. (2016). Water User Associations and the Politics of Water in Jordan. *World Development*, *79*, 164–176. https://doi.org/10.1016/j.worlddev.2015.11.008

Mwangi, E., & Dohrn, S. (2008). Securing Access to Drylands Resources for Multiple Users in Africa: A Review of Recent Research. *Land Use Policy*, *25*(2), 240–248. https://doi.org/10.1016/j.landusepol.2007.07.002

Nadiruzzaman, M., & Wrathall, D. (2014). *Participatory Exclusion–Elite capture of participatory approaches in the aftermath of Cyclone Sidr*. UNU-EHS Working Paper Series No. 3. https://doi.org/10.13140/2.1.2185.5529

Nath, A. (2014). *Political Competition and Elite Capture of Local Public Goods*. Working Paper, 38.

Oberlack, C., Tejada, L., Messerli, P., Rist, S., & Giger, M. (2016). Sustainable Livelihoods in the Global Land Rush? Archetypes of Livelihood Vulnerability and Sustainability Potentials. *Global Environmental Change*, *41*, 153–171. https://doi.org/10.1016/j.gloenvcha.2016.10.001

Olken, B. (2005). *Monitoring Corruption: Evidence from a Field Experiment in Indonesia*. NBER Working Paper No. 11753 November 2005.

Olowu, D. (2003). Local Institutional and Political Structures and Processes: Recent Experience in Africa. *Public Administration and Development*, *23*(1), 41–52. https://doi.org/10.1002/pad.258

Pacheco, P., de Jong, W., & Johnson, J. (2010). The Evolution of the Timber Sector in Lowland Bolivia: Examining the Influence of Three Disparate Policy Approaches. *Forest Policy and Economics*, *12*(4), 271–276. https://doi.org/10.1016/j.forpol.2009.12.002

Pan, L., & Christiaensen, L. (2012). Who is Vouching for the Input Voucher? Decentralized Targeting and Elite Capture in Tanzania. *World Development*, *40*(8), 1619–1633. https://doi.org/10.1016/j.worlddev.2012.04.012

Panda, S. (2015). Political Connections and Elite Capture in a Poverty Alleviation Programme in India. *The Journal of Development Studies*, *51*(1), 50–65. https://doi.org/10.1080/00220388.2014.947281

Persha, L., & Andersson, K. (2014). Elite Capture Risk and Mitigation in Decentralized Forest Governance Regimes. *Global Environmental Change*, *24*, 265–276. https://doi .org/10.1016/j.gloenvcha.2013.12.005

Pfeiffer, J. (2003). International NGOs and Primary Health Care in Mozambique: The Need for a New Model of Collaboration. *Social Science & Medicine*, *56*(4), 725–738. https://doi.org/10.1016/S0277-9536(02)00068-0

Phillips, D., Waddington, H., & White, H. (2014). Better Targeting of Farmers as a Channel For Poverty Reduction: A Systematic Review of Farmer Field Schools targeting. *Development Studies Research*, *1*(1), 113–136. https://doi.org/10.1080/2 1665095.2014.924841

Pitcher, A., Moran, M. H., & Johnston, M. (2009). Rethinking Patrimonialism and Neopatrimonialism in Africa. *African Studies Review*, *52*(1), 125–156. https://doi.org /10.1353/arw.0.0163

Platteau, J.-P. (2004). Monitoring Elite Capture in Community-driven Development. *Development and Change*, *35*(2), 223–246. https://doi.org/10.1111/j.1467-7660.2004 .00350.x

Platteau, J.-P. (2006). Chapter 12 Solidarity Norms and Institutions in Village Societies: Static and Dynamic Considerations. In *Handbook of the Economics of Giving, Altruism and Reciprocity* (Vol. *1*, pp. 819–886). Elsevier. https://doi.org/10.1016/S1574-0714(06)01012-8

Platteau, J.-P. (2009). *Information Distortion, Elite Capture, and Task Complexity in Decentralised Development*. Working Papers 1104, University of Namur, Department of Economics, 54.

Platteau, J.-P., & Gaspart, F. (2003). The Risk of Resource Misappropriation in Community-Driven Development. *World Development*, *31*(10), 1687–1703. https://do i.org/10.1016/S0305-750X(03)00138-4

Platteau, J.-P., Somville, V., & Wahhaj, Z. (2014). Elite Capture through Information Distortion: A Theoretical Essay. *Journal of Development Economics*, *106*, 250–263. https ://doi.org/10.1016/j.jdeveco.2013.10.002

Platteau, J.-P., & Abraham, A. (2002). Participatory Development in the Presence of Endogenous Community Imperfections. *Journal of Development Studies*, *39*(2), 104– 136. https://doi.org/10.1080/00220380412331322771

Power, G., Maury, M., & Maury, S. (2002). Operationalising Bottom-Up Learning in International NGOs: Barriers and Alternatives. *Development in Practice*, *12*(3/4), 272–284.

Powis, B. (2007). *Systems of Capture: Reassessing the Threat of Local Elites*. World Bank. Social Development Papers, South Asia Series, Paper No.109.

Price, J. I., Janmaat, J., Sugden, F., & Bharati, L. (2016). Water Storage Systems and Preference Heterogeneity in Water-Scarce Environments: A Choice Experiment in Nepal's Koshi River Basin. *Water Resources and Economics*, *13*, 6–18. https://doi.org/10 .1016/j.wre.2015.09.003

Prinsen, G., & Titeca, K. (2008). Uganda's Decentralised Primary Education: Musical Chairs and Inverted Elite Capture in School Management Committees. *Public Administration and Development*, *28*(2), 149–164. https://doi.org/10.1002/pad.487

Prokopy, L. S. (2009). Determinants and Benefits of Household Level Participation in Rural Drinking Water Projects in India. *The Journal of Development Studies*, *45*(4), 471–495. https://doi.org/10.1080/00220380802265504

Putzel, L., Kelly, A. B., Cerutti, P. O., & Artati, Y. (2015). Formalization as Development in Land and Natural Resource Policy. *Society & Natural Resources*, *28*(5), 453–472. https://doi.org/10.1080/08941920.2015.1014608

Rao, V., & Ibáñez, A. M. (2005). The Social Impact of Social Funds in Jamaica: A 'Participatory Econometric' Analysis of Targeting, Collective Action, and Participation in Community-Driven Development. *Journal of Development Studies, 41*(5), 788–838. https://doi.org/10.1080/00220380500145297

Ribot, J. C. (2004). *Waiting for Democracy: The Politics of Choice in Natural Resource Decentralization.* Washington: World Resources Institute.

Rigon, A. (2014). Building Local Governance: Participation and Elite Capture in Slum-upgrading in Kenya: Participation and Elite Capture in Kenya. *Development and Change, 45*(2), 257–283. https://doi.org/10.1111/dech.12078

Rusca, M., Schwartz, K., Hadzovic, L., & Ahlers, R. (2015). Adapting Generic Models through Bricolage: Elite Capture of Water Users Associations in Peri-urban Lilongwe. *The European Journal of Development Research, 27*(5), 777–792. https://doi.org/10.1057/ejdr.2014.58

Russell, A. J. M., & Dobson, T. (2011). Chiefs as Critical Partners for Decentralized Governance of Fisheries: An Analysis of Co-Management Case Studies in Malawi. *Society & Natural Resources, 24*(7), 734–750. https://doi.org/10.1080/08941920.2010.501432

Saguin, K. (2018). Why the Poor Do Not Benefit from Community-driven Development: Lessons from Participatory Budgeting. *World Development, 112,* 220–232. https://doi.org/10.1016/j.worlddev.2018.08.009

Saito-Jensen, M., Nathan, I., & Treue, T. (2010). Beyond Elite Capture? Community-based Natural Resource Management and Power in Mohammed Nagar Village, Andhra Pradesh, India. *Environmental Conservation, 37*(3), 327–335. https://doi.org/10.1017/S0376892910000664

Saul, M. (1983). Work Parties, Wages, and Accumulation in a Voltaic Village. *American Ethnologist, 10*(1), 77–96. https://doi.org/10.1525/ae.1983.10.1.02a00050

Scott, J. (1985). *Weapons of the Weak: Everyday Forms of Peasant Resistance.* New Haven: Yale University Press.

Sheely, R. (2015). Mobilization, Participatory Planning Institutions, and Elite Capture: Evidence from a Field Experiment in Rural Kenya. *World Development, 67,* 251–266. https://doi.org/10.1016/j.worlddev.2014.10.024

Sitko, N. J., Chamberlin, J., & Hichaambwa, M. (2014). Does Smallholder Land Titling Facilitate Agricultural Growth?: An Analysis of the Determinants and Effects of Smallholder Land Titling in Zambia. *World Development, 64,* 791–802. https://doi.org/10.1016/j.worlddev.2014.07.014

Sitko, N. J., & Jayne, T. S. (2014). Structural Transformation or Elite Land Capture? The Growth of "emergent" Farmers in Zambia. *Food Policy, 48,* 194–202. https://doi.org/10.1016/j.foodpol.2014.05.006

Smoke, P. (2003). Decentralisation in Africa: Goals, Dimensions, Myths and Challenges. *Public Administration and Development, 23*(1), 7–16. https://doi.org/10.1002/pad.255

Sovacool, B. K. (2018). Bamboo Beating Bandits: Conflict, Inequality, and Vulnerability in the Political Ecology of Climate Change Adaptation in Bangladesh. *World Development, 102,* 183–194. https://doi.org/10.1016/j.worlddev.2017.10.014

Spurr, D. (1993). *Colonial Discourse in Journalism, Trav~l Writing, and Imperial Administration.* Durham: Duke University Press.

Tai, H.-S. (2007). Development Through Conservation: An Institutional Analysis of Indigenous Community-Based Conservation in Taiwan. *World Development, 35*(7), 1186–1203. https://doi.org/10.1016/j.worlddev.2006.09.015

Takasaki, Y. (2011a). Targeting Cyclone Relief within the Village: Kinship, Sharing, and Capture. *Economic Development and Cultural Change, 59*(2) (January 2011), 387–416.

Takasaki, Y. (2011b). Do Local Elites Capture Natural Disaster Reconstruction Funds? *Journal of Development Studies*, *47*(9), 1281–1298. https://doi.org/10.1080/00220388.2010.509786

Thomas, G. M., Chhetri, N., & Hussaini, K. (2008). Legitimacy and the Rise of NGOs: The Global and Local in South Asia. *Journal of Civil Society*, *4*(1), 31–42. https://doi.org/10.1080/17448680802051139

Thompson, B. S. (2017). Can Financial Technology Innovate Benefit Distribution in Payments for Ecosystem Services and REDD+? *Ecological Economics*, *139*, 150–157. https://doi.org/10.1016/j.ecolecon.2017.04.008

To, P. X., Dressler, W. H., Mahanty, S., Pham, T. T., & Zingerli, C. (2012). The Prospects for Payment for Ecosystem Services (PES) in Vietnam: A Look at Three Payment Schemes. *Human Ecology*, *40*(2), 237–249. https://doi.org/10.1007/s10745-012-9480-9

Townsend, J. G., Porter, G., & Mawdsley, E. (2002). The Role of the Transnational Community of Non-government Organizations: Governance or Poverty Reduction? *Journal of International Development*, *14*(6), 829–839. https://doi.org/10.1002/jid.928

Tschakert, P. (2016). Shifting Discourses of Vilification and the Taming of Unruly Mining Landscapes in Ghana. *World Development*, *86*, 123–132. https://doi.org/10.1016/j.worlddev.2016.05.008

UNDP. (2010). The Real Wealth of Nations: Pathways to Human Development. Human Development Report 2010 20th Anniversary Edition, 238.

Vajja, A., & White, H. (2008). Can the World Bank Build Social Capital? The Experience of Social Funds in Malawi and Zambia. *The Journal of Development Studies*, *44*(8), 1145–1168. https://doi.org/10.1080/00220380802242404

van Geen, A., Ahmed, K. M., Ahmed, E. B., Choudhury, I., Mozumder, M. R., Bostick, B. C., & Mailloux, B. J. (2016). Inequitable Allocation of Deep Community Wells for Reducing Arsenic Exposure in Bangladesh. *Journal of Water, Sanitation and Hygiene for Development*, *6*(1), 142–150. https://doi.org/10.2166/washdev.2015.115

Verbrugge, B. (2015). Decentralization, Institutional Ambiguity, and Mineral Resource Conflict in Mindanao, Philippines. *World Development*, *67*, 449–460. https://doi.org/10.1016/j.worlddev.2014.11.007

Verma, R. (2014). Land Grabs, Power, and Gender in East and Southern Africa: So, What's New? *Feminist Economics*, *20*(1), 52–75. https://doi.org/10.1080/13545701.2014.897739

Vicol, M., Neilson, J., Hartatri, D. F. S., & Cooper, P. (2018). Upgrading for Whom? Relationship Coffee, Value Chain Interventions and Rural Development in Indonesia. *World Development*, *110*, 26–37. https://doi.org/10.1016/j.worlddev.2018.05.020

Walsh, E., & Lenihan, H. (2006). Accountability and Effectiveness of NGOs: Adapting Business Tools Successfully. *Development in Practice*, *16*(5), 412–424.

Ward, C., Holmes, G., & Stringer, L. (2018). Perceived Barriers to and Drivers of Community Participation in Protected-area Governance: Protected-Area Governance. *Conservation Biology*, *32*(2), 437–446. https://doi.org/10.1111/cobi.13000

Warren, C., & Visser, L. (2016). The Local Turn: An Introductory Essay Revisiting Leadership, Elite Capture and Good Governance in Indonesian Conservation and Development Programs. *Human Ecology*, *44*(3), 277–286. https://doi.org/10.1007/s10745-016-9831-z

Wenar, L. (2006). Accountability in International Development Aid. *Ethics & International Affairs*, *20*(1), 1–23. https://doi.org/10.1111/j.1747-7093.2006.00001.x

Williams, G., Veron, R., Corbridge, S., & Srivastava, M. (2003). Participation and Power: Poor People's Engagement with India's Employment Assurance Scheme. *Development and Change*, *34*(1), 163–192. https://doi.org/10.1111/1467-7660.00300

Wilmsen, B. (2016). Expanding capitalism in Rural China Through Land Acquisition and Land Reforms. *Journal of Contemporary China*, *25*(101), 701–717. https://doi.org/10.1080/10670564.2016.1160504

Wong, S. (2010). *Elite Capture or Capture Elites? Lessons from the 'Counter-elite' and 'Co-opt-elite' Approaches in Bangladesh and Ghana. 21.*

Wong, Sam. (2013). Challenges to the Elite Exclusion–Inclusion Dichotomy—Reconsidering Elite Capture in Community-based Natural Resource Management. *South African Journal of International Affairs*, *20*(3), 379–391. https://doi.org/10.1080/10220461.2013.841800

Wong, S. (2012). *What Have Been the Impacts of World Bank Community-Driven Development Programs?* The World Bank Social Development Department Sustainable Development Network.

Yilmaz, S., & Venugopal, V. (2013). Local Government Discretion and Accountability in Philippines. *Journal of International Development*, *25*(2), 227–250. https://doi.org/10.1002/jid.1687

Zulu, L. (2013). Bringing People Back into Protected Forests in Developing Countries: Insights from Co-Management in Malawi. *Sustainability*, *5*(5), 1917–1943. https://doi.org/10.3390/su5051917

Appendix

(Adhikari & Goldey, 2010; Alatas et al., 2010; Andersson et al., 2018; Araujo et al., 2008; Arnall et al., 2013; Aspinall, 2014; I. G. Baird, 2014; S. Baird et al., 2013; Bernard et al., 2008; Bodin & Crona, 2011; Chemouni, 2014; Chomba et al., 2015, 2016; Chome, 2015; Classen et al., 2008; Cooper & Wheeler, 2015; Crespo et al., 2014; Crook, 2003; Darrow & Tomas, 2005; Dasgupta & Beard, 2007; Daum & Birner, 2017; Findley et al., 2017; Finkel, 2015; Fritzen, 2007; García-López, 2019; German et al., 2013; Ghuman & Singh, 2013; Grillos, 2017; Gurung et al., 2013; Hall & Kepe, 2017; He, 2016; Hernández-Trillo & Jarillo-Rabling, 2008; Herrmann, 2017; Higgins et al., 2018; Hinnerich & Pettersson-Lidbom, 2014; Holden & Otsuka, 2014; Iversen et al., 2006; Jackson, 2011; Kamoto et al., 2013; Khatun et al., 2015; Kundu, 2011; Labonte, 2012; Lake, 2017; Lange & Kinyondo, 2016; Lebert & Rohde, 2007; Lee, 2018; Lewis, 2005; Liu et al., 2016; J. F. Lund, 2015; J. F. Lund & Saito-Jensen, 2013; MacArthur & Matthewman, 2018; Mapedza & Bond, 2006; Martinez-Bravo et al., 2017; Mattingly, 2016; McMillan et al., 2014; Minamoto, 2010; Mohammed & Inoue, 2014; Morck et al., 2011; Mustafa et al., 2016; Mwangi & Dohrn, 2008; Nadiruzzaman & Wrathall, 2014; Oberlack et al., 2016; Olken, 2005; Olowu, 2003; Pacheco et al., 2010; Pan & Christiaensen, 2012; Panda, 2015; Persha & Andersson, 2014; Phillips et al., 2014; Jean-Philippe Platteau, 2004; Jean-Philippe Platteau et al., 2014; Jean-Philippe Platteau & Gaspart, 2003; Price et al., 2016; Prinsen & Titeca, 2008; Prokopy, 2009; Putzel et al., 2015; Rigon, 2014; Rusca et al., 2015; Russell & Dobson, 2011; Saito-Jensen et al., 2010;

Sheely, 2015; Sitko et al., 2014; Sitko & Jayne, 2014; Sovacool, 2018; Tai, 2007; Takasaki, 2011a, 2011b; Thompson, 2017; To et al., 2012; Tschakert, 2016; Vajja & White, 2008; van Geen et al., 2016; Verbrugge, 2015; Verma, 2014; Vicol et al., 2018; Ward et al., 2018; Warren & Visser, 2016; Wilmsen, 2016; Yilmaz & Venugopal, 2013; Zulu, 2013).

6

'DEVELOPMENT' PERSPECTIVES FROM THE GLOBAL SOUTH

Learning from Ubuntu and Buen Vivir philosophies

Birgit K. Boogaard and Dorine E. van Norren[1]

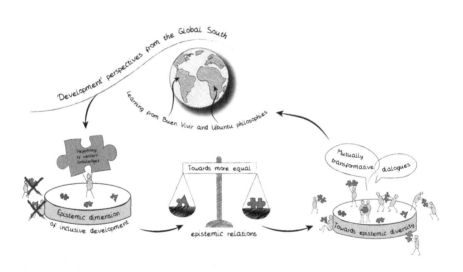

Introduction

While it is widely acknowledged that 'development' is an inherently Eurocentric concept (e.g. Ziai and Escobar, 2007), wellbeing concepts from perspectives of the Global South are less well known, let alone embraced.[2] The fact that development is a Eurocentric concept, however, may not necessarily mean that 'development' has to be thrown overboard entirely, though one should be open to accept pluralistic meanings of 'development'; thus, its mainstream meaning may evolve over time. For now, the term 'development' is still needed as a bridge to future conceptualisations. In general, development is largely based on mainstream Western ideas that are targeted at growth and progress (Bateye

DOI: 10.4324/9781003112525-6

et al., forthcoming; Kimmerle, 1998), including Western-based concepts such as 'capitalist, modernist, neoliberal, monocultural, extractivist and patriarchal' paradigms (Vásquez-Fernández and Ahenakew pii tai poo taa, 2020, p. 65).

The initial intention behind the concept of inclusive development was 'to counter the dominant neoliberal capitalist agenda' (Gupta et al., 2015, p. 541), based on the central idea that all stakeholders involved should benefit more equally. This was, however, only partly successful. Over time, inclusive development gained various meanings; for example, some put emphasis on inclusive growth while others put emphasis on ecological modernisation (Gupta and Pouw, 2017). A review by Gupta and Pouw (2017, p. 100) shows that despite the differences in meanings and approaches to inclusive development, it 'becomes apparent […] that many of these approaches have been designed within the growth paradigm.' As such, inclusive development does not undermine mainstream Western ideas on growth and progress, but tries to repair its flaws by including actors who previously were excluded. Subsequently, Gupta and Pouw recommend that critical social science scholars should try to avoid thinking within this growth paradigm. Instead, Gupta and Pouw propose a shift is needed in which development is more discursively defined and emphasises the social, ecological, and relational (power) dimensions of development. In this chapter we aim to contribute to this shift in thinking by addressing the epistemological and ontological dimensions of inclusive development, which have gained little attention so far.

We explore to what extent 'inclusive development' can accommodate philosophies from the Global South and how the definition of inclusive development needs to be adjusted. We will do this by presenting perspectives from the Global South through two indigenous philosophies: *Ubuntu* and *Buen Vivir*. We present some characteristics and critiques on both philosophies as well as parallels and differences between the two—based on a literature study and Van Norren's PhD research (2017). We then explore how these two indigenous philosophies relate to the concept of 'inclusive development' and raise several issues to pay attention to when moving towards epistemic diversity.

The epistemological dimension of inclusive development

To start with, a central point of inclusive development is the need to involve all stakeholders and their knowledge—in particular, marginalised groups. As Gupta et al. (2015) write: 'inclusiveness includes the knowledge and aspirations of local people in the development process […] and enhances their participation in decision-making' (Gupta et al., 2015, p. 546); meaning that indigenous knowledge should be included in the decision-making process. However, one can question the extent to which this also happens, in practice, in decisions about the concept of development itself. Inclusive development projects and policies may invite more diversity and marginalised people to the table even while, simultaneously, historically marginalised epistemologies continue being excluded (Boogaard, 2021). For example, a recent study of a livestock development project in a multi-stakeholder platform in Mozambique showed that the involved research organisation, the NGO, and the donor had set the definition of development prior to the start of the project, and this definition was not open to debate throughout the project (Boogaard, 2021).

The epistemological dimension of inclusive development thus refers to the involvement of indigenous people and their knowledge in development processes, especially with regard to the development concept itself. In the same line as the example above, we see that the majority of Sustainable Development Goals (SDGs) lean heavily on Western ideas about 'development' that are rooted in modernist economics and 'sustainable' growth—such as the target of 7% (sustained, inclusive) growth in SDG8—which largely excludes indigenous worldviews (Van Norren, 2017; Vásquez-Fernández and Ahenakew pii tai poo taa, 2020). As such, we see few attempts to include the knowledge of indigenous peoples in SDGs despite the formidable multi-stakeholder process that took place to draw up SDGs under the auspices of the United Nations (Van Norren, 2017). The exclusion and systematic and structural suppression of African, Latin American, Asian, and other indigenous philosophies and ways of knowing and doing constitutes epistemic injustice (Ramose, 2019; Sousa Santos, 2014). It is worrisome that development scholars have paid limited attention to African philosophies such as *Ubuntu* and Latin American philosophies such as *Buen Vivir*. For example, until today African philosophies are largely absent in debates on agricultural development in Africa (Boogaard, 2019).

In the current chapter, these two philosophies have been selected for the following reasons: (1) both have been historically excluded from mainstream development theories; (2) both have different epistemological roots compared to mainstream Western (economic) scientific knowledge; and (3) both offer a counter-hegemonic view on mainstream development views of economic progress and growth, meaning that they embrace concepts which go against the underpinnings of these paradigms. In addition to these three commonalities, there are also important differences between the two philosophies which we will address further on. We selected several characteristics as well as critiques that we deemed relevant in relation to the epistemological dimension of development, while being aware of the width and depth of both philosophies.[3]

Ubuntu philosophy

The term *Ubuntu* is found in many Sub-Saharan African languages; such as *botho* which has the same meaning in Sotho language, and *hunhu* in Shona language. *Ubuntu* is the fundamental ontological and epistemological category in the African thought of the Bantu people and as such can be described as the roots of African philosophies (Ramose, 1999, 2020). In Ramose's (2003, p. 271) words, 'The African tree of knowledge stems from ubuntu with which it is connected indivisibly.' In this section, we first describe *Ubuntu* philosophy by analysing three important African proverbs.[4]

To start with, *ubu-ntu* is a hyphenated word. *Ubu-* means the universe of being as enfolded—it is waiting to unfold. This is crucial, as it means that the philosophical point of departure is motion (not rest) and whole-ness (not fragmentation). The suffix *-ntu* refers to the process of unfolding through the knowing and speaking of humans. *Umuntu* can then be described as the living—a human being—in the visible world, while the living dead and yet-to-be-born are part of the invisible world, which together form the African community. It shows that relationality is central in African community, which is also expressed in the maxim '*umuntu ngumuntu nga bantu*' in Zulu—translated as 'to be human is to affirm one's humanity by recognizing the humanity of others and, on that basis, establish human relations with them' (Ramose, 1999, p. 37). Throughout life and in relations with others, one needs to learn 'being human.' With regard to development, this means that development is not about accumulating wealth at the costs of other human beings or Nature.[5] Instead, the maxim '*feta kgomo o thsware motho*' in Sotho states that 'if and when one must make a choice between preserving human life and accumulating wealth then one ought to opt for the preservation of human life' (Ramose, 1999, p. 109). Thus, instead of accumulating and safeguarding individual wealth, mutual sharing and caring is more important. This means that personal accumulation of wealth is far less important than the economic and social wellbeing of the community. African life and philosophy thus focus on harmonious and inclusive human relations. Several philosophers place speculative capitalist practices—often for personal gain—as going against the interest of the collective (Ramose, 1999); this includes financial speculation but also property (housing) speculation[6] or any speculation with other basic necessities, such as food. Equality and equity are moreover seen as cardinal values.

The importance of mutual caring and sharing is emphasised by a third Sotho maxim referring to the extended family: '*bana ba motho ba ngoathogana tlhogoana ya tsie*,' meaning that the children of one family share even the head of a locust (Ramose, 2021): one has an ethical obligation to share even the smallest portion (the locust is small and its head even smaller), or as Wiredu (2003) stated, 'life is mutual aid.' Family here should not be narrowed to the Western concept of a household, but accept a broader meaning of the extended family, the clan and furthermore, fellow human beings in general. Mutual care not only relates to fellow human beings, but also to Mother Earth and non-humans (Ramose, 2004). Land is sacred, and the living dead should be thanked for leaving behind a healthy land, while the living should leave the land behind in a good condition and pay respect to it for the following generations (Kelbessa, 2015). Humans additionally have a moral responsibility towards Earth (Behrens, 2014). In terms of development this means that resources—and especially land—cannot be exploited endlessly, but should be treated with respect and harmony with the Earth and land should be maintained.

Summarising, these three maxims show that in *Ubuntu* philosophy relationality in the visible and invisible world—the spiritual, the ancestral, and the yet-to-be-born—as well as mutual sharing and caring are more important than the accumulation of individual wealth, or national growth of wealth, if this does not benefit the community including Nature as a whole.

Buen Vivir (Sumak Kawsay) philosophy

Buen Vivir (Good Living) originates from the Andean Quecha people from Peru, Bolivia, Ecuador, Chile, whose concept is called *Sumak Kawsay*, meaning the best way of living, living in plenitude, or the right way of living. *Buen Vivir* is both an indigenous concept and an environmental and political movement rooted in indigenous philosophies. Both Ecuador and Bolivia enshrined it in their Constitutions and national policies. It is a biocentric concept in which all life forms are considered equal and revolves around living in harmony with Nature, which is posited as leading to harmony in relations with others and with oneself. Mother Earth (*Pachamama*) is revered as the life-giver and considered sacred—and therefore written with a capital letter, just like Nature. It encapsulates a cyclical way of thinking, as opposed to mainstream Western linear thinking, and calls for balancing spiritual and material wealth (Acosta, 2015; Akchurin, 2015; Hidalgo-Capitán and Cubillo-Guevara, 2014; Government of Ecuador, 2013; Gudynas, 2011).

Because *Pachamama* is sacred, she has rights—just like all other living creatures in Nature, including humans. Therefore, the (right of) Mother Earth is the main principle on which all life is based and from this all other (human) systems are derived, such as law, governance, economics, and culture, which all need to operate in harmony with Nature/Earth. After the relationship with the Cosmos, Earth and Nature follows the relationship with the (human) community. The community of life encompasses all of the above (Villalba, 2013). Thus, there is no distinction between culture and Nature (Van Norren, 2017). For indigenous people *Sumak Kawsay* is not only tied to spirituality, but also to interculturality and plurinationality—namely the recognition of indigenous nations and territories within the state (Sousa Santos, 2014 given that their collective way of life cannot be practised without ties to the land, Nature, and territory.

As *Sumak Kawsay* is cyclical and not linear, it does not strive at accumulation of goods or economic growth; the main goal is balance and harmony through reciprocity—between humans and with Mother Earth and all living beings. As in Nature everything grows and decays, the idea of sustainability is, like growth, a false notion because sustainability suggests a system that is stable (with consistent linear growth) whereas in Nature everything moves in cycles. Hence *Buen Vivir* poses as an alternative to 'sustainable development' (Acosta, 2015; Thomson, 2011; Villalba, 2013). Like Ubuntu, *Buen Vivir* strives towards a self-sustaining and life-nurturing economy without growth in terms of accumulation of production and consumption. Instead, it sees economic speculation and centrality of capital as the greatest cause of the current exploitation of humans and Nature (Acosta, 2015). As such, it looks for solidarity and equal exchange whereby all living subjects are complementary to one another. This is called collective capability by Deneulin (2012); a capability which includes living in reciprocity with Nature. The capability theory was first developed by Amartya Sen in 'Development as Freedom' (Sen, 1999), which nevertheless looks only at individual human capabilities rather than collective capabilities, including all life.[7]

Building on this work, Van Norren (2017) proposes 'development as service' in addition to 'development as freedom.' Development could be redefined in terms of mutual service or reciprocity to one another and Earth/Nature. To this end, academic knowledge should be combined with knowledge of indigenous peoples (Oviedo-Freire, 2011) so that reciprocity in human relations as well as with Nature becomes central—and not the economy. Progress is then defined differently and this might lead to the abolishment of the word 'development' altogether. Such an approach would lead to a whole new economy which strives amongst others things at the redistribution of wealth and income; promoting post-extractivist economies and (community) markets, based on use value; decentralising production; realising energy and food sovereignty; inclusion of leisure and creativity; recognising domestic and reproductive work; and measuring the economy in terms of full employment (Acosta, 2015; Dávalos, 2008; Van Norren, 2020; Waldmüller, 2014).

Several critiques on both philosophies

Because this chapter does not allow for an in-depth discussion of detailed philosophical debates on the application and significance of *Ubuntu* and *Buen Vivir*, we will present a few more general critiques of both philosophies that are relevant in relation to knowledge and development. There is similarity between the critiques corresponding to each. One of the main criticisms of *Ubuntu* philosophy is that it romanticises the past and presents a one-sided view of who Africans are today. For example, the ethical imperative of mutual care and sharing may be read as presenting Africans as communitarian and Westerners as individualists. However, many publications have provided a more nuanced view in which one also finds individualism in African philosophies, as well as communalism in Western philosophies, though the emphasis is different in both cultures (Eze, 2008; Kimmerle, 2008; Oyeshile, 2006). *Buen Vivir* is subject to similar criticisms for romanticising the past. According to Bretón et al. (2014, p. 12) 'Medina […] and Oviedo-Freire […], from Bolivia and Ecuador respectively, have deployed a noticeable effort to build an archetypal, decontextualized and mystical image of a kind of carrier "Andean civilization" […] uncontaminated for centuries by western culture,' so that '[t]his type of approach to the subject has been ironically described as "pachamamista" from anti-essentialist visions.' Even though indigenous people are not immune to modernisation, they undeniably have a strong link to the land and Nature.

In addition, *Buen Vivir* and *Ubuntu* are criticised for being anti-market and anti-growth (Van Norren, 2017), while in many African and Latin American contexts there is a desire for improved standards of living. As such, an alternative view on growth and development should not mean that 'Africa should remain in a position of severe disadvantage' (Kimmerle, 1998, p. 27), but it means that wellbeing of the community is more important than personal accumulation of wealth. If applied on a world scale, this would imply a better distribution of worldwide economic gains (Oruka, 1995).

Some parallels and differences between the two philosophies

From the previous section's considerations, it becomes clear that there are several parallels between the two philosophies. In both philosophies, relationality is central in the sense that both philosophies have a sense of an expanded community derived from a cosmic unity that reaches into ancestral and future lives and includes Nature. From this follows a notion of equality between humans as well as other living beings. Relations are then at the heart of development, in which none is dominant over the other. In addition, both philosophies emphasise the reciprocity of life, and the need to recognise this and respect it as a fundamental principle. In *Ubuntu* we see that life is mutual aid—including reciprocity to the ancestors—and in *Buen Vivir* it is living in harmony with, and respect for, Mother Earth (Van Norren, 2017). Hence, both philosophies are not concerned with the idea of progress or development in purely material means but instead stress the importance of harmony and (spiritual) relations.

If we zoom in on both philosophies there are also differences, for example, in the importance of human and non-human relations.[8] In *Ubuntu* philosophy inclusion of the human community comprises the living, the living dead and the yet-to-be-born, and the principle of mutual care also extends to Mother Earth and non-humans. It is, however, argued that African philosophies are essentially human-centred, as they mainly focus on relations between humans (e.g. Gyekye, 1997). In general, *Ubuntu* derives its relationship to Earth from the human interrelationships and dependence on land, as well as from its relationship with future generations as part of the 'bantu' community and the ancestors who are identified within the Earth (Van Norren, 2017). One could say that there are various interpretations of *Ubuntu* among Africans, which represent a position between anthropocentrism and biocentrism in which rural dwellers tend to be more biocentric. In *Buen Vivir* we saw that inclusion entails the whole community of life—with Nature and all living beings on an equal footing—that need to live in harmony with one another: humans are a tiny part of the spectrum. As such, *Buen Vivir* can be considered as biocentric (Acosta, 2015; Van Norren, 2017). Considering knowledge, in *Ubuntu* knowing is about 'being in relation' and 'feeling engaged with the other,' i.e., humanness. In *Buen Vivir*, knowing is being in harmony with the universe, Earth and Nature, and connecting to the Earth (Van Norren, 2017).

Towards epistemic diversity

Ubuntu and *Buen Vivir* are therefore inherently inclusive cosmologies, in the sense that they emphasise interrelationship and embrace diversity as basic tenets: in the 'rainbow nation' and 'holoculturality' (*Ubuntu*); and in plurinationality and interculturality (*Buen Vivir*). As such, the term 'inclusive development' can be seen as a tautology from an *Ubuntu* and *Buen Vivir* perspective. In fact, 'inclusive development' is a Western-developed concept that was deemed necessary, as a model aiming for economic progress and meritocracy is inherently exclusive. Inclusive development definitions that are trapped 'within the neo-liberal fast growth paradigm' (Gupta and Pouw, 2017, p. 97), and that take 'big-D development logic' such as inclusive growth as a starting point, have a fundamentally different view compared to the described indigenous philosophies. In *Ubuntu* and *Buen Vivir* philosophies, the economy is not central in development. For *Ubuntu*, it is developing human relations and moral responsibility; for *Buen Vivir* it is developing harmony with Nature and Earth. Thus, *Ubuntu* and *Buen Vivir* may lead to an altogether different 'development' or, rather, wellbeing paradigm in which the 'harmony of all life' may become more central; based on reciprocity and relationality between human and non-humans, including Mother Earth, and the present, past, and future generations (Van Norren, 2017).

As such, *Ubuntu* and *Buen Vivir* philosophies can be a source of inspiration for degrowth scholars because 'ubuntu offers the philosophical basis for an alternative imaginary to growth and development' (Ramose, 2015, p. 213). In addition, there are some parallels between *Buen Vivir* and environmental justice and deep ecology (Van Norren, 2017). In that sense, *Ubuntu* and *Buen Vivir* philosophies may be not entirely incommensurable with alternatives within the inclusive development discourse, though their scope is much wider.

However, there is a high risk of knowledge appropriation if one seeks to include indigenous philosophies in current narratives. This would make other knowledges part of dominant existing—and often Eurocentric—concepts. This was partly the case in Ecuador, where the extractive economy remained and became more dominant during *Buen Vivir* government policies instead of emulating the intrinsic value of Nature. Walsh (2010, p. 17) states that *Buen Vivir* may not 'disentangle Ecuador from its colonial past, but possibly entangles it with the development paradigm in a more complex way. It is in danger of becoming part of "the European push to humanize capitalism."' Likewise, the targets and indicators in the SDGs, are based on the idea that 'knowing is measuring,' whereas indigenous philosophies are not exclusively based on empiricist measuring but on other ways of knowing.

The concept of 'inclusive development' can become less Eurocentric by making room for, and subsequently being transformed by, indigenous philosophies: not as tokens or knowledge appropriation but by fundamentally questioning the concept of development (Vásquez-Fernández and Ahenakew pii tai poo taa, 2020). How can we move towards epistemic diversity? To start with, it would be a misunderstanding to assume that epistemic diversity is a harmonious process of bringing different knowledges seamlessly together. Instead, it is a process of negotiation and struggle between epistemologies, in which a reality of diversities is accepted; there may be overlaps as well as gaps and tensions between values, epistemologies, and ontologies (Ludwig and El-Hani, 2019). For example, both *Ubuntu* and *Buen Vivir* emphasise the importance of the relationship with the land (Vásquez-Fernández and Ahenakew pii tai poo taa, 2020), but there are huge tensions between such relationality to the land of indigenous peoples and current legal and economic systems revolving around private property and ownership of land; this includes the individualist human rights tradition that holds private property sacred. As such, negotiation between diverse types of knowledge and ways of knowing is needed to create space and recognition for epistemic diversity in the first place (Roothaan, 2019).

From this departure point, we propose to engage in mutually transformative dialogues between development scholars and philosophers in the Global South and North (following Kimmerle, 1998, 2012). Until today, international development debates tend to be dominated by narratives originally formulated by Western-trained scholars who—consciously or unconsciously—exclude indigenous philosophies. However, over the past decades, African and Latin American philosophers and other intellectuals have been—and continue to be—deeply engaged in questioning, thinking, discussing, reflecting, and acting on what development means from African or Latin American perspectives (Acosta, 2015; Agbakoba, 2019; Diagne and Kimmerle, 1998; Hountondji, 2004). To include the epistemological dimensions of development means to decolonise people's mindsets. Historically dehumanising experiences of slavery and colonialism still influence international relations between the Global South and Global North in the sense that these relations continue to be characterised by highly unequal power relations. While it is widely acknowledged that economic relations between the Global South and North are unequal, inequality in epistemological relations has gained less attention so far. In response to ongoing forms of dehumanisation, Ramose (2020) therefore argues that we need '*mothofatso*'; to re-humanise human relations, as echoed by authors like Acosta (2015).

A dialogical approach towards the epistemological dimensions of inclusive development may ask a more modest attitude from Western-trained scholars, and requires a willingness to listen and learn from indigenous philosophies (Kimmerle, 2012), in order to avoid that these philosophies are declared irrelevant and forgotten altogether or framed unjustly and too quickly in a dominant Western concept of inclusive development.

Conclusion

Based on the above, we argue that as long as African, Latin American, and other indigenous philosophies remain excluded from the concept of inclusive development, we will reproduce Eurocentric and neo-colonial ideas of development based on Western frameworks and theories that are easily imposed on 'non-Western' contexts.[9] Learning from *Ubuntu* and *Buen Vivir* philosophies, the present study provides at least four points on the epistemological and ontological dimensions of 'inclusive development':

(1) A need to broaden the concept and definition of 'inclusive development,' which includes fundamental and critical questions about the epistemologies on which the current concept of 'inclusive development' is founded. This requires a recognition of the existence, the value, and a better understanding of philosophies from the Global South.

(2) A need to recognise epistemic diversity and to question the concept of 'development,' which from a perspective of indigenous philosophies of the Global South would be more adequately described through (human) wellbeing, relationality, and harmony. This includes the requirement to re-humanise human relations, so that reciprocity in human relations as well as with Nature is central.

(3) A need to avoid knowledge appropriation, but instead engage in mutually transformative dialogues. This is perhaps the greatest danger: that *Ubuntu* and *Buen Vivir* will be paid lip service in future development reports and schemes, such as the SDGs, without taking full cognisance of them.

(4) A need to put harmony with Nature and respect for the Earth central to human thinking and to recognise the rights of the Earth and Nature as intrinsic and equal to that of human rights, as is done in *Buen Vivir* and the constitution of Ecuador.

Notes

1 Both authors contributed equally to this article.
2 'Development' is a contested and Eurocentric concept; therefore, we purposely put it between inverted commas. Likewise, we also purposely put the terms 'developing' and 'developed' between inverted commas.
3 Such a selection process is not neutral, especially given the Western educational and cultural background of both authors.
4 Over the past two decades, *Ubuntu* has been widely debated among African philosophers, particularly in South Africa, e.g. in the South African Journal of Philosophy.
5 Written with a capital to denote its sacredness for indigenous communities.
6 South African jurisprudence also offers very strong protection against eviction from housing, so that the interest of the private owner is subservient to the interests of the renters (Cornell and Muvangua 2012; Van Norren, 2017).
7 Sen (1999) articulates individual capabilities to reach valuable functionings and doings and to realise human rights and freedoms. Sen redefined development/progress thinking into actualising one's individual valuable states of being and doing, while 'development as service' adds the collective dimension.
8 We will mention some salient differences here. For a more extensive list see Table 9.3 'Comparison of SDG, Ubuntu, Happiness, Buen Vivir approach" in Van Norren (2017, p.320).
9 The term 'non-Western' is problematic in itself: it is a Eurocentric view towards indigenous philosophies that continues to refer to 'the West' as reference point.

References

Acosta, A. (2015). *Buen Vivir. Vom Recht auf ein gutes Leben.* Munich: Oekom Verlag.

Agbakoba, J. C. A. (2019). *Development and modernity in Africa: An intercultural philosophical perspective.* Cologne: Rüdiger Köppe Verlag.

Akchurin, M. (2015). Constructing the Rights of Nature: Constitutional reform, mobilization, and environmental protection in Ecuador. *Law and Social Inquiry,* 40(4), 937–968.

Bateye, B., Masaeli, M., Müller, L., and Roothaan, A. (forthcoming) (eds.). *Beauty in African thought: A critique of the Western idea of development.* Lanham: Lexington.

Behrens, K. (2014). An African relational environmentalism and moral considerability. *Environmental Ethics,* 36(1), 63–82.

Boogaard, B. K. (2019). The relevance of connecting sustainable agricultural development with African philosophy. *South African Journal of Philosophy,* 38(3), 273–286.

Boogaard, B. K. (2021). Epistemic injustice in agricultural development: Critical reflections on a livestock development project in rural Mozambique. *Knowledge Management for Development Journal.* 16(1), 28–54.

Breton, V., Cortez, D. and García, F. (2014). En busca del Sumak Kawsay: In search of Sumak Kawsay, introduction to the dossier. Íconos. *Revista de Ciencias Sociales,* 48, 9–24.

Cornell, D. and Muvangua, N. (eds.). (2012). *Ubuntu and the law: African ideals and post-apartheid jurisprudence.* New York: Fordham University Press.

Dávalos, P. (2008). *Reflexiones sobre el Sumac Kawsay (Buen Vivir) y las teorías del desarrollo.* ALAI (Agencia Latino Americana Informaciones). http://www.alainet.org/es/active /25617

Deneulin, S. (2012). Justice and deliberation about the Good Life: The contribution of Latin American Buen Vivir social movements to the idea of justice. *Bath papers in international development and wellbeing,* 17, Centre for Development Studies, University of Bath.

Diagne, S. B. and Kimmerle, H. (eds.). (1998). Time and development in the thought of Subsaharan Africa. *Studies in Intercultural Philosophy,* 8, Rodopi B.V.

Eze, M. O. (2008). What is African communitarianism? Against consensus as a regulative ideal. *South African Journal of Philosophy,* 27(4), 386–399.

Government of Ecuador (2013). *National development plan, National Plan for Good Living 2013–2017, a better world for everyone.* Summarized Version. Republic of Ecuador.

Gudynas, E. (2011). Good life: Germinating alternatives to development. *Latin America in Movement,* (ALAI), July 14. http://www.alainet.org/es/node/151207

Gupta, J. and Pouw, N. (2017). Towards a trans-disciplinary conceptualization of inclusive development. *Current Opinion in Environmental Sustainability,* 24, 96–103.

Gupta, J., Pouw, N. R. M. and Ros-tonen, M. A. F. (2015). Towards an elaborated theory of inclusive development. *The European Journal of Development Research,* 27(4), 541–559.

Gyekye, K. (1997). *Tradition and modernity. Philosophical reflections on the African experience.* Oxford: Oxford University Press.

Hidalgo-Capitán, A. L. and Cubillo-Guevara, A. P. (2014). Six open debates on Sumak Kawsay. *Íconos Revista de Ciencias Sociales,* 48, 25–40.

Hountondji, P. (2004). Knowledge as a development issue. In: Wiredu, K. (2007) *A companion to African philosophy.* Oxford: Blackwell Publishing, 529–537.

Kelbessa, W. (2015). African environmental ethics, indigenous knowledge, and environmental challenges. *Environmental Ethics,* 37(4), 387–410.

Kimmerle, H. (2012). Dialogues as form of intercultural philosophy. Irian Society of Intercultural Philosophy. http://isiph.ir/en/?p=27

Kimmerle, H. (2008). The concept of person in African thought: A dialogue between African and Western philosophies In: Wautischer, H. (ed.). *Ontology of Consciousness.* Cambridge: MIT Press, 507–524.

Kimmerle, H. (1998). The concept of time as key-notion for new ideas about development. In: Diagne, B. and Kimmerle, H. (eds.). *Time and development in the thought of Subsaharan Africa. Studies in intercultural philosophy 8.* GA. Amsterdam: Rodopi B.V.

Ludwig, D. and El-Hani, C. (2019). Philosophy of ethnobiology: Understanding knowledge integration and its limitations. *Journal of Ethnobiology,* 40(1), 3–20.

Oruka, H. O. (1995). Ecophilosophy and the parental Earth ethics (on the complex web of being). In: Oruka, H. O., Graness, A. and Kresse, K. (eds.). *Sagacious Reasoning: Henry Odera Oruka in Memoriam,* Bern: Peter Lang, 119–131.

Oviedo-Freire, A. (2011). *Qué es el Sumakawsay. Más álla del capitalismo y el socialismo. Camina alter-nativo al desarollo. Una propuesta para los 'indignados' y démas desencantados de todo el mundo.* La Paz: Sumak Editores.

Oyeshile, O. (2006). The individual-community relationship as an issue in social and political philosophy. In: O. Oladipo (ed.). *Core issues in African philosophy.* Hope Publications, 102–116.

Ramose, M. B. (2003). The philosophy of ubuntu and ubuntu as a philosophy. In: Coetzee, P. H. and Roux, A. P. J. (eds.). *The African philosophy reader.* Second edition. London: Routledge, 270–280.

Ramose, M. B. (2004). The Earth 'mother' metaphor: An African perspective. In: Elders, F. (ed.). *Visions of nature. Studies on the theory of Gaia and culture in ancient and modern times.* Brussels: VU University Press, 203–206.

Ramose, M. B. (2015). Ubuntu. In: D'Alisa, G., Demaria, F. and Kallis, G. (eds.). *Degrowth, A vocabulary for a new era.* London: Routledge, 212–213.

Ramose, M. B. (2020). Critique of Ramon Grosfoguel's 'The epistemic decolonial turn'. *Alternation,* 27(1), 271–307.

Ramose, M. B. (1999). *African philosophy through Ubuntu.* Harare: Mond Books Publishers.

Ramose, M. B. (2021). Ethical responsibility for the other arrested by epistemic blindness, deafness and muteness: An ubuntu perspective. In: Standish, K., Devere, H., Suazo, A. and Rafferty, R. (eds) *The Palgrave Handbook of Positive Peace.* Singapore: Palgrave Macmillan, 1–25.

Ramose, M. B. (2019). A philosophy without memory cannot abolish slavery: On epistemic justice in South Africa. In: Hull, G. (ed.). *Debating African philosophy. Perspectives on identity, decolonial ethics and comparative philosophy.* Routledge, 60–72.

Roothaan, A. (2019). *Indigenous, modern and postcolonial relations to Nature: Negotiating the environment.* London: Routledge.

Sen, A. (1999). *Development as Freedom.* Oxford: Oxford University Press.

Sousa Santos, B. de (2014). *Epistemologies of the South. Justice against epistemicide.* London: Routledge.

Thomson, B. (2011). Pachakuti: Indigenous perspectives, Buen Vivir, Sumaq Kawsay and degrowth. *Development,* 54(4), 448–454.

Van Norren, D. E. (2017). *Development as service. A Happiness, Ubuntu and Buen Vivir interdisciplinary view of the Sustainable Development Goals.* PhD dissertation, Tilburg University.

Van Norren, D. E. (2020). The sustainable development goals viewed through gross national happiness, Ubuntu, and Buen Vivir. *International Environmental Agreements: Politics, Law and Economics*. 20(3), 431–458.

Vásquez-Fernández, A. M. and Ahenakew pii tai poo taa, C. (2020). Resurgence of relationality: Reflections on decolonizing and indigenizing 'sustainable development'. *Current Opinion in Environmental Sustainability*, 43, 65–70.

Villalba, U. (2013). Buen Vivir vs development: A paradigm shift in the Andes? *Third World Quarterly*, 34(8), 1427–1442.

Waldmüller, J. M. (2014). *Buen Vivir, Sumak Kawsay, Good Living: An Introduction and Overview*. Alternautas, (Re)Searching Development: The Abya Yala Chapter, extended version. http://www.alternautas.net/blog/2014/5/14/buen-vivir-sumak-kawsay-good-living-an-introduction-and-overview.

Walsh, C. (2010). Development as Buen Vivir. Institutional arrangements and (de) colonial entanglements. *Development*, 53(1), 15–21.

Wiredu, K. (2003). The moral foundations of an African Culture. In: Coetzee, P. H. and Roux, A. P. J. (eds.). *The African philosophy reader*. Second edition. London: Routledge, 287–296.

Ziai, A. and Escobar, A. (2007). *Exploring post-development: Theory and practice, problems and perspectives*. London: Routledge.

PART III

Learning for transformative change

Creating space for diversity and dialogues

7

LEARNING AND CHANGE IN AND THROUGH ACTION-ORIENTED RESEARCH

Barbara van Mierlo, Annemarie van Paassen, Rico Lie, Elias Damtew, and Loes Witteveen

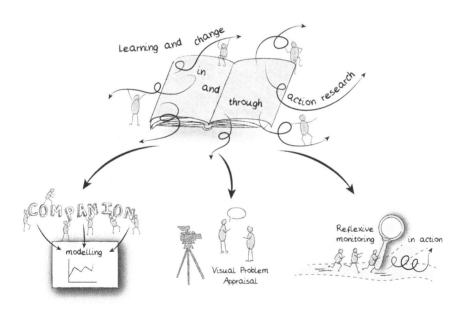

Introduction

Learning is a process involving changes in knowledge, practices, and aspirations, also potentially influencing the institutional setting in which actors operate. Learning takes place in and through communication. It can be observed in interaction and in this way inform research that is aiming for inclusive innovation. In this chapter, we tap into our personal experiences with action research

DOI: 10.4324/9781003112525-7

approaches for stimulating learning and transformative change, considered as sources of inspiration for researchers (interested in) engaging in action research.

Undertaking action-oriented research is a pathway ridden with challenges. It is hard to develop a good understanding of the factors influencing learning processes, or the links between learning processes and outcomes. Intervening is also not simple. Scholars tend to overstate the value of organised learning settings, while learning is often unduly assumed to be merely progressive and positive (Reed et al., 2010; Van Mierlo and Beers, 2020). Moreover, researchers are rarely supported by their institutions to conduct this kind of research (Fazey et al., 2018). These challenges call for transparency regarding the guiding conceptual notions and underlying theories, as well as empirical evidence of relations between interventions, learning, and the outcomes of action research.

In this chapter, we show how learning can provide a relevant entry point for inclusive innovation and transformative change and also how important a system perspective is for dealing with complex issues. Three well-elaborated methodologies that the authors have helped develop are presented and discussed: Companion Modelling, Visual Problem Appraisal, and Reflexive Monitoring in Action. The methodologies have been applied extensively in a diversity of domains; in small projects as well as in large programmes. They all recognise the importance of participation of actors with diverse perspectives and interests in the inclusive process of research, learning, and change. The methodologies are described in terms of methodological design, actor participation, and researcher roles, as well as in terms of their proven value in problem situations.

System perspectives in action-oriented research

Action research ideally concerns iterative cycles of action-observation, reflection, and planning, which are used together to understand and improve practice. Action-oriented research traditions all focus on learning of the present to act for the future by creating new ideas, building relationships to overcome societal challenges, and experimenting for societal transformation. Stakeholders are involved in the research to learn about a situation in its interconnectedness in order to define actions for desired societal change. Many traditions thus explicitly embrace a system perspective.

The word 'system' comes from a Greek verb meaning 'to stand together' and refers to the interconnection or relationships of things. Considering that the whole is greater than the sum of the parts, from a systems perspective, phenomena need to be understood as an emergent property of an interrelated whole (Flood, 2010). Systems thinking began in the 1940–50s, when scientists of different disciplines realised they were looking at similar phenomena and could benefit from an integrated system perspective. They engaged in 'hard system' research, which included studying functions and relationships between sub-systems, and also the effect of amplifying and balancing feedback loops; this was done in order to gain insight into the system dynamics and to find options for reaching a certain goal. Around the 1960s, epistemological awareness grew, and Checkland (2000) introduced 'soft system thinking' based on the social constructivist paradigm. In this perspective, 'a system' refers to a way of thinking about the connections between things after making a boundary judgment that defines 'the system of interest.' The purpose of soft system thinking is, with the aid of methodological tools and facilitation, to exchange knowledge and perspectives of stakeholders involved so as to enhance learning (a) about the human activity systems that offer insight into the problem situation; and (b) actor's perspectives, values, and interests to create change. In this way, proposals for change can be defined based on a change of mindsets and on the accommodation of interests (Checkland, 2000; Senge et al., 1999).

Soft system thinking focuses on meaning construction and the changing of mindsets, but it barely touches upon economic and political structures in the world determining the dominance of some mindsets and actions over others (Jackson, 1991), or those that distort meaningful dialogues and social transformation (Flood, 2010). In the 1980s, critical system thinking emerged putting concerns about power relations and inclusive and fair innovation on the agenda. Critical system thinkers embrace four major commitments (Jackson, 1991; Ulrich, 1983): critical awareness, by questioning one's own assumptions and values and/ or exploring the empowering effects of research methodologies; social awareness, by considering the acceptability of social rules and practices with a given society; human emancipation, by expressing a concern for people's well-being and fair development; and theoretical and methodological complementarity.

Soft system thinking, particularly—and to a lesser extent critical system thinking—have influenced ideas of action research (Greenwood and Levin, 2007). Reason and Bradbury (2001) distinguish three types of inquiry and learning related to systems thinking: single-loop learning concerns fact-finding about system dynamics to know what action leads to a valued goal; double-loop learning concerns an inquiry into actors' values, beliefs, and assumptions through dialogue leading to changed thinking and strategies; in third-loop learning, the purposes, identities, and the understanding of a situation as a whole (biophysical and societal system) are questioned and changed.

In good action research, these types of inquiry (fact-finding, dialogues, and whole system analysis for societal transformation) are interwoven. Hence, the task of action-oriented researchers—facilitating multi-level, social learning and change—is a delicate one, as they engage in 'systemic self-reflective scientific inquiry' (McKernan, 1996, p. 5). 'Self-reflective' means here the sense of being aware of one's own position, partial view, and preferred action; while 'systemic' considers the interconnectedness of issues, people, perspectives, and actions when exploring problem situations and action for change.

Companion Modelling

Since 1996, a group of agronomic, water, forest ecology, and social modelling scientists have applied a participatory modelling approach called Companion

Modelling (ComMod) (Bousquet et al., 2007). ComMod researchers embrace soft system thinking and the subjectivity of knowledge, and engage in iterative action research through initiating and facilitating social learning for NRM (Barreteau, 2003; Bousquet et al., 2007). Social learning refers to a process in which groups from different backgrounds, knowledge, and interests share perspectives to attain a more comprehensive knowledge on the issue-at-stake; gain insight into each other's perspectives and concerns; and develop mutual trust and commitment; all in order to arrive at convergent views for action (Röling, 2002).

Central to the ComMod approach is participatory modelling (see Figure 7.1). A model is a simplified representation of a system, which is built to discuss the relevance of the representation for the different stakeholders and subsequently to simulate and learn about the behaviour of the system. After a first scoping, local stakeholders are invited to formulate the issue-at-stake. After in-depth research of the social and biological system dynamics, scientists develop a conceptual model of the issue and translate this into a Role-Playing Game (RPG): natural resources (water, agricultural fields, forest, products, etc.) are located on the more-or-less abstract game board, and the various types of players are assigned an amount of resources (fields, money, labour, etc.) to play out their respective livelihood strategies. Game rules represent resource-use practices, farm practices, crop prices, while chance cards introduce contextual events. Every game round then simulates an agricultural season. RPGs allow multiple stakeholders to observe and better understand each other's behaviour, to examine the effects, and to react. In a game, players can easily swap roles and test the effect of alternative options for problem solving. As RPGs are time-consuming, ComMod

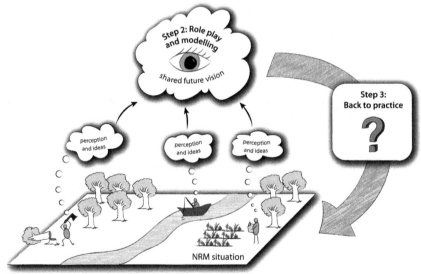

FIGURE 7.1   Soft system methodology of ComMod Collective (adapted from ComMod, source: https://www.commod.org/en)

scientists design a related Agent-Based computer Model (ABM) to simulate the long-term trade-offs of the proposed alternative practices in different scenarios.

The aim of modelling and RPGs is to enhance social learning and action. First, the RPG is used for stakeholders to mobilise their knowledge and to criticise and adapt the conceptual model of the NRM dynamics 'to make it realistic.' Then participants are encouraged to gain understanding of the situation of different types of actors, the rationality of their behaviour, and underlying norms and values; but also to gain an overview of how different practices and processes interrelate and work out at higher system levels (e.g. community, watershed level, etc.). RPGs are iterated with individual interviews and focus group discussions to stimulate and monitor the learning of players and stakeholder group/organisation representatives, as well as the interaction with their constituencies. The first RPG focuses on the actual NRM situation, but then stakeholders are asked to propose new options for change. Adapted RPGs (and ABMs) are prepared to explore these scenarios with the stakeholders, assess trade-offs for the different actors and the collective, and to agree on what actions to take.

All ComMod researchers engage in the action research: they initiate dialogue and learning with stakeholders related to NRM; closely study and analyse the effect of their intervention on learning, underlying beliefs and values, relationships, engagement, and action; and design the next steps for facilitating further communication and learning for more inclusive NRM. Care is taken to give voice to the concerns of the marginalised and to show consequences of scenarios for their livelihood. ComMod opts for a collaborative research approach, which means that researchers put themselves on equal footing in the knowledge exchange process. They share power in the definition of the problem and decision-making on the change process, while being responsible for the design of the research and communication process (Probst et al., 2003). An important principle for them is to be aware of, and transparent about their research and societal aims (Barreteau, 2003).

The approach developed by CIRAD in France has been applied globally to better understand the forces driving the evolution of farm and livelihood systems and natural resource use (Bousquet et al., 2007); as a tool to support mediation of resource conflicts (D'Aquino, 2003); and as a normative reflection and action for equitable, sustainable NRM (Barnaud et al., 2010). In the last decade, researchers in agriculture and the NRM domain have become increasingly interested in 'serious gaming' and applying ComMod.

In an in-depth evaluation of ComMod, participants underscored that learning has taken place, and individual farming practices—such as mulching or borrowing money—changed. This, however, did not lead to a change of policies as defined by the authorities involved (Barnaud et al., 2010). In consequence, researchers started recognising the influence of power asymmetries as well as the need for more reflection on the empowerment of marginalised groups and bottom-up policy processes within a political-institutional context. ComMod researchers were called upon to pay more attention to this context and its influence on process outcomes (Hassenforder et al., 2019). Several of them have begun using a critical system approach; strategically selecting stakeholders and designing knowledge sharing processes aiming for empowerment of marginalised actors while engaging in advocacy and informal mediation for fair and sustainable solutions.

Visual Problem Appraisal

Visual Problem Appraisal (VPA) is a film-based learning strategy used to enhance a multi-stakeholder analysis of complex issues and facilitate the development of action plans. VPA is used in workshops and creates a learning environment to 'meet' diverse stakeholders through watching filmed narratives. VPA is: (a) a learning strategy, (b) concerned with complex and wicked problem settings, (c) used for problem analysis and policy design, (d) focused on dialogue and participation, and (e) to enhance the participation of stakeholders—primary stakeholders who are socially segregated or at a distance from stakeholders in power or at a physical distance, as well as secondary stakeholders who are the decision makers and future practitioners.

The material core of a VPA learning strategy is a VPA set, which consists of a series of filmed interviews or portraits (between 20 and 30), complemented with documentaries in relation to a complex issue. These filmed narratives are produced in a specific film style with ethnographic and deliberative qualities, thereby providing a diversity of perspectives on the contextual and perceived reality of individual stakeholders. These filmed interviews and the accompanying documentaries offer VPA learners a chance to explore the complex and conflictive arena of problems such as coastal zone management, HIV/AIDS and rural development, and climate change adaptation.

VPA emphasises the positioning of various stakeholders. It combines soft systems thinking with critical systems thinking in the sense that the methodology articulates power positions and addresses unequal access to having a voice and making a difference. It does so by letting the stakeholders share their own perspective on parts of the system and the system as a whole. It is therefore used in the policy domain to gain insight into the different perspectives on a complex issue-at-stake. In higher education, VPA is used in training programmes for transdisciplinary problem analysis, policy design, and stimulating systems thinking in general.

Participants in a VPA workshop go through a three-tier programme: scoping, stakeholder consultation, and developing options for action (see Figure 7.2). The scoping stage varies from a quick scan to a desk study, starting with a kick-off meeting. Once participants have a basic idea of the VPA process, they first watch a documentary which explores subject-matter knowledge. Reflective forms guide this scoping. Participants answer reflective questions about their personal objectives (whether their questions were answered or not). The facilitators then provide procedural feedback on these reflective forms. These forms allow the learners and facilitators to assess and reflect on the knowledge gained, searching for individual accountability in the unfolding of the learning process.

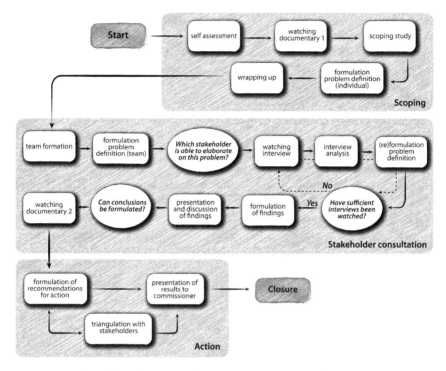

FIGURE 7.2   Flow chart depicting the VPA process (adapted from Lie and Mandler, 2009, p. 16)

VPA films are extended narratives, with only the interviewees on screen, in long steady frames, and filmed on location and during activities in their daily environments. The interviewees tell their story, filmed in such a way that the audience experiences the role of interviewer. Reflective forms guide the process: each team must convince the facilitators about the appropriateness of the selected interviewee before they can 'meet him or her.' After each interview, teams fill-in a form articulating their actions and decisions as a basis for the feedback session with facilitators. In the final stage, the learners analyse and structure the information encapsulated in the interviews and formulate recommendations for action.

Various VPAs are used in the policy domain as well as in different programmes at various universities in the Netherlands and abroad. The motivation of using VPA for enhancing learning about complex problems in transdisciplinary settings is fuelled by the facts that VPA can (a) bring overlooked stakeholders into the classrooms and place them next to policy makers, (b) address learning about various stakeholder positions, (c) create a safe space for learning, and (d) profit from the additional value of the visual (Witteveen and Lie, 2018).

The impact of VPA has mainly been explored in higher education. Course evaluations indicate that the diversity of learning activities is appreciated; the students gain insights into complex issues and transdisciplinarity, experiencing VPA as challenging but safe. A major repositioning over the years concerns aspects of reality that are no longer considered as a simulation because the reflexive actions by VPA users are not simulated but real 'since it [VPA] allows students to experience and reflect differently on their common images and on their usual behaviour when meeting farmers, fishermen and women' (Witteveen, Put, and Leeuwis, 2010, p. 53; Witteveen and Lie, 2018).

In the governance domain, the impact of the VPA AIDS & Rural Development in Sub-Saharan Africa and the VPA Kerala's Coast was evaluated by participating researchers (see https://www.visualproblemappraisal.org/). The space for dialogue and learning was positively evaluated in diverse international and intercultural settings; the impact in terms of action and relevance for filmed stakeholders was also evaluated positively, albeit only assessed in the short term. The facilitation is highlighted in evaluations, as facilitators need expertise with the methodology to be daring and confident for supporting 'learning on the edge.'

Reflexive Monitoring in Action

Reflexive Monitoring in Action (RMA) is an integrated methodology for addressing complex problems by encouraging innovating groups or networks to work towards aligned institutional changes, i.e., system innovation (Van Mierlo et al., 2010). Reflection and learning are interwoven in the process of change. Appointed reflexive monitors stimulate recurrent collective reflection in the network and the design and adaptation of actions targeting a future system change. In this way, while facing the everyday struggles of an ongoing transformative change process, system innovation initiatives are expected to increase their reflexivity—that is, their ability to interact with and affect the institutional setting in which they operate. It can be recognised as the emergence of new aligned practices and new associated rules enabling these practices, within the initiative and in wider networks (Beck et al., 1994; Beers and Van Mierlo, 2017).

Learning as a social, reciprocal process may thus occur in different locations (see Figure 7.3): among diverse actors involved in a local experiment or project (1); among such initiatives (2); at a more global level, for instance in a large policy programme (3); and between the local and the global level (4).

In order to monitor and stimulate the learning processes from the perspective of system innovation at these places, existing theories were adapted. To observe learning in regular project meetings, for example, a model was developed combining learning theories from Natural Resource Management and educational studies. The model suggests that learning in the context of system innovation interweaves: (1) new knowledge about problems or solutions; (2) relevant partners or opponents; and (3) which actions to take (Beers et al., 2016). Learning thus enables taking coordinated physical actions and influencing the process of (system) change.

Every (research) activity associated with reflexive monitoring is also a dedicated intervention to encourage reflection and learning. It involves a series of activities, preferably in iterative cycles: observation, analysis, reflection, and

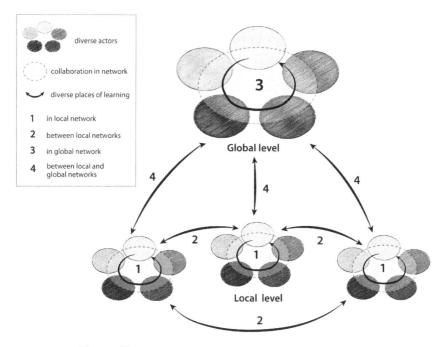

FIGURE 7.3   Places of learning in system innovation initiatives (adapted from Beers et al., 2019)

design and adjustment of actions. The monitoring is often an assigned role and responsibility of 'reflexive monitors' who act as analysts, sparring partners, process managers, and much more. This role could be performed by a researcher, consultant, policy maker, or by anyone else who is able to reflect, listen, and actively observe, summarise and integrate, handle diversity, and introduce relevant theories in a clear way. Specific RMA tools complement well-known research activities such as conducting interviews and process facilitation. The dynamic learning agenda, for instance, helps to link long-term aims to concrete perspectives for actions by putting challenges that arise on the agenda, as well as keeping track of how they are addressed and changed (Van Mierlo et al., 2010).

In principle, monitoring activities are—as far as possible—conducted collectively by all actors involved in the initiative, and as far as circumstances allow, embedded in activities that were already planned by the initiators. For instance, regular project meetings or other social encounters can be observed and reflected upon; or gatherings of value-chain actors can be designed to include analysis of the institutional setting so as to decide how to grasp windows of opportunity.

Over the past decade, the methodology has been applied in a diversity of domains including sustainable agriculture, health, international development, the knowledge infrastructure, and education for sustainability. RMA stimulated the diverse participants to reframe issues and problems, redesign strategies, grasp windows of opportunity, enhance collaboration, and overcome stagnation in the change process in projects like *Telen met Toekomst* (Farming with Future) in the Netherlands and Primary Innovation in New-Zealand (Fielke et al., 2017).

There are also examples of RMA becoming part of local and national policy making in the Netherlands and Belgium, as well as of education activities regarding sustainable development in schools and systems for policy analysis and evaluation. Most of all, it has supplemented the repertoire of many academic and applied researchers across the world. For the Dutch Research Institute for Transitions (DRIFT), for instance, it has become a visible element of their work, mainly by helping put flesh on a key component of transition management.

The above results indicate the emergence of new practices within system innovation initiatives, occasionally spilling from the initiatives' boundaries into their wider networks. Signs of new associated rules enabling these practices showcase the reflexivity of the methodology; albeit, an evaluation has shown that learning in a system innovation initiative does not necessarily increase its reflexivity (Beers and Van Mierlo, 2017). Initiatives were found to operate in three different modes depending on the extent to which they share an orientation towards structural change with their institutional environments. Also, only in a few situations did learning pave the way for systemic change in context. Still, in the rest, reflexivity within the institutional setting preceded learning in the initiative; either by providing room for fundamental change, or by limiting it and hindering change. This all underlines the dependence of action research success on external developments.

Reflection

How does action-oriented research instigate learning, inclusive innovation, and transformative change? Table 7.1 provides an overview of the core features of the three action-oriented research strategies applied by our group. The nature of their methodological design and concrete activities is diverse; ranging from multi-step approaches to develop potential scenarios in multi-stakeholder groups; to a film-based strategy in which learning is stimulated by mediated participation of stakeholders; to the monitoring of an ongoing process of (system) change. Despite this, they also build on similar basic ideas. Here we ponder their value for learning and systemic change from a bird's eye view.

System perspectives acknowledging and addressing complexity

Addressing complex problems on the basis of a system perspective is at the heart of the three methodologies. They all acknowledge the complexity of invasive biophysical and societal issues by taking their emergent properties as a starting point, as well as the inherent uncertainty and their contested nature because of competing claims, various positions and concerns, and diversity in backgrounds and knowledge.

TABLE 7.1 Overview of the three action-oriented research methodologies

	ComMod	VPA	RMA
Methodology	A structured process of joint-demand articulation, problem survey, a role-playing game, and simulation model to explore future NRM scenarios. Agreement on goals and actions. Community development through iterative cycles of problem identification, exploration, and actions.	Uses a staged process of preparing for, watching, and reflecting on filmed narratives of stakeholders in a complex problem. Learners understand various stakeholder positions and are expected to develop recommendations for actions.	Flexible, tailor-made interventions (from feedback on planned activities to workshops) to stimulate collective reflection on effects of actions in the light of a desirable future and the institutional setting. Iterative cycles *ex dure* the process of change to increase the capacity to work on system innovation.
Temporality	Initiated when NRM problem is flagged. Through iterative problem formulation, exploration scenarios, and dialogue for action, sustainable and inclusive NRM and community development is pursued.	One-off cyclical event ranging from a one or two-day workshop to a full course. Situated at the moment in time that the stakeholders were interviewed. Connects to contemporary and future situation.	Ideally during the course of system innovation initiatives. Backcasting from desired long-term future situation.
Inclusion of actors	Diverse local stakeholders involved in a NRM problem, or other related problem forwarded. Different types of NR users in community and related policy makers.	Primary stakeholders presenting individual perspectives and realities on a complex problem. Secondary stakeholders, decision makers, and future practitioners watching the filmed interviews.	Groups or networks of innovators: with researchers, consultants, policy makers, and other professionals; rarely also civil actors.

(Continued)

TABLE 7.1 (*Continued*)

	ComMod	VPA	RMA
Roles of researchers	Design conceptual model and game, with relevant socio-ecological knowledge. Facilitate and monitor learning and negotiation around scenario explorations and towards inclusive, sustainable NRM.	Dual role researchers: build a video set as VPA producers or learn from the videos as audience	Social scientists or experienced consultants in a variety of roles, as team partner operating 'from a distance.'
Documented impact	Learning about issue, others' perspectives, and community preferred future. Changed individual practices. Community level propositions for new policy rules.	Learning about issue and others' perspectives (including disadvantaged actors). Research ethics in practice. Learning about the relevance of public participation for transformative and inclusive action.	Adaptations of actions and changes in understanding and practices in concrete innovation trajectories. Changes in practices and rules of pursuing transformative change (monitoring and evaluation, research, and policy making).

While all methodologies build on soft system thinking, there are also interesting differences: VPA builds primarily on a critical system perspective by contrasting deprived actors with (future) decision makers; RMA combines soft system thinking with a touch of hard systems thinking when analysing social and institutional dimensions of a complex problem, thus also addressing the persistency of problems; ComMod combines soft with hard system thinking by paying attention to the biophysical dimension regarding the ecological system surrounding the endangered natural resources because of which natural scientists are included in the research process. Diversity in the key roles of researchers is partly related to these differences, with VPA being primarily process oriented. Interventions in ComMod and RMA navigate also on the basis of desirable futures and plausible directions of the change process.

Valuing the group for learning and action

Learning about novel information, such as other actors' perspectives and experiences by bringing together—directly or indirectly—multiple actors in a group setting is key to all three strategies. To stimulate collective learning, VPA and ComMod involve both actors experiencing a problem and actors who are expected to have the responsibilities and means to address this problem. The main aim is to develop a richer perspective on the complex issue and a mutual understanding of stakes, based on which actions could be envisioned and designed. RMA, in contrast, works primarily with the actors involved in a system innovation initiative who have already started to take action; this enables the monitoring of physical actions and their effects on the change process, while other relevant actors are regarded as part of the context targeted by the initiators. Most importantly, this way of thinking rearranges the participation-philosophy of action research: actors are not invited to participate in research, but researchers are allowed to participate in change processes.

In all cases, the (proposed) actions are related to who, exactly, are involved in the research project or change initiative. They thus build, by definition, on a selective group's ideas, knowledge, and aspirations. This points to the importance of reflection on the consequences of the selection of participants, as well as on the exclusion of multiple other actors.

Direct changes, but intangible impact

The evaluation of the impact of the methodologies shows that much learning about the participants' perspectives, the targeted system, and possible solutions, has taken place and several practices have changed. The research activities did not lead to the envisioned fundamental system changes during the research. One explanation is that system changes can hardly be expected in the short time span of a research. Another is that learning does not necessarily lead to actions and a change of practices and institutions; it may even just be follow-up on other changes instead of being their prelude (Beers and Van Mierlo, 2017). The relevance and results of action-oriented research depend on the kind of change pursued, the resources available, and the existence of numerous preconditions including the expectations regarding research and researchers. Modesty regarding their own expectations to evidently contribute to systemic change characterises researchers embarking on the path of action-oriented research. Nonetheless, the induced changes in thinking and acting can be seen and treated as preliminary preparations for wider change.

The essence of facilitation and monitoring

Action-oriented research can operate as a catalyst in change processes. The desirable direction and the reference frame for the interventions should be defined in a flexible, collaborative process and adapted on the basis of recurrent reflections in the group. Whether this happens is highly dependent on the quality of facilitation and monitoring, thus putting researchers in a delicate role. While being actively engaged in the process of learning from change-oriented actions and changing research practices which are often part of the complex problems in modern society (Fazey et al., 2018), researchers should also take sufficient distance in order not to pursue individual goals and be acceptable as a facilitator or monitor to a diversity of actors. The presented methodologies show some of the ways in which these stakes could be balanced; from structured role descriptions to a high variety of roles that build on explicit principles.

References

Barnaud, C., Van Paassen, A., Trébuil, G., Promburom T. and Bousquet, F. (2010). Dealing with power games in a companion modelling process: Lessons from community water management in Thailand highlands. *The Journal of Agricultural Education and Extension*, 16(1), 55–74.

Barreteau, O. (2003). The joint use of role-playing games and models regarding negotiation processes: Characterization of associations. *Journal of Artificial Societies and Social Simulation*, 6(2), 16.

Beck, U., A. Giddens and Las S. (1994). *Reflexive modernization: Politics, tradition and aesthetics in the modern social order.* Stanford: Stanford University Press.

Beers, P. J., Turner, J. A., Rijswijk, K., Williams, T., Barnard, T. and Beechener, S. (2019). Learning or evaluating? Towards a negotiation-of-meaning approach to learning in transition governance. *Technological Forecasting and Social Change*, 145, 229–239.

Beers, P. J., Van Mierlo, B. and Hoes, A. C. (2016). Toward an integrative perspective on social learning in system innovation initiatives. *Ecology and Society*, 21(1), 33.

Beers, P. J. and Van Mierlo, B. (2017). Reflexivity and learning in system innovation processes. *Sociologia Ruralis*, 57(3), 415–436.

Bousquet, F., Castella, J.-C., Trébuil, G., Barnaud, C., Boisseau, S. and Kam, S. P. (2007). Using multi-agents systems in a companion modelling approach for agro-ecosystem management in south-east Asia. *Outlook on Agriculture*, 36(1), 57–62.

Checkland, P. B. (2000). Soft systems methodology: A thirty year retrospective. *Systems Research and Behavioral Science*, 17(S1), S11–S58.

D'Aquino, P., Le Page, C., Bousquet, F. and Bah, A. (2003). Using self-designed role-playing games and multi-agent system to empower a local decision-making process for land use management: The Self Cormas experiment in Senegal. *Journal of Artificial Societies and Social Simulation*, 6(3), 1–5.

Fazey, I., Schäpke, N., Caniglia, G., Patterson, J., Hultman, J., Van Mierlo, B., et al. (2018). Ten essentials for action-oriented and second order energy transitions, transformations and climate change research. *Energy Research and Social Science*, 40, 54–70.

Fielke, S., Nelson, T., Blackett, P., Bewsell, D., Bayne, K., Park, N., Rijswijk, K. and Small, B. (2017). Hitting the bullseye: Learning to become a reflexive monitor in New Zealand. *Outlook on Agriculture*, 46(2), 117–124.

Flood, R. L. (2010). The relationship of 'systems thinking' to action research. *Systemic Practice and Action Research*, 23, 269–284.

Greenwood, D. J. and Levin, M. (2007). *Introduction to action research. Social research for social change*, 2nd edition. Sage, Thousand Oaks.

Hassenforder, E., Clavreul, D., Akhmouch, A. and Ferrand, N. (2019). What's the middle ground? Institutionalized vs. emerging water-related stakeholder engagement processes. *International Journal of Water Resources Development*, 35(3), 525–542.

Jackson, M. C. (1991). *Systems methodology for the management sciences*. Plenum.

Lie, R. and Mandler, A. (2009). *Video in development. Filming for rural change*. Wageningen: CTA/FAO.

McKernan, J. (1996). *Curriculum action research*. London: Kogan Page.

Probst, K., Hagmann, J., Fernandez, M. and Ashby, J. A. (2003). *Understanding participatory research in the context of natural resource management; paradigms, approaches and typologies*. Agren Network paper 130.

Reason, P. and Bradbury, H. (eds.) (2001). *Handbook of action research; Participative inquiry and practice*. New York: Sage.

Reed, M. S., Evely, A. C., Cundill, G., Fazey, I., Glass, J., Laing, A., et al. (2010). What is social learning? *Ecology and Society*, 15(4), 1–10.

Röling, N. (2002). Beyond the aggregation of individual preferences; Moving from multiple to distributed cognition in resource dilemmas. In: Leeuwis, C. and Pyburn, R. (eds.), *Wheelbarrows full of frogs. Social learning in rural resource management*. Assen: Koninklijk van Gorcum, 25–48.

Senge, P., Kleiner, A., Roberts, C., Ross, R., Roth, G. and Smith, B. (1999). *The dance of change*. London: Nichols Brealey Publishing.

Ulrich, W. (1983). *Critical heuristics of social planning*. Bern: Haupt.

Van Mierlo, B., Regeer, B., Van Amstel, M., Arkesteijn, M., Beekman, V., Bunders, J., et al. (2010). *Reflexive monitoring in action: A guide for monitoring system innovation projects*. Amsterdam: Boxpress.

Van Mierlo, B. and Beers, P. J. (2020). Understanding and governing learning in sustainability transitions: A review. *Environmental Innovation and Societal Transitions*, 34, 255–269.

Witteveen, L., Put, M. and Leeuwis, C. (2010). Learning about complex multi-stakeholder issues: Assessing the visual problem appraisal. *The Journal of Agricultural Education and Extension*, 16(1), 39–54.

Witteveen, L. and Lie, R. (2018). Visual problem appraisal. An educational package, which uses filmed narratives. In: Griffith, S., Bliemel, M. and Carruthers, K. (eds.), *Visual tools for developing student capacity for cross-disciplinary collaboration, innovation and entrepreneurship*. Transformative Pedagogies in the Visual Domain: Book No. 6. Common Ground Research Networks.

8

TOWARDS DESIGN PRINCIPLES FOR DIVERSITY SENSITIVE LEARNING

Rico Lie, Birgit K. Boogaard, and Loes Witteveen

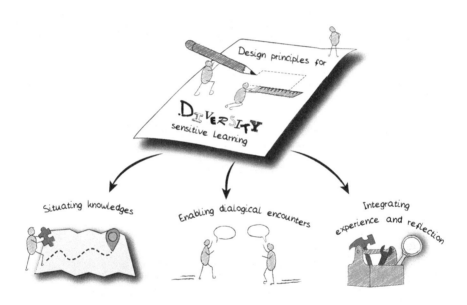

Introduction

With the increasing recognition of science and society interfaces in times of the Anthropocene and with complex sustainability challenges, authors like Scholz and Steiner (2015) and Gilbert (2016) have explored transforming the role of research and education. Such a societal perspective proposes an alignment of Higher Education policies and practices with contemporary issues. A changing world order and the recent attention to Black Lives Matter (BLM) protests added even more urgency to the perspective of diversity sensitive learning addressed in

DOI: 10.4324/9781003112525-8

this chapter. Diversity is increasingly seen as a factor that needs to be considered to make knowledge work in our current educational systems and beyond; in a globalised world (university) cultures become increasingly heterogeneous, with students and teachers originating from and working in international and culturally diverse contexts. Considering Higher Education as an imperative place where knowledge is (re)produced, based on ontological assumptions of objectivity and normative truths, the chapter explores design principles for diversity sensitive learning in a Netherlands university setting.

In August 2020, the Ministry of Education, Culture and Science in the Netherlands launched the National Action Plan for Greater Diversity and Inclusion in Higher Education and Research. This action plan sets various goals for Higher Education and Research for 2025 to achieve 'an inclusive, diverse and safe learning and working environment in which everyone has the opportunity to flourish' (Ministry of Education, Culture and Science in the Netherlands, 2020, p. 5). Through the implementation of the action plan, the Ministry aims 'to increase diversity both among students and staff and in research and educational content' (ibid, p. 9).

This increase in diversity is needed to align with societal developments and especially fits the perspective of Wageningen University and its slogan: 'Quality needs diversity' (WUR, 2020). Wageningen University explicitly states in the document that the university values diversity and, to implement this, it adheres to four principles when it comes to working in multicultural settings: (1) empathy; (2) respect for each other; (3) scope for authenticity; and (4) communication and, in particular, listening carefully (WUR, 2020). Its scope nevertheless falls short on the recognition of systemic problems, and so it neglects the content focus and learning strategies which are implicitly being favoured.

Taking the above critique into account while considering societal processes of globalisation and localisation, this chapter addresses diversity by focussing on what we have termed 'diversity sensitive learning.' The chapter has a focus on learning designs in formal Higher Education and aims to identify (foundational) design principles for such diversity sensitive learning. The assumption is that in making these principles explicit, they become accessible and can enhance the quality of learning designs. As an illustration, this chapter probes three courses offered by the Social Sciences Department at Wageningen University. The chapter envisions through an empirical approach to formulate design principles that can be useful for courses offered by the Social Sciences Department of Wageningen University and beyond.

An empirical approach to explore learning spaces for diversity

The empirical foundation for this chapter is the analysis of three specific courses: Intercultural Communication (CPT-35806 by Rico Lie), African

Philosophy (CPT-58306 by Birgit Boogaard), and Visual Research Methods (CPT-58802 by Loes Witteveen). Three reasons underlie the choice of these courses. First, the authors of this chapter were the main actors involved in the design and teaching of these courses. The second is the diverse scientific groundings of the three courses: Intercultural Communication is grounded in communication science, intercultural and cross-cultural communication, social anthropology, and cultural studies; African Philosophy follows an intercultural philosophical approach; and Visual Research Methods, as a methodology course, is founded on methodology studies combined with sociology, cultural studies, and media studies. Finally, all three courses embark on aspects of diversity sensitive learning in relation to (cultural) content, and they address the relationship between content matters and cultures in various ways. In all three courses, learning from diversity refers to processes and outcomes to enhance the quality of learning. These three reasons enhance the presence and visibility of design principles.

The chapter does not detail the learning goals and setup of each course. Instead, it exemplifies diversity sensitive learning in a reflective and open, explorative way, highlighting several features of the courses which contribute to 'diversity sensitive learning.' In each feature—i.e. each sub-heading—it is first explained *why* a particular learning strategy is included in the course and subsequently *how* it is applied in the course. The next section presents the three courses; we then describe the underlying principles which emerged from comparing and analysing the features that address diversity sensitive learning in each course.

Intercultural Communication

Know the knowledge that already exists

The course used the knowledge that people already acquired through earlier experiences (experiential learning) and combined this with learning new knowledge produced by others. The course focused on theories of globalisation, theories about cultural mixing, theories about acculturation, and identity construction, with the students learning about the differences between stereotypes and prejudices.

In the course, we shared Joyce Osland's acculturation theory based on Joseph Campbell's work on mythic heroes in which the ex-pat (the hero) travels a six-part journey: (1) the call to adventure; (2) the belly of the whale (being in an unknown culture); (3) the magical friend (a cultural mentor); (4) the road of trials (paradoxes); (5) the ultimate boon (the transformation of self); and (6) the return (things have changed) (Osland, 1995). Students recognised the parts of the journey, felt that they shared that in the group and that they do have similar experiences. Having this shared frame of knowledge enabled students to project their own experiences.

Intersubjectivity

Objectivity does not exist. All actions and all learnings are biased, and a first step in realising this is making biases as explicit as possible. However, this epistemological positioning does not mean that there is no value in subjectivity. We can share and agree on the kind of subjectivity and the content of subjectivity. Intersubjectivity is agreeing with different subjects that a particular interpretation is valid, makes sense, or is even true.

In the 'Museum Assignment' called Representing the Other, students visited an ethnographic museum in groups and conducted semiotic analyses of 'the Other.' Students selected an ethnographic museum and an object (statue, painting, photograph) or a specific exhibition within the museum. The groups in which they conducted the assignment were formed by the teacher based on diversity in (1) nationality, (2) study programme, and (3) gender. This diversity leads to discussions in the group about interpretations, and it was especially these discussions that should somehow be written down and reflected upon in the student report.

Sensitivity

This aspect addresses how to become sensitive to differences, without knowing the exact form of the differences. As with the previous two aspects, becoming sensitive requires making things explicit.

Sensitivity was trained in role play through analysing films and by applying theories from the field of intercultural communication to one's interests and/or experiences in an essay. In the essay assignment, students were asked to select a specific intercultural experience that they had, that confused them, or that in another way made an impression. Alternatively, they could choose a popular text. Once they made their choice, they then analysed that situation (or popular text) through applying compulsory literature analyses, which included one peer-reviewed academic article of their own choosing. In this way, they became sensitive through reinterpretation, using different (academic) perspectives.

African Philosophy

Learning about and from a diversity of knowledge

The historical exclusion and systematic suppression of African philosophy in academic curricula maintains and reinforces epistemic injustice (Boogaard, 2019; Ramose, 2019). The need for epistemological diversity in academic curricula is in line with a wider call for 'mental decolonisation' and 'decolonising universities' (Bhambra et al., 2018). In this course, students therefore learned about African philosophies, such as Henry Odera Oruka's (1995) sage philosophy and *Ubuntu* philosophy (Ramose, 1999).

Students read texts written by African philosophers and watched videos with interviews of African philosophers. This is crucial: hearing perspectives and reasoning from African philosophers themselves; and not just by talking about people or their knowledges. Students highly appreciated the content of the course, as it provided perspectives that they hardly ever encountered in their regular study program.

Eurocentrism and self-reflectivity

Many students from Wageningen University will work in international and culturally diverse contexts and desire to affect social change across the globe. Especially for those students, it is important to critically reflect on their views and assumptions about Africa, which often tend to be Eurocentric. African philosophy demands that we critically reflect on Eurocentric ways of perceiving and reasoning about the world (Kimmerle, 2016).

By reading and discussing Hegel's Eurocentric concept of philosophy (Kimmerle, 2016), students learned that Africans had historically been portrayed as 'the Other' who do not have a philosophy. In addition, the teacher and students jointly reflected how Eurocentrism continues to exist until today, particularly in international development in Africa. This was done via storytelling, where the teacher told her experiences in a research for development project in Mozambique (Boogaard, forthcoming). Students answered the question 'In what ways was my [the teacher's] thinking Eurocentric?' The power of this exercise lies in the combination of the content, people, and process: diversity sensitive learning is not only about 'other' people far away (Mozambican goat keepers), but even more so about ourselves (the Western-trained researcher). By jointly reflecting on how the teacher's thinking was Eurocentric, the process provided a safe learning environment, which is a prerequisite for truthful—and sometimes confronting—self-reflectivity.

Methodology of listening

General academic skills tend to focus on debating, in which one aims to convince another of a particular viewpoint. However, culturally sensitive learning requires dialogical encounters, in which one tries to understand a different way of reasoning and different kinds of knowledges apart from one's own. As such, intercultural dialogues can lead to mutual understanding between dialogue partners. To be able to engage in mutually respectful intercultural dialogues, we need to first listen; not in terms of 'good' or 'bad,' but in terms of being different from each other and with a willingness to learn from others (Kimmerle, 2012).

Students conducted empathic interviews with fellow students in pairs. They talked about their (future) study and work ambition, particularly in relation to Africa. The key point was that they practised listening to each other without providing their own experiences and judgments. Subsequently, students switched roles so that each student practised with the methodology of listening.

Visual Research Methods (VRM)

Portrayal of diversity in society

For students to gain insight on the dynamic continuum of semiotic and socio-cultural constructionist approaches, De Saussure's models of sign and language systems, a Foucauldian perspective on the socio-cultural and political context of media industries, and a model of 'sites and modalities for interpreting visual materials' (Rose, 2016) are theorised and practised.

Students analysed the portrayal of diversity in Dutch society with the covers of the ninth volume (22 covers, A4) of the Wageningen University and Research (WUR) magazine *Resource* and an underwear brochure by retailer Zeeman (33 pages, A5). The analysis of *Resource* covers illustrated how diversity of ethnicity and gender is hardly observable: one lady with a veil is seen in the background, but overall women's visibility is limited; meanwhile, white men are portrayed as travelling, doing hard science, and as decision-makers. Findings for the Zeeman-campaign showed diversity expressed for socio-economic categories with the inclusion of outdoor workers, a grandmother, and diverse representations of ethnicity, age, gender, and body shape. Students hesitantly concluded that the retailer 'represents diversity in the Netherlands, even more when compared to the WUR magazine.' It was also resolved that '*Resource* covers portray the WUR community in a patriarchal style, in a very Dutch and "tongue in cheek" way,' and that 'If the content analysis of the covers of *Resource* would indicate diversity in practice at WUR, it gives a bleak picture' (VRM student reports).

Reversal of representation and orientalism

Following Stuart Hall's terminology, all media materials are 'encoded,' but visuals are often read while taking the coding for granted (Hall, Evans, and Nixon, 2013; also Witteveen and Lie, 2019). Through reversal and a focus on production, students gain sensitivity to systemic processes of symbolic meaning creation.

Students explored the production of 'Updating Cocoa Stories' (Witteveen and Van, Rijn, 2014) a short film presented by the Dutch Minister for Agriculture during her opening speech at the World Cocoa Conference on 10 June 2014. The initial script for the film summarised a 1952 film. A group of Ghanaian WUR students rejected the outdated and colonial representation of Ghana and proposed another script, which was accepted for production by the Dutch commissioning ministry. Exploring the production unveils continuity of 'orientalism' and 'othering,' even when unintentional.

Continuous reflection on learning

To support a continuous process of reflection on one's biases concerning processes of encoding and decoding, a wide array of diverse portrayal and visual discourses are enacted in all course materials, including interwoven 'making-of' documentation, audience evaluations, and production diaries.

Students assembled a repository of visuals and continuously jotted down their reflections. 'While I am writing this short reflection on how I'm learning about visual methods, I'm also very aware of how my own frame of mind/looking determines my interpretation of these two images.' The shortest version of learning and reflection is the student statement: 'I cannot even watch a silly Netflix series at the moment without thinking about the making' (VRM student reports).

Designing diversity sensitive learning

Learning is about creating a space for learning and designing appropriate learning strategies and materials within that space (Lie and Witteveen, 2013). Learning in diversity means that the learning strategy and activities are deliberately designed to make use of cultural diversity in one way or the other. Learning in a cultural diversity sensitive way has been explicitly considered in the three selected courses, as the design addressed cultural diversity as embodied in student groups, and in the methods and knowledges with deliberate contributions to the learning space. The three courses reveal various aspects of diversity sensitive learning including aspects of learning *in* diversity, *about* diversity, and aiming to learn *from* diversity. From the courses we can now address diversity in a learning space at three domains: *people*, *content*, and *process*. Focusing here on the learning design of courses does not give many options to address how diversity sensitive learning is a systemic aspect of the educational institution. We will address this wider setting later.

Based on identifying parallels between the courses, the next sections elaborate on underlying principles. We thereby follow the distinction made between people, content, and process to indicate aspects of diversity sensitive learning. Following this distinction, we identify three design principles. These principles are not mutually exclusive but overlap and complement each other. We will, under each principle, describe a specific parallel, which emerged from the analyses of the courses. After that, we reflect on the principle so that it becomes of relevance to learning design at course level at universities as well as to other institutional levels aiming to design learning in a culturally and diversity sensitive way.

Principle 1: Situating knowledges

In terms of content, the three courses showed parallels in learning about diversity of knowledges. For example, the course Intercultural Communication addressed theories of globalisation, cultural mixing, acculturation, and identity construction, which students then apply to their field of expertise. In the course African Philosophy, students learned about perspectives and reasoning of African philosophers, which are less known to many students. The Visual Research Methods course built almost literally on different views focussing on theories and models for visual analysis. These courses emphasised the reinterpretation and re-construction of knowledges as central processes in learning and diversity.

Knowledges are situated in the sense that they are embedded in pre-existing situations, which also influence the design of the learning system. These knowledges are operational as epistemic and procedural lenses in the learning system (Kenter et al., 2019) as they interact with each other and create synergy or conflict between the learners, and as they react to the underlying values in the learning design and thereby influence the learning process. Such a perspective on learning experiences in the classroom has consequences for the imperatives of perspectives on learning. Looking through a lens of diversity sensitive learning is about recognising the complete epistemological context of selected knowledges and the designed learning strategies, and not only about bringing diverse knowledges on stage. Therefore, the learning situation is conceptualised as a space where different cultural embedded knowledges meet and are explicitly challenged to reach an articulated hybridisation of a diversity of knowledges and learning outcomes. The essential point is that knowledge and learning are not neutral or objective but that—as Paulo Freire (1970) remarked years ago—knowledge is political. This point is in line Banks et al.'s (2001) 12 principles on education for policymakers and practitioners aiming for appropriate educational practices in a multicultural societies; namely, that 'students understand that knowledge is socially constructed' (Banks et al., 2001, p. 198).

Principle 2: Enabling dialogical encounters

In terms of process, the three courses share the need for what we have termed enabling dialogical encounters, which emphasises engaging in dialogical encounters with 'the Other.' Although the African Philosophy course did not create direct dialogical encounters between students and philosophers, students practised with the methodology of listening to each other—an essential first step of such an encounter. In this same line, students in Intercultural Communication were engaged in dialogues with each other about different intercultural experiences and theories. Students in the Visual Research Methods course work in groups and are exposed to mediated encounters with diverse people and communities during the assignments.

Each of the three courses explicitly paid attention to how 'the Other' is represented and approached within a dominant Western perspective. For example, the course Intercultural Communication used a museum assignment in which students made a semiotic analysis of 'the Other,' which led to discussions among students about different interpretations of this representation. The Visual Research Methods course included a visual analysis of media outings and (cultural) diversity. In the same course, students analysed the production stages of a short film, which provided a system view on the continuity of 'Orientalism' and 'othering.'

Practising to reverse 'othering' by changing positions in a cultural system underlines 'otherness' as a relational concept, thereby addressing roles and accountability of all actors involved. In the African Philosophy course, students learned how in Hegel's Eurocentric concept of philosophy, Africans were portrayed as 'Others without philosophy.' Thus—although differently approached—all three courses deconstruct how 'the Other' is portrayed, represented, and framed. As such, all three courses contained crucial aspects of what we like to call 'Looking through a lens of diversity sensitive learning.' Awareness is created among students about dominant (Western) world views, which enables them to move beyond stereotypes and open up to other types of knowledge and ways of knowing.

Bringing this learning further, it will be challenging to practically engage in dialogue with distant others. However, ample opportunities exist to practice with dialogues among students themselves; a practice to establish human relations with others. Nevertheless, we remark how options for dialogue should explicitly take into account design principles to explore if or how dialogical encounters with 'the Other' can be created, for example, by creating online encounters with people who are geographically far away from the university.

In terms of people and process, it is essential to mention that diversity sensitive learning does not seek to create a homogenous group out of this diversity, but instead to offer a safe learning environment where diversity can be explored. The underlying idea is that there is a difference between people and cultures, while at the same time there is equality (Kimmerle, 2012). The relation 'equal, but different' may sound contradictory to some (Kimmerle, 2011) because our world is characterised by many unequal (power) relations between men and women, Western and 'non-Western' cultures, and students and teachers, among others. Such inequalities are founded on hierarchical thinking of 'superiority' of one group towards 'inferiority' of 'the other,' which is not conducive for diversity. The point is not to ignore existing inequalities, but instead, to insist on how equality entails that 'the ontological equality of all human beings ought to be realised in practice' (Ramose, 2020, p. 303).

From this it follows that in learning processes it is central to enhance the realisation that 'the other' is a human being. Although this may sound obvious, it is not as straightforward as it may seem. History shows—for example, in Western colonisation and in the current BLM protests—that to date there is a 'stubborn refusal to treat "the other" as a human being' (Ramose, 2020, p. 303). As the *Ubuntu* maxim *umuntu ngumuntu nga bantu* says, 'to be a human being is to affirm one's humanity by recognising the humanity of others and, on that basis, establish humane relations with them' (Ramose, 1999, p. 37).

Ramose pleads for a process of 're-humanisation of all human relationships' in which we learn to be human. How can we incorporate such a learning process in the design of intercultural education? Following Ramose (forthcoming) and Kimmerle (2011, 2012), we need an intercultural dialogical approach. A basic premise is the methodology of listening in which the listener takes the position that 'the others tell me something, which I could not have told myself by any means' (2012). It means that there is a willingness and openness to try and understand the other, even if this may not happen (Kimmerle, 2012).

Principle 3: Integrating experience and reflection

All three courses showed that 'integrating experience and reflection' are important aspects of diversity sensitive learning. For example, in Intercultural Communication students wrote an essay about a specific intercultural experience they went through, and they used theories from the course to critically describe and reflect on this experience. In the African Philosophy course, students reflected critically on a livestock development project in Mozambique through which students identified Eurocentric thinking in international development. In Visual Research Methods, students were requested to write down their reflections throughout the course. The main aim of these exercises in each course was that students gain insight into the origins and presence of their assumptions, while also learning through and from their experiences. All started from the premise that learning is about integrating experiences and reflection and not only about gaining theoretical and cognitive knowledge.

This principle is grounded in general learning theories and is termed by us as 'Integrating experience and reflection.' The principle of Integrating experience and reflection has been identified in many cases as a principle that guides learning and certainly is of value when it comes to 'diversity sensitive learning.' Lie and Witteveen (2019) write about this principle:

> [what] stands out is the centrality of experiences and reflexivity. Kolb's experiential learning and Mezirow's transformative learning have both emphasised the importance of experiences, and reflections and reflexivity is widely seen as an important condition for collaborative learning. Having many experiences is a strong asset in adult learning processes. Experience is the key word in experiential learning, and old and new experiences lead – by the act of reflecting – to learning. Learning can therefore be seen as an interactive play between experiences and reflections and between observations and interpretations. Reflexivity is to be seen as a condition for learning. (Lie and Witteveen, 2019, p. 14)

Looking through a lens of diversity sensitive learning: conclusion and recommendations

Empathy, respect, and authenticity are commonly acknowledged principles (e.g. WUR, 2020) that hardly anyone would oppose. Still, they seem to be grounded in a linear and oppositional perspective on communication and learning, based also on a paradigm of binary thinking and 'othering' of minority groups. In this same line, cultural diversity in education is too-often approached and operationalised as a 'tick-the-box' exercise—in numbers of 'diverse students and staff,' which are complemented with special services such as student counsellors and social events. However, thinking about learning and cultural diversity in Higher Education requires a paradigm-shift towards a systemic, inclusive perspective on designing educational activities.

We aim to contribute to this shift and argue that meaningful diversity sensitive learning requires specific design principles to prepare for contemporary learning spaces in a changing world. It thereby positions learning as a designed and situated space. Based on the empirical analyses of courses in different arenas of social sciences, the overarching principle emerges that meaningful diversity sensitive learning requires an integrative transformative educational approach that works on three domains simultaneously: content, people, and process. Diversity sensitive learning is thus about teaching in diversity (people) about diversity (content) and learning from diversity (process). More specifically, to enhance diversity sensitive learning in learning spaces, the following three design principles have been discerned:

- *Situating knowledges.* This is the most fundamental principle, when it comes to content. It recognises that the re-interpretation and the re-construction of a diversity of knowledges are central in learning processes.
- *Enabling dialogical encounters.* This principle emphasises that learning processes occur through dialogical interactions between people.
- *Integrating experience and reflection.* This principle identifies experience and reflexivity as essential conditions for collaborative learning.

In our view, the focus on process—the *how*—is essential, as it is within the process that diversity in people and content come together as reflected in the two principles 'enabling dialogical encounters' and 'integrating experience and reflection.' The analyses revealed that all three courses explicitly focus on processes, whereas in policy arenas and society at large it is often only diversity in people and content that is addressed. This is also the case in the National Action Plan for Greater Diversity and Inclusion in Higher Education (Ministry of Education, Culture and Science in the Netherlands, 2020) in which only people and content are considered, with process never explicitly referred to.

Our proposed integrative and transformative approach involves a specific perspective on inclusive education; that is, looking through a lens of diversity sensitive learning. Rather than focussing on empathy values and pampering—which reinforces 'otherness'—it is about re-positioning 'the cultural other' and paves the way for understanding and acting on a diversity of epistemologies and cultural practices, which allows 'being different.' Global communities can no longer be defined by ethnicity, and therefore knowledge institutes have to acknowledge contemporary societal diversity concerns and take their share in dealing with debates surrounding dissonant heritage, discrimination and exclusion, cultural appropriation, and the most recent activated concept of cancel-culture. This is an ongoing transformation process. All learning manifestations—ranging from courses to programmes—require a deliberately designed learning space and policy in which diversity is a fact to consider. Diversity is thus a systemic aspect of learning spaces and should be treated as such: one cannot add diversity simply as a supplementary aspect to education. Instead, it is an integral part of the learning space and the institutional setting in which it is embedded. Diversity is not context: it is text.

References

Bhambra, G. K., Gebrial, D., and Nişancıoğlu, K. (2018). *Decolonising the University.* London: Pluto Press.

Banks, J. A., Cookson, P., Gay, G., Hawley, W. D., Irvine, J. J., Nieto, S., … Stephan, W. G. (2001). Diversity within unity: Essential principles for teaching and learning in a multicultural society. *Phi Delta Kappan*, 83(3), 196–203.

Boogaard, B. K. (2019). The relevance of connecting sustainable agricultural development with African philosophy. *South African Journal of Philosophy*, 38(3), 273–286.

Boogaard, B. K. (forthcoming). Epistemic injustice in agricultural development: critical reflections on a livestock development project in rural Mozambique. *Knowledge Management for Development Journal.*

Freire, P. (1970). *Pedagogy of the Oppressed. 30th Anniversary Edition (2005).* London: Continuum International Publishing Group.

Gilbert, J. (2016). Transforming science education for the Anthropocene—is it possible? *Research in Science Education*, 46(2), 187–201.

Hall, S., Evans, J., and Nixon, S. (eds.) (2013). *Representation.* 2nd edition, New York: Sage.

Kenter, J. O., Raymond, C. M., van Riper, C. J. et al. (2019). Loving the mess: Navigating diversity and conflict in social values for sustainability. *Sustainability Science*, 14(5), 1439–1461.

Kimmerle, H. (2011). Respect for the Other and the refounding of society: Practical aspects of intercultural philosophy. In: Oosterling, H. and Ziarek, E. P. (eds.). *Intermedialities: Philosophy, Arts, Politics.* Lanham: Lexington Books, 137–152.

Kimmerle, H. (2012). *Dialogues as form of intercultural philosophy.* Iranian Society of Intercultural Philosophy. http://isiph.ir/en/?p=27

Kimmerle, H. (2016). Hegel's Eurocentric concept of philosophy. *Confluence, Journal of World Philosophies*, (1), 99–117.

Lie, R. and Witteveen, L. (2013). Spaces of intercultural learning. In: Mertens, S. (ed.). *Internationale Perspectieven op Journalistiek.* Ghent: Academia Press, 19–34.

Lie, R. and Witteveen, L. (2019). ICTs for learning in the field of rural communication. In: Servaes, J. (ed.). *Handbook of Communication for Development and Social Change.* Dordrecht: Springer.

Ministry of Education, Culture and Science in the Netherlands (2020). *National Action Plan for Greater Diversity and Inclusion.* Den Haag: Ministry of Education, Culture and Science in the Netherlands.

Ramose, M. B. (1999). Ecology through Ubuntu. In: Ramose, M. B. (ed.). *African Philosophy through Ubuntu.* Harare: Mond Books, 105–110.

Ramose, M. B. (2019). A Philosophy without memory cannot abolish slavery: On Epistemic Justice in South Africa. In: Hull, G. (ed.). *Debating African Philosophy. Perspectives on Identity, Decolonial Ethics and Comparative Philosophy.* London: Routledge, 60–72.

Ramose, M. B. (2020). Critique of Ramon Grosfoguel's 'The Epistemic Decolonial Turn'. *Alternation Journal. Interdisciplinary Journal for the Study of the Arts and Humanities in Southern Africa*, 27(1), 271–307.

Rose, G. (2016). *Visual Methodologies. An Introduction to Researching with Visual Materials.* 4th edition, New York: Sage.

Scholz, R. W. and Steiner, G. (2015). The real type and ideal type of transdisciplinary processes: Part I—Theoretical foundations. *Sustainability Science*, 10(4), 527–544.

Oruka, H. O. (1995). Ecophilosophy and the parental Earth ethics (on the complex web of being). In: Graness, A. and Kresse, K. (eds.) (1997). *Sagacious Reasoning: Henry Odera Oruka in Memoriam*, Bern: Peter Lang, 119–131.

Osland, J. S. (1995). *The Adventure of Working Abroad: Hero Tales from the Global Frontier.* San Francisco: Jossey-Bass.

Witteveen, L. and Lie, R. (2019). Visual communication and social change. In: Servaes, J. (ed.). *Handbook of Communication for Development and Social Change.* Dordrecht: Springer.

Witteveen, L. and Van Rijn, A. (2014). *Updating Cocoa Stories* [film]. Den Haag: Ministry of Economic Affairs, Directorate General Agro. https://www.youtube.com/watch?v=-tSsIOT4OAc

WUR (2020). *Guidelines for Working in Multicultural Settings. 'Quality Needs Diversity. Student Charter 2019–2020.* Wageningen University and Research Centre. https://www.wur.nl/en/Education-Programmes/Current-Students/student-charter-2019-2020.htm

9

LEARNING FROM HISTORIES OF GENDER AND RACIAL SEGREGATION IN AGRICULTURAL EDUCATION AND EXTENSION WORLDWIDE

Margreet van der Burg

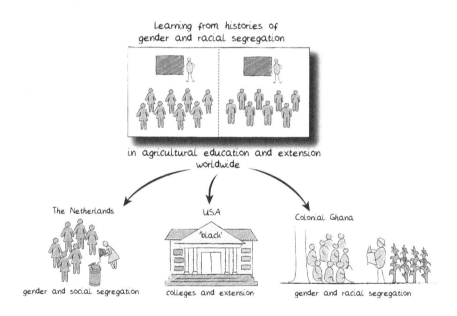

Agricultural education under debate: segregation and built-in biases

Agricultural education, including extension,[1] is highly praised for contributing to the prosperity of farmers and nations through science-based agriculture. Enrolment in agricultural education and participation in extension are widely considered key to advance modernisation, development, or innovation. Agricultural education has commonly been referred to as a crucial part of the

DOI: 10.4324/9781003112525-9

triptych of *research*, *education*, and *extension* through which states and agricultural organisations institutionalised and internationalised their cooperation to endorse agriculture-related policies.

For more than 150 years, critical insiders and outsiders have been debating the content and structure of agricultural education. Nevertheless, critiques and alternatives evoked by emancipatory movements of organised small-holders, wage labourers, women, religious minorities, and colonised and former enslaved peoples have been mostly forgotten. According to Van der Burg (2002, 2010), leaders of the first feminist wave urged to fully serve women and let them participate and profit equally as educated change agents. Instead, state-supported agricultural education started with specific programmes for women in the early 20th century which focused on home economics adapted to farm and rural life. Few schools successfully offered professional qualification in agricultural domains to women as propagated by first-wave feminists, and then mostly without state support. The feminist-inspired professional qualification centred on specialisation in women's traditional agricultural domains, such as dairy processing, poultry raising, and horticulture. However, it was not easy for graduates—mainly women from better-off families—to gain recognition or employment as women professionals.

Agricultural education systems appeared to serve the farming populations but were, in fact, segregated systems: along with social stratification related to farm types and sizes, segregation manifested also globally according to gender and in the USA also by race. Similar segregation principles were later adopted by colonial regimes and their successors as 'adapted education' (Domosh, 2015). Segregation was justified as adaptation to the life and circumstances in respective farm and rural lives.

From the 1970s onwards, growing global solidarity and social equality claims, as well as the second feminist wave, inspired to highlighting the unfairness and ineffectiveness of segregated education. Margaret Mead (1976, p.11), for example, put the finger on structurally built-in biases and the disastrous effects of this segregated agricultural education system. In a speech she called it discrimination and emphasised the need to combine all farming skills without gender distinction:

> What is needed are departments or schools in which all the skills related to food—including plant genetics, animal husbandry, veterinary skills, nutrition, child development, food management, etc.—are taught without discrimination to both men and women.

Since then, small-scale initiatives have resulted in minor increases in the participation of women in formerly male-dominated branches of agricultural education. Nowadays, addressing food insecurity and climate change is widely considered impossible without substantially advancing social and gender equality (Quisumbing et al., 2014). Furthermore the UN Sustainable Development Goals (SDGs) 5 (gender equality) and 10 (reduce inequalities) demand a systemic change away from segregation in agricultural education systems. Accordingly,

Afrina Choudhury and Paige Castellanos (2021) conclude after reviewing recent practices and suggestions that filling the participation gaps is not enough. They call for addressing social and gender norms in the curriculum.

This chapter argues that in-built gender and racial bias and segregation constrain systemic change in agricultural education despite common calls to ensure equal involvement in agricultural change. This chapter examines how 'adaption' or 'accommodation' (van der Burg, 2019) to diverse social groups constrains the advancement of equality in agriculture through the built-in segregation, including gender and race biases, in the foundation of agricultural education systems. Through a historical perspective, the chapter scrutinises how and why segregation has become part of the foundational roots of national agricultural education systems worldwide. It shows how agricultural education was part of politics fostering both a science-based agricultural sector and a smooth integration of farming populations into processes of modernisation, development, and innovation. These two aims were brought together, but separately addressed in agricultural education systems; accommodating and in parallel reinforcing segregation, based on gender, racial, and other social norms.

This chapter provides the example of three national historical cases—the Netherlands, USA, and colonial Ghana—to illustrate the transnational interconnectedness in views and underpinnings, in particular concerning gender and racial segregation. It then explicates the stickiness encountered in attempts to change built-in segregation and biases by discussing the provided options and the results of previous efforts for change. The chapter concludes by stressing the need for the combination and integration of formerly segregated curricula (Mead, 1976) and the need for a normative approach to achieve transformative change (Choudhury and Castellanos, 2021). This chapter concludes that *integration* as opposite to *segregation*—and not only *inclusion* as opposite to *exclusion*—is required to widen perspectives on knowledge to work for the advancement of both livelihoods and equality of farming people.

History of segregation in agricultural education

Education to effect agricultural innovation and rural development

From around the 1850s, rural and farming elites in Europe and the Americas pushed agricultural innovation and rural development in close connection with their peers in politics and the government. Around the 1900s, farmers firmly joined to influence policies through their organisations, syndicates, and unions. Through national and international publications, study visits, and conference exchange, together they created a growing and further professionalising international community of practice in the Christian Western world. In this transnational context they shared their visions and set out the direction, basic lay-outs, and adaptations for national and regional specifics. They invested in learning from the natural sciences and promoted innovation based on new scientific insights gained through experimentation and systematic data collection. They obtained state support for their initiatives to promote research and diverse types of agricultural education (e.g. van der Burg, 2002, 2010).

The Netherlands: gender and social segregation

The case of the Netherlands is exemplary for many European countries. Earlier work (Van der Burg, 2002, 2010, 2017) reveals the Dutch discussions and changes in detail, and contextualise them in a transnational context. The Dutch study by Van der Burg (2002, 2017) showed that among agricultural policy-makers a distinction was made between the better-off 'decent' male farmers advancing or newly taking up farming and the existing majority of less prosperous small-holding farmers. Science-based agricultural education was set up for this first group with the option to become a professional in the agricultural sector, for instance to teach others as part of the moral obligation to support less privileged farmers. The latter group was often depicted as 'others' to care for, as rough and backward, kept in the dark, and deprived of new findings and insights. They were not to be blamed for their 'ignorance' but surely considered in need for support to 'better' lives. Learning to practice science-based agriculture was the way set up to have them integrated into the modern economy and nation. This was accompanied by formative campaigns and especially educating the women as 'spiritual mothers' was considered crucial to strengthen the farming population in their patriotic, moral, and religious virtues (van der Burg, 2002, 2010, 2017).

In 1909, a new type of state-supported agricultural education was established for women which put their work and life in the centre. Along with traditionally women's farm tasks, also hygiene, first aid, healthy diets, clean and airy living conditions, and later ergonomically sound working methods, were taken into the curriculum as adopted to farm circumstances. Also, as in many European countries, the agricultural identity was kept in the name: *landbouw-huishoudonderwijs* (Netherlands and Flemish Belgium), *écoles ménagères agricoles* (France and French Belgium), and *Landwirtschaftliche Haushaltungsschule*, later *Ländliche Haushaltschule* (German speaking countries) (e.g. van der Burg, 2002, 2017; Van Molle, 2006; Caniou, 1983; Wörner-Heil, 1999).

Various education types, which differed in duration and subjects, were created to accommodate not only to gender but also social background and type of farming. In this way, agricultural education reflected in its horizontal and vertical set up the gender division of farm tasks in correspondence with family farming and rural gender norms, and social status of a regional farm type. Accommodation to these gender norms appeared in the normalisation of the segregation. Although no specific law prohibited individuals from enrolling in education marked for other groups, this was not done in practice as was best visible for gender segregation. Besides differences in course duration and subjects, the segregation additionally included institutional inequality, since there were smaller budgets for women's than men's education.

Gradually, Dutch *landbouw-huishoudonderwijs* expanded within the Dutch agricultural education system, to include women-oriented schools and courses, teacher qualifications, and governmental inspection. Girls of the farming and rural elite were especially called to qualify as *landbouw-huishoudteachers* to educate their less fortunate 'sisters.' Meanwhile, while working within the same education system alongside male peers—including brothers and fathers—in functions such as agricultural counsellors, they could internally bridge and coordinate. Through this *landbouw-huishoudonderwijs*, these female teachers created a strong foundation for extension, organisation, community development, and social work for and with farm women. After World War II, the farm women's education branch gradually became the education trajectory for rural girls by removing the agricultural components, until it was discontinued in 1968. As part of the Western agricultural development process towards specialisation, farm women and their specific responsibilities and potential in farming disappeared from sight.

Farm family ideology reflected in gender-specific orientation and segregation

For the start of the women-specific *landbouw-huishoudonderwijs*, the national agricultural conference of 1905 in the Netherlands was decisive. Male participants based their decision on economic grounds. They argued that improvement of farm men's work could only be successful if farm women would cooperate to their full potential as well. Connections were made between a future of an economically viable agricultural sector, securing a stable and healthy rural population and 'modern' living conditions, whilst also addressing problems of growing rural outmigration. Farm women's domains were acknowledged as important to secure healthy farm families. Education in home gardening and the processing of milk, meat, and vegetables would enable women to produce quality food for their own household use and for sale. This was extended to the work done by women under male control, like milking cows, watering cattle, feeding young animals, chickens, and pigs, as well as weeding, haying, and harvesting.

By distinguishing gender-specific domains in the farm as a whole, the underlying approach was holistic and systemic. At the same time, the segregated system contributed to the formalisation and reinforcement of normative gender borders that had been quite fluid in the various farm practices before. Its formative character to support modernisation resonated and reinforced the existing gender norms as well. Farm family ideology was successfully merged with bourgeois ideals of complementarity between partners in married couples. The agricultural education system supported that the male head of the farm family was 'the' farmer; there was no place for a 'second' farmer. The hidden curricula encouraged women to act as the safekeepers of good farm family virtues. They were kept away from learning to master farm management and male farm domains. In practice, they nevertheless experienced how the interests of the farm business, the farmhouse, and the farm family often overlapped and easily conflicted.

The alleged complementarity heavily mismatched with reality if a partner was absent, got sick, or died, or if two women intended to partner together. The segregation also discouraged to anticipate how women's work was affected by new methods taught to men. This was never substantially redressed: neither the underlying gender-specific rules and arrangements of family farming, nor any gender-specific impacts or (in)equalities.

USA: 'black' colleges and extension for formerly enslaved men and women

Agricultural education in the USA developed along structures of racial segregation in American society. The first Morill Act, from 1862, granted land to every state for establishing colleges for agricultural and industrial (mechanic) education—the so-called Land Grant colleges. As explained by Marcus Comer et al. (2006), the Southern states were authorised to establish separate colleges for African Americans, but due to slavery and a lack of specific earmarking, only three so-called black institutes were established. After the Civil War in 1865 and the abolition of slavery, five new 'black' colleges followed. After recession and fierce racial riots, most new biracial laws were again overturned in the 1880s, including the Civil Rights Act of 1875. The Southern states made it illegal for African Americans to vote and attend schools with white Americans. When passing a second Morrill Act in 1890 to increase land grants, Southern obstruction was prevented by adding a 'separate but equal' provision for black colleges. Seventeen states received funding for these so-called 1890 Land Grants, plus the Tuskegee Institute—the latter did not receive a land grant but had a similar curriculum. Soon the Land Grant colleges also knew home economics to serve agricultural and rural development.

The Smith-Lever Act of 1914 regulated extension work on agriculture and home economics (Ramussen, 1989), formally establishing the Cooperative Extension System under the US Department of Agriculture (USDA) and resonating the Commission of Country Life's mission to revitalise agriculture and rural life. The Land Grant colleges had to support the services and work together to reach out to the 'black' population. This faced much resistance (Harris, 2008), such as brusque racial statements against equal budgeting from Southern senators. The final arrangement was that the USDA could withhold funds if any injustice was claimed. This 'triumph in prejudice' has been long criticised as stagnating the African American extension work. Despite continuous calls for rectifying discrimination and exclusion (e.g. Wilkerson, 1938), it took until the 1960s to enact. Although racial and gender segregation has been formally rejected and redressed in the US since the late 1960s, a 2009 report points to decreasing gender gaps, yet also to continuing underrepresentation of Black, Hispanic, and Native American students in agricultural education (National Research Council, 2009).

Underlying racial and gender norms as part of the social and cultural agenda

The Cooperative Extension came under the care and supervision of the USDA Farm Bureau with a division for Home Economics, which became an independent Bureau of Home Economics in 1923. Farm and home demonstrations as well as clubs were organised for segregated groups of farmers according to gender, race, and generation. Mona Domosh (2015) emphasises the underlying social and cultural agenda of modernising USA agriculture, which included all aspects of farm and rural life. Domosh argues that the 'black' branches were instrumental in teaching African Americans how to assimilate to white, middle-class Americans. This resonates with how in the Dutch example middle-class views were coupled to farm family ideology.

Domosh finds specific racially defined differences between white and black racialised home demonstration since the 1920s. As in the Dutch example, USA home demonstration or clubs covered home food production, health and sanitation, and life conditions. White women were increasingly approached as modern consumers, while African American women were trained in sanitation, health, and 'improvement' of life. This coincided with the new practice in Federal policy to mark African Americans farm and home demonstration agents by race. Carmen Harris (2008) has found appointment forms that named their functions as 'Negro Home Demonstration Agent' or 'Negro Agent' and forbade the use of any other title. Following Harris among other scholars, Domosh (2015) connected this racial approach to the underlying belief that African Americans were inherently and bodily 'problematic' and in need of 'improvement' within the dominating culture of segregation and white supremacy. Therefore, beyond teaching better farming techniques, this education was set up to prevent malnutrition and diseases and ever growing outmigration among African Americans by ensuring they would have 'fit bodies' and 'morality' so crucial to increase agricultural productivity. More systematic research is needed to assess how strict the lines were kept in varying socio-economic contexts such as the Great Depression. Various examples evidenced that non-white women's extension agents ignored the divisions and encouraged women to income generation activities in South Carolina, Alabama, East Tennessee, and New Mexico (e.g. Harris, 2009; Walker, 1996; Jensen, 1986).

Colonial Ghana: gender and racial segregation as mirrored in colonial areas

The final case, colonial Ghana, exemplifies how colonial powers around the turn of the 19th century responded to the growing need to secure qualified plantation managers and stable food supply. For the latter, the model of 'adapted education' based on the USA Tuskegee Institute for African Americans was considered applicable to Africa and piloted in colonial Ghana. Various authors point to the model's appeal by demonstrating that Tuskegee received study visits and job invitations from all over the world. Three Tuskegee graduates were employed in colonial Togo (German Togoland) to boost agricultural productivity. In 1909, the idea of founding a 'Tuskegee-in-Africa' in Liberia was launched. Later, the British transferred the model into other colonial areas, including the Pacific and Cyprus (Comer et al., 2006; Steiner-Khamsi and Quist, 2000; Domosh, 2015). US writings, lectures, and Tuskegee visit reports were also published in Dutch with comments to consider the model for educational efforts in the Dutch colonies Surinam and Indonesia (Dutch East Indies) (e.g. Schmalhausen, 1909, esp 209–218; Bromet, 1905).

Gita Steiner-Khamsi and Hubert Quist (2000) address how Achimota College in colonial Ghana (Gold Coast) was showcased by the British colonial power to advance education programming in colonial Africa. They characterise 'adapted' education as implemented in Achimota according to the Tuskegee model, i.e., as 'adapted to the mentality, aptitudes, occupations and traditions of the various peoples' (Steiner-Khamsi and Quist, 2000, p. 274). They critically examine how the Tuskegee model was adjusted and received in colonial Ghana in the 1920s. According to Steiner-Khamsi and Quist, Achimota College prompted the Africanisation of the curriculum, adapted it to its rural environment, and emphasised appreciation and mastery of techniques, and industriousness in new labour methods. This caused tensions, being publicly contested as segregationist and racist. Mistrust was expressed about the aim to let students return to their villages as chiefs, teachers, housewives, farmers, medical assistants, or artisans, instead of moving into towns. The colonised educated elite critiqued Achimota College for settling generations for a life in the rural areas, of servitude to the colonial master and of confinement to tribal life. It was also criticised for revitalising tribal practices that resonated with the colonisers' fantasies of the idyll of savage life. The suspicion was voiced that 'adapted' education implied a 'backward' orientation instead of a 'forward' cultural adaptation to join in national pride, urbanisation, and modernisation. Similarly, the newspaper *Gold Coast Leader* in 1924 equalled adapted education with inferior education. And the missionaries critiqued that Christian converts would be confused to learn what was first abandoned as 'pagan' practices. Interestingly, the colonised elite challenged the potential racial bias but not the gender one, nor the embedded gender segregation. In the end, the promise of Achimota in colonial Ghana was not upheld; in the 1950s the features of rural and cultural 'adaption' were reduced to the African languages, history, and arts.

Qualifying 'adaption' as rural accommodative approach

Steiner-Khamsi and Quist recount how in 1926 the *Gold Coast Leader* directly attacked the US-based Phelps-Stokes Fund for having promoted the Hampton-Tuskegee model as a blueprint for Achimota College. The influence of a study mission journey by the Fund through West Africa and visiting Ghana was considered crucial. The Fund aimed to apply methods which had proved helpful for African Americans to 'the members of their race in Africa' (Jones, 1922, p. xii). It aspired to address many prevailing gaps, such as between white and black, African Americans and their distant African cousins, European and African civilisation, educational theory and practice, and Christian faith and work. Its study mission report by mission leader Jones provides insight into the underlying vision; it persistently refers to the 'adaption' concept labelled as 'African adjustment' with explicit reference to the Tuskegee Institute.

According to the report, the study commission hardly found any schools providing agricultural education or education for girls. Its recommendations were accompanied by detailed examples of schools, farm and home demonstrations, and study clubs in the African American education system. The report stressed focussing on the rural community, since Africa was overwhelmingly rural and superimposed by urban education already. The report recommended using the daily and wider African context in school materials and lessons; for instance, village market transactions and problems encountered in the dairy, barn, market, or home. Regarding home life, both boys and girls were said to be included in formative education regarding habits, attitudes, and homemaking in which the copying of Western lifestyles was critically questioned. This education was considered most important for girls, since women were considered key to changing village and economic life. In this, the report matched Western ideas for women's education.

The critical article in the 1926 *Gold Coast Leader* referred to a well-known adversary of 'adapted education,' W. E. B. Du Bois. The newspaper echoed Du Bois's argument that the white world wanted the black world to study agriculture, keeping Africans in country districts and depriving them of a decent income (Steiner-Khamsi and Quist, 2000). Later, Du Bois (1932) bridged the controversy. He also acknowledged the shortcomings of 'classical' black colleges and incorporated this into his earlier critique of institutes like Tuskegee. The first were ridiculed for including useless education in Latin and Greek. The latter were rejected for depriving black students of intellectual challenges and making careers. The dependency of these institutes on endowments by white philanthropists was detested since the training of an industrious black labour force was considered in their economic interest. In 1932, Du Bois claimed that the radically changing world required him to switch and call for having all black youth prepared and equipped for modern citizenship; and to change the curricula for both types of institutes by including economics, trades, and social-political awareness. He politicised segregation as a means to downplay black voices who he called upon to become independent and well-educated and informed citizens.

Mabel Carney (1936) nevertheless kept fiercely defending the Tuskegee model as not racial. She stressed that the model comprised 'rural' adaption, similar to that offered to the white rural population in the US. She emphasised the connection to what rural living offered, compared to what was normal for urban students: taking this background into account was the way towards equality.

The man behind the Tuskegee model, African American first director Booker T. Washington seemed to have followed the same reasoning and cautiously warned against claiming social equality, instead of gradually gaining it (Bromet, 1905).

Beyond segregation and bias in agricultural education

Also after the Second World War, most states and philanthropic and other international organisations adapted agricultural education as 'technical assistance' in cooperation with Western colleges and universities. The invested tradition of gender segregated agricultural education was largely continued. FAO as a new player to ensure food security internationally also started with separate units for 'home economics' and 'agriculture.' The period can be characterised by further expansion of transnational copying as already demonstrated regarding the three historical cases. The striking parallels, for which the cases served as examples, reflect built-in bias and inequalities in the agricultural development agenda until today. These were also repeatedly challenged and therefore provided many suggestions and pilots to learn from.

Addressing structurally built-in inequalities in the development agenda

Ester Boserup (1970) is often cited as the first feminist scholar questioning farm women's limited options and the underlying history of farm women's education. Boserup pointed at the impact of having overlooked women in agriculture politically and epistemologically. Others have stressed how women's agricultural contributions became obscured as part of Western middle-class ideals and practices of domestication (Rogers, 1980) or 'housewifisation' (Mies, 1986). Cornelia Flora (1985) has underlined how colonial powers and later postcolonial national governments continued to build their national agricultural education system on the long-standing assumption that men were the primary producers.

Meanwhile, new studies exposed how gender, class, and racial segregation and bias were built in colonial and post-colonial agricultural education systems, e.g. for Belgian Congo, Kenya, Egypt, Nigeria, and German Togo (resp. Yates, 1982; Staudt, 1982; Jensen, 1994; Osuala, 1987; Zimmerman, 2010). Research further demonstrated its worldwide spread and impacts (Berger et al., 1984; Saito and Weidemann, 1990; FAO, 1993). All mentioned authors claimed to offer women extensive agricultural education instead of home economics even if it included some agricultural components since these merely focused on food for household food security.

However, this criticism did not prompt radical change. Janice Jiggins et al. (1997) reported limited success but also warned about decreasing investments in agricultural research and extension to affect particularly farm women in developing countries. Similar claims were made and not fulfilled for Western countries, as Gloria Leckie (1996, p. 311) expressed in the case of North America:

> Farm women today need sound agricultural information and knowledge [...] since 'farmer' represents the most non-traditional role that women in agriculture can have, they continually confront a system which has not been attuned to their talents, needs or viewpoints. The barriers they face prompt many questions about how women gain the information and expertise [...] to farm successfully in the long run.

The interest in improving agricultural education for women revived in the 2000s. It coincided with the urgency to address severe food shortages and revive small-holding agriculture, especially in Africa. In 2011, the FAO renewed its mission by combining agricultural productivity with gender equality in agriculture, and the world-wide ranging CGIAR institutes of the Consortium of International Agricultural Research launched a full-blown gender strategy, with gender as cross-cutting theme (van der Burg, 2019). Shortly after, the FAO and CGIAR gender experts compiled a diagnostic volume, *Gender in Agriculture. Closing the Knowledge Gap* (Quisumbing et al., 2014), which also restated the importance of agricultural education for women to achieve the formulated development aims. Still, recent research overviews provide evidence of the continuation of gender issues and gaps in agricultural and rural development programming. These again highlight ways to overcome the neglect of women in farming and of their knowledge bases (Bock and Shortall, 2017; Fletcher and Kubik, 2017; Sachs, 2019; Sachs et al., 2021).

Suggestions and initiatives to overcome divides

Although FAO responded right at the start of the UN Decade for Women in 1975 by fully integrating women in its rural and agricultural development programmes and projects (van der Burg, 2019; FAO, 1993), renewed action was needed in 2011. Still, many of the older recommendations remain valuable. For instance, Berger et al. (1984) suggested focussing on farm couples and include both partners' activities, in line with Mead's proposal. They stressed to also include women farm managers in such an integrative approach. Berger et al. also warned against falling back to a home-economics orientation, or substituting male agricultural extensionists with female ones without levelling their position and changing the programme contents. Jiggins et al. (1997) added the need for recognising diversity and not sticking to a single universal model for all. They explicated male bias as constraining reforms. They also suggested group extension to smoothen access for women as it would 'calm the fears of male extension agents, husbands, and women about transgressing norms of approved social contact' (Jiggins et al., 1997, s.p.). In the end, mainly small-scale pilots with practical solutions and efforts to interrelate research, development, and extension were initiated. No solid focus or recommendations to reform or transform the agricultural education institutions or systems as such were found.

Choudhury and Castellanos (2021) have recently taken up the question again of how to produce agricultural change while including all in farming. Based on a robust literature review, they applaud the continuous stream of suggestions but highlight the need to take it further and include targeting social inequalities with transformative intent. They assess the Farmer Field Schools (FFS) as having most potential since they already offered, from the 1980s onwards, hands-on agricultural training for agriculture producer groups and claim to include participants' own knowledge, experiences, and needs while balancing between local knowledge and adapting scientific concepts to the local context. Choudhury and Castellanos suggest, from a gender transformative approach, to tackle community and household gender dynamics and norms by addressing societal inequities and power relations within the curriculum. Based on pilots, they explain how gender roles, norms, and practices were addressed in combination with production-focused agricultural training to also enable men to optimally engage in such discussions. Awareness and discussion sessions were built upon the trust fostered between participants and facilitators during the technical agricultural part. Especially women's effectivity could be raised by understanding the constraints or barriers to their agriculture productivity. However, Choudhury and Castellanos also warn that donors' focus on limited project time and short-term results needs to be challenged.

Discussion and conclusion

In this chapter, the historical and global biases in the foundations of agricultural education systems were made visible by pointing at their gender, social, and racial segregated roots, in various examples as being worldwide transferred, taken up, and internalised. Decision-makers created different types of education to adapt or accommodate to existing practices and underlying norms concerning family, income generation, farm labour, and care arrangements as a point of departure. Such an accommodative approach was certainly not serving claims to equally profit from new opportunities. In fact, the types mirrored hierarchies along gender, race, and other forms of social stratification—in budgets, teachers' positions, and educational contents—despite the fact that many participants also experienced their marginal and segregated inclusion as a window of opportunity to another world. Through time, these foundational premises appeared hard to change, even if highly debated by society. The underlying norms have been solidly reinforced, engrained, and internalised. Meanwhile, small-scale alternatives could not obtain enough support to scale up sustainably to enforce durable change.

The chapter concludes that lifting *segregation* without *integration* of all farm-related persons and subjects into teaching contents and methods, will not provide transformative results. Crucial farm activities and the underlying normative basis that was formerly overlooked, need to be addressed in the integration process. A *transformative* approach would match with a systemic approach of awareness raising that agriculture, farm types, and education are interwoven as social systems including social hierarchical positions and notions. It is time to fundamentally discuss and address not only the inclusion of women but also the integration of formerly called farm men's and women's domains while addressing restraining gender and racial norms and biases based in farm family ideology. The attitudes related to former racial segregated agricultural education deserve more research to explore further detailing of how institutional racial bias in subjects, teaching contents, and methods is present and can be redressed. When taking up agricultural education as a way forward to integrate farming populations into urgent needed change, this must be taken seriously to optimally profit from new investments. The SDG goals for gender equality and reduced inequalities (5 and 10) can provide direction to transform agricultural education systems to work with the various farming groups in socially just and respectful, and in agriculturally productive and ecologically sound ways.

Note

1 This includes both formal (certified) and informal forms of education organised and subsidised by institutions such as governments, (I)NGOs or grassroots organisations, and commercial parties (Ragasa, 2014).

References

Berger, M., V. DeLancey and A. Mellencamp (1984). *Bridging the gender gap in agricultural extension*. Washington, DC: ICRW.

Bock, B.B. and S. Shortall (eds.) (2017). *Gender and rural globalization. International perspectives on gender and rural development*. Wallingford/Cambridge, MA: CABI.

Boserup, E. (1970). *Women's role in economic development*. New York: St. Martin's Press.

Bromet, M.S. (1905). *De Neger-Kwestie. Een lezing over Booker T. Washington*. Amsterdam: S.A. Van Looy.

Burg, M. van der (2019). 'Change in the making': 1970s and 1980s building stones to gender integration in CGIAR Agricultural Research. In: Sachs, C.E. (ed.). *Gender, agriculture and Agrarian transformations: Changing relations in Africa, Latin America and Asia*. London: Routledge, 35–57.

Caniou, J. (1983). Les fonctions sociales de l'enseignement agricole féminin. *Études Rurales* 92, 41–56.

Carney, M. (1936). Desirable rural adaptations in the education of negroes. *Journal of Negro Education* 5(3), 448–454.

Choudhury, A. and P. Castellanos (2021). In: Sachs, C.E. et al. (eds.). *Routledge handbook of gender and agriculture*. London: Routledge, 251–263.

Comer, M.M., T. Campbell, K. Edwards and J. Hillison (2006). Cooperative Extension and the 1890 land-grant institution: The real story. *Journal of Extension* 44(3), 1–6.

Domosh, M. (2015). Practising development at home: Race, gender, and the "development" of the American South. *Antipode* 47, 915–941.

Du Bois, W.E.B. (1932). Education and work. *Journal of Negro Education* 1(1), 60–74.

FAO (1993). *Agricultural extension and farm women in the 1980s*. Rome: FAO.

Fletcher, A.J. and W. Kubik (eds.) (2017). *Women in agriculture worldwide. Key issues and practical approaches.* London: Routledge.

Flora, C. (1985). Women and agriculture. *Agriculture and Human Values* 2(1), 5–12.

Harris, C.V. (2008). "The Extension Service Is Not an Integration Agency": The idea of race in the cooperative extension service. *Agricultural History*, 82(2), 193–219.

Harris, C.V. (2009). "Well I just generally bes the president of everything": Rural Black Women's empowerment through South Carolina home demonstration activities, *Black Women, Gender and Families* 3(1), 91–112.

Jensen, J.M. (1986). Crossing ethnic barriers in the Southwest: Women's agricultural extension education, 1914–1940. *Agricultural History* 60(2), 169–181.

Jensen, K. (1994). Who carries the load? Who carries the cash? Work and status among Egyptian farm women. *Frontiers: A Journal of Women Studies* 15(2), 133–152.

Jiggins, J.R., K. Samanta, J.E. Olawoye, J. Aguilera, and D.E. Tempelman (1997). Improving women farmers' access to extension services. In: Swanson, B.E., R.P. Bentz and A.J. Sofranko (eds.). *Improving agricultural extension. A reference manual.* Rome: FAO, 73–80.

Jones, T.M. (1922). *Education in Africa. A study of West, South, and Equatorial Africa by the African Education Commission, under the Auspices of the Phelps-Stokes Fund and Foreign Mission Societies of North America and Europe.* New York: Phelps-Stokes Fund.

Leckie, G.L. (1996). 'They Never Trusted Me to Drive': Farm girls and the gender relations of agricultural information transfer. *Gender, Place & Culture* 3(3), 309–326.

Mead, M. (1976). A comment on the role of women in agriculture. In: Tinker, I., and M.B. Bramsen (eds.). *Women in development.* Washington, DC: AAAS / Overseas Development Council, 9–13.

Mies, M. (1986). *Patriarchy and accumulation: Women in the international division of labour.* London: Zedbooks

National Research Council (2009). *Transforming agricultural education for a changing world.* Washington, DC: The National Academies Press.

Osuala, J.D. (1987). Extending appropriate technology to rural African women. *Women's Studies International Forum* 10(5), 481–487.

Quisumbing, A., R. Meinzen-Dick, T.L. Raney, A. Croppenstedt, J.A. Behrman and A. Peterman (eds) (2014). *Gender in agriculture. Closing the knowledge gap.* Rome/Dordrecht: FAO/Springer.

Ragasa, C. (2014). Chapter 17. Improving gender responsiveness of agricultural extension. In: Quisumbing et al. (eds.). *Gender in agriculture. Closing the knowledge gap.* Rome/Dordrecht: FAO/Springer, 411–431.

Ramussen, W.D. (1989). *Taking the university to the people: Seventy-five years of cooperative extension.* West Lafayette: Purdue University Press.

Rogers, B. (1980). *The domestication of women. Discrimination in developing societies.* London: Kogan Page.

Sachs, C.E. (ed.) (2019). *Gender, agriculture and Agrarian transformations: Changing relations in Africa, Latin America and Asia.* London: Routledge.

Sachs, C.E., L. Jensen, P. Castellanos and K. Sexsmith (eds.) (2021). *Routledge handbook of gender and agriculture.* Oxon/New York: Routlegde.

Saito, K., and C.J. Weidemann (1990). *Agricultural extension for women farmers in Africa.* Washington, DC: WorldBank.

Schmalhausen, H.E.B. (1909). *Over Java en Javanen. Nagelaten geschriften.* Van Kampen.

Staudt, K. (1982). Women farmers and inequities in agricultural services. In: Bay, E. (ed.). *Women and work in Africa.* Boulder, CO: Westview, 207–224.

Steiner-Khamsi, G. and H.O. Quist (2000).The politics of educational borrowing: Reopening the case of Achimota in British Ghana. *Comparative Education Review* 44(3), 272–299.

Van der Burg, M. (2002). *'Geen tweede boer'. Gender, landbouwmodernisering en onderwijs aan plattelandsvrouwen in Nederland, 1863–1968*. Hilversum: Verloren.

Van der Burg, M. (2010). Rural women's voices and the identification of rural women's issues within the landscape of international organisations, 1889–1940. In: Ernst, W. (ed.). *Grenzregime. Geschlechterkonstellationen zwischen Kulturen und Raumen der Globalisierung*. Berlin: LIT Verlag, 203–227.

Van der Burg, M. (2017). Professionalising farm women, recognizing their integrated food roles: The Netherlands, 1880–1950. In: Ambrose, L.M. and J. Jensen (eds.). *Women and agriculture. Professionalizing rural life in North America and Europe, 1880–1965*. Ames, IA: University of Iowa Press, 65–85.

Van Molle, L. (2006). Gendering through agricultural education in Belgium, c. 1860–1914: A Matruska Model, Conference paper XIV International Economic History Congress, Session 14.

Walker, M. (1996). Home extension work among African American Farm Women in East Tennessee, 1920–1939. *Agricultural History* 70(3), 487–502.

Wilkerson, D.A. (1938). The participation of Negroes in the federally-aided program of agricultural and home economics extension. *Journal of Negro Education* 7 (3), 331–344.

Wörner-Heil, O. (1999). Die Wirtschaftlichen Frauenschulen des Reifensteiner Verbandes als neuer Schultyp in der modernen Berufsbildung. Ein Beitrag zu den Anfängen des ländlich-hauswirtschaftlichen Bildungswesens. In: Heidrich, H. (Hg.). *Frauenwelten. Arbeit, Leben, Politik und Perspektiven auf dem Land, Bad Windsheim*, Bad Windesheim, 99–119.

Yates, B.A. (1982). Colonialism, education and work: Sex differentiation in Colonial Zaïre. In: Bay, E. (ed.). *Women and Work in Africa*, London: Routledge, 127–152.

Zimmerman, A. (2010). *Alabama in Africa: Booker T. Washington, the German Empire, and the globalization of the new south*. Princeton: Princeton University Press.

PART IV

Rethinking evidence in development

10

THEORISING THEORIES OF CHANGE IN INTERNATIONAL DEVELOPMENT

What counts as evidence?

Katarzyna Cieslik and Cees Leeuwis

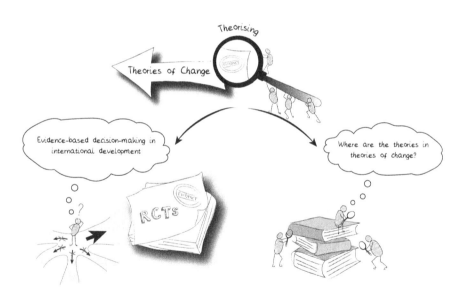

Introduction

Development projects are based on explicit or implicit assumptions of how and why a certain intervention will work. Over the past three decades, these assumptions have captured the attention of academics and practitioners alike, sparking interest in the so-called *theories of change* (Brown, 2020; Prinsen and Nijhof, 2015). In the most common sense, theories of change (ToCs) are explanations of how groups of stakeholders expect to reach a commonly understood long-term goal (Brest, 2010; Stein and Valters, 2012; Weiss, 1995). Depending on

DOI: 10.4324/9781003112525-10

their purpose (designing, monitoring and evaluation, or scaling interventions), theories of change might be developed and deployed at the level of a singular intervention, a complex program, or an entire organisation (Mason and Barnes, 2007). Currently, many development donors demand that projects and initiatives are based on an explicit and credible theory of change, turning it into a widely used planning and assessment tool in international development.

Interestingly, to date, the relationship between theories of change (as tools in development practice) and social scientific theories *about* change has not been investigated in academic literature. In most cases, theories of change rely on the common-sense logic of the implementers and on experimental evaluations of similar interventions (Brest, 2010; Astbury and Leeuw, 2010), referred to as 'evidence.' As evidence-based decision-making has become the cornerstone of sustainable development, so have theories of change; both promising to replace ideologically driven policy with rational planning (Donovan, 2018).

In this paper, we explore the links between theories of change and scientific knowledge, theories, and methods. In the context of international development, a scientific theory would describe the 'how' and 'why' of achieving positive social change. It should also fulfil two conditions: adherence to a scientific method, and a certain level of generalisability. At the same time, in lay terms, a 'theory' is understood as a hypothesis, or a 'hunch,' that has little to do with science. By scrutinising how these 'hunches' and 'evidence' both guide ToC development, we critically assess the use of knowledge and science in the design, monitoring and assessment of development interventions. Our contribution is as follows.

First, we establish conceptual clarity over the existing conceptualisations of ToCs, positioning them against similar approaches: Logical framework approaches (LFAs) and program logic models (PLMs). Broadly categorised as development management 'tools,' all of these approaches were driven by the quest for increased efficacy and accountability within the development sector. We argue that while LFAs and PLMs belong to the realm of development management, strategic planning, and evaluation, ToCs originated from the discipline of critical development studies.

Second, we show that the use of 'evidence' in ToCs development rarely goes beyond looking at existing assessments of similar interventions. These are generated through randomised controlled trials (RCTs) and systematic research syntheses. We argue that experimental evaluations ('evidence'), while useful to policy makers, do not, in fact, advance theory formation, as they do not consider the auxiliary assumptions and their results are not generalisable. As such, they can guide policy makers to evaluate and assess social interventions, but they do not substantially further our understanding of the outside world, nor do they capitalise on validated scientific theories about how change happened in the past.

Third, we introduce alternative sources of 'evidence' that should be considered complementary to positivist approaches in pursuit of improved decision-making. Instead of discarding 'hunches' and 'common-sense logic' as unscientific, we propose broadening the spectrum of perspectives engaged in ToC development and use. Drawing on the tradition of participatory development, we suggest that inclusive project governance can lead to more robust ToCs based on contextual knowledge. While including local-level stakeholders' perspectives results in more locally relevant ToCs, including social science theories *about* change (the 'how' and 'why') allows insight into potential auxiliary assumptions.

With this, we argue that experimental assessments are not the only way in which science may contribute to 'theories of change' in international development. We urge policy makers to look beyond what is considered 'hard evidence,' carving space for more qualitative, inclusive, and deliberative approaches that highlight the 'why' and 'how' of the change process (Murdach, 2010). In so doing, we undermine the positivist notion of 'evidence-based' policy, arguing instead for broader 'evidence-informed' decision-making. With these contributions, we complement the existing literature on the role of scientific knowledge in international development with a nuanced analysis of the interplay of different functions of theory building and their evolving legitimacy within the legacy of development studies.

Evidence-based decision-making in international development

In the name of accountability

The 2019 Nobel Prize in Economic Sciences, awarded to Abhijit Banerjee, Esther and Michael Kremer 'for their experimental approach to alleviating global poverty,' put 'evidence-based' policy in the spotlight. Their Abdul Latif Jameel Poverty Action Lab (J-PAL) has been conducting rigorous assessments of social interventions through randomised experiments in developing countries for almost 20 years, and building a 'theory of change' is the first step in their approach. To J-PAL, theory of change provides a structured way of 'thinking about impact,' integrating program design, implementation, monitoring and evaluation, and communication. The concerted movement to enhance development effectiveness through better planning and increased accountability builds on the assumption that, through the application of experimental evaluations, the development industry can rid itself of ineffective interventions and scale-up those that do work. Apart from J-PAL, a plethora of similar organisations started conducting or commissioning RCTs and systematic syntheses of them, e.g. the International Initiative for Impact Evaluation (3ie) and Innovations for Poverty Action, aiming to quantitatively prove what works, for whom, why, and at what cost in low-and middle-income countries (Pahlman, 2014).

The growing popularity of evidence-provisioning organisations like J-PAL runs parallel to increasing transparency and accountability pressures within the international development sector, which Ramalingam et al. (2014, p. 3) call an 'accountability revolution.' Similarly, the transformations within the aid industry—including the economisation of development and the retreat from macro-planning, created the opportunity for the 'rise of the randomistas,' or proponents of applying experimental evaluations to social program in development contexts (Donovan, 2018, p. 27; Leigh, 2018). Delivering development results has become a prominent topic within the development industry. Referred to as 'the golden age of evidence-based policy' (APPAM, 2015) or 'the quiet movement to make government fail less often' (Leonhard, 2014), the new millennium was marked by an interest in better planning, strategic management, and continuous, rigorous assessment of projects, interventions, and policies (de Souza Leão and Eyal, 2019).

Importantly, as noted by Baguios (2019), the increased use of planning and of assessment tools such as theories of change was not meant to increase accountability towards the aid receivers, but to provide clarity and reassurance to the donors. Brest (2010, p. 47) explains that '[...] a funder has a legitimate interest in knowing whether an organization is on the path to success and, at some point, whether it is actually achieving impact.' Accordingly, experimental assessments gain popularity as authoritative means of achieving certainty over 'what works.' For RCTs to take place, however, the relationship between the intervention and the desired outcome needs to be explicated. This is where logframes, logic models, and theories of change come in. In the next two sections, we first look how logframes evolved into theories of change, and then scrutinise the 'evidence' that they are meant to build on.

Logframes, logic models, and theories of change

Chronologically, logframes and logic models much preceded theories of change. Broadly speaking, logframes, and the management approach that followed (the logical framework approach, or LFA) are a program design methodology that delineates the core elements of an intervention (see Figure 10.1):

FIGURE 10.1.   Logical framework: core components, from 'inputs' to 'impacts'

The core elements are inputs (the resources, contributions, and investments that go into a program), outputs (the visible and tangible consequences of program project input), outcomes (the short-term effects of the program/ project), and impacts (long-term, generalised goals) (Gasper, 2000). When portrayed in a 4x4 matrix, logframe becomes a 'logic model' or program logic model (PLM). Logic models are hypothesised chains of causes and effects, leading to a generalised long-term goal, often taking the form of 'if-then' relationships between the core elements. In this sense, LFA and PLM both include implicit or explicit assumptions regarding the contextual conditions in which interventions take place (see Figure 10.2). In addition, both tools enable monitoring and evaluation process by specifying quantifiable indicators for each of the implementation stages (Gasper, 2000).

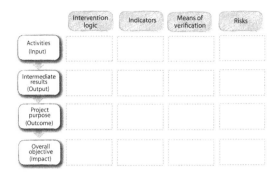

FIGURE 10.2   Logic model known as a 4x4 matrix

As an entry point to structured evaluations, LFA/PLM are often seen as a way to plausibly demonstrate impact, and hence of increasing transparency and accountability of the development industry. At the same time, they impose a pre-defined project logic on stakeholders with potentially different—or even conflicting—worldviews. A number of development organisations refer to their logframes as 'roadmaps' or 'blueprints,' discounting any alternative trajectories that their interventions might have (Dale, 2003). As narrative framing tools, LFA/PLM are also target-driven and invariably positive (Büscher, 2014) (Table 10.1).

From the point of view of social science theory, LFA/PLM reflects a strong belief in rational planning and control as a mechanism for orchestrating positive change, as it assumes that change and transformation can be engineered, predicted, and designed by means of systematic thinking about hierarchies of goals and means (inputs, outputs, outcomes, impacts). However, numerous studies in development sociology suggest that development and change arise from a capricious process of social struggle over resources, meanings, goals, and identities with inherently uncertain outcomes (Leeuwis, 2000). Similarly, historians studying transformation over longer periods have concluded that meaningful change emerges from competition between those supporting and those challenging the status quo, with success depending on the quality of coalition formation and adaptive learning in the context of ever changing circumstances (Klerkx et al., 2010). Thus, we see that logic models may be informed by modes of thinking at a more abstract level (e.g. on whether change emerges from 'planning,' 'learning,' or 'social struggle'; see Leeuwis, 2000) allowing us to question whether a 'rational planning and control' paradigm is an adequate reflection of how change occurs.

Specifically, from within the discipline of development studies came a strong critical narrative, juxtaposing LFA/PLM and bottom-up inclusive approaches like Participatory Rural Appraisal (PRA) and Participatory Learning and Action (PLA) (Aune, 2000; Kumar and Corbridge, 2002). As a response, theories of change (ToC) were meant to bridge structured planning and local participation

TABLE 10.1 The three uses of project planning tools: overview of main criticisms

Three main uses of LFA/PLM	Criticisms
Designing interventions	• Fail to consider historical and social science theories about how change happened in the past. • Based on 'expert hunches' and, at best, some of the existing 'evidence' (RCTs). • Promote a singular project trajectory, disregard alternative pathways. • Hamper innovation and creativity at the local level.
Monitoring and evaluation	• Create implementation bottle necks, slow down project maturation. • Discount externalities ('unintended effects').
Scaling up and out	• One-fits-all solution ('blueprint' approach). • Disempower local stakeholders (a 'straightjacket').

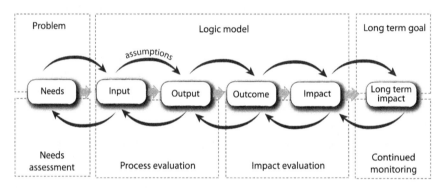

FIGURE 10.3 Basic setup of a theory of change

(Weiss, 1995). Though the principal components of ToCs resemble LFA/PLM, their originality lies in recognising the importance of tacit, or only partly articulated assumptions, of how and why an intervention is supposed to work (Astbury and Leeuw, 2010; Weiss, 1995). As Figure 10.3 illustrates, ToCs start with problem framing ('needs assessment') which influences the course(s) of action taken ('assumptions' towards input-output-outcome-impact relationships). While within a limited program-timeframe of several years a ToC would usually end with an 'impact evaluation,' further 'assumptions' need to be elaborated to explain how and why the project will achieve lasting change ('long-term goal').

By involving the different level stakeholders, ToCs encourage local organisations to take ownership of, and the responsibility for, the course of the interventions (Sullivan and Stewart, 2006). This requires sensitivity to perennial power imbalances within project structures, which in reality is rarely achieved

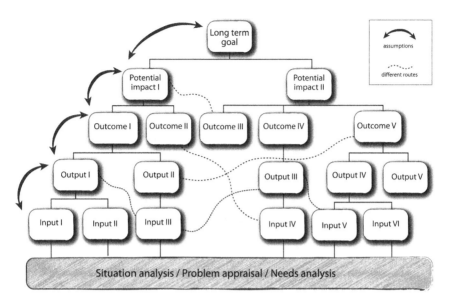

FIGURE 10.4   Theory of change template graph

(Ferguson et al., 2010). As Figure 10.4 illustrates, ToCs acknowledge that relationships between inputs and outputs are not straightforward and may take different routes (see dotted lines on the graph).

The brief reconstruction of the evolution of logical frameworks, logic
models, and theories of change points to the constant tension between stability and flexibility in project management (Hersoug, 1996). While development
studies scholars argue that standardisation of the project approach is detrimental
to local agency, constrains innovation, and is prone to ignore contextual dynamics of power and competition, development managers point out that the lack of
structure confuses evaluation and hampers scale-up efforts (Crawford and Bryce,
2003; Curtis and Poon, 2009).

While adopting any of the LFA, PLM, and ToC tools may help development practitioners attenuate some of the projects' operational uncertainties, it
does nothing for contextual uncertainty (Hersoug, 1996). When trying to decide
what kind of intervention is most likely to lead to the desired long-term goal
and in mapping out the project trajectory, founders, managers, and implementers turn to research to provide them with 'evidence' of 'what works.' In order
to avoid bias and formulating 'unfounded' assumptions, ToCs are meant to be
'evidence-based.' In the sections that follow, we take a critical look at what kind
of scientific outputs are used to construct theories of change for development
interventions.

TABLE 10.2 The three uses of theories of change: comparing disciplinary perspectives

Three main uses of LFA, PLM, ToC, and PoC	Framing by development management	Framing by critical development studies
Designing interventions	Action plans, roadmaps, blueprints.	Participatory needs assessment, co-creation, co-design, negotiating differences.
Monitoring and evaluation	Results-based management, performance review, cost-benefit analysis.	Reflexive critique and feedback loops, participatory evaluation, flexibility, adaptation to take in unforeseen surprises.
Scaling up and out	Impact acceleration, value maximisation.	Learning, context-specificity, communities of practice.

What counts as evidence? Hierarchies of evidence and the 'gold standard' of RCTs

While 'evidence-based policy' has become the dominant paradigm in policy circles, it is often performed with perfunctory attention. In a comprehensive report commissioned by the King's Fund, UK, Coote et al. (2004, p. xi) find that 'major social programs,' were not, in fact based on rigorous evidence: 'Interviews with those in central government make it clear that they (social programs) have been designed, by and large, on the basis of informed guesswork and expert hunches, enriched by some evidence and driven by political and other imperatives'; see also Mason and Barnes (2007).

The issue of what constitutes 'evidence' for research-informed policy triggered considerable academic debates (Oakley, 2000). When applied to theories of change, however, the answer appears much more straightforward: 'evidence' refers to evaluations of similar interventions and proofs that a certain logic 'works' (Pahlman, 2014). While, taken in its entirety, evaluation can generate many kinds of knowledge, not all knowledge is routinely defined as evidence: there is a clear tendency to put systematic reviews of RCT studies at the top of the hierarchy, followed by single RCT studies and quantitative survey results. Qualitative research (e.g. ethnographic studies, expert interviews) may also be used (Coote et al., 2004), though it would count as 'soft evidence' (Murdach, 2010; Oakley, 2000). Evidence that comes low in such hierarchies is likely to be ignored, including local knowledges and lived experience documented through ethnography and anthropology.

RCTs are a type of impact evaluation that randomises access to a particular social intervention to produce an unbiased and internally valid impact estimate. There are a number of reasons why RCTs as scientific outputs rank highly in policy makers' hierarchies of evidence. First, RCTs demonstrate a clear causal relationship between an intervention and its outcomes. This is because randomisation eliminates the bias inherent in comparative studies: as all potentially impactful variables are equally distributed in treatment and control groups, any possible difference in outcome can only be attributed to the intervention. Second, RCTs allow for the quantification of uncertainly. If the sample that undergoes randomisation is large enough, RCTs provide a quantifiable degree of certainty about the accuracy of the captured effect. Third, by comparing more than one treatment, RCTs allow researchers to determine which components of a program (or, in ToC language, which 'inputs') are necessary for it to be effective in a *ceteris paribus* context. Fourth, they allow for a thorough cost-benefit analysis, by setting the price (cost of activities, or inputs) of achieving incremental change in a chosen indicator (quantifiable outcome and/or impact).

These four features make RCTs powerful tools for evaluation. At the same time, RCTs do exactly what they are designed to do: they assess single projects, in particular contexts. In other words: though a highly effective evaluation methodology, RCTs do not show 'what works,' but 'what was observed to work under specific circumstances,' without saying anything about these circumstances. Against this background, and considering that RCTs and RCT-syntheses are almost exclusively used as base for 'evidence-based policy,' it is crucial to determine what contribution RCTs actually make to theory-building.

Where are the theories in theories of change?

RCTs as means to test theories

A scientific theory is an explanation of a chosen aspect of the world that can be repeatedly tested using accepted protocols of observation, measurement, and evaluation of results. Just as laboratory experiments are set up to test scientific theories, RCTs are meant to test program theories: to establish whether a certain intervention brings about the desired effect. In laboratory conditions, each testing of a theory entails 'auxiliary assumptions,' which are all the propositions that are assumed to be accurate or in place in order for the test to work, such as a particular temperature or humidity as measured by certain devices in a biophysical experiment. Field experiments, on the other hand, do not, and cannot, consider auxiliary assumptions, as it is impossible to enlist all the specifications of social reality (Cartwright, 2007). To the contrary, as rigorous evaluation tools, RCTs are meant to detect the effect of an intervention *regardless* of the external conditions, such as the unique socio-cultural characteristics of a given region. Thanks to randomisation, these will affect the control and treatment groups in exactly the same way, and hence can be ignored for the purpose of assessment. They do matter, though, for external validity. This, in fact, is the function of the counterfactual: as long as the control and treatment groups are exposed to the same, undetermined set of influences, these influences do not matter, as the experiment will only consider the difference in outcome. A positive result of a

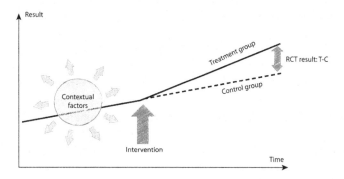

FIGURE 10.5 A schematic representation of an RCT set-up and outcome

rigorously executed RCT will always detect the appropriate causal conclusion— and only that (Figure 10.5).

While strikingly effective for evaluations, this feature of RCTs translates into a serious flaw when assessing their theory-building potential. RCT results are limited to the exact temporal and special context where they were conducted, and can never be generalised. Cartwright (2007, p. 11) writes that 'the benefit that the conclusions follow deductively in the ideal case comes with a great cost: narrowness of scope. This is an instance of the familiar trade-off between internal and external validity. RCTs have high internal validity but the formal methodology puts severe constraints on the assumptions a target population must meet to justify exporting a conclusion from the test population to the target.' When applied to social science research, the absence of auxiliary assumptions in RCTs renders generalisation of results virtually impossible. Accordingly, using experimental assessment of one intervention as 'evidence' to support another is methodologically unsound. In addition, while RCTs detect causality, they remain a 'black box' in terms of the ways by which the intervention exerted its impact.

Against this background, the relationship between theories of change and randomised controlled trials is problematic at best. First, program theories are tested through RCTs: in the case of a positive assessment, a ToC is considered to 'have worked.' Second, in accordance with the evidence-based policy paradigm, these results are used to guide the development of ToCs for future interventions, in new places, and by different actors. Both inferences are questionable to some degree. While the first may be appropriate in the sense that RCTs can provide robust and rigorous assessment that an intervention has worked, it still remains possible that the intervention has worked in a different way than its theory of change suggests. For example, a theory of change might state that community meetings to promote technology create awareness of the positive consequences of technology use (in line with scientific theories about diffusion of innovations), while in practice they may have served to resolve conflict or promote collective action in support of technology uptake (in line with systemic theories about innovation). Thus, a positive assessment of the intervention provides no definitive evidence that the explicated theory of change was in fact correct. As explained above, the second inference—that the intervention is likely to lead to similar effects elsewhere—is even more questionable, as RCT results cannot be generalised.

Importantly, as discussed above, theories of change are supposed to 'spell out' project propositions and make implicit assumptions explicit. At the same time, without proper tools and procedures of capturing the 'auxiliary assumptions,' these can only comprise what Coote et al. (2004, p. xi). call 'informed guesswork and expert hunches.' In the next section, we propose what these tools and procedures might be, and develop a more comprehensive evidence–policy model.

Theorising theories of change: broadening out and opening up

In the practitioner and grey literature cited in this paper, evidence-based theories of change are presented as the 'gold standard' and other approaches are often dismissed. At the same time, experience-based insights of the local staff are also not considered: 'a common element across professions is the extent to which the legitimacy of professional decision-making is no longer based on what might be accounted as professional wisdom, often founded in tradition. Instead, it is thought to reside in the weight of evidence, produced by other members of the community or by the researcher community, independently sifted through external review' (Clegg, 2007, p. 417). This singular logic mindset and expert supremacy, however, is precisely the problem that the theories of change were meant to address by engaging with multiple-level stakeholders (Sullivan and Stewart, 2006). Once an intervention is considered 'successful'—often with the help of an RCT—its theory of change is taken out of its original context and implemented in another through scaling up; losing both its place specificity and its participatory credentials. Against this background, we propose that the original, stakeholder-driven theory of change model should not only be reinstated, but also further opened up and broadened out to include both more local stakeholders, and a wider range of interdisciplinary scholarship.

In defence of common sense

The 'opening up' entails inviting different level stakeholders to participate in the theory of change process, besides policy makers and practitioners. In a critical piece on ToCs uses and misuses, Mason and Barnes (2007, p. 162) ask rhetorically, 'should we assume that a ToC generated by social scientists on the basis of a review of research evidence is necessarily better than that produced by staff and community members directly involved in the program itself?,' further observing that 'if services (within international development organizations) are commissioned solely on the basis of research evidence, there may be little space for innovation.' Local communities and frontline staff may be better positioned to judge or make assumptions about where and how a ToC needs to be tweaked in order to achieve a better fit with the local context, even though it is based on 'common-sense logic' rather than research evidence. This applies to ToC development, but also to deployment (on-the-go adaptation of project activities and thresholds) and to evaluation (designing locally relevant indicators of project 'success' which may be different from the onset assumptions). While concerned communities are at times participating in the ToC development workshops, at later stages their engagement is usually limited to 'consulting' and 'informing.' This is at odds with the central idea of participatory development practice, where a broad, public, deliberative conversation is essential for reaching a shared understanding of the problems and monitoring the process of change over time. Central to the process is creating a shared space through transparency and openness, and actively resisting the systemic power pressures. Apart from content-enrichment and enhanced insight into locally relevant conditions, including more local voices would contribute to what Baguios (2019) calls the 'decolonization of the project management in the aid sector.' At the same time, romanticising and glorifying 'local voices' bears the risk of raising unrealistic expectations as well as losing sight of the 'big picture': the organisational mission.

Carving space for social science theories about change

Broadening the range of social science approaches to ToC development requires undermining the hierarchy of 'research evidence.' As indicated earlier, evidence from RCTs falls short on the question of 'how and why' change happens. There is a plethora of historical, sociological, and anthropological meta-level theories that shed light on processes that matter in change trajectories (e.g. complexity theories of societal change, progressive change theory, or innovation theory). Although such theories tend to be validated through methodological approaches other than RCTs (e.g. systematic process tracing, historiography, discourse analysis, participant observation, etc.) they may be usefully introduced in discussions with stakeholders for purposes of ToC construction, adaptation, and testing. For example, if social science theories suggest that meaningful transformation depends on the quality of coalition formation and adaptive learning, then such a theory could enrich the stakeholder consultations by questioning whether suggested 'inputs, outputs, and outcomes' in the theory of change (and indicators used to assess these) indeed refer to such parameters at all.

For this reason, we argue that applying a range of social scientific approaches to ToC development, implementation, and evaluation ultimately leads to better projects based on well-grounded theories and assumptions about how change happens. Different theoretical traditions have complementary insights and functions, allowing practitioners and scholars to challenge the conventions and innovate. Combining experimental assessment with a comprehensive and inclusive

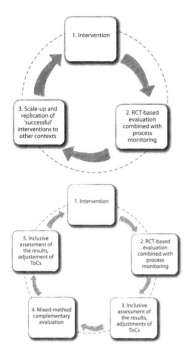

FIGURE 10.6   Currently dominant (a) and proposed (b) use of methods in ToC evaluation cycles

local participation leads to both more locally relevant projects, and more meaningful evaluations. Conceived as such, participatory assessment of the RCT results could help the researchers uncover the contextual factors—or the auxiliary assumptions—that could have contributed to the intervention's success/ failure results, as well as shed light on the change process (the 'why' and 'how', see Figures 10.6a and 10.6b).

Conclusions

In the recently published *Navigation by Judgment Why and When Top Down Management of Foreign Aid Doesn't Work*, Honig (2019) provides a strong critique of development management tools and donor control. Drawing on a database of over 14,000 development projects, he argues that a narrow focus on reaching pre-set targets limits frontline workers from solving problems on the ground, seriously undermining the projects' performance. Conscious of these critiques, in this paper, we traced the evolution of logic models, logframes and theories of change, highlighting the trade-offs between transparency and accountability on one hand, and flexibility and adaptation on the other. We showed how the growing popularity of theories of change is linked to different concerns regarding accountability within the development sector.

While ToC was initially developed as a method to induce greater accountability to local-level stakeholders with appropriate knowledge and understanding of relevant conditions, we now witness that they are increasingly used as a point of reference in the development and identification of 'evidence-based' policies and interventions that can be generalised across contexts. We critically discussed the concept of evidence-based policy making, arguing that focusing solely on experimental methods (RCTs) as evidence sources is not just epistemologically limiting, but also methodologically unsound. The relationship between policy and evidence is far more complex than a linear evidence-to-policy chain suggests. Central to making evidence more meaningful to the policy process is re-evaluating the process through which the 'evidence' is constructed. While evidence-based policy tends to be portrayed as a neutral and objective policy tool, the very act of evidence selection is, in itself, affected by hierarchical structures governing knowledge systems. The current dominance of RCTs in evidence construction comes with the risk of making development projects blind to both stakeholder perspectives and social science theories on 'how and why' change may happen. Against this background, we argued that theories of change may be useful instruments, if applied with caution, encouraging broad and deep participation of different level stakeholders as well as offering opportunities to engage with a variety of social science disciplines throughout the research cycle.

Considering that evidence-based policy and the prevalence of RCTs were modelled on the 'gold standard' of medical experiments, perhaps it is again within the realm of natural science that social scientists should look for inspiration for the way forward. In a recent study in *the Lancet*, Jones and Podolsky (2015, p. 1503) write that

> The past several years have seen increasing calls for an ecumenical approach to clinical research, with more flexible standards for what counts as acceptable study designs. Physicians have developed new methods to extract robust analyses from patient registries and from the ever-growing databases provided by electronic medical records. Will this erode the status of RCTs as a gold standard?

References

APPAM (2015). Association for Public Policy Analysis and Management 37 Annual Research Conference: The Golden Age of Evidence-Based Policy, November 12–14, Miami, Florida, the US.

Astbury, B. and Leeuw, F. L. (2010). Unpacking black boxes: Mechanisms and theory building in evaluation. *American Journal of Evaluation*, 31(3), 363–381.

Aune, J. B. (2000). Logical framework approach and PRA - mutually exclusive or complementary tools for project planning? *Development in Practice*, 10(5), 687–690.

Baguios, A. (2019). It's time to decolonise project management in the aid sector. Aid Re-imagined for *Medium*. https://medium.com/@aidreimagined/its-time-to-de colonise-project-management-in-the-aid-sector-da1aa30c5eee.

Brest, P. (2010). The power of theories of change. *Stanford Social Innovation Review*, 8(2), 47–51.

Brown, M. (2020). Unpacking the theory of change. *Stanford Social Innovation Review*. https://ssir.org/articles/entry/unpacking_the_theory_of_change?fbclid=IwAR2 GsxxaLimnwQmG3doQJWTdRa7m-rhbTJkfnWlEAQN6XHwLuP0EtUzOwLo.

Büscher, B. (2014). Selling success: Constructing value in conservation and development. *World Development*, 57, 79–90.

Cartwright, N. (2007). Are RCTs the Gold standard? *BioSocieties*, 2(1), 11–20.

Clegg, S. (2007). Evidence-based practice in educational research: A critical realist critique of systematic review. *British Journal of Sociology of Education*, 26(3), 415–428.

Coote, A., Allen, J. and Woodhead, D. (2004). Finding out what works. Building knowledge about complex, community-based initiatives. King's Fund Publications. https://www.kingsfund.org.uk/sites/default/files/field/field_publication_file/fi nding-out-what-works-community-based-inititatives-nov04.pdf.

Curtis, D. and Poon, Y. (2009). Why a managerialist pursuit will not necessarily lead to achievement of MDGs. *Development in Practice*, 19(7), 837–848.

Dale, R. (2003). The logical framework: An easy escape, a straitjacket, or a useful planning tool? *Development in Practice*, 13(1), 57–70.

de Souza Leão, L. and Eyal, G. (2019). The rise of randomized controlled trials (RCTs) in international development in historical perspective. *Theory and Society*, 48, 383–418.

Donovan, K. P. (2018). The rise of the randomistas: On the experimental turn in international aid. *Economy and Society*, 47(1), 27–58.

Ferguson, J., Huysman, M. and Soekijad, M. (2010). Knowledge management in practice: Pitfalls and potentials for development. *World Development*, 38(12), 1797–1810. doi:10.1016/j.worlddev.2010.05.004

Gasper, D. (2000). Evaluating the "logical framework approach" towards learning-oriented development evaluation. *Public Administration and Development*, 20(1), 17–28.

Hersoug B. (1996). Logical framework analyses in an illogical world. *Forum for Development Studies*, 2, 377–404.

Honig, D. (2019). *Navigation by judgment: Why and when top-down management of foreign aid doesn't work*. Oxford: Oxford University Press.

Jones, D. S. and Podolsky, S. H. (2015). The art of medicine. The history and fate of the gold standard. *The Lancet*, 385, 1502–1503.

Klerkx, L., Aarts, N. and Leeuwis, C. (2010). Adaptive management in agricultural innovation systems: The interactions between innovation networks and their environment. *Agricultural Systems*, 103, 390–400.

Kumar, S. and Corbridge, S. (2002). Programmed to fail? Development projects and the politics of participation. *Journal of Development Studies*, 39(2), 73–103.

Leeuwis, C. (2000) Re-conceptualizing participation for sustainable rural development. Towards a negotiation approach. *Development and Change*, 31, 931–959.

Leigh, A. (2018). *Randomistas. How radical researchers are changing our world*. New Haven: Yale University Press.

Leonhardt, D. (2014). The quiet movement to make the government fail less often. *The New York Times* – The Upshot 2014/07/15. https://www.nytimes.com/2014/07/15/ upshot/the-quiet-movement-to-make-government-fail-less-often.html

Mason, P. and Barnes, M. (2007). Constructing theories of change: Methods and sources. *Evaluation*, 13(2), 151–170.

Murdach, A. D. (2010). What good is soft evidence? *Social Work*, 55(4), 309–316.

Oakley, A. (2000). *Experiments in knowing: Gender and method in the social sciences.* Cambridge: Polity Press.

Pahlman, K. (2014). A critical examination of the idea of evidence-based policymaking. *ANU Undergraduate Research Journal*, 6, 83–94.

Prinsen, G. and Nijhof, S. (2015). Between logframes and theory of change: Reviewing debates and a practical experience. *Development in Practice*, 25(2), 234–246.

Ramalingam, B., Laric, M. and Primrose, J. (2014). *From best practice to best fit.* Understanding and navigating wicked problems in international development. Overseas Development Institute. https://www.odi.org/publications/8571-best-pr actice-best-fit-understanding-and-navigating-wicked-problems-international-devel opment.

Stein, D. and Valters, C (2012). Understanding 'Theory of Change' in international development. A review of existing knowledge. Justice and Security Research Programme, London School of Economics and Political Science.

Sullivan, H. and Stewart, M. (2006). Who owns the theory of change? *Evaluation*, 12(2), 179–199.

Weiss, C. H. (1995). Nothing as practical as good theory: Exploring theory-based evaluation for comprehensive community initiatives for children and families. In: Connell, J. P. (eds.). *New approaches to evaluating community initiatives. concepts, methods, and contexts. Roundtable on comprehensive community initiatives for children and families.* Aspen: Aspen Institute, 65–92.

11

THE POLITICS OF EVIDENCE-BASED ADVOCACY BY CIVIL SOCIETY ORGANISATIONS

Margit van Wessel

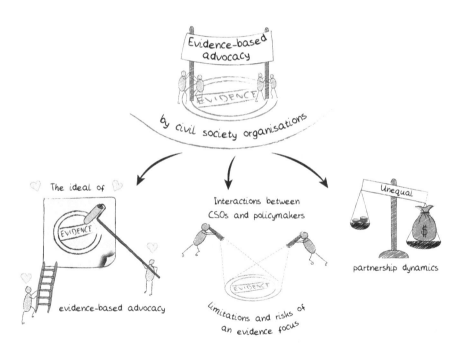

Introduction

This chapter discusses the nature and role of evidence in advocacy for development by civil society organisations (CSOs). It focuses on the ways the production and use of evidence in this context should be understood: as relational, dynamic, and political, with important implications for whether, and

DOI: 10.4324/9781003112525-11

how, different forms of evidence can come to be seen and taken into account. After showing the important and diverse roles of evidence in CSO advocacy, this chapter problematises the supposed objectivity of evidence and the neutral nature of its usage, as well as the implications for inclusive development. It does this by identifying the ways in which evidence creation and usage is shaped in relational dynamics between CSOs and the policymakers they target, and between CSOs that are differently positioned in power relations. The chapter further considers the implications of these issues for inclusion, ownership, representation, and legitimacy, and presents possible advances based on these insights.

The ideal of evidence-based advocacy

Over the past two decades, the ideal of 'evidence-based policymaking' has been firmly established across policy domains and policymaking arenas (Parkhurst, 2017), including international development. Evidence-based policymaking has found its way into practice and legitimation processes, through an increased focus on 'what works,' results, efficiency, and accountability in development (Anderson, 2010; Goldman and Pabari, 2021; Hayman, 2016, p. 131; Storeng and Béhague, 2014). Leading international development think tank Overseas Development Institute (ODI) exemplifies the weight prominent actors in the sector give to this ideal in a report promoting evidence-based working:

> Better use of evidence by CSOs is part of the solution to increasing the policy influence and pro-poor impact of their work. Better utilisation of research and evidence in development policy and practice can help save lives, reduce poverty and improve the quality of life […] In order to have a greater impact, civil society must improve their interaction with, and effect on, public institutions, actors and policies—and do so based on rigorous evidence.
>
> *(Court et al., 2006, p. 1)*

This statement speaks directly to CSOs involved in advocacy for development, defined in this chapter as a 'wide range of activities conducted to influence decision-makers at different levels, with the overall aim of combatting the structural causes of poverty and injustice' (Barrett et al., 2016). The definition follows the widely held belief that CSO advocacy is a tool to fight the causes of poverty and injustice and influence structural change, aiming to alter social, political, and policy structures that sustain inequalities (ibid). Policymakers are a key target of many CSOs' advocacy for development, with the diverse roles for evidence widely embraced by the latter.

Evidence was already fundamental to civil society advocacy in the context of international development before the advent of the evidence-based policy movement. Early leading publications emphasised the prominent role of information, mainly in the shape of information politics, or 'the ability to quickly and credibly generate information and move it where it will have the most impact' (Keck and Sikkink, 1999, p. 95); Jordan and Van Tuijl (1998, p. 2052) go so far as to define advocacy as 'an act of organizing the strategic use of information to democratize unequal power relations.'

While some CSOs give it a more prominent role than others, 'evidence-based advocacy' is a common strategy. To illustrate: websites of leading CSOs in international development commonly show that they have adopted not only working with information but also the language of evidence-based policy, commonly stating 'evidence' as fundamental to their advocacy.

Evidence can take multiple forms. CSOs carry out research of their own, or may hire dedicated experts (Eagleton-Pierce, 2015). Research is also commonly carried out through collaborations, such as between 'Northern' and 'Southern' CSO partners, between CSOs and universities, and by CSO networks (Travers, 2016). Research can be on local or regional realities in the Global South (Motta and Nilsen, 2011); on international or global dimensions of issues (Eagleton-Pierce, 2015); or combinations of both, as when global issues like climate change or land grabbing are illustrated by case studies of local realities or solutions (Arensman et al., 2015). Research can involve new data, or centre on synthesis of existing data and analyses. In addition, research can also centre on the humanisation and concretisation of issues and their solutions by testimony and visuals, bringing in the 'voices' of those affected.

Evidence can come in with advocacy in different stages of policymaking. It can play a role in agenda-setting, policy formulation, implementation, and evaluation (Court et al., 2006). However, relatively much of the effort and influence of advocacy appears to lie in agenda-setting, with CSOs seeking to draw attention to specific problems and solutions; proposing understandings of their nature and importance; and seeking to advance their political salience to policymakers by embedding CSOs' voices into policy processes (Arensman et al., 2015, p. 584–585).

Research on evidence-based advocacy by CSOs mostly shows roles in agenda-setting (Arensman et al., 2018; Arensman et al., 2015; Eagleton-Pierce, 2015). Some research also shows roles of evidence in advocacy by CSOs towards policy formulation, seeking uptake of CSO ideas and results—particularly once CSOs have succeeded in establishing themselves as valuable partners and their agendas as agreeable (Stroup and Wong, 2017). CSO advocacy addressing policy implementation and evaluation has been less researched (but see Barnes et al., 2016 for an example), so we know little of the role of evidence in that. However, many CSOs active in service delivery may seek to influence policy through the entry points provided by such roles, as some research at least indicates (Van Wessel et al., 2019), and evidence may be important here. This is of particular interest with civic space for CSO advocacy increasingly constricted in many contexts (CIVICUS, 2020).

Using evidence: different strategies and approaches

Much of the emphasis on agenda-setting in civil society advocacy can be illustrated by pointing out how CSOs in international development commonly seek to attain a voice for relatively marginalised groups, and their understandings, agendas, and solutions. For civil society, it takes multiple actions and often significant time before advocacy can move from agenda-setting into contributing to actual policy formulation and beyond. Evidence can thus support efforts to gain access and close contact with policymakers and other audiences, which has strategic significance for the way evidence is employed. CSOs' engagement with questions of evidence can be relatively open ended, seeking to identify and understand issues that may subsequently guide advocacy (Gooding, 2016; Travers, 2016). However, evidence creation, interpretation, and use are often guided by strategic considerations: evidence is commonly brought in to back up and legitimate established positions (Gooding, 2016; Mably, 2006; Thrandardottir, 2016). Evidence is thus employed to convince policymakers and others of truth claims, rather than to facilitate learning based on unbiased consideration of the best available information. Evidence is utilised to convince policymakers of the nature of an issue and its effects on specific groups or public goods; its pressing nature; the nature of its causes; the effectiveness of certain solutions; or the way current policies or forms of implementation are wanting. This last use of evidence is very visible in campaigning, as in Oxfam's use of what it calls 'killer facts' to provoke, draw attention, mobilise, and set agendas on issues such as economic inequality (Oxfam, 2019).

Another format, the case study, illustrates a problem and/or its solution by presenting exemplars for upscaling (often by the State), such as Hivos' case study of Sumba Island—meant to inspire actors elsewhere by proposing an exemplary way of reducing communities' dependency on fossil fuel, while developing access to locally produced renewable energy (Hivos, 2016).

Evidence can thus be central to advocacy in different ways. At the same time, CSOs have different approaches when it comes to the role of evidence in their advocacy. While some, like Oxfam, take an activist stance, openly employing evidence for supporting truth claims and explicit attempts at influencing, others rather take the stance of being a relatively neutral provider of information. Fundamental underlying values and missions may then take a back seat in communications, relatively speaking, as can be seen in the case of African Child Policy Forum (ACPF). ACPF positions itself primarily through its research, providing policy-relevant information and recommendations for policymakers. ACPF is appreciated among key target actors for performing this role, and is a sought-after knowledge partner. At the same time, by performing this role, ACPF does voice concerns and plays the role of an agenda-setter (Arensman et al., 2015; Arensman et al., 2018). The boundaries between activist and knowledge provider roles thus seem fluid. In any case, CSOs acting from both such stances are faced with the same need to build and maintain credibility with policymakers when it comes to the evidence they

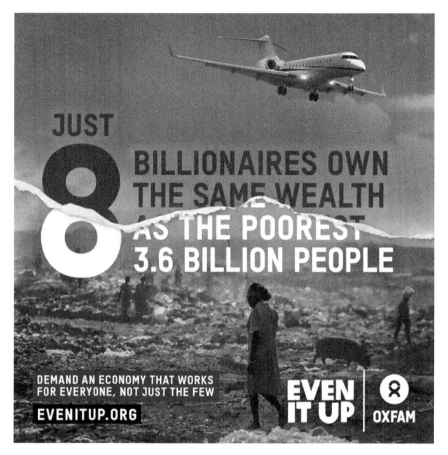

FIGURE 11.1   Oxfam's usage of evidence as 'killer facts.' *Source:* https://oxfamblogs.o
rg/fp2p/8-men-now-own-the-same-as-the-poorest-half-of-the-world-t
he-davos-killer-fact-just-got-more-deadly/

advance. When accepted as credible, CSOs can be attractive interlocutors for policymakers because of the information they can provide on problems, solutions, and
constituencies' views; as experts providing quality policy analyses; and as organisations having privileged access to information 'from the ground up' (Tallberg et al.,
2018; Travers, 2016; Van Wessel et al., 2017). Doing so successfully can help them
fulfil policymakers' needs, while advancing their own agendas.

Interactions between CSOs and policymakers: limitations and risks of an evidence focus

Literature discussing evidence-based advocacy by CSOs commonly stresses
their capacity to provide convincing information to policymakers, rooted

SUMBA: AN ICONIC ISLAND TO DEMONSTRATE THE POTENTIAL OF RENEWABLE ENERGY

Poverty reduction, economic development and energy access combined

With update June 2011

Hivos
people unlimited

FIGURE 11.2 Hivos' usage of an exemplar. *Source:* https://issuu.com/hivos/docs/b rochuresumba_iconic_island

in engagement with policy process and practices and digestibly packaged. Policymaking is presented as a rational process, with the quality of evidence and objectivity both playing key roles (Court et al., 2006; Mably, 2006).

However, these requirements can also constrict civil society advocacy by narrowing its scope. Storeng and Béhague (2014) show how international maternal health advocacy has evolved from drawing on feminist and social justice arguments for legitimation, to using number-based evidence on maternal mortality or morbidity rates, and the cost-effectiveness of targeted interventions. This shift has contributed to the depoliticisation of the issue, while constricting valuable knowledge to whatever is measurable: policymakers can thus be convinced of targeted interventions' effectiveness, rather than of broader transformations. This is an example of 'issue bias' that 'can arise when promotion of evidence skews agendas to those issues which are measured rather than those which are important to affected populations' (Parkhurst, 2017, p. 28).

Privileging 'expertise' as objective can similarly hamper representation. Rodriguez (2010), writing on a global policy process on migration and development, shows how civil society was brought into the arena to represent migrants— yet organisers privileged selected 'experts,' who provided knowledge much more fitting to the interests of states and corporate actors than those of critical grassroots migrant organisations, whose knowledge was excluded. By affecting creation, selection, and interpretation of evidence (Parkhurst, 2017) that can be used to identify and address policy questions, the foundations of policy processes can be affected: What are people's exact needs? Which needs matter most? Asking for what kind of policy or policy change?

Other research argues that the role of evidence in civil society advocacy is relative, with evidence much less in the lead than one might think looking at the status that it is commonly accorded. First, an approach to civil society advocacy that puts provision of quality evidence at the heart of advocacy work easily reduces it to an effort centred on the expertise policymakers ostensibly value CSOs for, ignoring the complex nature of advocacy. It does not acknowledge the strategic nature of advocacy, which in important ways rests on the capacity to monitor and engage with political dynamics (Arensman et al., 2015), build and maintain relations with targets, allies, constituencies, and publics (Barnes et al., 2016; Motta and Nilsen, 2011), and create and benefit from opportunities (Barrett et al., 2016).

Such an approach may also ignore the fact that advocacy need not centre on provision of evidence. Keck and Sikkink (1999), for example, also identify accountability politics (holding targets to account, appealing to norms or laws such as human rights); symbolic politics (involving organising around symbols of systematic injustice such as the killing of George Floyd); and leverage politics (drawing on CSOs' ability to call upon powerful actors to affect a situation where weaker members of a network are unlikely to have sufficient influence, such as Dutch NGOs appealing to the Dutch state to influence another state where partner CSOs within that country are helped with that influence). For example, Dutch CSOs working with CSO partners in Nigeria working on oil pollution might ask the Dutch government to try and use its influence with the Nigerian government concerning the management of pollution caused by oil production in which Shell has been involved, using information provided by Nigerian partners.

Second, an approach to civil society advocacy that puts provision of quality evidence at the heart of the work also ignores the way policymakers operate. Policymakers often do not approach evidence or its providers neutrally, limiting the chances of objective evidence playing a leading role. The likelihood of engagement with CSOs' evidence, and the CSOs providing it, thus seems higher when there is agreement between CSO and policymaker views (Mably, 2006; Parkhurst, 2017; Rodriquez, 2010; Weible, 2008). Additionally, Gourevitch and Young (2012) show that CSOs' resources for credibility are varied, including virtue, common interest with audiences, and being subjected to verification. The role of evidence is thus relative. This is in line with broader literature on the role of evidence in policymaking that shows that knowledge use in policymaking is shaped in political process (Keeley and Scoones, 2014; Parkhurst, 2017). The actual importance of evidence and its objectivity is therefore open to questioning, as are the conditions under which evidence is afforded objectivity by policymakers.

Third, evidence creation, interpretation, and use are a result of dynamics between CSOs and their targets. Mayne et al. (2018) consider how, for Oxfam, these dynamics shape their way of working with evidence. For Oxfam, evidence is integrated into influencing strategies that involve closely engaging with specific policy processes; designing evidence to maximise influence; designing and using additional influencing strategies; adapting the presentation of evidence and influencing strategies to changing contexts; and embracing trial and error.

The capacity to use evidence in advocacy thus concerns not only evidence as such, but also the development and execution of effective advocacy strategies in political interaction with targets. Eagleton-Pierce (2015), writing on Oxfam's trade policy advocacy, describes as a key strategy its connecting with sanctioned knowledge in the World Trade Organisation's context, i.e. working with theories, principles, modes of reasoning, agendas, and histories connected to trade policymaking. Being able to relate to economics and law as key academic fields proved important to develop their access—and therefore, exercising a form of power. Eagleton-Pierce (2015, p. 163) further explains that 'the Oxfam writer is traditionally imbued with a social justice sensibility, including a capacity to unearth and trace forms of human suffering beneath a veneer of orthodox knowledge,' and that 'pure forms of economic and legal knowledge are not the only sources of symbolic power that are nurtured by Oxfam authors to mount their trade campaigns. We also see explicit and tacit appeals to other systems and techniques of legitimation, notably Christian values of care and compassion for "distant suffering" beyond the West.'

Even when employing differentiated and contextualised influencing strategies, civil society advocacy is still shaped by the readiness of targets to allow them an influencing role. This can relativise the role of evidence by shaping the way CSOs conduct their advocacy. Stroup and Wong (2017) seek to explain how it is that only a very small number of INGOs (International Non-Governmental Organisations) are highly influential, and how this position then traps them into roles of advocates for moderate change, shaping their strategies to this effect. They argue that the leading role of certain INGOs depends on their authority: the deference they have managed to secure from multiple audiences. In their analysis, authority is relational, built up over time, and involves audiences (such as states) stopping, over time, 'evaluating the merits of every single case' (Stroup and Wong, 2017, p. 27). To maintain this status, leading INGOs need to moderate their demands making authority a 'trap,' leading only to incremental 'vanilla victories,' as the authors describe it. In this view, authority implies a limited role for evidence as a source of influence (even though repeated persuasion, as by evidence, can result in deference to the INGO).

Unequal partnership dynamics

The lion's share of development funding for civil society is controlled by CSOs in the Global North. In 2018, less than 4% of international funding for humanitarian assistance went to local and domestic CSOs (Development Initiatives, 2019). This means that a very small subgroup of CSOs—INGOs that are mostly Northern-based—control by far the most resources for evidence-building, interpretation, and use for advocacy in the context of international development. This likely contributes to a phenomenon described by Hayman (2016) and Fransman (2019): a global push towards rigorous, expertise-intensive research as a form of evidence, with advantages for those having the capacity to provide such evidence. As Court et al. (2006, p. 20) state, 'CSOs have significant constraints on technical and financial capacities that can limit their ability to engage with policy processes and use evidence effectively,' further noting that 'given their resources, big international NGOs sometimes crowd out the voices of smaller, indigenous ones.' However, this dominance is a complicated matter, involving a range of ways in which ties between CSOs shape the role of evidence in advocacy.

INGOs are closely involved with evidence-building in the Global South. Much of the research they commission and carry out is conducted in the countries where they work (often through partners, consultants, and/or national-level chapters of their organisations), as these are the sites where problems are being experienced, and in which locally viable solutions need to be built. In addition, Southern-based case studies, exemplars, and testimony are helpful to build policy-relevant knowledge and persuasive arguments (Travers, 2016, p. 115). This includes forms of evidence beyond research. Southern-based knowledge in the form of testimony, case studies, and visuals also helps build persuasive cases targeting Northern states and international institutions.

For example, Eagleton-Pierce (2015, p.164), writing on Oxfam's reporting on trade policy, points out the 'use of select quotes (along with photographs) from the field, whereby the voice of a farmer or producer helps to justify the overall argument.' Their privileged access to local partners and constituencies can further build up INGOs' reputation as actors having access to important development knowledge 'from the ground' (Van Wessel et al., 2017), contributing to their credibility and access to policymakers.

Well-resourced INGOs often also seek to facilitate participation of Southern CSOs in international arenas, so that their voices may be heard. Many such efforts involve genuine attempts to work together, and support and empower the latter. INGOs commonly use their funding, convening power, and access to policymaking arenas to give space to their Southern partners to engage advocacy targets. For example, during its programme *Women Leadership in Peace and Security*, Cordaid has opened up political space for Colombian women's organisations to push their government to embrace UNSCR 1325 (on women, peace, and security); and to include women in the peace negotiations by strategically linking a women's group with Margot Wallström, UN Secretary-General Special Representative on Sexual Violence in Conflict (Arensman et al., 2015). Another common way of providing space to 'local voices' is through facilitating Southern partners to speak at important international-level meetings (ibid).

How Southern CSOs' roles can be constrained

However, four issues potentially limit the role of Southern CSOs in evidence-based advocacy. First, considering control of access to events and meetings, and engagement with prevalent norms in specific policymaking arenas: INGOs can take up roles of gatekeepers and translators, exclusively bringing in partners that fit the kind of policy process they are engaging with, and in line with their own understandings and agendas, or those of the policymakers they target (Arensman et al., 2015, p. 470). As Keck and Sikkink (2014) explain:

> The process by which testimony is discovered normally involves several layers of prior translation. Transnational actors may identify what kinds of testimony would be valuable, then ask an NGO in the area to seek out people who could tell those stories. They may filter the story through expatriates, through traveling scholars like ourselves, or through the media. There is frequently a huge gap between the story's original telling and the retellings—in its socio-cultural context, its instrumental meaning, and even its language.
>
> *(Keck and Sikkink, 2014, p. 19)*

An example is provided by Gibbings (2011), who discusses how CSOs working closely with the United Nations act as mediators, bringing women from conflict zones into UN arenas as 'grounded voices' to speak on women's role in peace and security. Such efforts commonly involve preparation of speeches, so that the language employed by these 'grounded voices' matches discursive UN norms, e.g. framing women as agents of peace able to work across political and ethnic divisions; rather than, for example, giving space to women for expressing accusations against states, or other forms of confrontational language.

Second, and more fundamentally, INGOs' control over funding also implies considerable control over agenda-setting and thus control over which evidence matters. International funding also helps to build the research capacities of Southern CSOs in ways that support their ownership of issues and the development of advocacy (Travers, 2016). However, the way programmes are often set up 'centrally' can work against this. For example, an INGO alliance that the author worked with recently carried out a multi-country and multi-level programme on advocacy on disaster management, advocating for the integration of disaster risk reduction, ecosystems management and restoration, and climate change adaptation. Being a knowledge-intensive programme, research and evidence-based advocacy were intrinsic elements. However, with knowledge questions and aims geared towards the starting points of the programme, this also defined research priorities worldwide. Working with partners in this programme in India, the author experienced several cases of engagement with disaster problems through the prism of local social inequalities. For example, they engaged with locally marginalised groups' poor access to resources and assistance, as compared to more powerful and well-off groups. While this was accommodated, it was outside of the programme framework and knowledge questions on this front were thus not invited through the programme.

A third issue is the emphasis among many INGOs on internationally relevant issues and their resolution, e.g. leading themes such as 'climate change,' 'food security,' and 'gender.' However, this raises the question of what space remains for domestic dimensions and understandings of development issues and politics around these, with states as key actors and targets, and domestic CSOs as the more legitimate and knowledgeable advocates. A key example is that of caste, a form of social hierarchy that contributes to large-scale discrimination and deprivation in India, while largely ignored by the development sector (Mosse, 2018). While some scholars and CSOs acknowledge this role of domestic conditions and politics (Gaventa and McGee, 2010; Goodman, 2016), the need for domestic knowledge development to support this advocacy has not received much attention yet. This may easily lead to failure in addressing Southern partner organisations' knowledge needs in connection to domestic advocacy and potential opportunities. It may also lead to relegating knowledge from Southern partners to experiential knowledge, case studies, and testimonies that must fit internationally predefined programmes and theoretical frameworks.

A fourth issue concerns standards of evidence that may be imposed through aid systems. As Hayman et al. (2016, p. 153) note, 'trends in the development system are tipping the balance of knowledge conceptualization in development discourse, policy and practice towards the more scientific, normative, and elitist.' This can happen in ways that disqualify some forms of knowledge, raising problems of representation. Gooding (2016, p. 22) points to ongoing discussions on this that express 'concerns that the focus on research privileges issues that can be addressed through research and affects whose voices are valued.' As discussed above, such approaches may depoliticise, but here we can also point out that those advocates able and willing to abide by such imposed standards may more easily gain access to policymaking processes than those who do not.

Ways forward

The creation, interpretation, and use of evidence in evidence-based advocacy is the result of political processes between the actors involved that include the exercise of their power, the protection of organisational interests, and an important role for actors' perspectives in their ways of approaching evidence. These processes may easily lead to privileging certain types of evidence over others. While this is ostensibly portrayed in terms of evidence quality, it may lead to the exclusion of less powerful groups and marginalised interests. Some scholars and practitioners recognise that objectivity of evidence is a problematic notion, given the political dimensions of knowledge processes in policymaking, and argue we better speak of evidence-informed policymaking rather than evidence-based policymaking. Moving beyond this, from different vantage points, scholars urge us to address the problems involved, and make a turn towards more inclusiveness when it comes to engagement with actors and knowledges.

First, there are appeals to subvert current forms of domination of actors and approaches, asking to engage with local knowledge systems (Hayman et al., 2016), create space for different forms of knowledge (Gooding, 2016), and recognise the capacity of Southern civil society actors to develop their own alternative subjectivities. An illustrative example of this approach is provided by Prashant and Kapoor (2010), writing about the importance of theoretical knowledge production by a movement bringing together Dalit and Adivasi (i.e., indigenous) groups in the Indian state of Odisha, providing them with a contextually shaped understanding of the root causes of their plight and what response to their oppression should look like. Such knowledge development may be at odds with the (often more moderate) approaches of INGOs, and the question of how to engage with this is fundamental to the broader issue of how the development sector approaches development and the question what space there is for alternative understandings of development and the knowledge and knowledge development it requires.

Second, there is increasing recognition of the political nature of knowledge processes in development (see e.g. Georgalakis et al., 2017), and, in line with this, the development sector can be advised to engage more deeply with the political dimensions of knowledge creation, interpretation, and utilisation. It is important for donors and CSOs involved to recognise that these processes are informed by values and ideological positions, and involve questions of representation and legitimacy (Gooding, 2016; Parkhurst, 2017; Porter, 2010).

Third, the issues raised here are closely connected to the wider debate on ownership of development. It has been widely established that control over civil society as exercised by donors and INGOs acting as 'fundermediaries' has detrimental effects on the autonomy and political role of CSOs in development (Banks et al., 2015). Sector acceptance of this issue is increasingly evident. This acceptance has led to searches for solutions and some experiments involving changes in control over funding, as with the current Netherlands policy programme *Power of Voices* (Netherlands Ministry of Foreign Affairs, 2019), which requires Southern Partners to be part of the CSO alliances controlling the funding. Another example is the *#Shiftthepower* movement that started out from appeals to build CSO independence from powerful donors through community philanthropy. There are also calls to rethink INGO and donor roles, for example, proposing roles towards facilitation and support (Banks et al., 2015) and appeals to link up with existing networks and ongoing civil society processes in order to 'Start from the South' (Van Wessel et al., 2019). Also when it comes to questions around knowledge, engaging such structural conditions and embedded imaginaries, practices, and norms shaping development efforts are at the basis of the challenges, which would have to be acknowledged in order to be overcome.

References

Anderson, M. (2010). Turning evidence into policy: Challenges facing UK aid. *Journal of Development Effectiveness*, 2(4), 556–560.

Arensman, B., Van Waegeningh, C. and Van Wessel, M. (2018). Twinning 'practices of change' with 'theory of change' room for emergence in advocacy evaluation. *American Journal of Evaluation*, 39(2), 221–236.

Arensman, B., Barrett, J., Van Bodegom, A., Hilhorst, D., Klaver, D., Van Waegeningh, C. and van Wessel, M. (2015). *MFS II joint evaluation of international lobbying and advocacy*. Endline report. Wageningen University and Research. https://edepot.wur.nl/356079

Banks, N., Hulme, D. and Edwards, M. (2015). NGOs, states, and donors revisited: Still too close for comfort? *World Development*, 66, 707–718.

Barnes, C., Van Laerhoven, F. and Driessen, P. P. (2016). Advocating for change? How a civil society-led coalition influences the implementation of the forest rights act in India. *World Development*, 84, 162–175.

Barrett, J. B., Van Wessel, M. G. J. and Hilhorst, D. (2016). *Advocacy for development: effectiveness, monitoring and evaluation*. Wageningen University. https://edepot.wur.nl/375995

CIVICUS (2020). *The state of civil society report*. Available at: https://www.CIVICUS.org/index.php/state-of-civil-society-report-2020

Court, J., Mendizabal, E., Osborne, D. and Young, J. (2006). *Policy engagement: How civil society can be more effective*. London: Overseas Development Institute.

Development Initiatives. (2019). *Global Humanitarian Assistance report 2019*. Development Initiatives. Available at: https://devinit.org/publications/global-humanitarian-assistance-report-2019/

Eagleton-Pierce, M. (2015). Symbolic power and social critique in the making of Oxfam's trade policy research. In: Hannah, E., Scott, J. and Trommer, S. (eds.). *Expert knowledge in global trade*. Routledge, 84–102.

Fransman, J. (2019). *Engaging with research for real impact: The state of research in the INGO sector and ways forward for better practice*. Bond.

Gaventa, J. and McGee, R. (2010). Introduction: Making change happen. Citizen action and national policy reform. In: Gaventa, J. and McGee, R. (eds.). *Citizen action and national policy reform: Making change happen*. London: Zed Books, 1–43.

Georgalakis, J., Jessani, N., Oronje, R. and Ramalingam, B. (2017). *The social realities of knowledge for development: sharing lessons of improving development processes with evidence*. IDS/The Impact Initiative.

Gibbings, S. L. (2011). No angry women at the United Nations: Political dreams and the cultural politics of United Nations Security Council Resolution 1325. *International Feminist Journal of Politics*, 13(4), 522–538.

Goldman, I. and M. Pabari (eds.). (2021). *Using evidence in policy and practice. Lessons from Africa*. Abingdon: Routledge.

Gooding, K. (2016). What do we mean by evidence-based advocacy? Ideas from NGOs in Malawi. In: Hayman, R., King, S., Kontinen, T. and Narayanaswamy, L. (eds.). *Negotiating knowledge: Evidence and experience in development NGOs*. Rugby: Practical Action Publishing, 129–145.

Goodman, E. S. (2016). *Changing advocacy practices in a changing world: An evaluation of Oxfam America's influencing work in a shifting international NGO culture*. Available at: https://digitalcollections.sit.edu/capstones/2884/

Gourevitch, P. A., Lake, D. A. and Stein, J. G. (eds.) (2012). *The credibility of transnational NGOs: When virtue is not enough*. Cambridge: Cambridge University Press.

Hayman, R. (2016). NGOs and the evidence-based policy agenda. In: Hayman, R., King, S., Kontinen, T. and Narayanaswamy, L. (eds.). *Negotiating knowledge: Evidence and experience in development NGOs*. Rugby: Practical Action Publishing.

Hayman, R., King, S., Kontinen, T. and Narayanaswamy, L. (eds.) (2016). *Negotiating knowledge: Evidence and experience in development NGOs*. Rugby: Practical Action Publishing.

Hivos (2016). *Case study for Sumba Iconic Island Programme*. Available at: https://www.hivos.nl/assets/2016/06/CD-case-study-Sumba-Island.pdf

Jordan, L., & van Tuijl, P. (1998). Political Responsibility in NGO Advocacy: Exploring emerging shapes of global democracy. New York: Europe's Forum on International Cooperation.

Keck, M. E. and Sikkink, K. (1999). Transnational advocacy networks in international and regional politics. *International Social Science Journal*, 51(159), 89–101.

Keck, M. E. and Sikkink, K. (2014). *Activists beyond borders: Advocacy networks in international politics*. Cornell University Press.

Keeley, J. and Scoones, I. (2014). Understanding environmental policy processes: A conceptual map. In: Keeley, J. and Scoones, I. (eds.). *Understanding environmental policy processes: Cases from Africa*. Routledge, 21–39.

Mably, P. (2006). *Evidence based advocacy: NGO research capacities and policy influence in the field of international trade*. Available at: https://idl-bnc-idrc.dspacedirect.org/bitstream/handle/10625/45959/132438.pdf?isAllowed=yandsequence=1

Mayne, R., Green, D., Guijt, I., Walsh, M., English, R. and Cairney, P. (2018). Using evidence to influence policy: Oxfam's experience. *Palgrave Communications*, 4(1), 1–10.

Mosse, D. (2018). Caste and development: Contemporary perspectives on a structure of discrimination and advantage. *World Development*, 110, 422–436.

Motta, S. and Nilsen, A. G. (eds.) (2011). *Social movements in the global south: Dispossession, development and resistance.* London: Palgrave McMillan.

Netherlands Ministry of Foreign Affairs (2019). *Grant instrument Power of Voices partnerships.* Available at: https://www.rijksoverheid.nl/documenten/beleidsnotas/2019/11/28/b eleidskader-versterking-maatschappelijk-middenveld

Oxfam (2019). *Creating killer facts and graphics.* Available at: https://policy-practice.oxfam. org.uk/publications/creating-killer-facts-and-graphics-253013

Parkhurst, J. (2017). *The politics of evidence: From evidence-based policy to the good governance of evidence.* Routledge.

Porter, C. (2010). *What shapes the influence evidence has on policy? The role of politics in research utilisation.* Young Lives. Available at: https://www.younglives.org.uk/content/what -shapes-influence-evidence-has-policy-role-politics-research-utilisation

Prasant, K. and Kapoor, D. (2010). Learning and knowledge production in Dalit social movements in rural India. In: *Learning from the ground up.* London: Palgrave Macmillan, 193–210.

Rodriguez, R. M. (2010). On the question of expertise: A critical reflection on 'civil society' processes. In: Choudry, A. and Kapoor, D. (eds.). *Learning from the ground up.* London: Palgrave Macmillan, 53–68.

Storeng, K. T. and Béhague, D. P. (2014). 'Playing the numbers game': evidence-based advocacy and the technocratic narrowing of the safe motherhood initiative. *Medical Anthropology Quarterly,* 28(2), 260–279.

Stroup, S. S. and Wong, W. H. (2017). *The authority trap: Strategic choices of international NGOs.* Ithaca: Cornell University Press.

Tallberg, J., Dellmuth, L. M., Agné, H. and Duit, A. (2018). NGO influence in international organizations: Information, access and exchange. *British Journal of Political Science,* 48(1), 213–238.

Thrandardottir, E. (2016). Legitimacy and knowledge production in NGOs. In: Hayan, R., King, S., Kontinen, T., Narayanaswamy, L. (eds.). *Negotiating knowledge: Evidence and experience in development NGOs.* Rugby: Practical Action Publishing, 47–58.

Travers, S. (2016). Canadian civil society organizations using research to influence policy and practice in the Global South. In: Mougeot, L. J. A. (ed.). *Putting knowledge to work: Collaborating, influencing and learning for international development.* Rugby: Practical Action Publishing, 107–142.

Van Wessel, M. G. J., Katyaini, S., Mishra, Y., Naz, F., Balasubramanian, R., Manchanda, R., ... and Sahoo, S. (2019). *Civil society dynamics: Shaping roles, navigating contexts.* Wageningen University and Research. Available at: https://library.wur.nl/WebQuer y/wurpubs/fulltext/511476

Van Wessel, M., Schulpen, L., Hilhorst, T. and Biekart, K. (2017). *Mapping the expectations of the Dutch strategic partnerships for lobby and advocacy.* Wageningen University and Research. Available at: https://edepot.wur.nl/410800

Weible, C. M. (2008). Expert-based information and policy subsystems: A review and synthesis. *Policy Studies Journal,* 36(4), 615–635.

PART V

Negotiating technological change and digitalisation

12

A PROBLEMATISATION OF INCLUSION AND EXCLUSION

Trade-offs and nuances in the digitalisation of African agriculture

Mariette McCampbell, Kelly Rijswijk,
Hannah Wilson, and Laurens Klerkx

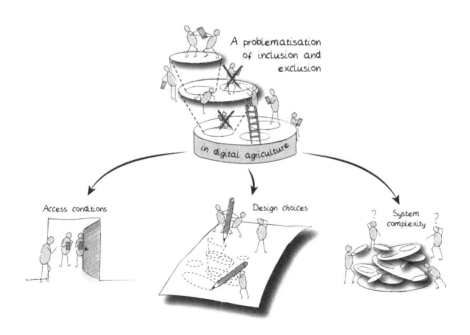

Introduction

The use of digital technologies to enhance efficiency of production, processing, and trade, aiming to improve the profitability and sustainability of organisations and industries, has become a global trend in a wide range of industries including in African smallholder agriculture (Klerkx et al., 2019; Munthali et al., 2018). The digitalisation process concerns the use of digital technologies

DOI: 10.4324/9781003112525-12

and infrastructures in businesses, economy, and society, restructuring social and professional life through digital communication and social media (Rijswijk et al., 2020). Another important concept related to digitalisation is datafication, defined as the transformation through which objects, relationships, events, and processes become data points that are machine-readable and analysable by digital technologies using data analytics, machine learning, and complex algorithms (Williamson, 2018).

A popular assumption is that digitalisation is ultimately beneficial for everyone, and truly transforms agriculture (Klerkx et al., 2019). This discourse is especially commonplace in the context of digitalisation efforts for humanitarian, aid, and development objectives (Cinnamon, 2020; Mann, 2018), like many of the present-day digital interventions in African agriculture (Mann and Iazzolino, 2019; Tsan et al., 2019). In practice, the true socio-economic impact of digitalisation processes in Africa's agricultural system is yet to be seen, and recent critical analyses of digitalisation in agriculture point to unequal distribution of benefits and harm (Rotz et al., 2019; Van der Burg et al., 2019). This unequal distribution relates to mechanisms of social inclusion and exclusion, terms that are generally used to organise people (or groups) according to criteria that define who is 'in' and who is 'out' (Graham and Sweller, 2011). For example, when assessing access of African farmers to weather information via a mobile phone, one could take geography, gender, age, wealth, etc. into account; but in practice, processes of inclusion and exclusion are more complex.

This chapter has the objective to unravel this complexity in digitalisation processes in African smallholder agriculture in three levels: (1) access conditions in relation to a specific digital technology; (2) design choices in relation to a digital innovation package; and (3) system complexity in relation to the digital agricultural system. To date these potential causes and impacts of inclusion and exclusion are underexplored in an African smallholder agricultural context, especially when looking beyond access conditions. There is a knowledge gap about the understanding of inclusion and exclusion surrounding digitalisation of agriculture in the African context. With such a focus on Africa, this chapter builds on lessons learned from both a Global North and South context, providing a broad overview of factors causing inclusion and exclusion and establishing a more nuanced discourse around inclusion and exclusion related to digital agriculture—understood as broad digitalisation both on- and off-farm, e.g. in the broader value chain—and its impact on people's lives.

Conceptual framing of social inclusion and exclusion

Notions of inclusion and exclusion in sociology address structural inequalities faced by different groups; traditionally mostly women, and also disabled, illiterate, indigenous, or (rural) poor people. Inclusiveness has long been promoted as a strategy to alleviate poverty, increase economic growth, generate employment, progress horizontal and vertical (gender) equality, and improve well-being

(McKinley, 2010). In the African context, there is significant attention for inclusive development, innovation, and business (Opola et al., 2020; Pouw et al., 2019). Inclusion and exclusion are often used as binary distinctions that are defined by people either falling inside or outside specific social categories, and above or below specified limits (Mascareño and Carvajal, 2015). Within this context the *good*, *expectable*, and *normal* are attributed to inclusion, with exclusion being the negative opposite (Parsons, 1965). However, modern societies allow for a people and groups to be simultaneously included and excluded: hence inclusion and exclusion are not an 'either-or' matter, since no person is fully included or excluded (Mascareño and Cavajal, 2015). Stichweh and Windolf (2009) add a distinction between *including exclusion* and *excluding inclusion*, i.e., how inclusion in one group can result in (indirect) exclusion from another and vice versa. Hence, the distinction between inclusion and exclusion is more complex than a static observation of who is 'in' versus 'out' (Fitoussi and Rosanvallon, 1997) and should be approached as a process taking place within a particular social context, instead of a dichotomy between insiders and outsiders.

The thinking about inclusion and exclusion should move beyond binary terms and pay particular attention to the formation and maintenance of various kinds of power Du Toit (2004). In this regard, Sen (2000) identified unfavourable forms of inclusion; for example, as pointed out by Joseph (2014), a subordinated type in which inclusion is not evenly distributed. Another example is seen in agricultural value chains in which the profits are unevenly distributed between farmers, traders, and sellers.

Digital responses to address subordinated inclusion comprise applications that connect producers and buyers that bypass the middlemen (Aker, 2016) and e-auctions (Joseph, 2020). Unfavourable inclusion can also be illusive, so that the outcome of being included is then the same as the outcome of being excluded (Joseph, 2014). An example of illusive inclusion is when a farmer is selected to participate in a survey of a development project and expects to benefit from this. Yet, in practice the farmer never hears from this project again, nor witnesses results.

Sen's (2000) framework also recognises constitutive, instrumental, active, and passive exclusion (and unfavourable inclusion). Constitutive exclusion has a direct impact on the person excluded, such as female farmers not being invited for agronomic training and therefore not developing the same knowledge as male farmers. Instrumental exclusion leads to exclusion through causal linkages, for instance, when a farmer cannot access credit to buy inputs and equipment to increase farm production and escape poverty. Active exclusion is deliberate, as in purposely not inviting women for agronomic training, while passive exclusion is non-deliberate and the result of social processes. In the latter case, exclusion is an unintended consequence of some decision or action, such as early-warning messages about the outbreak of a crop disease not reaching poorer farmers because they cannot afford the smartphone needed to receive the message. Nevile (2007) argues that when active forms of exclusion (or unfavourable inclusion) act as

causal factors, focus should be on reasons and possible justifications for the deliberate decision to exclude. For passive forms of exclusion (or unfavourable inclusion), the focus should be on ways to mitigate unintended consequences.

Observing mechanisms of inclusion and exclusion in digital agriculture

Existing digital development discourse characterises (data) inequalities as 'a
basic problem of inclusion/exclusion, based on the notion that inequality in
diffusion of, access to, and use of data can widen development gaps between
individuals, groups, and nations' (Cinnamon, 2020, p. 215), a framing that is
criticised for being insufficient for explaining or addressing causes, forms, and
consequences of inequalities. Hence, digital and data inclusion and exclusion
always occur in a specific context. Figure 12.1 presents three contextual levels
at which inclusion and exclusion takes place: the level of a (single) digital technology; a digital innovation package (i.e., a design of digital hardware and/or
software, and the institutional arrangements to use it); and a digital agricultural
system (i.e., the configuration of various rival and/or adherent and/or syner-
getic innovation packages and the socio-cultural context in which they need
to operate).

Illustrates how these contextual levels relate to each other. The digital technology level represents the most tangible and transparent level. Studies with an
African focus have primarily concentrated on this level, studying who can and
who cannot access a digital technology, and the conditions required for access.
This access can be further divided into five sub-categories: availability, affordability, awareness, abilities, and agency (Roberts and Hernandez, 2019).

Digital technologies and access conditions: looking at digital divides

In the following sections, we further unravel the three contextual levels introduced in the conceptual framework based on existing literature. Starting with
the contextual level of digital technologies, we discuss different forms of inclusion and exclusion that together present a variety of (potential) areas of concern
in relation to digital agriculture as identified in Table 12.1.

The advantage of focusing on a specific digital technology, and access to
it, is that inclusion and exclusion are then relatively tangible and transparent.
But as seen in Figure 12.1, only the tip of the iceberg is then visible. Negative
socio-economic impacts of digitalisation have often been summarised under the
umbrella of the so-called 'digital divide.' Access issues in Africa are generally
recognised as key reasons for digital divides between the Africa/Global North,
urban/rural, and rich/poor pairings (Trendov, 2019). This leads to social and
economic marginalisation and uneven socio-economic development (Rijswijk
et al., 2020; Rotz et al., 2019; Salemink et al., 2017). Thus, known factors like

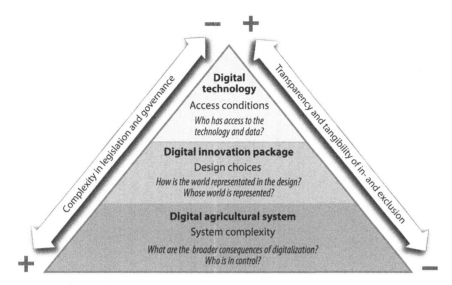

FIGURE 12.1   Relationship between the three levels at which digital and data inclusion and exclusion may appear, with increasing or decreasing complexity in the vertical axis governing the digital systems, and marking how tangible and transparent inclusion and/or exclusion are

location, age, gender, ethnicity, wealth status, and education level, determine access to and use of digital technologies by individuals, and they foster individuals' inclusion or exclusion to potential or assumed benefits of digitalisation.

Digital divides are born from inequalities in access, literacy, cost, or service relevance, and continue to exist despite being a key challenge for achieving developmental and economic goals, regardless of whether a country is rich or if nation-wide access has increased (USAID, 2020). The disadvantage of women in African smallholder farming communities has received particular attention (OECD, 2018). Studies systematically show the existence of a gender digital divide, with men nearly always being better off (Porter et al., 2020) and women benefitting less than they could (GSMA, 2019).

Additionally, the increasing importance of data (that is, of datafication) has led to the emergence of a specific new type of divide: the data divide. The data divide refers to asymmetries between the 'data haves' and 'have-nots' (Scholz et al., 2018). According to Cinnamon (2020, p. 228), data divides matter because 'access to data production and analytics in some cases actually has the reverse effect, the instantiation of new harms and the widening of inequalities.'

Challenges arising from digital divides

Availability here implies various forms of access: material (digital hardware, software, and data); infrastructure (required to access and use those hardware,

TABLE 12.1 Overview linking the three contextual levels (digital technology; digital innovation package; digital agricultural system), forms of inclusion and exclusion that can arise, and existing or future areas of concern that were identified

Contextual level where inclusion and exclusion takes place	Specific digital technology	Digital innovation package	Digital agricultural system
Overarching reason for inclusion and exclusion at this level	Access conditions.	Design choices.	System complexity.
Related data inequality	Access to data.	Representation of the world as data.	Control over data flow.
Likely forms of exclusion and unfavourable inclusion	Active, passive, constitutive, inclusion; subordinated inclusion.	Active, passive, constitutive, instrumental exclusion; subordinated, illusive inclusion.	Passive, instrumental exclusion; subordinated, illusive inclusion.
Opportunities	Increased equal access to digital technologies.	Decisions and solutions that anticipate unintended consequences (e.g. based on fair and responsible data principles).	Establishing synergies between digital technologies and innovation packages.
Threats	Digital divides; data divides.	Design related risks.	Digital traps: data originators or users become stuck in/with a particular system or digital technology.
Factors influencing existence of inclusion and exclusion	(Mostly) tangible aspects determining a person's access to a technology.	Risks and prospects related to design decisions.	Socio-technical organisation and integration with the digital innovation package(s).

| Current or future areas of concern for unintended consequences and inclusion and exclusion | *Availability of:* hardware, software, data, infrastructure, rules/regulations, demand/supply. *Affordability:* income/wealth, cost of material, value proposition, ease of use and learning. *Agency:* autonomy, norms/values/beliefs, identity as a farmer. *Ability:* digital literacy, general literacy, human physical ability, type of farm/geography. | Obsolescence of skills, individual and group privacy, (data) security, concentrated/private data ownership, profiling, data processing location, data aggregation, regulations for digital development, choice vs. obligation to participate/be included, distribution of technological benefits, associated economic/social arrangements/contracts, product/service sustainability, technological bias. | Information overload, information quality issues, loss of human control and oversight over technology, human/animal–machine interaction, addictions, cybercrime, blurring of roles of organisations, ethical dilemmas. |

software, and data); institutional (rules and regulations); market (demand and supply); and suitability context (is the digital technology a good and fair fit for the context?). Availability of hardware, software, infrastructure, and suitable policies are outstanding issues in African countries (Ezeomah and Duncombe, 2019; Mann, 2018; Trendov, 2019;) leading mostly to passive and constitutive exclusion although active exclusion is also possible. Concerns arise that universal access and the increasing power of data in economic governance, together with the lobby of big tech companies for strategically advantageous regulation, puts African countries at risk of data extraction that benefits foreign rather than domestic economies (Mann, 2018). In such cases there is a risk of unfavourable inclusion; specifically, of subordinated inclusion.

Affordability relates to economic capacity: capital required to access digital technologies; one-off or recurring material investments; and whether the technology delivers profit. Inclusion and exclusion here result from economic inequalities between farmers and farmers and other stakeholders, thus resulting in passive and constitutive exclusion. Affordability challenges may exacerbate with extremely high initial investments, or recurring expenses. Continuous investments become more problematic in case of technological lock-in and path-dependency, tying a farmer to one particular company or organisation due to proprietary software, inability to access farm data without a subscription plan, or inoperability with competitive offers (Bronson, 2018). Considering the income levels of African smallholder farmers combined with general absence of loan facilities, practically any investment may be considered 'extremely high' in this context. In addition, social needs and values influence perceptions about affordability. For example, the common conception that 'time is money' in high-income countries legitimates investments in labour and time saving technologies. Most African farmer's time or labour however is considered 'for free,' especially women's time, resulting in a totally different cost-benefit calculation (Grassi, 2015). Additionally, whether investments guarantee profit return or not matters, especially in volatile markets with fluctuating agriculture produce prices (Rotz et al., 2019). These affordability issues may all result in exclusion of farmers' access to digital technologies, by definition (e.g. unable to buy a phone) or by choice (e.g. unwilling to invest in a phone).

Another issue for digital agricultural technologies in the context of African smallholder farming is users' capabilities, ease of learning and using a digital technology, and whether farmers can afford investment in additional training and resources (e.g. time, effort, physical strength). A reason for poor adoption is that farmers—especially the elderly, and females—struggle with using digital tools, particularly when smartphone based (Ezeomah and Duncombe, 2019). This relates to user ability in terms of digital and general literacy, and physical ability. Literacy is a well-known challenge in agricultural development, creating barriers for farmers with limited or no education. Digital literacy is a newer issue relating to skills and knowledge required to use digital technologies, such as using hardware and software, and making sense of data produced or received.

In other words, digital technologies need to fit farmers' level of tech savviness so as to prevent passive and constitutive exclusion.

Agency and awareness about the socio-cultural context are less tangible issues that are often embedded in the socio-cultural make up of agricultural communities and therefore not directly observable. However, they are critical factors that influence adoption decisions and passive as well as constitutive exclusion, especially in cases of non-adoption or de-adoption, regardless of good availability, affordability, and ability of users. An example of constitutive exclusion is when it is considered socio-culturally inappropriate for a woman to use digital technologies.

Reasons for inequalities in access to digital technologies and data are not limited to observable, tangible, or seemingly individual factors (like age, gender, and wealth) but extend to more unobservable, intangible, and aggregated issues too, which, as we will see in the next sections, relate to the other contextual levels of Figure 12.1, viz. the digital innovation package, and the digital agricultural system.

Digital innovation packages and design choices: deciding about the design and anticipating design consequences

Digital technologies and interventions are designed with a specific objective and desired outcomes in mind. Decisions about the design determine, for example, the physical, front-end design (e.g. the hardware and software interface) and system or back-end design (e.g. programming languages used, location of databases, interoperability with other systems). These design choices around digital technologies and innovation packages are always accompanied by risks, as it requires decision making about the world that the technology and the collected data collected represents, i.e., whose world is represented, and how this is done. These decisions alter our physical world and how we operate in it, potentially causing unequal opportunities (Cinnamon, 2020). Hence, design related impacts intended; unintended consequences are likely, which in turn can lead to all forms of exclusion and unfavourable inclusion. Design choices are ultimately accompanied by trade-offs; saying 'yes' to one design feature usually equals saying 'no' to other features. Those trade-offs make exclusion almost inevitable as design-for-all or one-size-fits-all solutions are highly complex and oftentimes simply impossible. An example trade-off is the anticipation that progressing digitalisation in African agriculture will reduce demand for traditional farm-labourers, but that digitalisation could be a net job-creator too, offering opportunities for those with the right skills, like the many highly educated African youth (Heeks, 2020; Tsan et al., 2019). This non-deliberate loss of particular jobs is, in turn, an example of unequal distribution of benefits as well as instrumental and passive exclusion. Design choices should ideally anticipate unintended consequences that could become design related risks (Rijswijk et al., 2020). In this, transparency and accountability are desirable.

Designing digital innovation packages is also about distributing power among actors, with some becoming more influential than others. But how are benefits from digital technologies distributed among different actors, such as technology developers, users, data originators, and data owners? Do design choices contribute to reducing inclusion and equal distribution of benefits, or do they create marginalisation of individuals or groups? These questions relate to subordinated inclusion, e.g. one actor will benefit more from an innovation design than another. Digital agriculture is often associated with high-tech, smart technologies and large-scale, input-intensive farms. Scholars have observed that wealthier, large-scale, commercial farmers benefit more from digitalisation in agriculture (Bronson, 2018). Hence digitalisation may support a limited number of specific agricultural production systems at the expense of others (Bronson and Knezevic, 2016; Klerkx et al., 2019). Others argue that visions for the role of digital technologies support perpetuation of a status quo that prioritises maximisation of global agricultural production (Lajoie-O'Malley et al., 2020). Then again, in the absence of large numbers of commercial farms to date, current digitalisation initiatives in Africa focus mostly on reaching smallholder farmers. The widespread use of smartphone-based applications and platforms in digitalisation processes, for now, makes the socio-economic status of users less influential. Nevertheless, in practice wealthier or more literate farmers have the advantage of an overall larger capacity to buy fertilisers, hybrid seeds, get credit, or access digital hardware and infrastructure required to get access to information in the first place (Mann, 2018); therefore they are better able to benefit from what digital technologies have to offer. This as an example of illusive inclusion; the design of a digital technology may be inclusive for all farmers, yet they cannot all benefit from it because of the inability to truly use or act upon it.

Digital agricultural systems and system complexity: emerging mechanisms of inclusion and exclusion in digital agriculture

In this section we cover the third level, system complexity, or the composition of elements that together make up the digital agricultural system and the sociotechnical organisation within it. The digital agricultural system is complex in multiple ways: variations in crop production systems and value chains; national and international jurisdictions; the multitude of actors involved; and the ever-growing diversity of digital technologies and technological packages which may or may not be interconnected or interoperable. The complexity and motions of digital systems make prediction and visibility of different forms of inclusion and exclusion challenging.

System complexity also increases uncertainty about issues such as the quality of data and information as input and output of digital systems. A possible response is more technological integration. Integration offers opportunities for synergies and reduced complexity, yet a lack of integration can become a digital trap (Rijswijk et al., 2020). For example, a user may become stuck with a particular piece of hardware or software that is not interoperable with other items, or cannot be updated. Interoperability and coupling of systems is critical. In contrast, too tight coupling of systems leads to vulnerability and potential domino effects, i.e., if one system fails all fail. How do digital traps and domino effects relate to inclusion and exclusion? The first can result in perpetuating inclusion or exclusion: those included remain included, those excluded remain excluded. Instrumental exclusion may be the outcome of the latter because of the causal linkages between systems.

The presence of digital technologies and data-based decision making inherently affects real-life interactions, such as between people or people and animals. Traditional human-to-human interactions become moderated or replaced by machines, changing relationships between humans and their natural, technical, and social environments and allowing for less empathy, trust building, and judgment of intentions and preferences (Scholz et al., 2018). In cultures where human-to-human interaction has important cultural value, like most African cultures, trust is important for acceptance of (digital) technologies (Aker et al., 2016). According to Scholz et al. (2018), data can be a disturbing variable and distractor for sharing experiences and knowledge, taking away agency from the human individual.

More concretely, digital systems rely on data input to operate. However, data inconsistency is a known problem, especially with large datasets from heterogeneous sources, needing investment in rigorous efforts to reduce data noise and correct inconsistencies (Philip Chen and Zhang, 2014). Another challenge with data aggregation is the need to consider variances in how data is interpreted. Although mainstreaming interpretations enhances interoperability, it also raises the question of whether 'hybrid' interpretations are trustworthy or provide a new form of interpretative doubt (Mansour et al., 2016), and whether they support or undermine equality. For example, the outcome of interpretational mistakes may be that people are passively included or excluded, which is hard to control for and may have unforeseen consequences.

But, who is responsible for those consequences? Governing digital agricultural systems is inherently difficult, especially when they are coupled or operating across-borders. Yet this also influences control over digital technologies and, more importantly, control over who uses data, where, when, and for what purposes (Cinnamon, 2020) as well as who can be held accountable. In combination with uncertainty about emerging effects of digitalisation, accountability leads to various concerns about misuse of data and blurring roles and responsibilities in the digital agriculture system. Currently, roles, actors, and data owners are not clearly defined; neither are governance models, establishing who is accountable for what. Additionally, actors in the agricultural sector need to redevelop their identity and build new capacity and expertise, moving from being classical agricultural or humanitarian organisations working on crop improvement, face-to-face extension services, or emergency support to people, to designers and operators of digital platforms and systems which requires different skillsets and expertise. Within this complex and opaque environment it is easy for all kinds of inclusion and exclusion to emerge, being at the same time difficult to anticipate. Additionally, taking action against exclusion or unfavourable inclusion may not be in the interest of the actors who are in control, yet institutional arrangements fall short in effectively controlling this.

Rethinking inclusion and exclusion for the context of digital agriculture

The previous sections showed that as opportunities to capture unique properties about individuals, their farm, and their behaviour (habits, norms and values, likes and dislikes, recurring decisions) expand, it more and more matters who you are and what you do, both as an individual and a company or organisation. We have seen that digital technologies may lead to various mechanisms of inclusion and/or exclusion of actors and that increasingly these mechanisms may be intangible in nature (e.g. algorithmic bias, or user profiling). Intangible factors, resulting from design choices and system complexity, become powerful determinants of who is included or excluded and whether inclusion and exclusion is beneficial or harmful due to e.g. expanding access to data, aggregation of data, and capacity for data computation and manipulation. We previously noted that in relation to African agriculture, focus has been biased towards access conditions, while attention for design choices and system complexity lags behind. The latter two are rarely considered, or only in form of critique—such as exclusion of actors in the design process and of actors from the benefits of data generated outputs—without offering solutions to the emerging challenges. Digital technologies meanwhile present themselves as a double-edged sword: being included may be both beneficial and harmful. Similarly, included individuals may gain agency at one contextual level, but lose it at another level.

In this chapter, we unravelled the known and future impacts of digitalisation processes on inclusion and exclusion in African agriculture and showed the difficulty to identify 'right' from 'wrong.' Ultimately, digitalisation comes with trade-offs: people generally lack control in being included somewhere and excluded elsewhere, and vice versa. Although designers and implementers of digital technologies may anticipate many unintended consequences, some fall into the category of unknown consequences and simply cannot be predicted beforehand. Additionally, it is not always possible to control for all unintended consequences, especially when they require transformations beyond the technological design such as in the institutional or socio-cultural environment. Hence, the dichotomy of inclusion and exclusion and the inherent normative assumption that inclusion is always good and exclusion always bad, demands revisiting. The perception that technology and technological progress are inherently good and needed for growth is fundamentally flawed when it comes to digital technologies. Instead, the trade-offs and unintended consequences that come with digitalisation and datafication at the three contextual levels that we discussed in this chapter should receive more recognition and consideration.

Acknowledements

This chapter was partly based on and funded through the DESIRA project. This project received funding from the European Union's Horizon 2020 research and innovation programme under grant agreement No 818194. Additional support for this work came from the CGIAR Research Program on Roots, Tubers and Bananas (RTB) supported by CGIAR Trust Fund contributors. Disclaimer: the content of this chapter does not reflect the official opinion of the European Union, RTB, or CGIAR. Responsibility for the information and views expressed therein lies entirely with the author(s).

References

Aker, J. C., Ghosh, I. and Burrell, J. (2016). The promise (and pitfalls) of ICT for agriculture initiatives. *Agricultural Economics*, 47, 35–48.

Bronson, K. and Knezevic, I. (2016). Big data in food and agriculture. *Big Data & Society*, 3(1), 2053951716648174.

Bronson, K. (2018). Smart farming: Including rights holders for responsible agricultural innovation. *Technology Innovation Management Review*, 8(2), 7–14.

Cinnamon, J. (2020). Data inequalities and why they matter for development. *Information Technology for Development*, 26(2), 214–233.

Philip Chen, C. L. and Zhang, C.-Y. (2014). Data-intensive applications, challenges, techniques and technologies: A survey on Big Data. *Information Sciences*, 275, 314–347.

Du Toit, A. (2004). "Social exclusion" discourse and chronic poverty: A South African case study. *Development and Change*, 35(5), 987–1010.

Ezeomah, B. and Duncombe, R. (2019). The role of digital platforms in disrupting agricultural value chains in developing countries. International Conference on Social Implications of Computers in Developing Countries, Springer, 231–47.

Fitoussi, J. P. and Rosanvallon, P. (1997). *La nueva era de las desigualdades*. Buenos Aires: Manantial.

Graham, L. J. and Sweller, N. (2011). The inclusion lottery: Who's in and who's out? Tracking inclusion and exclusion in New South Wales government schools. *International Journal of Inclusive Education*, 15(9), 941–953.

Grassi, F., Landberg, J. and Huyer, S. (2015). *Running out of time. The reduction of women's work burden in agricultural production*. Rome: Food and Agriculture Organization of the United Nations.

GSMA. (2019). *Connected women: The mobile gender gap report 2019*. GSMA.

Heeks, R. (2020). ICT4D 3.0? Part 2—The patterns of an emerging "digital-for-development" paradigm. *The Electronic Journal of Information Systems in Developing Countries*, 86(3), e12123.

Joseph, K. J. (2014). Exploring exclusion in innovation systems: Case of plantation agriculture in India. *Innovation and Development*, 4(1), 73–90.

Joseph, K. J. (2020). *Commodity markets, computers and inclusive development: A Study of Marketing and Price Formation of Cardamom with e-Auctions*. Dordrecht: Springer.

Klerkx, L., Jakku, E. and Labarthe, P. (2019). A review of social science on digital agriculture, smart farming and agriculture 4.0: New contributions and a future research agenda. *NJAS—Wageningen Journal of Life Sciences*, 90-91, 100315.

Lajoie-O'malley, A., Bronson, K., Van Der Burg, S. and Klerkx, L. (2020). The future(s) of digital agriculture and sustainable food systems: An analysis of high-level policy documents. *Ecosystem Services*, 45, 101183.

Mann, L. (2018). Left to other peoples' devices? A political economy perspective on the big data revolution in development. *Development and Change*, 49(1), 3–36.

Mann, L. and Iazzolino, G. (2019). *See, nudge, control and profit: Digital platforms as privatized epistemic infrastructures*. Bangalore: IT for Change.

Mansour, I., Sahandi, R., Cooper, K. and Warman, A. (2016). Interoperability in the heterogeneous cloud environment: A survey of recent user-centric approaches. In: *ICC 2016 proceedings of the International Conference on Internet of Things and Cloud Computing*, 62: ACM.

Mascareño, A. and Carvajal, F. (2015). The different faces of inclusion and exclusion. *Cepal Review*, 116, 127–141.

McKinley, T. (2010). *Inclusive growth criteria and indicators: An inclusive growth index for diagnosis of country progress*. Manila: ADB Sustainable Development.

Munthali, N., Leeuwis, C., van Paassen, A., Lie, R., Asare, R., van Lammeren, R. and Schut, M. (2018). Innovation intermediation in a digital age: Comparing public and private new-ICT platforms for agricultural extension in Ghana. *NJAS - Wageningen Journal of Life Sciences*, 86/87, 64–76.

Nevile, A. (2007). Amartya K. Sen and social exclusion. *Development in Practice*, 17(2), 249–255.

OECD (2018). *Bridging the digital gender divide - include, upskill, innovate*. Paris: OECD.

Opola, F.O., Klerkx, L., Leeuwis, C., & Kilelu, C. W. (2021). The hybridity of inclusive innovation narratives between theory and practice: A framing analysis. *The European Journal of Development Research*. 33, 626–648. https://doi.org/10.1057/s41287-020 -00290-z@

Parsons, T. (1965). Full citizenship for the negro American? A sociological problem. *Daedalus*, 94(4), 1009–1054.

Porter, G., Hampshire, K., Abane, A., Munthali, A., Robson, E., De Lannoy, A., et al. (2020). Mobile phones, gender, and female empowerment in sub-Saharan Africa: Studies with African youth. *Information Technology for Development*, 26(1), 180–193.

Pouw, N., Bush, S. and Mangnus, E. (2019). Editorial overview: Inclusive business for sustainability. *Current Opinion in Environmental Sustainability*, 41, A1–A4.

Rijswijk, K., Bulten, E., Klerkx, L., Dessein, J., Debruyne, L., Brunori, G., . . . Metta, M. (2020). Digital transformation of agriculture, forestry and rural areas: Developing a futureproof socio-cyber-physical system. Retrieved from http://desira2020.eu/wp -content/uploads/2020/07/D1.1_CAF-report_I.pdf

Roberts, T. and Hernandez, K. (2019). Digital access is not binary: The 5 'A's of technology access in the Philippines. *The Electronic Journal of Information Systems in Developing Countries*, 85(4), e12084.

Rotz, S., Duncan, E., Small, M., Botschner, J., Dara, R., Mosby, I., … Fraser, E. D. G. (2019). The politics of digital agricultural technologies: A preliminary review. *Sociologia Ruralis*, 59(2), 203–229.

Salemink, K., Strijker, D. and Bosworth, G. (2017). Rural development in the digital age: A systematic literature review on unequal ICT availability, adoption, and use in rural areas. *Journal of Rural Studies*, 54, 360–371.

Sen, A. (2000). *Social exclusion: Concept, application, and scrutiny.* Social Development Papers No. 1, Mandaluyong: Asian Development Bank.

Scholz, R. W., Bartelsman, E. J., Diefenbach, S., Franke, L., Grunwald, A., Helbing, D., ... Montag, C. (2018). Unintended side effects of the digital transition: European scientists' messages from a proposition-based expert round table. *Sustainability*, 10(6), 2001.

Stichweh, R. and Windolf, P. (eds.) (2009). *Inklusion und Exklusion: Analysen zur Sozialstruktur und sozialen Ungleichheit.* VS Verlag für Sozialwissenschaften.

Trendov, N. M., Varas, S. and Zeng M. (2019). *Digital technologies in agriculture and rural areas—Status report.* Rome: FAO.

Tsan, M., Totapally, S., Hailu, M. and Addom, B. (2019). *The digitalisation of African agriculture report 2018-2019.* Wageningen: CTA.

USAID. (2020). *USAID Digital Strategy 2020–2024.* https://www.usaid.gov/digitalstrategy

Van der Burg, S., Bogaardt, M. J. and Wolfert, S. (2019). Ethics of smart farming: Current questions and directions for responsible innovation towards the future. *NJAS - Wageningen Journal of Life Sciences*, 90/91, 100289.

Williamson, B. (2018). *10 definitions of datafication (in education).* Accessed June 8, 2020, https://codeactsineducation.wordpress.com/2018/03/17/10-definitions-datafication/

13

RESPONSIBLY DESIGNING DIGITAL AGRICULTURE SERVICES UNDER UNCERTAINTY IN THE GLOBAL SOUTH

The case of Esoko-Ghana

Andy Bonaventure Nyamekye, Laurens Klerkx, and Art Dewulf

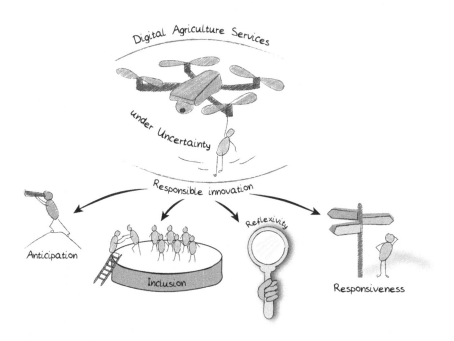

Introduction

With the world population expected to reach close to 10 billion by 2050, innovation in African agriculture is a critical topic (Nelson et al., 2009, Barrett, 2020; Reardon et al., 2019; Hounkonnou et al., 2012). Innovations include new crop

DOI: 10.4324/9781003112525-13

varieties, smart irrigation systems, drone technology, and blockchain and other internet-based solutions driven by mobile technology (Robertson et al., 2016; Wolfert et al., 2017; Shepherd et al., 2020), broadly captured under the banner of 'digital agriculture' (Klerkx et al., 2019). The agricultural sector in Africa is currently experiencing major transformation enabled by digital innovation. Digital services are expected to improve productivity in value chains, in the management of diseases, the efficient use of resources, and the reduction of labour. A surge in public and private enterprises in digital services is providing access to capital, market, weather, extension, and insurance services, mostly through mobile technology (Agyekumhene et al., 2020, Nyamekye et al., 2020, Evans, 2018, Munthali et al., 2018, Fabregas et al., 2019). Many of the proposed benefits of digital agriculture hinge on increased efficiency using precise mechanisation, automation, and improved decision-making. Digital agriculture has the potential to become a game changer in both the Global North and South; but it is also likely that resulting industry-wide digital transformation will create existential questions for agricultural stakeholders as they learn to grasp new ways of working (Barrett, 2020; Herrero et al., 2020; Klerkx and Rose, 2020; Reardon et al., 2019).

Both in the Global North and Global South—though perhaps a better distinction would be between high-income and low- and middle-income countries—such issues have been noted regarding ethics, justice, and exclusion: for example in relation to data ownership and design of digital devices (Barrett, 2020; Fielke et al., 2020; Klerkx et al., 2019; Steinke et al., 2020), so that calls have been made for taking up responsibility in research and innovation (Bronson, 2018; Reardon et al., 2019; van der Burg et al., 2019). RRI is one of the recent frameworks projected to help address these challenges and to streamline innovation by ensuring a well-coordinated innovation process at regional, national, or subnational or organisational levels (De Saille, 2015; Lubberink et al., 2017; Owen et al., 2013; Von Schomberg, 2013).

RRI is underpinned by the argument that present modes of innovating with science and technology are unsuccessful because they fail to sufficiently account for social needs and values (Van Oudheusden, 2014). Furthermore, organisations and individuals innovate in environments characterised by uncertainties as a result of changes in social, economic, and environmental factors, even when these are accounted for (Klerkx et al., 2010; Meijer et al., 2006), and this has also been noted for digital agriculture (Bryant and Higgins, 2020; Eastwood and Renwick, 2020). The RRI framework is expected to help circumvent, eliminate, or manage such uncertainties (Pavie and Carthy, 2015; Tallacchini, 2014; Van Oudheusden, 2014). Furthermore, the RRI framework has now been applied in different national contexts (De Campos et al., 2017; De Hoop et al., 2016; Doezema et al., 2019; Macnaghten, 2020).

Recent literature has paid attention to how RRI principles can be applied to digital agriculture with a focus on high-income countries in Europe, North America, Australia, and New Zealand (Bronson, 2019; Eastwood et al., 2019;

Fielke et al., 2020; Klerkx and Rose, 2020; Rose and Chilvers, 2018). Currently, the application of a framework such as RRI for the Global South (or low- and middle-income countries) is virtually non-existent, but rather concentrates on pockets of generic instruments aimed at strengthening institutions and guiding the innovative process at the country level (Oluwatobi et al., 2015; Sanginga et al., 2009). However, RRI is not always carried out as an organised and discrete process, but may also occur in a more loose or implicit fashion—at least in the early stages—and it remains to be seen how to best operationalise it in the different contexts where digital agriculture is developed (Bronson, 2019; Eastwood et al., 2019) by taking into account the particularities of the field (Rose and Chilvers, 2018).

This chapter focuses on Ghana, where Esoko (a social enterprise) has over the past 12 years provided digital services to farmers and value-chain actors. This includes the introduction of innovative products supported by digital technology amidst institutional, social, and economic changes which have consequences on their operations and services. The study sets out to establish the applicability of RRI framework elements under these conditions in Ghana: we explore how innovation occurs under uncertainty in social enterprises providing digital services to support actionable knowledge creation in food systems.

Nyamekye et al. (2020) in their study of food systems in northern Ghana define actionable knowledge as 'indigenous and scientific knowledge that is locally relevant, trustworthy, and produced in a fair, transparent way.' Whilst Nyamekye et al. approach the study from an actionable knowledge lens as outcome of digital agriculture services, this chapter attempts to unpack the black box of the process of responsible innovation towards digital agriculture services, rather than its outputs. Hence, we investigate how responsible innovation is organised under conditions of uncertainty by the target organisation.

Theoretical framework and research methods: investigating responsible innovation in uncertain conditions

Von Schomberg (2013, p. 19) defines RRI as a 'transparent, interactive process by which societal actors and innovators become mutually responsive to each other with a view to the (ethical) acceptability, sustainability and societal desirability of the innovation process and its marketable products (to allow a proper embedding of scientific and technological advances in our society).' Operationalising RRI as a governance framework, Stilgoe et al. (2013) mention four-dimensions: anticipation, responsiveness, reflexivity, and inclusion.

Anticipation prompts researchers and organisations to ask, 'what if ...?' questions, and to consider contingency, what is known, what is likely, what is plausible, and what is possible. Systematic thinking should shape the agenda of organisations. Anticipation requires foresight and forward-looking decision-making in an attempt to shape expected future states. In what the authors refer to as 'second-order' *reflexivity*, institutions should recognise the value systems (formal or informal) that define their innovation and governance systems. As innovation evolves, it could become essential to reflect on what values should be held, prioritised, or reformed. *Responsiveness* means that institutions as agents of innovation recognise the insufficiency of knowledge and control and can respond to new knowledge, perspectives, and norms. *Inclusion* involves embracing and drawing in multiple stakeholders through partnerships and different forms of collaboration in the innovation process.

Developing digital agriculture innovations happens in a complex and rapidly changing environment (Eastwood et al., 2017; Fielke et al., 2020), and this has implications for organisations (Rijswijk et al., 2019). This makes it critical to establish how the process of responsible innovation occurs within organisations in the face of uncertain developments and unknown futures. Uncertainties challenge organisations in how they deal with complex problems (Dewulf and Biesbroek, 2018; Klijn and Koppenjan, 2016). In establishing what objects of uncertainty arise, Klijn and Koppenjan highlight three objects of uncertainty: substantive, strategic, and institutional. Substantive uncertainty refers to uncertainty about the nature of a problem, its causal factors, and solutions. Strategic uncertainty refers to uncertainty about actors, their interests, and their strategies in engaging with each other; this could involve competition, collaboration, or coalition-building in achieving goals (Dewulf and Biesbroek, 2018). Institutional uncertainty refers to uncertainty about formal and informal rules of the game in the relevant network (Klijn and Koppenjan, 2016).

Uncertainty thus appears to be a challenge for organising RRI. For example, whilst Stilgoe et al. (2013) recognise institutional and cultural resistance to *anticipation*, such resistance could be due to institutional uncertainty about how formal and informal rules might evolve. Stilgoe et al. argue that *institutional reflexivity* holds the promise of self-awareness of lags and limits of knowledge about rules and how they could evolve. The *inclusion* dimension occurs in a condition of strategic uncertainty where organisations, as part of the governance process, have to deal with actor interests and varying ideas in deciding to compete, collaborate, or build coalitions. This makes the pursuit of an inclusive innovative process a high-risk endeavour under conditions of uncertainty (Dewulf and Biesbroek, 2018). About *responsiveness*, institutions' ability to change direction in response to stakeholder values and changing circumstances could occur under conditions of substantive uncertainty related to information—lack, incomplete, or conflicting—about problems they seek to address as innovative entities. Actors could also have different understandings of the problem being addressed.

Operators of digital agriculture services in the Global South, such as Esoko, can face these three objects of uncertainty, thus influencing the degree to which they can enact RRI in design and uptake of digital services (see Figure 13.1). Digital service providers are expected to enhance inclusive measures in their operations and service delivery. Engaging multiple actors also means being able to manage strategic uncertainty from collaborative arrangements and consultative processes. Similarly, adopting an anticipatory lens means they have the

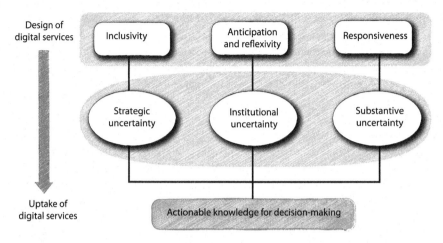

FIGURE 13.1 Conceptualising RRI in relation to design of digital services

ability to align digital innovation to a change in rules, to unpredictability in rules, and to how such transformation impact the innovation process. Hopefully, continuous reflexivity can accelerate instrumentation and strategy development in the governance of the innovative process to address institutional uncertainty in different forms. Accessing and leveraging agricultural data, information, and the translation of information into relevant knowledge whilst minimising substantive uncertainty also improves trust, reliability, and usability of knowledge produced. This is all, however, dependent on responsiveness in the innovation process.

Like Eastwood et al. (2019), we explore how the RRI framework can be made practical in digital agriculture services innovation—or what we will also refer to as responsible design, following Leeuwis et al. (2018). We specifically focus on the organisational level at Esoko.

Inaugurated in 2005 as Tradenet, Esoko was legally incorporated in Ghana with a vision to drive economic empowerment in rural areas by providing digital services. Headquartered in Ghana, the company has over the past years reached farmers in 20 countries with an established presence in Tanzania, Burkina Faso, Malawi, Zimbabwe, Benin, Cote d'Ivoire, Nigeria, and South Africa (See Figure 13.2). In Ghana, Esoko provides information services on market conditions, weather, cropping calendar, nutrition information, and agronomic advice to nearly 3.7 million rural inhabitants.

Our study of Esoko focused on how responsible innovation occurs under conditions of uncertainty in the design of digital services that enable actionable knowledge creation in food systems. The team designed semi-structured interview guides and engaged key staff of Esoko in Ghana. A total of 20 staff members were engaged, spanning technical, field, and administration units.[1] Data was

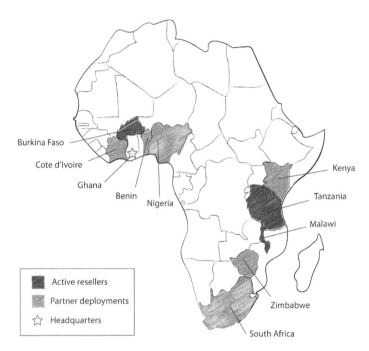

FIGURE 13.2   Geographical footprints of Esoko (2002–2020)

edited and processed, and a thematic analysis was undertaken to interpret the data, guided by the responsible innovation framework.

Enabling inclusivity under strategic uncertainty

Esoko's innovation process is guided by the so-called digital principles for sustainable development.[2] Based on feedback from end-users of digital solutions, the technical team at Esoko go through an iterative process of redesigning the digital solutions. Although the feedback loop is a late end approach to inclusivity, the process of engaging end-users from the product design stage is expensive in terms of time and capital. End-users such as farmers, mostly in rural areas, are perceived to have low technical know-how required to support the design of digital services. Thus Esoko faces strategic uncertainty about the willingness and capability of actors to be included in the technology design process

Following Tongia and Subrahmanian (2006), iterative feedback cycles must be accounted for during the specification of solutions. Although Esoko has a number of internally designed policy instruments (Quality Assurance Policy, Equality and Diversity Policy, Environmental Policy, Health and Safety Policy, Grievance Procedure Policy), a pathway to inclusive design and scaling of digital solutions is yet to be tabled. The absence of a clear strategy or 'regulative configuration' (Steinke et al., 2020) for inclusivity in the presence of the adopted digital principles creates a vacuum where a tailor-made strategy would have increased the stepwise and incremental approach to success in uptake of digital solutions and of services rendered. This, however, is yet to be appreciated, as the following quote illustrates:

> Esoko Operations Officer: Innovation is the foundation of Esoko. We always listen to our cherished customers and generate ideas to find solutions to their problems. To us, we innovate together with our customers because they introduce the problems and possible solutions to us.

Focusing on the external environment, Esoko is only required to satisfy regulations on data protection (Data Protection Act 2012—Act 843) enacted by the Parliament of Ghana in 2012 in the absence of a clear regulatory framework on digital agriculture—which are, however, emerging more broadly in recent times, e.g. Ayamga et al. (2020). Thus, before the enactment of the Data Protection Act, Esoko relied on internal ethical guidelines on data protection. Here, Esoko, like most enterprises set up before the enactment of the Data Protection Act, operated within a space of institutional uncertainty, with the interpretation of data protection limited to internal framing. Also, in the absence of a national framework on innovation in agriculture, the process of designing digital solutions is limited to the company's internal compliance measures informed by a list of international best practices deemed relatable to; a situation that an inclusive process could impact heavily towards creating responsible digital services that better contribute to actionable knowledge creation in food systems in which they are applied. Whilst Eastwood et al. (2019), Ortiz-Crespo et al. (2020), and Steinke et al. (2020) highlight strengthening user-centred design parameters for this purpose, Karpouzoglou et al. (2016), in their discussion of 'second generation' innovations, present co-creation and coordination as key elements for actor inclusivity.

   Thus, the fair and transparent production of knowledge begins with a conscious, inclusive process of engaging end-users in responsible design. With the state as a regulator, the absence of regulatory frameworks could be compensated for by a consultative process where operators engage state regulatory institutions, who, all things being equal, seek to protect the masses from ethical and moral concerns associated with technology adoption in agriculture (van der Burg et al. 2019).

Enabling anticipation and reflexivity under institutional uncertainty

The study also set out to understand how uncertainty about rules challenges anticipation and reflexivity in the innovation process. From the study, we see a combination of anticipatory and reflexive processes being employed by Esoko.

For example, following the deployment of digital solutions, market research is undertaken for feedback from end-users which is collated and presented by the marketing team to the product and operations team. Internal meetings are organised to discuss the relevance of feedback from the operations point of view. The product team then reports any relevant suggestions to the engineering team to ensure digital solutions are fit-for-purpose. Here, the enterprise uses a reflexive process to deal with informal rules in the user environment that were not anticipated. This allows the company to manage institutional uncertainty that is presented in the form of change in local conditions in user communities. The downside of this process, however, is the limited connection of the product review process to new debates in the digital landscape.

Esoko anticipates that rules on the operations of digital agriculture services might change across all levels of governance. For example, the buzz created by the government of Ghana concerning a digital economy might lead to the introduction of new rules in the near future. Furthermore, significant change is anticipated in conditions set by development agencies related to engaging private companies in programmes and project implementation in the fields of digital agriculture. However, until such changes are observed, anticipatory planning within the company is influenced strongly by end-user feedback.

Groves (2015), in referring to *reflexive* uncertainty and dealing with 'a double mind,' calls for an *ex-ante* approach in determining future responsibility, even though this is difficult when technological innovations are complex. As part of the prototyping and product development, Esoko could explore hypothetical scenarios to better establish existing uncertainties and new uncertainties that could arise. This includes addressing questions on usefulness and usability, with the logic that product innovation is not an end in itself but a continuous loop that must evolve as society evolves, or through forward decision-making (Bas and Guillo, 2015). In establishing a connection to actionable knowledge creation, the reflexive and anticipatory process enhances sharing, learning, and appreciation of rules and how they change, thereby enabling transparency and potential uptake and application of knowledge produced through user adoption of digital services.

Enabling responsiveness under substantive uncertainty

Part of Esoko's success hinges on its ability to minimise substantive uncertainty associated with information provided to end-users. For example, Esoko repackages weather forecasts from the Ghana Meteorological Agency and its partners as climate-smart agricultural information and channels it to farmers, extension officers, and water managers in its beneficiary communities. Esoko thus aims to inform farmer decisions on pre-season and in-season activities ranging from land preparation to harvesting. For the end-user, the accuracy of the forecast is crucial. The presence of a call centre at Esoko as a channel for direct interaction between farmers and experts helps manage ambiguities, misconceptions, and misinterpretation of forecast information. Farmers can also inquire directly

TABLE 13.1 Summary of findings on improving innovation in social enterprises

RRI principle	Related uncertainty	Esoko's challenges	Mechanisms to address challenges
Inclusivity.	Strategic Uncertainty.	Blurred frameworks on inclusion.	Define co-creation and coordination elements for engaging actors (Karpouzoglou et al., 2016). Strengthen user-centred design parameters (Eastwood et al., 2019, Steinke et al., 2020).
Anticipation and reflexivity.	Institutional uncertainty.	Changes in formal and informal rules.	Adopt a forward-looking decision-making approach (Bas and Guillo, 2015).
Responsiveness.	Substantive Uncertainty.	Information asymmetry and lack thereof.	Adopt citizen science approaches (Cieslik et al., 2017; Munthali et al., 2018). Integrate different knowledge systems in information framing (Nyadzi et al., 2019).

before receiving information on their mobile phones. The responsive process enabled by the call centre helps manage differences in framing, expectations, and trust.

Following Agyekumhene et al. (2020), however, the pursuit of trust and information symmetry on the side of service providers could be counterproductive given that farmers, due to limited inclusiveness in design, interpret this as surveillance and control. Also, Nyadzi et al. (2019) point to knowledge integration in dealing with substantive uncertainty due to information asymmetry. Nyadzi et al. confirm findings of enhanced trust for weather and seasonal information among farmers in northern Ghana when scientific and indigenous knowledge is integrated (see Table 13.1).

Conclusion

The RRI framework holds promise to support responsible innovation in digital agriculture now and in the future. Whilst appreciating its significance, this study nevertheless argues that an extension of the framework to digital service provision in Ghana, using Esoko as a case study, can be challenging given the existing strategic, institutional, and substantive uncertainty. Firstly, in the context of poor regulatory and policy frameworks around digital agriculture, the

RRI framework would be challenging to implement 'to the letter,' mainly due to strategic uncertainties with potential impact on inclusive design of digital services. The RRI framework must therefore be weighted with the state of strategic governance and the degree to which governance parameters serve as enablers. Secondly, changes in rules—just as much as their absence—shape practices and have consequences on the adoption of digital services, which are pertinent to reflexivity and anticipation in responsible innovation. Lastly, in contexts where unfavourable environmental and climatic conditions pose uncertainties with consequences on information provision, responsiveness in providing digital services could be hampered.

These uncertainties indicate as yet a limited 'readiness' to enact RRI in the setting that was analysed; this resembles the point made by Eastwood et al. (2019) that RRI, in settings where there is limited experience applying it, is initially patchy. In view of these uncertainties, as discussed by Rose and Chilvers (2018) and Bronson (2019), an RRI rubric for digital agriculture is needed. Such a rubric could not only foster the goals of reflexivity and inclusion in digital agriculture in the Global North where RRI has been mostly applied as a concept to support digital agriculture innovation, but also in North–South collaborations in the digital agriculture space. This would require due attention to making RRI locally applicable and culturally sensitive (Doezema et al., 2019; Klerkx et al., 2019; Macnaghten et al., 2014): in view of the global political economy of digital agriculture (Clapp and Ruder, 2020; Rikap and Lundvall, 2020), RRI in this case would need to increase attention to power dimensions and dependency relationships.

Notes

1 11 Technical Officers, 8 Market Enumerators and 1 Operations Officer.
2 These principles have been endorsed by over 54 international organisations led by the United States Agency for International Development. See: https://digitalprinciples .org/.

References

Agyekumhene, C., De Vries, J., Paassen, A. V., Schut, M. and Macnaghten, P. (2020). Making smallholder value chain partnerships inclusive: Exploring digital farm monitoring through farmer friendly smartphone platforms. *Sustainability*, 12, 4580.

Ayamga, M., Tekinerdogan, B., Kassahun, A., & Rambaldi, G. (2021). Developing a policy framework for adoption and management of drones for agriculture in Africa. *Technology Analysis & Strategic Management*. 33(8), 970–987.

Barrett, C. B. (2020). Overcoming global food security challenges through science and solidarity. *American Journal of Agricultural Economics*. Early view, available online. https://doi.org/10.1111/ajae.12160

Bas, E. and Guillo, M. (2015). Participatory foresight for social innovation. FLUX-3D method (Forward Looking User Experience), a tool for evaluating innovations. *Technological Forecasting and Social Change*, 101, 275–290.

Bronson, K. (2018). Smart farming: Including rights holders for responsible agricultural innovation. *Technology Innovation Management Review*, 8, 7–14.

Bronson, K. (2019). Looking through a responsible innovation lens at uneven engagements with digital farming. *NJAS-Wageningen Journal of Life Sciences*, 90, 100294.

Bryant, M. and Higgins, V. (2020). Securitising uncertainty: Ontological security and cultural scripts in smart farming technology implementation. *Journal of Rural Studies*, 81, 315–323.

Clapp, J. and Ruder, S.-L. (2020). Precision technologies for agriculture: Digital farming, gene-edited crops, and the politics of sustainability. *Global Environmental Politics*, 20, 49–69.

De Campos, A. S., Hartley, S., De Koning, C., Lezaun, J. and Velho, L. (2017). Responsible innovation and political accountability: Genetically modified mosquitoes in Brazil. *Journal of Responsible Innovation*, 4, 5–23.

De Hoop, E., Pols, A. and Romijn, H. (2016). Limits to responsible innovation. *Journal of Responsible Innovation*, 3, 110–134.

De Saille, S. (2015). Innovating innovation policy: The emergence of 'Responsible Research and Innovation'. *Journal of Responsible Innovation*, 2, 152–168.

Dewulf, A. and Biesbroek, R. (2018). Nine lives of uncertainty in decision-making: strategies for dealing with uncertainty in environmental governance. *Policy and Society*, 37, 441–458.

Doezema, T., Ludwig, D., Macnaghten, P., Shelley-Egan, C. and Forsberg, E.-M. (2019). Translation, transduction, and transformation: Expanding practices of responsibility across borders. *Journal of Responsible Innovation*, 6, 323–331.

Eastwood, C., Klerkx, L., Ayre, M. and Rue, B. D. (2019). Managing socio-ethical challenges in the development of smart farming: From a fragmented to a comprehensive approach for responsible research and innovation. *Journal of Agricultural and Environmental Ethics*, 32, 741–768.

Eastwood, C., Klerkx, L. and Nettle, R. (2017). Dynamics and distribution of public and private research and extension roles for technological innovation and diffusion: Case studies of the implementation and adaptation of precision farming technologies. *Journal of Rural Studies*, 49, 1–12.

Eastwood, C. and Renwick, A. (2020). Innovation uncertainty impacts the adoption of smarter farming approaches. *Frontiers in Sustainable Food Systems*, 4(24), 1–14.

Evans, O. (2018). Digital agriculture: Mobile phones, internet & agricultural development in Africa. *Actual Problems of Economics*, 7/8(205/206), 76–90.

Fabregas, R., Kremer, M. and Schilbach, F. (2019). Realizing the potential of digital development: The case of agricultural advice. *Science*, 366.

Fielke, S., Taylor, B. and Jakku, E. (2020). Digitalisation of agricultural knowledge and advice networks: A state-of-the-art review. *Agricultural Systems*, 180, 102763.

Groves, C. (2015). Logic of choice or logic of care? Uncertainty, technological mediation and responsible innovation. *NanoEthics*, 9, 321–333.

Herrero, M., Thornton, P. K., Mason-D'croz, D., Palmer, J., Benton, T. G., Bodirsky, B. L., Bogard, J. R., Hall, A., Lee, B. and Nyborg, K. (2020). Innovation can accelerate the transition towards a sustainable food system. *Nature Food*, 1, 266–272.

Hounkonnou, D., Kossou, D., Kuyper, T. W., Leeuwis, C., Nederlof, E. S., Röling, N., Sakyi-Dawson, O., Traoré, M. and Van Huis, A. (2012). An innovation systems approach to institutional change: Smallholder development in West Africa. *Agricultural Systems*, 108, 74–83.

Karpouzoglou, T., Zulkafli, Z., Grainger, S., Dewulf, A., Buytaert, W. and Hannah, D. M. (2016). Environmental virtual observatories (EVOs): Prospects for knowledge co-creation and resilience in the information age. *Current Opinion in Environmental Sustainability*, 18, 40–48.

Klerkx, L., Aarts, N. and Leeuwis, C. (2010). Adaptive management in agricultural innovation systems: The interactions between innovation networks and their environment. *Agricultural Systems*, 103, 390–400.

Klerkx, L., Jakku, E., & Labarthe, P. (2019). A review of social science on digital agriculture, smart farming and agriculture 4.0: New contributions and a future research agenda. *NJAS-Wageningen Journal of Life Sciences*. 90–91, 100315.

Klerkx, L. and Rose, D. (2020). Dealing with the game-changing technologies of Agriculture 4.0: How do we manage diversity and responsibility in food system transition pathways? *Global Food Security*, 24, 100347.

Klijn, E.-H. and Koppenjan, J. (2016). The shift toward network governance. In: de Walle, S. and Groeneveld, S. (eds.). *Theory and practice of public sector reform*. Milton Park: Routledge, 158–177.

Leeuwis, C., Cieslik, K., Aarts, M., Dewulf, A., Ludwig, F., Werners, S. and Struik, P. (2018). Reflections on the potential of virtual citizen science platforms to address collective action challenges: Lessons and implications for future research. *NJAS-Wageningen Journal of Life Sciences*, 86, 146–157.

Lubberink, R., Blok, V., Van Ophem, J. and Omta, O. (2017). A framework for responsible innovation in the business context: Lessons from responsible-, social-and sustainable innovation. *Responsible Innovation*, 8, 181–207.

Macnaghten, P. (2020). *The making of responsible innovation*. Cambridge: Cambridge University Press.

Macnaghten, P., Owen, R., Stilgoe, J., Wynne, B., Azevedo, A., De Campos, A., Chilvers, J., Dagnino, R., Di Giulio, G. and Frow, E. (2014). Responsible innovation across borders: Tensions, paradoxes and possibilities. *Journal of Responsible Innovation*, 1, 191–199.

Meijer, I. S., Hekkert, M. P., Faber, J. and Smits, R. E. (2006). Perceived uncertainties regarding socio-technological transformations: Towards a framework. *International Journal of Foresight and Innovation Policy*, 2, 214–240.

Munthali, N., Leeuwis, C., Van Paassen, A., Lie, R., Asare, R., Van Lammeren, R. and Schut, M. (2018). Innovation intermediation in a digital age: Comparing public and private new-ICT platforms for agricultural extension in Ghana. *NJAS-Wageningen Journal of Life Sciences*, 86, 64–76.

Nelson, G. C., Rosegrant, M. W., Koo, J., Robertson, R., Sulser, T., Zhu, T., Ringler, C., Msangi, S., Palazzo, A. and Batka, M. (2009). *Climate change: Impact on agriculture and costs of adaptation*. International Food Policy Research Institute.

Nyadzi, E., Werners, E. S., Biesbroek, R., Long, P. H., Franssen, W. and Ludwig, F. (2019). Verification of seasonal climate forecast toward hydroclimatic information needs of rice farmers in Northern Ghana. *Weather, Climate, and Society*, 11, 127–142.

Nyamekye, A. B., Dewulf, A., Van Slobbe, E. and Termeer, K. (2020). Information systems and actionable knowledge creation in rice-farming systems in Northern Ghana. *African Geographical Review*, 39, 144–161.

Oluwatobi, S., Efobi, U., Olurinola, I. and Alege, P. (2015). Innovation in Africa: Why institutions matter. *South African Journal of Economics*, 83, 390–410.

Ortiz-Crespo, B., Steinke, J., Quirós, C. F., van de Gevel, J., Daudi, H., Gaspar Mgimiloko, M., & van Etten, J. (2020). User-centred design of a digital advisory service: Enhancing public agricultural extension for sustainable intensification in Tanzania. *International Journal of Agricultural Sustainability*, 1–17. Online first, https://doi.org/10.1080/14735903.2020.1720474

Owen, R., Bessant, J. R. and Heintz, M. (2013). *Responsible innovation: Managing the responsible emergence of science and innovation in society.* New York: John Wiley & Sons.

Pavie, X. and Carthy, D. (2015). Leveraging uncertainty: A practical approach to the integration of responsible innovation through design thinking. *Procedia—Social and Behavioral Sciences*, 213, 1040–1049.

Reardon, T., Echeverria, R., Berdegué, J., Minten, B., Liverpool-Tasie, S., Tschirley, D. and Zilberman, D. (2019). Rapid transformation of food systems in developing regions: highlighting the role of agricultural research & innovations. *Agricultural Systems*, 172, 47–59.

Rijswijk, K., Klerkx, L. and Turner, J. A. (2019). Digitalisation in the New Zealand agricultural knowledge and innovation system: Initial understandings and emerging organisational responses to digital agriculture. *NJAS-Wageningen Journal of Life Sciences*, 90, 100313.

Rikap, C. and Lundvall, B.-Å. (2020). Big tech, knowledge predation and the implications for development. *Innovation and Development.* Online first, https://doi.org/10.1080/2 157930X.2020.1855825.

Robertson, M., Kirkegaard, J., Rebetzke, G., Llewellyn, R. and Wark, T. (2016). Prospects for yield improvement in the Australian wheat industry: a perspective. *Food and Energy Security*, 5, 107–122.

Rose, D. C. and Chilvers, J. (2018). Agriculture 4.0: Broadening responsible innovation in an era of smart farming. *Frontiers in Sustainable Food Systems*, 2, 87.

Sanginga, P. C., Waters-Bayer, A., Kaaria, S., Wettasinha, C. and Njuki, J. (2009). *Innovation Africa: enriching farmers' livelihoods.* London: Earthscan.

Shepherd, M., Turner, J. A., Small, B. and Wheeler, D. (2020). Priorities for science to overcome hurdles thwarting the full promise of the 'digital agriculture' revolution. *Journal of the Science of Food and Agriculture*, 100, 5083–5092.

Steinke, J., Van Etten, J., Müller, A., Ortiz-Crespo, B., Van De Gevel, J., Silvestri, S. and Priebe, J. (2020). Tapping the full potential of the digital revolution for agricultural extension: an emerging innovation agenda. *International Journal of Agricultural Sustainability*, 1–17, DOI: 10.1080/14735903.2020.1738754

Stilgoe, J., Owen, R. and Macnaghten, P. (2013). Developing a framework for responsible innovation. *Research Policy*, 42, 1568–1580.

Tallacchini, M. (2014). Between uncertainty and responsibility: Precaution and the complex journey towards reflexive innovation. In: Van Asselt, M. B. A., Everson, M. and Vos, E. (eds.). *Trade, Health and the Environment: The European Union put to the test.* Earthscan, 74–88.

Tongia, R. and Subrahmanian, E. (2006) Information and Communications Technology for Development (ICT4D). A design challenge? *International Conference on Information and Communication Technologies and Development, 200*, IEEE, 243–255.

Van Der Burg, S., Bogaardt, M.-J. and Wolfert, S. (2019). Ethics of smart farming: Current questions and directions for responsible innovation towards the future. *NJAS-Wageningen Journal of Life Sciences*, 90, 100289.

Van Oudheusden, M. (2014). Where are the politics in responsible innovation? European governance, technology assessments, and beyond. *Journal of Responsible Innovation*, 1, 67–86.

Von Schomberg, R. (2013). A vision of responsible innovation. In: Owen, R., Heintz, M. and Bessant, J. (eds.). *Responsible Innovation.* Hoboken: John Wiley.

Wolfert, S., Ge, L., Verdouw, C. and Bogaardt, M.-J. (2017). Big data in smart farming–a review. *Agricultural Systems*, 153, 69–80.

14

MOBILISING KNOWLEDGE SHARING IN THE AGRICULTURAL ADVISORY SYSTEM

The case of ICT-facilitated plant doctor chat groups

Šarūnas Jomantas, Nyamwaya Munthali, Annemarie van Paassen, Conny Almekinders, Anna Wood, Christine Alokit, Birgitta Oppong-Mensah, Willis Ochilo, and Dannie Romney

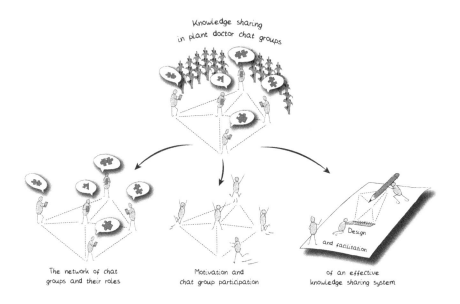

Knowledge sharing in plant doctor chat groups

| The network of chat groups and their roles | Motivation and chat group participation | of an effective knowledge sharing system |

Introduction

The cornerstone of a well-functioning agricultural advisory service is the ability to efficiently reach out; diagnose problems; advise; and disseminate solutions, with the end goal of supporting sustainable livelihoods of the farmers served.

DOI: 10.4324/9781003112525-14

These activities represent the front-office interface of the advisory services. To assure high levels of expertise in meeting information demands presented by farmers, advisory staff attend capacity-building and refresher courses to obtain, share, and absorb the latest knowledge. These are considered back-office operations. Informal networks of expert communities and the horizontal exchange of their collective knowledge and gathered experiences therein play a crucial role in developing and strengthening the skills of the advisory staff (Adolwa et al., 2017; Klerkx and Proctor, 2013; Labarthe and Laurent, 2013; Landini, 2020).

When calls are made to improve agricultural advisory service—through crowdsourcing of agricultural data for research or environmental monitoring (Minet et al., 2017), e-agriculture (FAO, 2015, 2019), or ICTs in general (Barber et al., 2016; Tsan et al., 2019)—the implicit aim is often to improve farmer–advisor exchanges. The rural contexts of developing countries in which these front-office advisories operate are characterised by inadequate internet and energy infrastructure, limited device ownership, and expensive internet access, which pose more hurdles than opportunities to harness ICTs (Aker et al., 2016; Mbagwu et al., 2017). At the same time, means to support advisor–expert interactions within back-office operations remains understudied. One of the advocated innovations to enhance backstopping which merits further exploration is the use of social media (Suchiradipta and Saravanan, 2016) and specific applications such as WhatsApp and Telegram that support chat groups. The potential of these platforms to facilitate interaction among geographically widespread actors makes them especially attractive for decentralised collection and sharing of data among agricultural advisory services. Advisors may benefit from the online sharing of resourceful content supporting informal learning (Teo et al., 2017), while discussion with experts may lead to resolution of arising issues and challenges in the field (Saravanan & Vasumathi, 2016). Although ambitions and expectations for the use of chat groups in advisory services are high, research on their actual use remains marginal and anecdotal (Ifejika et al., 2019; Raj et al., 2020; Thakur and Chander, 2017). We therefore share and reflect on the CABI-led Plantwise programme experiences with chat group use to benefit agricultural advisory services and consider how they can be more deliberately used and integrated to support service delivery.

Plantwise: ICT-enhanced advisory services in practice

Plantwise transitioned from a CABI project into a global programme in 2012. Its goal is to strengthen national plant health advisory systems from within, enabling countries to provide farmers with the knowledge they need to lose less crops and feed more people (www.plantwise.org). Plantwise is active in 26 countries worldwide (at the time of writing) and is working closely with national agricultural advisory services. The programme establishes and actively supports the national agricultural ministries of each country through a network of plant clinics, run by two or three national advisory staff who are trained for an additional job title of *plant doctor*. In these plant clinics, farmers get free practical advice about specific crop pests and diseases and their respective treatments (Bentley et al., 2018; Majuga et al., 2018). Plant clinics are organised near busy rural markets on a rotating basis once every 1–2 weeks, but sometimes also less often. They function like human health clinics, as affected crop samples brought by farmers are diagnosed by plant doctors who then provide evidence-based recommendations on correct treatment/management. Even when they are not running plant clinics, plant doctors use the acquired knowledge to follow up and advise farmers. In case emerging crop problems identified at the clinics show the potential to affect a large numbers of farmers, mass extension campaigns using plant health rallies, radio, video, or mobile messaging are employed to maximize overall outreach.

Having trained 11,000 plant doctors and established 4,500 plant clinics worldwide, Plantwise estimates its direct reach in 2019 alone was around 2.6 million farmers with approximately 27,000 farmer visits to the plant clinics (CABI, 2020), with the remainder reached through mass extension campaigns. Several studies indicate that the initiative is delivering impact at farm level. In Rwanda, plant clinics were able to improve the household food security of the farmers who sought advice, decreasing the food shortage period by a month (Tambo et al., 2019). The clinics have also led to significant yield and income increases—28% and 23% respectively—for maize alone (Tambo et al., 2020). In Zambia, clinic attendees were shown to share clinic advice with friends and neighbours, thus expanding the programme's reach and impact (Danielsen et al., 2020). An evaluation of the Plantwise programe in Kenya (Bonilla et al., 2018) observed that farmers within a 1.5 km radius of a clinic had 9% higher maize yields and net benefits compared to other farmers, estimating returns to investment in the Plantwise programme of 3:1.

To further improve the advisory services of the plant doctors, Plantwise has been integrating tablets into plant clinic operations across several African countries: Kenya, Uganda, Rwanda, Mozambique, Malawi, Zambia, Ethiopia, and Ghana. The purpose of these devices is twofold: first, they provide plant doctors with online and offline access to pest diagnosis and management information within the global Plantwise Knowledge Bank; second, the devices are used by plant doctors to collect data during plant clinic consultations, rapidly uploading them to nationwide databases, providing key information to monitor and manage pests' emergence, and supporting decision-making and policy. To support the rollout stage of the tablet adoption and to troubleshoot any soft- or hardware related issues of the geographically widespread workforce, the tablets came with a preinstalled Telegram[1] chat application. In Uganda, where tablets were not given out, plant doctors use their smartphones to collect data, access the knowledge bank, and participate in Plantwise initiated online chat groups.

On their own initiative plant doctors began to use these chat groups to communicate on a wide range of topics, sharing observations on pest incidence, seeking advice on treating less-common plant pests, discussing logistics, and also socialising with colleagues. A Plantwise survey in Ghana found that plant doctors adapted the use of the chat groups because they were user-friendly, enabled interaction with otherwise busy colleagues, and facilitated immediate two-way communication in large groups (Munthali et al., 2021). Although varying from country to country, Plantwise adopted the practice of adding new trainees to both dedicated small groups of local trainees and larger national chat groups.

These online spaces facilitating interactions became nationwide peer-to-peer support groups of geographically dispersed plant doctors, with additional input provided by national experts in plant protection and research. To monitor unanswered diagnostic queries and provide additional support CABI's international plant disease experts also joined the chat groups. This further accelerated vertical information flows within national plant health systems.

In 2017 these online communities contributed to the early identification, flagging, and tracking of the fall armyworm (FAW)—an invasive pest feeding on over 80 different crops that first appeared on the African continent in 2016 (Abrahams et al., 2017; Day et al., 2017). Interestingly, although the national government had not yet officially identified the pest, the plant doctor chat groups began communicating on a strange sightings affecting the maize suspecting it to potentially be a case of FAW. Looking at these chat group exchanges, national staff and international experts were quickly able to confirm this to be the case. Once the pest was formally recognised at the country level as FAW, methods for diagnosis and management were rapidly disseminated across the very same chat groups.

Likewise, chat groups raised awareness about regional occurrences of maize lethal necrosis disease (MLND) and the tomato leaf-miner (*Tuta Absoluta*), and more recently the desert locust (*Schistocerca gregaria*). The chat groups have partially also led to an early detection and agile interception at the early phase of these outbreaks contributing to the overall management of pests such as FAW across Kenya, Rwanda, and Uganda (Bundi et al., submitted) and other African countries where Plantwise was active. Furthermore, connections between experts, advisors, and field staff across a national advisory system chat groups can serve as horizontal and vertical information exchange networks, where knowledge sharing supports learning and capacity building of the advisory staff (Adolwa et al., 2017; Klerkx and Proctor, 2013; Labarthe and Laurent, 2013; Landini, 2020). In line with such findings, in Ghana in 2019, knowledge sharing related to pest identification and control across chat groups was accompanied with approximately 20 lectures on relevant pest management topics. Although experts contributed during lectures, interestingly, all but one was prepared and delivered by plant doctors (CABI Internal Communication). However, to structurally embed and to further support the functioning of Plantwise chat groups, more understanding of the social dynamics and roles of Plantwise and related chat groups is needed.

The functioning of chat groups in the agricultural advisory system

In this section, we use scientific literature, the research of Munthali et al. (2021) on chat groups in Ghana's agricultural advisory system, and other insights from Plantwise to reflect on documented Plantwise chat group experiences. These insights are used to consider possible future dynamics and functioning of the Plantwise backstopping chat groups across pluralistic agricultural advisory systems in Africa.

The network of chat groups and their roles

CABI supports plant doctor chat groups in eight of the 12 African countries where Plantwise is active. In each country, there are both large national Plantwise chat groups (230 members in Ghana, 200 in Kenya, and 140 in Uganda) and smaller ones (less than 50) functioning parallel to each other. The Plantwise groups differ in both size and actor composition with larger national Plantwise groups constituted by geographically dispersed frontline plant doctors and their supervisors, who are supported by CABI, other diagnostic experts from various crop protection services, research and teaching institutions, input supply companies, and in some cases, representatives of NGOs and other organisations involved in advisory service delivery (CABI internal reports). In contrast, the smaller Plantwise groups are more homogenous, comprising plant doctors from specific districts or those recently trained, with members of these groups having tighter-knit personal connections (CABI internal reports). Besides these chat groups, plant doctors also participate in District Extension Office (DEO) chat groups of field staff, specialised officers, and district directors (Munthali et al., 2021). Similar to smaller Plantwise groups, the members of the DEO chat group are also relatively homogeneous and highly connected as they work in the same locality and/or organisation.

The size and composition of the chat groups more or less determine the focus and communication dynamics. In Ghana, Munthali et al. (2021) found that the DEO group was ten times smaller than the Plantwise national group (n=38 vs. n=235) and the interaction was more frequent and egalitarian, with a substantially higher number of social and informal messages (Table 14.1). In comparison, the much larger national Plantwise group, connecting geographically widespread actors, was more task-oriented. Plantwise members were also asked to share social content on alternative, private channels, and the chat group was mainly used for knowledge sharing to creatively solve emerging (new) problems.

In both chat groups, the high average clustering coefficient for receiving messages combined with the lower coefficient for sending messages shows a relative centralised communication structure (Table 14.1). The average degree for sending was considerably higher for the DEO chat group than for the national

TABLE 14.1 Type and frequency of messages in the DEO and National Plantwise chat group in Ghana, 2018

	District Extension Office chat group (n = 38, July 2017–June 2018 = 11 months)	National Plantwise chat group (n = 235, April 2017–June 2018 = 14 months)
Types of messages		
Social messages	372 (61%)	5 (1%)
Work notifications	166 (27%)	114 (24%)
Knowledge sharing for problem solving	45 (7%)	295 (63%)
Knowledge dissemination	15 (2%)	23 (5%)
Pest/disease monitoring	7 (1%)	32 (7%)
Total number messages	605 (100%)	469 (100%)
Average number messages per month	55	33.5
Average number messages per month, per person)	1.4	0.14
Clustering coefficient of receiving messages★	>0.6	>0.6
Clustering coefficient of sending messages★	0.51	0.13

Source: Munthali et al (2021)

★Clustering coefficients show the extent to which actors connect to each other. Measuring involves establishing for each actor (the ego) the actors it is linked to (neighbours), calculating the ratio to which the ego's neighbours are connected to each other. If the node's neighbours are fully connected the clustering coefficient is 1, whilst 0 means there are no connections among neighbours and they are pendant to the ego. The coefficient can be measured in terms of in-coming connections (receiving messages) and out-going connections (sending messages)

Plantwise group, indicating a more egalitarian communication structure. The average number of messages per month, per person, was also much higher (1.4 against 0.14). Although Colfer and Baldwin (2016) suggest that heterogeneous actors from different organisational backgrounds tend to have less restrained interactions as they are less susceptible to follow the institutional hierarchies of a specific entity, Plantwise data suggests the opposite.

When we look at the group structures that emerged from the members' interactions in the DEO and national Plantwise chat group, the former tends to display more *bonding* social capital and the latter more *bridging* social capital. Bonding social capital is associated with strong ties: long-term relationships within relatively homogeneous networks, characterised by trust and informal collaboration and access to similar information and resources (Claridge, 2018). Bridging social capital is associated with weak ties: relationships between heterogeneous actors or communities that lack a sense of belonging but have access to broader information and resources (Claridge, 2018; Putnam, 2000). These distinct chat group characteristics enable the groups to play different but complementary roles in knowledge sharing: local chat groups, displaying strong bonding, focus on routine practices and advice; while the national chat groups can be characterised as 'bridging,' with a high diversity of knowledge for creative problem solving. The different group structures enable both bridging and bonding social capital to be used in fulfilling different, complementary roles in knowledge sharing (Cofré-Bravo et al., 2019; Klerkx and Proctor, 2013).

Findings from Munthali et al. (2021) show that in Ghana the local and national chat groups did indeed play active complementary mutual supporting roles in the advisory system. Local chat groups were primarily used in coordinating 'the last mile' extension—logistics, plant clinic organisation, and other agricultural department announcements. The local and practical orientation of the smaller groups also makes them useful for maintaining adequate knowledge, for routine problem solving, and for operational effectiveness. The national Plantwise chat groups with a higher number of members, including experts with specific types of experiential and scientific knowledge, served as a rich source of guidance for non-routine problem solving. Data showed that the local chat groups provided an overview of pest/disease occurrences in their area, and when forwarded to the national chat group, provided a timely overview of the situation, enabling national plant health staff to determine threats and knowledge gaps, and share possible solutions. Furthermore, the act of sharing of information also served to link the actors (mainly plant doctors). Whether other chat groups of local advisory officers across Africa demonstrate similar communication dynamics and roles with respect to the national Plantwise chat groups requires further research.

Motivation and chat group participation

What drives chat group members to participate in the different platforms related to Plantwise, enhancing knowledge sharing? Relatively little is known about the individual motivations for participation. A survey amongst plant doctors in Ghana alludes to the desire to report new problems and also offer viable solutions to problems posted by colleagues—especially in cases of managing new pests, such as fall armyworm (Munthali et al., forthcoming). Similar results by Chaouali (2016) and Huang et al. (2017) demonstrate that participation in institutional chat groups is often based on feelings of being useful, resulting in positive emotions of enjoyment and satisfaction.

However, despite these motivations, it was established that in the national Plantwise group and DEO chat groups relatively few users actively posted content (Munthali et al., forthcoming). A network analysis of the communication patterns for the national Plantwise chat group in Ghana showed that the majority of messages were generated by a few active users, with a significant difference between the number of senders and receivers highlighting a centralised communication structure (Table 14.1). Similarly, looking at hundreds of thousands of Persian chat groups on Telegram, Hashemi and Chahooki (2019) find that across professional chat groups it is common for fewer users to create the majority of exchanged content—similar to our Plantwise observations. In comparison to the large national Plantwise group, the smaller non-CABI DEO chat group had a higher average number of messages per month and per person, and showed a much more egalitarian communication structure. In terms of content, this group was very active in providing advice and guidance also marked by a much higher number of social message exchanges compared to work coordination and task- and knowledge-related messages (Table 14.1). District agricultural directors and specialised officers coordinating the work were the most active members. In the national Plantwise chat group, participants were asked to share only knowledge-related messages and abstain from posting social messages. Within these same chat groups Subject Matter Specialists—researchers and respected plant doctors—were was very active in providing advice and guidance, while ordinary extension offic-ers were of the view that they should mainly listen. It was also noted that when the specialists and researchers were silent or took longer to respond to queries, the number of plant doctor peer-to-peer exchanges increased (Munthali, 2021).

The design and facilitation of an effective knowledge sharing system

Though the functioning of the local and national chat groups may have relied on a few active members, it was observed that there were periods of high activity around new emerging pests and diseases such as FAW, MLND, and the tomato leaf-miner. However, later on chat groups initiated by Plantwise began display-ing periods of low activity. For example, in Kenya and Uganda the number of shared messages decreased after a peak in 2018, yet it was also noted that active facilitation of the groups—prompting experts to respond to queries and intro-ducing initiatives such as mini-lectures—had the effect of encouraging overall participation (CABI internal reports).

One question that remains is whether dwindling activity of a national Plantwise group is always an issue for concern. We found that offline and online meetings of DEOs and projects or local Plantwise groups complement and nur-ture national Plantwise chat groups, enhancing timely, relevant, and effective knowledge sharing systems for creative problem solving. If such localised groups with high levels of social capital and activity, and an interest in pest and disease management exists, it may be opportune for CABI to rely on these group for local level pest monitoring and to further concentrate on supporting national backstopping via online platforms.

As highlighted by Birner et al. (2009) as well as Faure et al. (2016), contex-tual factors such as the policy environment; agricultural production and market systems; and the farm community aspects define the needs for advisory services. Within this context, a pluralistic advisory service system is shaped by the type of actors providing advice (actors of the state, NGO/farmer organisation, or private sector); the actors' specific mission and funding requirements that they must comply with; their staff and financial capacity; and their internal styles of management and advisory communication. The various advisory service providers have their internal offline and online communication focus and styles, and they interact with other system actors in offline and online platforms. This leads to a self-organised system of offline and online platforms with specific focuses and interaction patterns; bonding and bridging characteristics, and roles performed within the advisory system.

Domain-specific backstopping chat groups, such as those initiated by Plantwise, need to strategically embed themselves in an existing pluralistic advisory system. Based on our findings, we recommend that national backstopping initiatives should (a) encourage the participation of communicative, responsible actors with strong and relevant local, organisation, or project-related advisory experience in nationwide exchanges; (b) encourage proactive exchange in smaller localised groups while raising unresolved issues to the national groups; and (c) integrate facilitation within all groups, ensuring that all queries get answered.

Regarding the latter, we observe several factors that warrant facilitation interventions over chat groups. We know that in Ghana and Uganda plant doctors are inclined to remain silent in chat groups to create room for expert opinions. Furthermore, it is a natural group dynamic to be active when issues need to be tackled, followed by phases of inactivity (Rybski et al., 2012). Temporary inactivity is not a problem, but group participation might be structurally affected when central users fall silent or leave groups when switching jobs, leading to a sudden drop in content that once was instrumental in catalysing active engagement. Prolonged periods of low activity may also decrease members' alertness or interest to share problems and knowledge in chat groups. Kelly et al. (2017), who studied online social media for agricultural advisory services in India and Australia, therefore concluded that continuous facilitation by experts was key for attaining knowledge sharing and learning.

A moderator can facilitate knowledge sharing and support learning, but needs participants to aggregate and analyse mobilised data and knowledge, adding insights from elsewhere to feedback into the dialogue for learning (Van Paassen et al., 2011). Moderators—as chat group administrators—have been shown to be key in keeping professional chat groups organised, while assuring that shared content meets overall institutional objectives (Hashemi and Chahooki, 2019). A chat group moderator within groups may therefore (a) stimulate sharing field experiences for monitoring of emerging problems; (b) encourage and guide knowledge sharing and learning about pests, diseases, and applied management practices; (c) invite (experiential and science-based) experts and researchers to aggregate the data, analyse, and feedback insights; (d) act as a conduit for anonymous queries or comments where junior staff feel uncomfortable posting on groups including senior staff or experts; and (e) discourage off-topic chats where needed.

With regard to facilitation, it is critical to encourage the more experienced plant doctors to contribute to discussions, as users' interest is often attracted not by content, but who is sharing it (think of social media influencers); this was explicitly reported in the Uganda network. Therefore, identifying influential/central group members within chat groups might be key to ensuring that users are cognizant of shared content. Likewise, one should consider encouraging participation of subject matter specialists and researchers, providing them with incentives such as remuneration for time spent, capacity-building opportunities, and career advancement/promotions (Bitzer, 2016). Priharsari et al. (2020) also conclude that such a reward system is essential to co-create value, when organisations seek to connect their workforce via online networks.

Conclusion

The experience with the Plantwise chat groups shows that, in contrast to other pre-defined and elaborate ICT apps, agricultural professionals tend to shape chat groups to functions complementary to existing offline (and online) meetings in their locality and/or organisation. More specifically, groups of newly trained plant doctors received tablets to collect data and access the knowledge bank, but soon started to use the chat function for nationwide troubleshooting on diagnosis and management of pests, and to raise awareness and rapidly share information on emerging pests. Recently, formal learning has been expanded to cover areas identified as desired by plant doctors and provided through 'mini-lectures'. More local (e.g. DEO or NGO project-related) chat groups are used, in contrast, for socialising and timely organisation of routine tasks. Hence, chat groups are self-organised, and play useful and important roles within organisations and between different actors in pluralistic advisory systems.

As chat groups proliferate, it is important to know how these platforms can be structurally embedded within organisational practices and how they can be facilitated and managed effectively. Looking at the interaction dynamics of the groups, we noted smaller groups encouraged bonding social capital; they also exhibited less restricted exchanges between group members that were more confident to post to a group of (mainly) peers or well-known individuals in the hierarchy, supporting the organisation of routine tasks. In contrast, large heterogeneous groups encouraged bridging social capital with the potential to access broader expertise outside immediate social groups to flag and timely solve emerging problems.

Facilitation and proper rewarding of experts could help to ensure the dynamism of the groups, encourage sharing of experiences, and the resolution of queries from the group, keeping the groups focused where necessary. In the longer term, guidelines defining official roles and responsibilities may support long-term sustainability and usefulness of groups. Although the value of spontaneous evolution of groups has been recognised, further work is required to understand and effectively support advisory group functions in different geographies and institutional contexts.

Note

1 At this time the firmware of the tablets could not support the use of WhatsApp.

References

Abrahams, P., Beale, T., Cock, M., Corniani, N., Day, R., Godwin, J., ... and Vos, J., (2017). *Fall armyworm status. Impacts and control options in Africa: Preliminary Evidence Note (April 2017)*. CABI, UK.

Adolwa, I. S., Schwarze, S., Bellwood-Howard, I., Schareika, N. and Buerkert, A., (2017). A comparative analysis of agricultural knowledge and innovation systems in Kenya and Ghana: Sustainable agricultural intensification in the rural–urban interface. *Agriculture and Human Values*, 34(2), 453–472.

Aker, J. C., Ghosh, I. and Burrell, J. (2016). The promise (and pitfalls) of ICT for agriculture initiatives. *Agricultural Economics*, 47(S1), 35–48.

Barber, J., Mangnus, E. and Bitzer, V. (2016). Harnessing ICT for agricultural extension. KIT Working Paper 2016, KIT Royal Tropical Institute.

Bentley, J. W., Danielsen, S., Phiri, N., Tegha, Y. C., Nyalugwe, N., Neves, E., Hidalgo, E., Sharma, A., Pandit, V. and Sharma, D. R. (2018). Farmer responses to technical advice offered at plant clinics in Malawi, Costa Rica and Nepal. *International Journal of Agricultural Sustainability*, 16(2), 187–200.

Birner R., Davis, K. E., Pender, J., Nkonya, E., Anandajayasekeram, P., Ekboir, J., Mbabu, A., Spielman, D. J., Horna, D., Benin, S. and Cohen, M. (2009). From best practice to best fit: A framework for designing and analyzing pluralistic agricultural advisory services worldwide. *Journal of Agricultural Education and Extension*, 15(4), 341–355.

Bitzer, V. (2016). Incentives for enhanced performance of agricultural extension systems. *Kit Sustainable Economic Development & Gender*, 6, 1–8.

Bonilla J., Coombes A., & Molotsky A. 2018. *Plantwise impact: Results and lessons from Kenya*. CABI, 8. https://doi.org/10.1079/CABICOMM-62-8090

Bundi, M., Oronje, M. L., Romney, D. and Hunt, S. (submitted). Social media and other ICT in early detection of crop pests and rapid response in advisory service delivery. Submitted to *Journal of Agricultural and Food Information*.

CABI (2020). *Plantwise annual donor report 2019*. https://www.cabi.org/wp-content/upl oads/Plantwise_Annual_Donor_Report_2019_PUBLIC.pdf

Chaouali, W. (2016). Once a user, always a user: Enablers and inhibitors of continuance intention of mobile social networking sites. *Telematics and Informatics*, 33(4), 1022–1033.

Claridge, T. (2018). Functions of social capital – bonding, bridging, linking. *Social Capital Research*, 1–7. Retrieved 24 November 2020. https://www.socialcapitalresea rch.com/difference-bonding-bridging-social-capital/

Cofré-Bravo, G., Klerkx, L. and Engler A. (2019). Combinations of bonding, bridging and linking social capital for farm innovation: How farmers configure different support networks. *Journal of Rural Studies*, 69, 53–64.

Colfer, L. J. and Baldwin, C. Y. (2016). The mirroring hypothesis: Theory, evidence, and exceptions. *Industrial and Corporate Change*, 25(5), 709–738.

Danielsen, S., Mur, R., Kleijn, W., Wan, M., Zhang, Y., Phiri, N., Chulu, B., Zhang, T. and Posthumus, H. (2020). Assessing information sharing from plant clinics in China and Zambia through social network analysis. *The Journal of Agricultural Education and Extension*, 26(3), 269–289.

Day, R., Abrahams, P., Bateman, M., Beale, T., Clottey, V., Cock, M., ... and Gomez, J. (2017). Fall armyworm: Impacts and implications for Africa. *Outlooks on Pest Management*, 28(5), 196–201.

FAO (2015). *e-agriculture 10 year Review Report: Implementation of the World Summit on the Information Society (WSIS) Action Line C7*. Food and Agriculture Organization of the United Nations.

FAO (2019). Digital technologies in agriculture and rural areas. Briefing paper. Food and Agriculture Organization of the United Nations.

Faure, G., Davis, K. E., Ragasa, C., Ranzel, S. and Babu S. C. (2016). Framework to assess performance and impact of pluralistic agricultural extension systems. The best-fit framework revisited. IFPRI Discussion paper 01567. IFPRI.

Hashemi, A. and Chahooki, M. A. Z. (2019). Telegram group quality measurement by user behavior analysis. *Social Network Analysis and Mining*, 9(1), 1–12.

Huang, H. Y., Chen, P. L. and Kuo, Y. C. (2017). Understanding the facilitators and inhibitors of individuals' social network site usage. *Online Information Review*, 41(1), 85–101.

Ifejika, P. I., Asadu, A. N., Enibe, D. O., Ifejika, L. I. and Sule, A. M. (2019). Analysis of social media mainstreaming in E-extension by agricultural development programmes in North Central Zone, Nigeria. *Journal of Agricultural Extension and Rural Development*, 11(4), 78–84.

Kelly, N., Bennett, J. M. and Starasts, A. (2017). Networked learning for agricultural extension: A framework for analysis and two cases. *The Journal of Agricultural Education and Extension*, 23(5), 399–414.

Klerkx, L. and Proctor, A. (2013). Land use policy beyond fragmentation and disconnect: Networks for knowledge exchange in the English land management advisory system. *Land Use Policy*, 30(1), 13–24.

Labarthe, P. and Laurent, C. (2013). The Importance of the back-office for farm advisory services. *Eurochoices*, 12(1), 21–26.

Landini, F. (2020). How do rural extension agents learn? Argentine practitioners' sources of learning and knowledge. *The Journal of Agricultural Education and Extension*, 27(1), 35–54. doi:10.1080/1389224X.2020.1780140

Majuga, J. C. N., Uzayisenga, B., Kalisa, J. P., Almekinders, C. and Danielsen, S (2018). "Here we give advice for free": The functioning of plant clinics in Rwanda. *Development in Practice*, 28(7), 858–871.

Mbagwu, F. C., Benson, O. V. and Onuoha, C. O. (2017). Challenges of meeting information needs of rural farmers through internet-based services: Experiences from developing countries in Africa. Paper presented a IFLA WLIC 2018, Agricultural Libraries SIG.

Minet, J., Curnel, Y., Gobin, A., Goffart, J. P., Mélard, F., Tychon, B., Wellens, J., Defournye, P. (2017). Crowdsourcing for agricultural applications: A review of uses and opportunities for a farmsourcing approach. *Computers and Electronics in Agriculture*, 142(A), 126–138.

Munthali, N., Van Paassen, A., Leeuwis, C., Lie, R., van Lammeren, R., Aguilar-Gallegos, N., & Oppong-Mensah, B. (2021). Social media platforms, open communication and problem solving in the back-office of Ghanaian extension: A substantive, structural and relational analysis. *Agricultural Systems*. 190, 103123.

Priharsari, D., Abedin, B. and Mastio, E. (2020). Value co-creation in firm sponsored online communities. *Internet Research*, 30(3), 763–788.

Putnam, R. D. (2000). *Bowling alone: The collapse and revival of American community*. New York: Simon and Schuster.

Raj, U. R., Satyanarayan, K., Jagadeeswary, V., Rathod, P., Kumar, S. N. and Mahadevappa, D. G. (2020). Utilization of social media for accessing scientific information by livestock farmers in Karnataka state. *The Indian Journal of Veterinary Sciences and Biotechnology*, 15(04), 80–83.

Rybski, D., Buldyrev, S. V., Havlin, S., Liljeros, F. and Makse, H. A. (2012). Communication activity in a social network: Relation between long-term correlations and inter-event clustering. *Scientific Reports*, 2, 560.

Saravanan, P., and Vasumathi, A. (2016). A Study of the Human-Resource Practices and Challenges Confronted by Human-Resource Experts in an Indian IT Firm, Bangalore. In Selected Papers from the Asia-Pacific Conference on Economics & Finance (APEF 2016). Singapore: Springer. 77–98.

Suchiradipta, B. and Saravanan, R. (2016). Social media: Shaping the future of agricultural extension and advisory services. GFRAS interest group on ICT4RAS discussion paper, Global Forum for Rural Advisory Service, 9.

Tambo, J. A., Uzayisenga, B., Mugambi, I. and Bundi, M. (2019). Do plant clinics improve household food security? Evidence from Rwanda. *Journal of Agricultural Economics*, 72(1), 97–116.

Tambo, J. A., Uzayisenga, B., Mugambi, I., Bundi, M. and Silvestri, S. (2020). Plant clinics, farm performance and poverty alleviation: Panel data evidence from Rwanda. *World Development*, 129, 104881.

Teo, H. J., Johri, A. and Lohani, V. (2017). Analytics and patterns of knowledge creation: Experts at work in an online engineering community. *Computers & Education*, 112, 18–36.

Thakur, D. and Chander, M. (2017). Use of social media for livestock advisory services: The case of WhatsApp in Himachal Pradesh, India. *The Indian Journal of Animal Sciences*, 87(8), 106–109.

Tsan, M., Totapally, S., Hailu, M. and Addom, B. K. (2019). *The digitalisation of African agriculture report 2018–2019*. CTA.

Van Paassen, A., Opdam, P., Steingröver, E. and Van den Berg, J. (2011). Landscape science and societal action. In: Van Paassen, A., van den Berg, J., Steingröver, E., Werkman, R. and Pedroli, B. (eds.) *Knowledge in action. The search for effective collaborative research for sustainable landscape development*. Wageningen: Mansholt series, Wageningen Publishers.

PART VI

Governing knowledge and innovation

15

MAKING DIALOGUE WORK

Responsible innovation and gene editing

Phil Macnaghten, Esha Shah, and David Ludwig

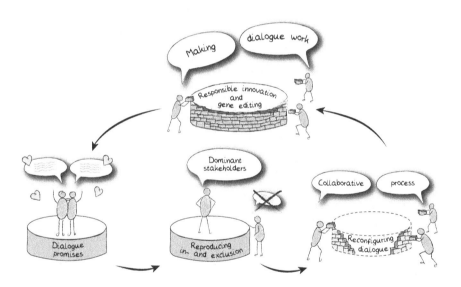

Introduction

Traditionally, it has been assumed that the institution of science needs little governance; that it should operate as if it was an autonomous republic (Polanyi, 1962). So, the argument goes, as long as internalist norms are upheld which are aimed at guaranteeing scientific integrity—including the Mertonian norms of universalism, communalism, disinterestedness, and organised scepticism—the pursuit of pure curiosity-driven science would operate as the seed from which applied research flourishes, the economy grows and society prosper (Godin, 2006). Yet,

DOI: 10.4324/9781003112525-15

as the 20th century progressed, this model came increasingly under strain as capable of providing robust governance in the face of real-world harms or unintended consequences that derived from scientific and technological innovation. The initial governance response was to acknowledge that science and technology—even when well conducted—could generate harms and undesired consequences, but that these could be evaluated in advance and within the bounds of scientific rationality through practices of risk assessment. Notwithstanding the efficacy of risk assessment to mitigate the harms associated with science and technology, it did little to anticipate or mitigate a number of high-profile technology disasters that took place throughout the latter half of the 20th century, including the Three Mile Island nuclear accident in the United States in 1979; the Bhopal Union Carbide gas disaster in India in 1984; the Chernobyl nuclear disaster in Ukraine in 1986; and the Fukushima Daiichi nuclear disaster in 2011. Nor did such a model provide authoritative governance in the face of major societal controversy to science and technology, such as the 'mad cow' BSE controversy in the UK and Europe throughout the late 1980s and 1990s, or the genetically modified (GM) food and crop controversy in the 1990s and 2000s first in Europe and then across much of the Global South.

One institutional response to such critique has been the development of initiatives aimed at aligning science priority and agenda-setting processes explicitly to societal challenges. The 'grand challenge' model of science governance best illustrates this approach by focusing the funding of science on core societal problems such as biodiversity loss, sustainable energy production, public health, or poverty reduction. Over the last decade, the grand challenge concept has become deeply embedded in science policy institutions as a central and organising concept that appeals to funding bodies, philanthropic trusts, think tanks, and universities alike. It is as much an organising device for research calls, as it is for research in organisations, notably universities. Yet, even though grand challenges by definition are attempts to respond to society and to public interest, the choice and framing of the challenges themselves tend to be chosen top-down by funding organisations (Calvert, 2013) and in ways that often lend themselves to 'silver bullet' technological solutions (Brooks et al., 2009).

If the *grand challenge science governance model* seeks to reconfigure the social contract of science such that its core value lies in providing solutions to the world's most pressing problems and not with the pursuit of pure knowledge, the *responsible innovation model* seeks to reconfigure the social contract in another direction. In contrast with earlier models of science governance, responsible innovation aims to align science and society through inclusive processes that engage with a wide range of stakeholders. In the last decade, responsible innovation emerged as a governance framework both to address grand societal challenges and as a way to 'make science more attractive, raise the appetite of society for innovation, and open up research and innovation activities; allowing all societal actors to work together during the whole research and innovation process in order to better align both the process and its outcomes with the values, needs and expectations of European society' (European Commission, 2013: 1). In developing a framework of responsible innovation, debates on responsibility in science are broadened to extend both to their collective and to their external impacts on society, covering both foreseen and unforeseen impacts, alongside assessment of their goals and purposes. More specifically, four dimensions of responsible innovation—anticipation (A), inclusion (I), reflexivity (R), and responsiveness (R): the AIRR framework—have been formulated to provide a scaffold for raising, discussing, and responding to questions of societal concern, deemed to be characteristics of a more responsible vision of innovation, and heuristically helpful for decision-making on how to shape science and technology in line with societal values (Owen et al., 2012; Stilgoe et al., 2013).

Reconfiguring the relation between science and society along dimensions such as AIRR requires public engagement strategies for opening research and innovation to dialogue among heterogeneous stakeholders. In this chapter, we explore the challenge of aligning science and technology with and for society through an exploration of two case studies that make use of societal dialogues on the future of gene editing.

Gene editing technique CRISPR/Cas is a novel technique for making changes to an organism's DNA. CRISPR is a short term for DNA sequences known as clustered regularly interspaced short palindromic repeats. Scientists use a specific Cas family of enzymes, Cas9 or Cas12, that uses CRISPR sequences as a guide to recognise and cleave specific strands of DNA that are then modified. The gene-editing technqique is thus named CRISPR/Cas, or specifically CRISPR-Cas9, depending upon the enzyme used to edit genes within any organism. The CRISPR/Cas techinques have made advances in gene-editing arguably more precise, efficient, flexible, and cheaper compared to previous technologies, generating an upsurge of interest in the technique and its multifarious applications. Even though the technique promises benefits—variously defined—it also raises technical, ethical, and societal questions. Since the technology is still largely to be developed into marketable products, it is opportune to open up a conversation with society now; both to better understand public concerns so as to be able to integrate societal values into the science, but more radically, to make the science genuinely more self-reflective, particularly in relation to global challenges such as food security that allow for different responses depending on how the issue is framed and defined.

In the first case, we analyse the dynamics of inclusion and exclusion at a recent CRISPRcon conference at Wageningen University, which had been set up as 'a unique forum bringing diverse voices together to discuss the future of CRISPR and gene editing technologies across applications in agriculture, health, conservation, and more' (CRISPRcon, 2020). Here, we scrutinise the linguistic devises, including the 'affective voice' of the conference, assumptions of how gene editing works, and assumptions of societal benefit that were deployed to frame the discussions on societal relevance of CRISPR/Cas gene editing and its products.

We then set out design principles for an anticipatory or 'upstream' public engagement methodology in deliberative research on new science and technology. Adopting a Science and Technology Studies (STS) perspective, a societal engagement methodology is presented that is aimed at anticipating the kinds of possible and plausible worlds that novel science and technology bring into being. These design principles are then put to use in our second case, a recently conducted focus group project, designed to explore public responses to gene editing in livestock. Reflecting on these two cases, we conclude the chapter on the challenges of making inclusion work in science governance debates, and on how a substantial account of responsible innovation can provide resources for addressing and navigating these challenges.

CRISPRcon: conversations on science, society, and the future of gene editing

CRISPRcon, hosted by Wageningen University and Research in June 2019, was the third so-called 'conversation' of its type organised in partnership with the Keystone Policy Centre. The aim of the conference was to discuss the future of CRISPR and related gene editing technologies across a variety of applications in agriculture, health, conservation, and more. The conference was attended by 156 participants of which the majority were from academia and industry, with 65% of participants aligned with the food and agriculture sector.

The conversation was hosted under the leadership of the Plant Science Group of Wageningen University and took place in the shadow of the ruling of the European Court of Justice (25 July 2018), at the time one-year old, that had declared that all products of genome editing would be subject to the European GMO Directive. Many scientists at Wageningen University were upset by this ruling because it meant that the elaborate legal control developed for the regulation of GMOs would also be exercised over research and marketing of gene-edited plants and animals. The ruling was received among scientists with a sense of disapproval. It was voiced repeatedly that the new science of gene-editing had rendered the old 2001 GMO directive outdated and in need of amendment, with some even going so far as to call the ruling 'anti-science.'

CRISPRcon at Wageningen was organised in an overall 'affective' frame of disappointment, frustration, disbelief, and irritation generated by the Court's ruling—especially among scientists. While this public and policy conversation was set up explicitly as an 'open dialogue,' promising an inclusive conversation 'aimed at the largest cross-section of society' on this new technology, it became a platform for showcasing CRISPR/Cas in a positive light and with immense potential to solve the problems of the world. A question in the opening poll provides a glance at this 'affective' composition of the conference. To the question 'How do you feel about the gene editing future?' The answers were: 44% *enthusiastic*, 50% *hopeful*, 4% *sceptical*, 2% *not sure*. We discuss two examples from the conference to explain our argument: first, how throughout the conference the science of the CRISPR/Cas gene-editing system was little debated or discussed but presented as a ground-breaking tool with immense potential; and second, how the CRISPR/Cas gene-editing system was discussed as a silver bullet that could solve societal problems, from malaria to food shortage, especially in Africa.

Importantly, in this dialogue on science and society hosted by the life sciences, the complex science of CRISPR/Cas, or even the science of the gene, was neither explained, discussed, nor debated, but exhibited in an overly positive light in what were called 'lightening presentations.' Each lightening presentation was scheduled only for five minutes, compared to an hour allotted to each panel discussion. The time management gave an impression that the conversations in panels were the mainstay of the conference, but looking differently, the lightening presentations highlighted and took for granted the current state of CRISPR/ Cas as a crisp, safe, clean, cheap, easy, and fast tool equipped to solve pressing problems in the agriculture and food and health sector.

For example, one particular lightening presentation posited the 'simple' and 'easy' tool of CRISPR/Cas using the metaphor of 'editing' as a written script at an 'exact' location with a 'precise' outcome explained in the following way: 'Green sea is native to China' is a gene/ text that needs to be edited. In this gene/ text, it is the 'sea' that does not fit and hence represents the 'wrong script'— analogous to a mutation causing deadly disease—in need of modification. The CRISPR/Cas tool then puts a cut at the right place and modifies 'the script' to 'Green | sea is native to China,' and then adds the correct script 'green tea is.' This correction, however, results in the incorrect expression 'Gree ntea is native to China,' which is then further repaired to 'Green tea is native to China.' This procedure was explained as analogous to how the system of Cas9 makes a precise cut exactly where it is needed, and how this can develop into one of two scenarios: after the cut either the cellular machinery kicks in to repair the cut by providing random letters that create mutations and thereby inactivate the gene; or, the cut opens a space for the scientists to 'precisely' provide a bare template that can be integrated into the gene, thereby repairing the gene to produce the desired effect. The CRISPR/Cas9 gene-editing tool was thus presented as easy, precise, cheap, fast, robust, and versatile. In both the lightening presentations and also in the panels the CRISPR/Cas system was frequently presented as a tool that could make only 'small' changes to create novel traits in a 'faster way' and hence that could 'speedily' and 'urgently' contribute to solving many of the world's pressing problems. This, we argue, was the first paradigmatic viewpoint of the conference.

'We shall move slowly and carefully' was, on the other hand, the second paradigmatic framing statement of the conference, which we observed to have a more limited effect than the first one. A cautious 'scientist's' voice did emerge in some of the lightening presentations and in the panel discussions. For instance, towards the end of the lightening presentation on the gene editing example discussed above, it was expressed that Cas9 can work only in some cells; that the scientist has to be sure about the availability of target sites to be edited; and that Cas9 can also create off-target unintended effects. However, none of these unintended consequences, nor the limits of Cas9, was explained or debated or reflected upon. In another panel discussion one such voice of caution did mention that several publications have shown that CRISPR/Cas9 can also produce unintentional mutations; that it can produce cell level mistakes in copying DNA; and that it can make major changes in the character of the genome. This voice of caution, however, was soon moderated by pointing out that such issues can be solved by locating the desired outcome through the technique of mapping the sequences or improving the protein engineering system from Cas9 to Cas12 to make the precise DNA cut, which can deal with the unintended additional mutations, for instance, in experimental field applications. The entire deliberation on the science of CRISPR/Cas gene-editing system was thus palpably presented as a success story with huge potential.

We argue that between these two competing paradigmatic framing statements of the conference—first, that we should enable CRISPR to solve urgent societal problems with speed; and second, that we should move slowly and carefully—the first frame dominated and shaped the overall 'conversation,' often turning into the voice of warning that European science will be left behind and diminished in the global race if so inhibited by the European Court of Justice's ruling.

The first paradigmatic framing statement often became the 'affective voice' of the panel. For example, one of the panellists, a business woman from Uganda, made an emotional appeal to solve the problem of malaria in Africa 'quick and fast,' 'in short time,' and 'now.' This, she claimed she was reliably informed, would be possible by releasing gene-edited mosquitoes into the environment through the technique of gene drives. Yet, surprisingly in a conference of world renowned scientists, there was no discussion of the ongoing debate in scientific communities concerning the growing body of experimental laboratory evidence and literature that has widely challenged the claim that CRISPR-based gene-drive technologies could rapidly eradicate diseases such as malaria, dengue, and zika by driving desired traits into mosquito populations (Alphey, 2016; Sarkar, 2018).

The ineffectiveness of the CRISPR gene-edited drives is attributed to the ontological complexity of the gene and the role of evolutionary processes to have made gene-editing develop into unintended directions (see also Shah et al., draft, for a full-length treatment of this argument). The promises of gene-drive technology to solve the problem of malaria, and of CRISPR gene-edited plant breeding to solve the problem of food shortage in Africa, was repeatedly mentioned several times in the conference. As another panellist pointed out, this 'hope and hype' was reminiscent of two decades of debate on GMOs, in which many similar claims now being made for CRISPR were also made with little success, such as the promise of GM agriculture 'feeding the world' (Macnaghten and Habets, 2020). From a social science perspective, and in the face of a considerable body of literature that has highlighted the need for technological innovation to be situated in larger debates on the socio-political history of agrarian development, it is remarkable that no such discussion was afforded in the CRISPRcon organised at Wageningen University, where generations of leading social scientists, from Norman Long to Paul Richards to Cees Leeuwis, have done pioneering work.

An anticipatory public engagement dialogue on gene editing

We have analysed above the dynamics of inclusion and exclusion at the 2019 CRISPRcon event at Wageningen University and Research. We found that far from providing reflexive and critical citizen input on a contested technology as a counterweight to technocratic decision-making, a form of public engagement had been developed that in practice had the effect of reinforcing existing relations of professional power and science policy institutional culture— solidifying dominant models of economic rationality, and reinforcing a quintessentially positive view of what the CRISPR/Cas system is and what it can do. But is such a model of participation as legitimation inevitable? Are other models of doing participation possible? Can reflexive social science move beyond the mode of critique and propose alternative models of doing public engagement for the public good?

In other research we have proposed three operating principles for the enactment of deliberative processes that mitigate against their use as tools of legitimation (Macnaghten, 2020). First, we need deliberative processes where societal actors are offered opportunities for dynamic expression and exploration, and where critique develops as an emergent quality of the process. Second, we need to guard against 'scientism,' the phenomenon where scientific and policy elites impose definitions on the meaning of public issues, foreclosing engagement with broader public meanings and their constituent normative and ontological underpinning. Importantly, these meanings need to emerge through endogenous processes, rather than being imposed either by expert scientific or corporate actors. And third, we need to develop spaces where participants can explore diverse arguments, affectivities, and forms of morality, and through which different identities and meanings can emerge as to the public issues associated with science and technology (Callon and Rabeharisoa, 2004). We now describe how these principles were operationalised in design criteria in a 2019/2020 Dutch NWO-funded project using focus groups—a particular kind of collective—the aim of which was to examine the conditions, if any, under which the technique of animal gene editing is socially acceptable.

The first design feature is sampling: determining who is involved in the deliberative research and the criteria for selection. For our research, using the focus group method, a sampling strategy was designed to be broad and deep. The project involved five groups, with each group meeting for between two hours and two hours 30 minutes. The groups were made up of between seven and nine participants, according to standard focus group norms, and professionally recruited to cover a diverse variety of backgrounds, localities, and demographics (age, gender, and socio-economic class) but with topic-specific or theoretically informed variants. These included a group of public sector professionals, another from rural locations, a group of foodies and outdoor enthusiasts, one more of 'involved' mums and dads, and a final one of private sector managers. The decision to involve uninformed participants, who had no particular *a priori* stake or position in the debate, and who did not know each other prior to the group, is a technique designed explicitly to produce an open-ended sociality, where people develop opinions and attitudes through structured interactive conversation in a safe and empowering space. In this way, the 'anticipatory' focus group methodology creates (albeit temporarily) 'technoscientific citizens' authorised to develop collective views and identities and to open up novel normative and ontological resources for thinking about emerging technology.

The second design feature is context, a neglected aspect in scholarship on deliberative methodology and science communication, but a core element of our methodological design. Given that, by definition, people are unfamiliar with an emerging technology and with the social and ethical issues it presents, it is necessary to explore the context out of which public responses are likely to emerge. Conceptually, it is assumed that it is through contextual factors that people develop an understanding and a relationship to technological innovations as they permeate everyday practice. For our research, the chosen context was animals. It was argued that deliberation on the social practices through which people experience and reflect upon animals in their daily lives—for example, as pets, as livestock, and as food—would illuminate the factors likely to shape responses to applications of gene editing to animals, including their sense of the issues, continuities, and discontinuities between gene-edited livestock and those determined by conventional selective breeding.

The focus groups started with a discussion on how people affectively relate to animals, particularly as pets. What do they like or not like about animals? What is it that builds a good relationship? What are key changes in how we are using and treating animals? What do people feel about eating meat? And how do people feel about different visions on the future of livestock farming represented in four models: an organic farming model, an industrial farming model, a no-livestock farming model, and a precision farming model. These contextual discussions proved enlightening. They revealed the affective and empathetic relations in which animals are regarded in much of daily life; the ambivalence many people feel in eating meat; and a tension between a global commercial system of livestock production and the wellbeing of animals and their rights to live a happy life. Such contextual deliberation helped in the formation of the group identity and underpinned the subsequent and overarching finding that the production of gene-edited livestock would, in the words of one participant, be akin to 'sticking a plaster on a self-inflicted wound.'

The third design feature is framing. Given that the representation of a technology is never neutral but always framed in particular ways and for particular purposes, care was exercised to introduce the technology by offering participants an inclusive range of rhetorical resources and frames, without closing down or narrowing the issue in the first place, or presuming that these align with dominant institutional frames and norms. For our research, the CRISPR/Cas system was introduced as a technique, and then in relation to possible and plausible applications both in agriculture and in the human/medical spheres. We then presented participants with four visions of how gene editing in livestock is represented: a positive and promissory vision; a negative and dystopian vision; a case-by-case vision; and a non-ideal vision.

The fourth design feature is moderation. A focus group is more than a group interview or the aggregation of individual opinions and preferences. It is a space in which a group identity and discourse can emerge; where the collective is empowered to articulate the issue at hand in its own terms, and to arrive where possible at the collective production of a group discourse through conversation. The moderator encourages the movement between argument and counter-argument in a spirit of mutual understanding. Facilitating a group dynamic and identity is an important accomplishment, as the group has to formulate shared understandings of issues that had been unfamiliar prior to the group discussion. In our research, to ensure that discussions are not framed by expert discourses and norms, the focus groups avoided the inclusion of technical experts. Nevertheless, codified information on what gene editing is, how it works, and what it means, was communicated by the moderator through the use of stimulus materials. Nevertheless, the practical meaning of the technology for the participants was derived through group discussion and deliberation.

The fifth design feature is analysis and interpretation. Our analytical approach is one where the role of the analyst is to become acquainted with the raw data; to organise rhetorical arguments into themes or discourses through the use of codes; to articulate the interplay between thematic concerns and wider social discourses and narratives; and to interpret this meaning within a framework of theoretical and policy concerns. What emerged in our analysis, generally, were thematic questions about purposes ('we need to have a good reason for it'), concerns that the technique in the agri-food domain would be driven principally by commercial imperatives ('this could be so lucrative that companies will move quickly'), about unnaturalness ('you are taking part of an animal's nature away [...] I am afraid nature will strike back'), about perfection ('sounds a bit like eugenics'), about a false solutionism ('maybe we get lax if we think this is an easy solution'), about unanticipated problems ('do we [really] know what it will do') and irretrievability ('if it goes wrong, it really goes wrong'), about the slippery slope ('where does this end'), about distribution of benefits ('the gap will get richer between rich and poor'), about ethical boundaries ('this will create new distinctions'), about control ('if we can decide everything life is no longer fun'), and about desire and excess ('we are so used to wanting more and more and more [...] we should train people "I have enough"—do I really need it'). Later, when we introduced different frames on the governance of animal gene editing and different styles emerging between the United States and Europe, participants expressed support for a restrictive European (and Dutch) approach, for time and care in considering impacts (social, ethical, economic), for public engagement, and for (the Dutch) government to take control.

To summarise, in this section we have described an anticipatory public engagement methodology aimed at structuring a societal dialogue on gene editing and its application to livestock. Through a carefully crafted methodology using focus groups we found a mismatch between: a dominant scientific and policy imaginary of gene editing, as evinced in the paradigmatic framing and affective voice dominating CRISPRcon described previously, evoking a characteristically positive view of the technology and its role in solving grand societal challenges; and a more cautious and sceptical approach and affective voice from our public respondents, advocating the need to slow research down, to search for a deeper analysis of our predicament (of which gene editing is a symptom), and to think about the kinds of society we value and wish science and innovation processes to collectively contribute towards. In the concluding section, we examine in more detail this comparison, and the implications for science governance and for a framework of responsible innovation.

Conclusion

Responsible governance requires responsible dialogues that conform, at least in principle, to the ideal of a free flowing group conversation in which participants attempt to reach a common understanding, and experience each other's point of view fully, equally, and non-judgmentally (Bohm, 1996; Gadamer, 2004). The case of gene editing illustrates both the importance and the challenges of establishing responsible dialogues about emerging technologies, at the intersection of wider hopes and worries about the relation between science and society. On the one hand, gene editing technologies such as CRISPR/Cas integrate into narratives about solving pressing societal problems such as the challenge of 'feeding the world' through cutting-edge science and technology (Gates, 2018; de Wit, 2020). On the other hand, gene editing also integrates into dystopian narratives of scientific hubris that produces outcomes that it can neither foresee nor control such as the infamous 'CRISPR babies' (Lovell-Badge, 2019; Macnaghten and Habets, 2020).

In the introduction, we outlined the development of science governance discourses through three phases: from curiosity-driven science that is detached from societal concerns, to 'grand challenges' science that is focused on solving social-environmental issues, to responsible innovation that aims to align science and society through public engagement. While inclusive dialogues are a crucial element of the responsible innovation model, our first case study of CRISPRcon demonstrates the challenges of making societal dialogue work in the context of emerging and contested technologies. CRISPRcon appealed to an inclusive dialogue through presenting itself as a forum for diverse voices to discuss CRISPR.

However, CRISPRcon clearly failed to represent these 'diverse voices,' as it assembled not only a group of stakeholders with overwhelmingly positive attitudes towards gene editing, but that also constructed an affective discourse and frame about revolutionary promises of CRISPR/Cas. The few dissenting voices were pushed to the periphery of this affective discourse later accused the organisers of 'a cleverly choreographed greenwashing rally, funded by corporations such as Bayer and Editas Medicine' (Arora et al., 2019).

The case of CRISPRcon highlights the need for caution in moving towards responsible innovation through science-society dialogues. Even frameworks of responsible innovation in terms of (A) anticipation, (I) inclusion, (R) reflexivity, and (R) responsiveness (Stilgoe et al., 2013) can become easily appropriated if not sufficiently specified. At least on the surface, CRISPRcon appealed to all four AIRR dimensions by promising an (A) anticipatory dialogue about opportunities and risks of gene editing that (I) included a 'a broad selection of diverse voices' and aimed to increase (R) reflexivity about the future of gene editing by (R) responding to various stakeholders from farmers to industry to the general public. The failure of CRISPRcon to actually create an inclusive dialogue reflects the challenges of moving towards responsible innovation through public engagement rather than reinforcing the perspectives of dominant stakeholders.

If dialogues about emerging technologies are more than a mechanism to legitimise dominant perspectives, they need to incorporate substantive interpretations of what it means to be anticipatory, inclusive, reflexive, and responsive in practice. Our second case study highlights opportunities for moving towards responsible innovation by incorporating these concerns into the design of science-society dialogues. Rather than departing from a vague appeal to 'a broad selection of diverse voices' (CRISPRcon), the focus group design used a clearly defined sampling strategy and topic guide to foster an open-ended dialogue. Rather than choreographing the affective mood through a focus on revolutionary promises or dystopian risks, the dialogue was designed to open up context, framing, and moderation for collaborative negotiation of heterogenous concerns and issue-framings. None of these design principles provides simple solutions to concerns about the instrumentalisation of dialogue, and they certainly do not lead to a value-neutral negotiation space free of biases. However, each of the five design principles constitutes a tool for navigating tensions in societal dialogues about emerging and contested technologies, for creating a safe space in which competing values and bias can be shared and negotiated, and as such for contributing to responsible, just, and inclusive innovation.

Finally, there is the political dimension to the above analysis. While deliberative processes inevitably involve the strategic use of arguments, the framing of engagement questions and formats, the inclusion and exclusion of particular actors and perspectives, and so on, it is also the case that some deliberative processes are by design more inclusive and reflexive than others. With this in mind, it is arguably the case that the implicit politics of the two cases were demonstrably divergent. While the politics of the CRISPRcon case was that of constituting dialogue as a means of *promoting* the technology not least through an overwhelmingly positive affective discourse, the politics of the anticipatory public engagement dialogue was that of designing an endogenous process aimed at developing a collective imagination of the possible worlds enabled by gene editing. How we configure the role of the public in early discussions of a technology—either as in Case 1 as a 'malleable subject' able to have its views and positions bent through the provision of information and argument from gene editing protagonists; or as in Case 2 as an 'exploratory' or 'reflexive' subject able to develop its own positions in its own terms (Macnaghten and Chilvers, 2014)—is ultimately a question for power and politics. Connecting dialogue processes to formal processes of democratic decision-making will be a formidable challenge for dialogue scholars and activists.

References

Alphey, L. (2016). Can CRISPR-Cas9 gene drives curb malaria? *Nature Biotechnology*, 34(2), 149–150.

Arora, S., van Dyck, B. and Wakeford, T. (2019). Choreographed consensus: The stifling of dissent at CRISPRcon 2019. *The STEPS Centre Blog*, 28, 2019.

Bohm, D. (1996). *On Dialogue*. London: Routledge.

Brooks, S., Leach, M., Lucas, H. and Millstone, E. (2009). *Silver Bullets, Grand Challenges and the New Philanthropy*. STEPS Working Paper 24, STEPS Centre. Accessed 17 June 2020. http://www.ids.ac.uk/files/dmfile/STEPSWorkingPaper24.pdf

Callon, M. and Rabeharisoa, V. (2004). Gino's lesson on humanity: Genetics, mutual entanglements and the sociologist's role. *Economy and Society*, 33(1), 1–27.

Calvert, J. (2013). Systems biology: Big science and grand challenges. *BioSocieties*, 8, 466–479.

European Commission (2013). Fact Sheet: Science with and for society in Horizon 2020. Accessed 17 June 2020. https://ec.europa.eu/programmes/horizon2020/sites/horizon2020/files/FactSheet_Science_with_and_for_Society.pdf

Gadamer, H.-G. (2004). *Truth and Method*. New York: Continuum.

Gates, B. (2018). Gene editing for good: How CRISPR could transform global development. *Foreign Affairs*, 97, 166.

Godin, B. (2006). The linear model of innovation: The historical construction of an analytical framework. *Science, Technology and Human Values*, 31(6), 639–667.

Lovell-Badge, R. (2019). CRISPR babies: A view from the centre of the storm. *Development*, 146(3), dev175778.

Macnaghten, P. (2020). Towards an anticipatory public engagement methodology: Deliberative experiments in the assembly of possible worlds using focus group. *Qualitative Research*, 29(1), 3–19, doi:10.1177/1468794120919096.

Macnaghten, P. and Chilvers, J. (2014). The future of science governance: Publics, policies, practices. *Environment and Planning C: Government and Policy*, 32(3), 530–548.

Macnaghten, P. and Habets, M. G. (2020). Breaking the impasse: Towards a forward-looking governance framework for gene editing with plants. *Plants, People, Planet*, 2(4), 353–365.

Owen, R., Macnaghten, P. and Stilgoe, J. (2012). Responsible research and innovation: From science in society to science for society, with society. *Science and Public Policy*, 39(6), 751–760.

Polanyi, M. (1962). The republic of science. *Minerva*, 1(1), 54–73.

Sarkar, S. (2018). Researchers hit roadblocks with gene drives. *BioScience*, 68(7), 474–480.

Shah, E., Ludwig, D. and Macnaghten, P. (draft). The complexity of the gene and the precision of CRISPR: What is the gene that is being edited?

Stilgoe, J., Owen, R. and Macnaghten, P. (2013). Developing a framework of responsible innovation. *Research Policy*, 42(9), 1568–1580.

de Wit, M. M. (2020). Democratizing CRISPR? Stories, practices, and politics of science and governance on the agricultural gene editing frontier. *Elementa: Science of the Anthropocene*, 8(1), 9.

16

MAKING KNOWLEDGE
WORK IN PRACTICE

An integrative methodology for researching
performance in global commodity
chains and local food markets

*Sietze Vellema, Faustina Obeng Adomaa,
and Mirjam Schoonhoven-Speijer*

Introduction

Making knowledge work needs to take place among real-life practices. These usually involve the work of groups of knowledgeable actors and sets of inter-linked purposeful actions that have material consequences. This chapter exam-ines a methodological perspective focusing on mutually constituting practices distributed in global commodity chains and in local food markets; the prac-tices accomplished by different groups of actors are also situated at different sites across the commodity chain or market system. These practices are the sites where 'knowing how to make things work' emerges. Moreover, making a set

DOI: 10.4324/9781003112525-16

of practices work reflects emerging organisational capacity to coordinate actions in a commodity chain or food market, which do not necessarily involve a coordinating agent. Therefore, this chapter also addresses the more general methodological question of how to study the process of making knowledge work in similar types of layered organisational settings.

To answer this methodological question, we build on literature in organisational studies that shifts the research gaze from a focus on individual knowledge and capacities to a focus on knowing that transpires in practices and their interrelationships (Nicolini, 2012). The methodological choice to study practices (Nicolini, 2009) combines with methodological perspectives in the field of technology studies that focus on the use of knowledge, skills, tools, and techniques in everyday and often mundane practices (Glover et al., 2017; Jansen and Vellema, 2011; Richards, 1989). This methodological choice resonates with anthropological work on the intrinsically social nature of learning, skills, apprenticeship, and competence (Jaarsma et al., 2011; Lave, 1993). Researching knowing as the joint accomplishment of a set of distributed, stabilised, routinised, or improvised practices opens methodological space to investigate the question of how social order is jointly established, maintained, and transformed; here specifically in the economic space of commodity chains or food markets (Jones and Murphy, 2011; Nicolini, 2012, p. 122). These perspectives research *knowing* as an organisational and collective accomplishment as a social phenomenon.

The chapter scrutinises the methodological choice to focus on practice and coordination in two cases based on in-depth empirical studies: first, on the sourcing of cocoa in Ghana; and second, on the collection of oilseed in Uganda. It posits *knowing* as an emergent outcome of a set of interdependent practices organised around achieving a practical goal, such as enhancing sustainability in commodity trade or ensuring consistency in food provisioning. The two cases zoom in on concrete social-material practices: the *pruning* of cocoa trees in smallholder farms in Ghana, and the *aggregation* of oilseed in small village stores in Uganda. Zooming in on problem-solving capacities in everyday practices enables one to identify how interconnected activities in global commodity chains or local food markets handle all kinds of errors and contingencies. Moreover, both situated practices are intrinsically connected to other practices distributed in the layered organisational set-up of commodity chains and food markets. This requires expanding the research gaze to modes of collaboration and governance that make organising possible in real markets. The case examples illustrate how a focus on knowing occurring in practice enables assessing and comparing the conditions for making knowledge work in the setting of a layered and spatially distributed organisational setup.

Next, the chapter presents the methodological perspective used for researching practices and introduces how material and institutional dimensions may be integrated into the study of knowing. The two case examples serve to analyse how knowing is brought about, which informs a discussion on how knowledge-based interventions, such as sustainability standards or contractual arrangements, may contrast or silence the processes from which knowing emerges. The chapter concludes by looking at how the methodological perspective offers a forward-looking agenda for a social science perspective to investigate the consequences of knowledge-based interferences associated with external organisations, including manuals, training, and managerial prescriptions and standards. The focus on knowing emerging from situated practices is appreciative of local problem-solving capacities; it contributes to detecting and opening spaces for inserting these capacities in the specialised knowing generated in mainstream science and technology institutes.

Methodological perspective

The methodological perspective used in this chapter includes three dimensions, which build on the systematics of doing technography (Jansen and Vellema, 2011). First, it focuses on knowing how to make practices work, which orients research towards the human capacity to make or transform, and includes materiality in the analysis. Second, it analyses knowing as a collective endeavour anchored in the configuration of distributed practices with explicit or hidden forms of coordination. Third, it associates knowing with forms of specialisation and professional rules embedded in a wider division of labour in society.

Making practice work

A focus on knowing how to make practice happen offers an alternative perspective on knowledge (Nicolini, 2011). Following Lave (1993), learning and knowing not only happens in the mind of the learner or the user. The human capacity to solve problems and achieve practical ends is traceable in the use of knowledge in team work and emerges in interactions of humans with natural or material objects. Hence, knowledge is an integral part of the package of techniques, machines, tools, physical layout, skills, or procedures, which mediate the interactions of society and materiality in everyday life.

The focus on everyday practices aligns the ethnographic tradition reflected in work on learning, skills, apprenticeship, and performance (Lave, 1993; Richards, 1989) with organisation and management literature analysing knowing and learning as socio-material interactions 'constituted and reconstituted' in everyday situated practices (Fenwick, 2006; Orlikowski, 2002). Knowing how to make practice happen is not limited to cognitive knowledge, which suggests that knowing is not a static capability or stable disposition of individual actors. Rather, knowing is an ongoing social accomplishment constituted, reshaped, and transmitted in actions performed to solve situated and often unanticipated problems. Zooming in on everyday practices opens space to include materiality in the study of knowing. Knowing how to handle material dimensions then becomes an integral element of the social analysis of how a set of actors make practice work. This is particularly relevant for analysing practices that interact, for example, with seasonal fluctuations in agricultural production, the spatial aspects of sourcing produce, or the influence of pests and diseases on yields and productivity in farms. These material dimensions make everyday practices partly unpredictable. Therefore, Lave (1993) and Barber (2007) emphasise the notion of skilled improvisation as an ongoing activity contributing to learning and knowing.

The methodological challenge is to recognise knowing, which is not always manifest in manuals or written instructions. People use prior experience to solve situated problems (Fenwick, 2006; Johri, 2011). Mastery transpires in what is done and how it is done (Nicolini, 2009). This makes it relevant to investigate knowing how to make a practice work, and to look closely at everyday activity, rather than seeking to generate an abstract conceptualisation of knowledge and its effects. A methodological consequence is that knowledge is essentially considered a tool used and reinforced in the performance of daily activities, which reflect purposeful and competent interactions with the real, social, and material worlds. The first dimension looks at knowing with an interest in handling errors and contingencies in evolving processes of (material) transformation with open-ended outcomes.

Connecting practices

The second methodological dimension shifts attention from a single practice to a bundle of practices knotted together. Multiple practices are usually located in different spaces, carried out at the same time or in a certain sequence. Hence, knowing is distributed in networks of people and material environments (Hutchins, 1995), which associates it with know-how distributed across task-oriented teams and mediated processes where activities are developed collaboratively (Paavola and Hakkarainen, 2005). This makes it relevant to investigate how interconnected groups, as small task-oriented units (McFeat, 1974), interpret, process, transmit, and transform information, both within and across the organisational boundaries of the smaller group.

Following Nicolini (2011), practices emerge around prospective outcomes, around which small groups organise their work, and around which activities are coordinated. Hence, making things work is a collective endeavour, which implies a multiplicity of paths, connections, antecedents, references, and deferrals, and brings to the fore the processes that make activities work together and establish associations. This implies a shift, from individual capacities to studying processes connecting practices, directing the movement of information, and creating relationships between practices. These configurations connect the accomplishment of local real-time practices to practices situated elsewhere (Nicolini, 2009). This raises the questions of how the combination of practices realises expected outcomes, or how it may generate unintended effects. This implies an interest in how interlinked and differently situated practices realise collaboration and collective endeavours, relying on the transmission of information, knowledge, and direction.

The methodological challenge is to expose those practices generating outcomes together, and to reveal patterns of coordination as an emerging property of global commodity trade or local food provisioning. Coordination may be the result of purposeful orchestration, but it may also emerge from a set of interconnected practices jointly producing a practical result. Accomplishing organisational knowing involves combining elements and weaving together dispersed knowing (Nicolini, 2011). Accordingly, the second dimension focuses on knowing how to organise, coordinate, form new alliances, and cooperate around specific and distributed tasks to produce order. This second dimension anchors the study of knowing on the configuration of interwoven practices performed and organised around prospective outcomes.

Interferences by non-localised specialisms

The third dimension looks at the presence of rules, procedures, and routines associated with non-localised specialisms in situated practices. This refers to institutionalised forms of knowing embedded in skill-based professions in the wider division of labour in society (Durkheim, 1957/2001). These are associations of people with specialised skills and knowledge that are joined together by the bonds of their profession. Members of a similar professional guild are inclined to solve problems in similar ways or make judgments on the basis of shared professional values (Mudambi and Swift, 2009). Therefore, membership of a professional field affects how specialised knowledge is differentiated from knowing manifest in situated practices.

Non-localised specialisms can interfere, possibly at a distance, with situated actions in various forms. This may refer to audits and checklists related to sustainability standards (Ponte and Cheyns, 2013) or to conventions associated with the professional fields of supply chain management and logistics (Gibbon and Ponte, 2008). These interferences can expose contrasts between knowing that is represented in formal learning and formal theoretical schemes through hand-and-eye-knowledge, when dealing with the material or social conditions of the practices (Richards, 1993). Knowledge reproduced in professional associations can take the form of prescribed practices, guidelines in contracts or standards, manuals, surveillance and monitoring procedures, or protocols for quality assurance. This knowledge influences the language of specialists used in the social selection of recipes or intervention pathways.

The methodological challenge is to detect processes generating tensions or accords between situated practices and non-localised specialisms. Combining specialised knowing and knowing accomplished in situated practices often involves dedicated institutional work (Lawrence and Suddaby, 2006). This comprises purposive actions that can lead to adjustments, adaptations, or compromises visible in localised day-to-day practices; or vice versa, to the insertion of context-specific solutions into mainstream science and technology, therefore enriching the portfolio of options available (Fressoli et al., 2014). Researching the practice of institutional work in layered organisational setups (Lawrence et al., 2009) makes it possible to diagnose the ways non-localised specialisms try to govern other practices, and relatedly, to what extent the blending of different practices is possible. The third methodological dimension looks at the manifestation of knowing associated with membership of professional fields and non-localised specialisms in localised practicing, which are not necessarily commensurable. The case examples below use the three methodological dimensions introduced in this section: (1) making practice work; (2) connecting practices; and (3) interferences by non-localised specialisms.

Knowing how to prune cocoa trees (Ghana)

In cocoa chains, sustainability standard and certification schemes drive sourcing and chocolate companies to organise training and extension services targeting smallholder producers and focusing on good agricultural practices such as pruning (Asare et al., 2018). These knowledge-oriented interventions connect on-farm pruning practices to the selection of pruning techniques higher up in the commodity chain and to research. A focus on practices exposes how pruning moves up and down this layered setting (Glover et al., 2017) and what institutional features enable or constrain fruitful interactions between knowledgeable actors at different sites.

Making practice work

Pruning is a skilful and essential management practice in tree crops (Govindaraj and Jancirani, 2017). It involves knowing which pruning techniques to apply and how to prune trees under specific local conditions. In cocoa, pruning can be undertaken to get young cocoa trees into shape, to shape the canopy of matured cocoa trees to a desired size and architecture, or to remove diseased and unnecessary branches and to control pests and diseases. Interviewed farmers explained that the choice of which type of pruning to do was highly situational and informed by their assessment of the state of the trees, the conditions in the farm, soil conditions, other trees in the farm, the presence of sunlight, and so on. Interviewed farmers highlighted the importance of learning from mistakes and looking closely at how other farmers were pruning. They explained that none of the farms in the area had similar conditions, and even in the same farm, different agro-ecological conditions need to be considered when pruning cocoa trees. Timing of pruning and maturity of trees were important, while knowing how trees have grown informed the selection of tools and techniques.

This technical knowing indicates that pruning entails the use of a combination of skills, tools, techniques, and knowledge, all of which is highly situational. At farm level, agricultural producers use and combine know-how, tools, techniques, and skills to achieve practical ends, such as controlling pests and diseases for producing enough beans. Pruning is one of the specific actions for achieving this, which assembles together with other actions for managing the agro-ecological conditions under which cocoa trees grow; the anticipated effect also depends on other practices, such as fertilisation. Moreover, pruning is labour intensive and requires skilful workers, which connects the practice to employment and market conditions in the environment of cocoa farmers.

Connecting practices

Achieving sustainable cocoa farming involves more than the application of good agricultural practices: it emerges from a web of practices, which jointly generate a steady supply of cocoa beans. Producing enough beans also includes managing workers available in the neighbourhood, some of whom may not be skilled to conduct the delicate task of pruning. Being able to sell cocoa beans entails connecting to purchasing clerks who mobilise working capital for making payments and maintain connections to the buyers licensed to operate in the Ghanaian cocoa market. At farm level, these practices, including work of land owners, farm managers, workers, and purchasing clerks, are knotted together, which reinforces a relatively stable configuration of institutional arrangements regarding land tenure, labour management, and local buying transactions.

Actions downstream in the cocoa chain involve the implementation of sustainability standards, accompanied by private and public investments in knowledge transfer and training targeting smallholder producers. This induces a stronger connectivity of local practices to sites located elsewhere. Manuals, audits, and checklists illustrate the governance mechanisms associated with standard setting and the associated form of knowledge transfer. A review of manuals produced in the Ghanaian cocoa sector since 1987 shows a bias towards one particular type of pruning, along with the absence of contextual factors to be considered during pruning. The orientation of manuals translated into the twofold purpose of extension and audits thus shapes the interaction between cocoa farmers and specialists. Mass training and coaching directs farmers towards one type of pruning and, in some instances, pruning was taken over by workers recruited by government or major firms. The members of these so-called 'pruning gangs,' according to farmers interviewed, did not have the skills and experience needed for proper pruning. Zooming out from on-farm pruning demonstrates how practices at sites downstream in the cocoa chain funnel pruning towards a narrower set of techniques, affecting productivity and sustainability levels in sourcing cocoa beans.

Interferences by non-localised specialisms

Public pressure for sustainability in global cocoa chains has led to the rise of standards and certification schemes, which are accompanied by trainings of smallholder producers in Good Agricultural Practices (Ponte and Cheyns, 2013). Sustainability standards and certification schemes prescribe pruning as a positive agricultural practice and consider it a low-cost choice for boosting productivity (Asare et al., 2018). Accordingly, knowledge is considered as a transferable item that brings scientific insights and prescribed ways-of-doing to farm management in multivariate agro-ecological conditions. The knowledge dimension is manifest in manuals, prescribed practices, check lists, and expert language appearing in the work of auditors and certifiers that monitor compliance to standards.

Agronomists employed at research institutes specialised in cocoa production acknowledged the situatedness of pruning and emphasised the contribution of pruning to conditions increasing productivity, which relate to aeration, light capture, and nutrient use. They also warned of the adverse effects of pruning when the practice is not learnt through hand-and-eye; a skilful pruner needs to carefully assess the status of the tree and its growing conditions before acting. Although these agronomic insights and the contextual understanding of pruning shared by farmers seem to be compatible, the real interactions between situated knowing and non-localised specialisms induced by standards and certification schemes indicate the opposite. The combination of training, monitoring, and auditing reduced the space for including context-specific practices.

The inclusion of pruning in protocols and procedures linked to standard setting and certification illustrates the institutional conditions for configuring skilful practices at one level in the layered organisational architecture, with knowledge-driven practices of controllers and managers at another level. The emphasis in the interactions seems to be on the adoption of prescribed practices, which limits space to jointly search for practices fit for the specific and variable conditions encountered in cocoa farming. Research on extension services in the cocoa sector in Ivory Coast (Muilerman and Vellema, 2017) exposes how institutional work embedded in the established cocoa bureaucracy created space for alternate arrangements, connecting the diversity at farm level and the *modus operandi* in the professional field of extension.

Knowing how to move produce from farm to market (Uganda)

In the case of oilseed, sourcing companies try out contractual arrangements for including smallholder farmers in agribusiness, which is combined with the provision of agricultural inputs and extension services. In addition to agricultural production, knowing how to ensure a consistent flow of produce to local markets is essential for food security. The following case focuses on intermediation between smallholders and downstream players within agri-food chains (Poulton et al., 2010). Access to food results from the intertwined practices of retailers, intermediary village traders, collecting agents in rural communities, and (smallholder) producers, which ensure a consistent flow of food from farms to markets often under conditions of scarcity and volatility.

Making practice work

Collecting and aggregating produce in this case is realised at sites where farmers bring their produce—oilseed—to village traders or collecting agents in rural communities (Vellema and Nakimbugwe, 2012). In the oilseed example, intermediary traders participated in local food markets through the practice of conduction (Legun and Bell, 2016): transporting, making payments, processing, and warehousing. The doorstep traders also knew where and when to get the supply. Given they were not able to be present everywhere all the time, they relied on close communication with informed farmers or sub-agents close to the farms informing them about oilseed ready for transport. This entailed securing presence in the villages in combination with the skills to handle the administering tasks associated with the transaction, such as weighing, writing down weights on bags and in notebooks, documenting any debts or remaining payments. Knowing how to organise storage capacity and transport was another crucial ingredient of the everyday work of the intermediary traders.

Besides the spatial dimension of conduction, traders also coped with the temporal dimension for ensuring consistency of supply. Seasonal fluctuation affected volumes available for trading. In addition, trading oilseed depended on choices made by farmers: reliability of the farmers' agent in the market formed an important consideration for what to plant. Farmers shifting to other crops or opting for a mixture of crops to spread risks generated a degree of uncertainty that local buying agents had to deal with. Traders themselves also diversified 'on-trade' and 'off-trade' practices, such as farming themselves, or renting out houses; or decided to diversify or specialise in certain crops, for example sesame or soybeans. Demonstrated capacity to ensure a consistent supply of oilseed under conditions of scarcity and seasonality, and therefore to sustain relationships with smallholder farmers, represents knowing how to bring food stuff from one place to another.

Connecting practices

Knowing how to bring food from farm to market entails addressing a variety of coordination problems relevant to staple food markets. Traders in the Ugandan markets for oilseed, which is linked to the edible oil food industry, face coordination problems due to the large number of small transactions, fluctuating production, and the need to travel long distances compounded by poor roads (Fafchamps and Minten, 2001). One important aspect of the practice of conduction is to be able to pay smallholder farmers for produce delivered. Timely and predictable payments to low-income farmers require availability of working capital. In an area where production is scattered over a large area with small farms, the doorstep traders need to pay on the spot and thus have cash readily available. The smaller village traders strongly rely on pre-financing by larger traders further downstream in the supply chain. The reliability of the village traders is constantly assessed by larger traders who make advanced payments. This usually starts with giving out small amounts to examine whether the receiving trader can be trusted and is able to handle larger amounts and handle financial risks intrinsic to buying and selling produce. More experienced village traders gradually receive higher amounts, which generate a degree of stability in the institutional arrangements in local markets. Mangnus and Vellema (2019) have observed similar processes shaping membership and inclusion in trading networks in Mali.

Knowing how to bring food from farms to markets emerges within a set of connected practices without the presence of a controlling agent. Trading oilseed encompasses several tasks performed by different people at different sites and entails less visible forms of coordination. Consequently, by knowing how to make the practice of conduction work, the intermediary village traders contribute to reliable and predictable market access at the farmer's doorstep (Chamberlin and Jayne, 2013). These skilful practices are part of a wider set of practices linked to an urban agri-food cluster assembling a stable group of larger traders in nearby towns (Schoonhoven-Speijer and Vellema, 2020). In dynamic market conditions, being able to rely on and partner with the practices of other actors proves to be instrumental for ensuring a continuous flow of produce. Knowing how to handle coordination problems is key to this.

Interferences by non-localised specialisms

In the early 2000s, one of Uganda's main food manufacturing companies supplying consumer markets with cooking oil decided to shift from importing palm oil to processing locally sourced sunflower seed. Initially, the company set up a contract farming scheme, provided farmers with hybrid sunflower seeds for planting, and started to source the produced oilseeds via their own agents. This initial step reflected the interventions and models proposed by NGOs, governments, and researchers, who aspire to shorten supply chains and replace intermediary traders. Eventually, the company recognised the role of intermediary traders in ensuring a consistent supply of oilseeds needed for meeting their increased processing capacity. Moreover, teaming up with the intermediary traders gave them access to actors knowing how to source from farmers, which was useful in an expanding competitive playing field after other companies arrived in the area.

In that sense, the processing company was added to the durable network of trading practices that already demonstrated the ability to handle a variety of coordination problems. The company recognised the skilful nature of knowing how to organise produce and cash flows; building and maintaining complex relationships; and handling unanticipated problems in food markets (Schoonhoven et al., 2017). They refrained from imposing alternate organisational models that are more favoured in the professional fields of market development and supply chain management. Seemingly, a functional relationship is conducive for productive interactions between the new demands of larger processing companies shifting to local sourcing and knowing accomplished in the situated practices of conduction responsive to changes in supply and fluctuating circumstances of farmers.

Conclusions

This chapter examined the methodological choice to take practices as an entry point for researching knowledge in the setting of layered commodity chains or food markets. Practices, such as pruning cocoa trees or sourcing oilseed, were investigated as situated and knowledgeable accomplishments, which reflect a form of mastery: pruning entails the mastery of selecting pruning techniques and assessing what works under specific agro-ecological condition; sourcing oilseed involves the mastery of handling coordination problems under conditions of fluctuation and scarcity. Zooming out from these time and place-specific practices reveals how they were part of a net of mutually constituting practices. The cases exemplify processes that are not always visible in making the distributed practices combine.

Unpacking the texture of practices is valuable for analysing whether and how a layered organisational set up, such as commodity chains or food markets, realises certain outcomes, such as sustainability or consistency in the sourcing of raw materials. Taking a specific practice as an entry point for research makes it possible to trace relationships in space and time that underlie organising. Hence, realising sustainability in commodity chains or consistency in food markets becomes a matter of knowing how to connect to established local practices, rather than transferring codified knowledge; for example, in the form of so-called good agricultural practices in standards, or prescribed use of inputs in contractual arrangements.

The chapter shows how to detect effects of interferences through knowledge-based interventions by non-localised specialisms. This offers a perspective on the politics of knowledge, which concentrates on rules and routines associated with knowing in professional fields anchored in evolving division of labour in society. The cases demonstrate that making the connection between the net of practices situated in specific contexts and non-localised specialisms is not automatically productive. Non-localised professionals, such as auditors, certifiers, or supply chain managers, are inclined to bring established practices in line with their preferred models and routines. In the case of the cocoa commodity chain in Ghana, training and extension were associated with the knowing included in standards and auditing and certification protocols. Their rigidity constrained making the connection to localised practicing and the knowledgeable activities of smallholder cocoa farmers. In the case of sourcing oilseed in Uganda, the leading food manufacturing company navigated different management styles and eventually opted for aligning with the net of established trading practices rather than concentrating on capturing efficiencies by way of direct control over the sourcing via induced contractual arrangements with smallholder farmers. Seemingly, the company recognised a proven capacity to handle coordination problems in the established network of trading practices.

The methodological perspective central to this chapter focuses on knowing how to make practice work. The perspective integrates a focus on localised attempts to repair errors, improvise workable action, and navigate unanticipated problems with a broader interest in explaining why and how a bundle of practices gains stability and permanence in dynamic markets and in agro-ecological environments. It enables discovering the trails between distributed practices and identifying the space for institutional work that make situated knowing and non-localised specialisms commensurable. This goes beyond contrasting, for example, local and scientific knowledge *per se* and encourages researchers to unravel the functional connections between knowing how to make practices work and durable processes shaping relationships between distributed practices from which social order emerges.

References

Aasare, R., Afari-Sefa, V., Muilerman, S. and Anim-Kwapong, G. (2018). Good agronomic practices in cocoa cultivation: Rehabilitating cocoa farms. In: Pathmanathan, U. (ed.). *Achieving sustainable cultivation of cocoa.* Cabridge: Burleigh Dodds Science Publishing, 1–28.

Barber, K. (2007). Improvisation and the art of making things stick. In: Hallam, E. and Ingold, T. (eds.). *Creativity and cultural improvisation.* Oxford: Berg Publishers.

Chamberlin, J. and Jayne, T. S. (2013). Unpacking the meaning of 'market access': evidence from rural Kenya. *World Development,* 41, 24–64.

Durkheim, E. (1957/2001). *Professional ethics and civic morals.* Milton Park: Routledge.

Fafchamps, M. and Minten, B. (2001). Property rights in a flea market economy. *Economic Development and Cultural Change,* 49(2), 229–267.

Fenwick, T. (2006). Learning as grounding and flying: Knowledge, skill and transformation in changing work contexts. *Journal of Industrial Relations,* 48(5), 691–706.

Fressoli, M., Arond, E., Abrol, D., Smith, A., Ely, A. and Dias, R. (2014). When grassroots innovation movements encounter mainstream institutions: Implications for models of inclusive innovation. *Innovation and Development,* 4(2), 277–292.

Gibbon, P. and Ponte, S. (2008). Global value chains: From governance to governmentality? *Economy and Society,* 37(3), 365–392.

Glover, D., Venot, J.-P. and Maat, H. (2017). On the movement of agricultural technologies. In: Sumberg, J. (ed.). *Agronomy for development: The politics of knowledge in agricultural research,* Milton Park: Routledge, 14–30.

Govindaraj, K. and Jancirani, P. (2017). Effect of pruning on cocoa (Theobroma cacao L.) on morphological, flowering and yield and quality of cocoa beans. *International Journal of Agricultural Science and Research,* 7(6), 113–118.

Hutchins, E. (1995). *Cognition in the wild.* Cambridge: MIT Press.

Jaarsma, T., Maat, H., Richards, P. and Wals, A. (2011). The role of materiality in apprenticeships: The case of the Suame Magazine, Kumasi, Ghana. *Journal of Vocational Education and Training,* 63(3), 439–449.

Jansen, K. and Vellema, S. (2011). What is technography? *NJAS Wageningen Journal of Life Sciences,* 57(3/4), 169–177.

Johri, A. (2011). The socio-materiality of learning practices and implications for the field of learning technology. *Research in Learning Technology,* 19(3), 207–217.

Jones, A. and Murphy, J. T. (2011). Theorizing practice in economic geography: Foundations, challenges, and possibilities. *Progress in Human Geography*, 35(3), 366–392.

Lave, J. (1993). The practice of learning. In: Chaiklin, S. and Lave, J. (eds.). *Understanding practice: Perspectives on activity and context*. Cambridge: Cambridge University Press.

Lawrence, T. B. and Suddaby, R. (2006). Institutions and institutional work. In: Clegg, R., Hardy, C., Lawrence, T. B. and Nord, W. R. (eds.). *Handbook of organization studies*, 2nd Edition. London: Sage.

Lawrence, T. B., Suddaby, R. and Leca, B. (2009). Introduction: Theorizing and studying institutional work. In: Lawrence, T. B., Suddaby, R. and Leca, B. (eds.). *Institutional work: Actors and agency in institutional studies of organizations*. Cambridge: Cambridge University Press.

Legun, K. and Bell, M. M. (2016). The second middle: Conducers and the agrifood economy. *Journal of Rural Studies*, 48, 104–114.

Mangnus, E. and Vellema, S. (2019). Persistence and practice of trading networks a case study of the cereal trade in Mali. *Journal of Rural Studies*, 69, 137–144.

Mcfeat, T. (1974). *Small group cultures*. Oxford: Pergamon.

Mudambi, R. and Swift, T. (2009). Professional guilds, tension and knowledge management. *Research Policy*, 38(5), 736–745.

Muilerman, S. and Vellema, S. (2017). Scaling service delivery in a failed state: Cocoa smallholders, Farmer Field Schools, persistent bureaucrats and institutional work in Côte d'Ivoire. *International Journal of Agricultural Sustainability*, 15(1), 83–98.

Nicolini, D. (2009). Zooming in and out: Studying practices by switching theoretical lenses and trailing connections. *Organization Studies*, 30(12), 1391–1418.

Nicolini, D. (2011). Practice as the site of knowing: Insights from the field of telemedicine. *Organization Science*, 22(3), 602–620.

Nicolini, D. (2012). *Practice theory, work, and organization: An introduction*. Oxford: Oxford University Press.

Orlikowski, W. J. (2002). Knowing in practice: Enacting a collective capability in distributed organizing. *Organization Science*, 13(3), 249–273.

Paavola, S. and Hakkarainen, K. (2005). The knowledge creation metaphor–An emergent epistemological approach to learning. *Science and Education*, 14(6), 535–557.

Ponte, S. and Cheyns, E. (2013). Voluntary standards, expert knowledge and the governance of sustainability networks. *Global Networks*, 13(4), 459–477.

Poulton, C., Dorward, A. and Kydd, J. (2010). The future of small farms: New directions for services, institutions, and intermediation. *World Development*, 38(10), 1413–1428.

Richards, P. (1989). Agriculture as a performance. In: Chambers, R., Pacey, A. and Thrupp, L. A. (eds.). *Farmer first. Farmer innovation and agricultural research*. Bradford: Intermediate Technology Publications.

Richards, P. (1993). Cultivation: Knowledge or performance? In: Hobart, M. (ed.). *An anthropological critique of development: The growth of ignorance*. Milton Park: Routledge.

Schoonhoven-Speijer, M. and Vellema, S. (2020). How institutions governing the economic middle in food provisioning are reinforced: The case of an agri-food cluster in northern Uganda. *Journal of Rural Studies*, 80, 34–44.

Schoonhoven, M., Mangnus, E. and Vellema, S. (2017). Knowing how to bring food to the market: Appreciating the contribution of intermediary traders to the future of food availability in Sub-Saharan Africa. In: Duncan, J. and Bailey, M. (eds.). *Sustainable Food Futures: Multidisciplinary Solutions*. Milton Park: Routledge.

Vellema, S. and Nakimbugwe, D. (2012). The Ugandan oilseed sub-sector platform. In: Nederlof, E. S., Wongtschowski, M. and Lee, F. V. D. (eds.). *Putting heads together: Agricultural innovation platforms in practice*. Amsterdam: KIT Publishers.

17

THE CONUNDRUM OF ARTICULATING SOCIETAL KNOWLEDGE AND TECHNOLOGY DEMAND

Cees Leeuwis

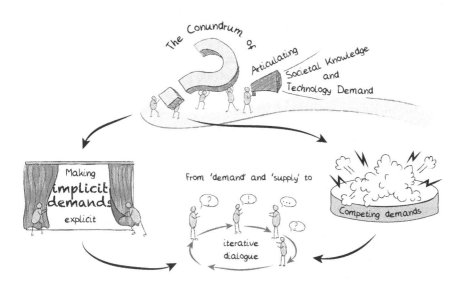

Introduction

Although there is considerable investment in the production and provision of applied knowledge and technology to beneficiaries in the context of international development efforts, there are many examples where such knowledge is often found less relevant and applicable to prospective users. Both agricultural research and extension organisations, for example, have been sharply criticised for generating and disseminating knowledge and technology that does not match with the needs, demands, and realities of large segments of farming populations (Birner and Byerlee, 2016; Klerkx and Leeuwis, 2008; Laborde et al., 2020).

DOI: 10.4324/9781003112525-17

In response to this, several authors have called for greater involvement of users in the setting of research and extension agendas. These developments in agricultural research for development resonate with developments in other sectors and contexts, where we see greater attention for democracy and public engagement in the formulation of research agendas (Boon and Edler, 2018). In the Netherlands, for example, this has resulted in a nationwide citizen consultation for the development of the Dutch 'national research agenda' (De Graaf et al., 2017).

Such strategies for 'making knowledge work' are frequently linked to the idea that the articulation of knowledge-demands in society needs to be enhanced. Here, the notion of 'demand' is used primarily in a substantive sense in referring to questions that citizens have, to gaps in understanding that they prioritise, or to criteria that they use in evaluating whether a new technology (e.g. a seed variety) meets their expectations (Almekinders, 2011). The assumption is that the articulation of such demands will serve to make research and extension systems more 'demand-driven' or 'demand-led' (Birner and Anderson, 2007; Kibwika et al., 2009), leading to the production (or co-creation) of more relevant knowledge and technology, and—eventually—to more effective knowledge utilisation and problem solving.

The next section presents several small case-studies that invite reflection on the notions of demand and demand-articulation. With reference to these empirical observations, I critically examine assumptions that underpin the idea of demand-articulation and the expectation that this will enhance the applicability of knowledge generated. In doing so, a better understanding on 'how knowledge works' is created.

In the final part of the paper, I discuss how we can 'make demand articulation work differently.' I propose that we need to embed demand-articulation in collaborative change initiatives, whereby knowledge provision becomes an integral part of efforts to strengthen discourse coalitions for change.

Formative experiences and reflections

Over a period stretching from the late 1980s to the present, I was involved in a number of studies that yielded insights into the notions of demand and demand-articulation. Below I summarise some of these experiences and the lessons learned from them.

Case 1: Developing software for horticulturists: discovering demands as a moving target

A first formative experience dates back to an early stage in the digital revolution, shortly after the introduction of the personal computer in agriculture in the 1980s. However, the story resonates with recent experiences in developing software for mobile Information and Communication Technology for Development (ICT4D).

In the early 1990s, a group of glasshouse horticulturists in the Netherlands managed to arrange a national subsidy in order to build a software package that would support them in exchanging data and comparing the performance of different glasshouse enterprises. A software company was hired to build the programme, and the process started with several meetings geared towards eliciting a programme of requirements. The growers explicated their interests regarding the functionalities of the software, and had to find a compromise on the data that the package would include. Glasshouse horticulturists specialise in different crops (tomato, cucumber, flowers, etc.) and each crop was associated with specific agronomic and production-related parameters of relevance, while all growers had an interest in analysing production parameters against climatic data. Since the project was supposed to benefit all, it was decided that the emphasis should be on exchanging climatic data since these were the same for all growers. When the programme of requirements was ready, the software developers build the software package.

Once the horticulturists began using the package, they immediately formulated a range of additional ideas, including a wish for graphic presentation of data (e.g. graphs comparing several parameters in selected time periods, cumulative graphs regarding production per week, etc.). However, the subsidy had been spent already, and there were no additional resources available. Meanwhile, a small group of cucumber growers had started a competing initiative because they were unhappy about the compromises made. They engaged a partially disabled arable farmer and computer amateur, developing tailor-made comparison software for cucumber growers in a relatively short time. This amateur continuously engaged with the users and rapidly developed new prototypes based on user feedback, including numerous graphical presentations that were desired by the growers. The costs were a fraction of the subsidised project. The users were very happy with the rapid uptake of their suggestions, but complained about numerous bugs and the continuous stream of updates (Leeuwis and Arkesteijn, 1991).

From this experience we can draw several lessons relevant to demand-articulation.

Demands are diverse. The experience makes clear that demands are diverse even within a group that may seem relatively homogeneous at first sight. In this case, glasshouse horticulturists specialising in different crops wanted the software package to include diverging crop-specific agronomic and production-related parameters. Without such crop-specific information the package had little added value to them. More in general, we know that users and audiences can differ along numerous lines (gender, aspirations, wealth, etc.) that cause them to pose different demands on knowledge and technology, and that a 'one-size-fits-all' solution rarely works.

Demands can be emergent and tacit due to limited experience. The experience demonstrates that the precise needs and demands of users may only become clear after they have been confronted with solutions (see also Bentley et al., 2007). In this case, growers were asked to formulate their demands in advance, but they could not articulate sharp and validated demands because it was inherently difficult for them to imagine what the new ICT technologies could do for them. It was only when they were confronted with a working version of the software that they realised and explicated what it was they really wanted. More generally, it is very difficult to formulate a demand in relation to something that one is not familiar with, and one cannot therefore assume that prospective users can always articulate in detail what they want.

The layered character of needs and demands. The experience shows that it is relevant to distinguish between 'needs' and 'demands' at different levels of abstraction. While the growers were able in advance to formulate a broad need at an abstract level ('we want a software package that supports exchange and comparison of on-farm data') they could not yet translate this into more detailed demands (the inclusion of specific parameters and graphic comparison facilities). Thus, demands can be seen as a further translation and operationalisation of a broader need. The formulation of a need (e.g. to have 'a viable farm' or 'a healthy living environment') is much easier than exerting specific and validated demands that will help to realise the broader need and ambition. By implication, processes of demand-articulation need to move beyond 'needs assessment' and find ways of digging deeper into the specific practices and rationales involved.

Participatory projects and methods differ in their capacity to incorporate emergent demands. Experience shows that technologies—in this case software—can be developed in different ways. Arguably, both projects were highly participatory and initiated by growers, but they differed in their approach and level of formality. In order to get access to a government subsidy, the national initiative was required to make use of a professional software company that used a linear development method that made a strict separation between the needs-articulation and the implementation phases. When the software was ready, it was no longer possible to make meaningful adaptations since the project resources were finished. The more localised and amateur-based initiative used an informal 'prototyping' (Vonk, 1990) approach that was very effective for discovering and meeting substantive demands, but at the costs of software technical elegance and sustainability. Thus, we see that formalised project environments can easily impose constraints that hamper the identification and uptake of demands. The challenge then is to fund and organise projects in such a way that emerging demands can be incorporated, i.e., that iteration between actual use and design is possible.

Case 2: Farmer funded research: a process resulting in disappointment

In 2004, I was approached by representatives of the Dutch Dairy Commodity Board (DCB) with a request to investigate their internal processes of demand-articulation for applied research. The DCB collected farmer levies (a fee per litre of milk produced) and used these to fund applied research on questions generated by farmers, and to translate the findings into extension materials that would assumedly be highly relevant to farmers. Despite the fact that farmers generated the initial questions, and even though a farmer committee (the Dairy Farming Committee, DFC) had full control over resources and fund allocation, the DCB had worries about the relevance of the knowledge being generated. Farmers were not appreciative of the research findings that were communicated, and questioned whether they should continue to collectively fund research at all. I was intrigued: how could it be that the relevance of knowledge generated seemed so poor in a situation where the degree of farmer ownership, participation, and control seemed so high?

We investigated the entire process from exploring farmer demands to research implementation and dissemination (Klerkx et al., 2008), and concluded that there were several missed opportunities for enhancing relevance. In a nutshell, possible questions for research were mostly solicited at the end of regional farmer meetings that had a much broader agenda. Questions from different regions were then collated and grouped by a DCB official. Subsequently, questions were passed on to researchers for assessment and advice, whereby most questions tended to be dismissed as being 'too operational and not requiring additional research.' Remaining questions would typically be prioritised by a committee of DFC farmers and DCB officials, after which researchers developed research proposals that were subsequently approved or rejected by the DFC, and then further operationalised and implemented in a research facility (for details, see Klerkx et al., 2008).

Strikingly, the farmers who had initially posed the questions were not included in these subsequent stages and had no opportunity to interact with officials or researchers to discuss the specific context or the 'questions behind the question.' In addition, research tended to be carried out in researcher facilities (and not on-farm) and without any direct involvement of farmers. Overall, it appeared that the process was organised in such a way that researchers had a high degree of influence on the eventual framing of the research questions, the methodologies used, and the conclusions drawn. At no point in the process was there serious interaction between the farmers posing the questions, other stakeholders that might be relevant to the perceived problem setting, and those who were mandated to generate answers. We concluded that an in-depth articulation of demand (and also 'supply') did not occur, and that the subtleties of the process and the institutional setting offered researchers a lot of opportunities to steer research in directions that fitted their rationales and preferences.

From the above example we can learn several things.

Demands are negotiated in an arena with unequal opportunities to exert influence. In this experience we see that the local questions and demands from farmers were filtered and transformed in a process that involved bureaucrats, researchers, and high-level farmer representatives. The assumptions, criteria, and interests of these parties became leading strands, resulting in research projects that largely reflected their needs and demands rather than those of the farmers. This was possible because those formulating questions had no voice in the transformation process, while others were empowered to make their expertise, preferences, and interpretations count in developing and implementing research proposals. Thus, the demands that are actually catered for are the outcome of a negotiation process that is affected by the way in which the interaction is organised (see also Bukenya, 2010).

Diverging lifeworlds complicate the formulation of demands for 'research.' In this example, we also see that prospective users were asked to formulate demands in relation to something abstract ('research') that they were not necessarily familiar with. Arguably, understanding what scientific researchers can or cannot do requires fairly intimate understanding of different scientific disciplines, methods, and available knowledge and research approaches. Clearly, most farmers had little awareness of these. It was therefore not surprising that bureaucrats and researchers could dismiss most issues raised as 'not requiring additional research' or 'non-researchable.' Similarly, bureaucrats and researchers tended to have limited contextual understanding of the challenges that emerge in everyday farming practice, and therefore had little to no access to the world from which the issue or question emerged. In essence, we see that users and researchers may live in different taken-for-granted worlds (or 'lifeworlds,' Schutz and Luckmann, 1974) that do not easily become connected and linked in a meaningful manner.

Case 3: Potato diseases in Ethiopia: the importance and limitations of knowledge

Potato production in Ethiopia (and elsewhere) is severely affected by several diseases, including late blight and bacterial wilt. The micro-organisms that cause the disease can spread through various routes (e.g. wind, water, soil, seed), which means that farmers can easily infect neighbouring farms if they do not burn diseased plants, disinfect tools and boots, prevent water run-off to other fields, buy clean seed (in case of bacterial wilt), and/or spray against the disease (in case of late blight).

A study by Tafesse et al. (2018) indicated that farmers had very limited knowledge about the existence of damaging micro-organisms and the mechanisms through which they spread, and that most farmers therefore did not realise that successful disease management was highly dependent on the behaviour of their neighbours. In response, several learning-oriented interventions were implemented to foster a greater understanding of the dynamics of the disease for farmers (Damtew et al., 2020).

Although these activities were indeed fruitful, having access to knowledge about disease symptoms, spreading mechanisms, and interdependence was far from sufficient, not least because effective application of such knowledge in Ethiopia essentially required the introduction of a community-based disease management system, rather than a system that relied on individual action only. Typically, collective forms of disease management would need to include an agreement about rules and bylaws to be applied, the establishment of committees monitoring both disease occurrence and adherence to agreements by community members, the implementation of a sanctioning system for those that violated agreed-upon rules, and the development of an organisational model to support all this (Tafesse et al., 2020).

Demands can be latent due to gaps in understanding. This experience confirms that it can be difficult to develop understandings and demands about phenomena (i.e., spreading mechanisms of bacteria and viruses) that are largely invisible to the eye (Bentley et al., 2007). Farmers could see the disease symptoms and identify a need for solutions, but few farmers could articulate a demand for knowledge about spreading mechanisms or for community-based disease management, even though this would be highly relevant to them from the perspective of scientists. Parallel to the case about ICT development described above (where growers knew about ICT but had limited experience) we see that it is very difficult to articulate demands about something one does not know about already. In such cases, we could say that users may have latent demands; demands that they cannot formulate in detail but that they would be likely to articulate if they had more usable and relevant information. This is of course a tricky area for researchers, as it offers ample opportunities for them to promote knowledge and technology under the pretext that 'users do not understand anyway.' While latent demands can certainly exist, it is important to realise that one still needs to validate and test what they look like in practice.

Fulfilling knowledge demands is not sufficient. The experience also makes clear that having knowledge about something at an individual level is not a sufficient condition for effective action. In this case, knowledge could only be made effective in concert with other farmers; that is, in a relational setting and in conjunction with institutional issues such as agreement, trust, rules, organisational arrangements, and sanctions. There are many examples showing that new knowledge and technology can only be applied when social and institutional environments are reconfigured (Adjeih Nsiah et al., 2008; Kilelu et al., 2014; Sartas et al., 2020) and achieving this requires radically different kinds of processes than simply detecting and addressing gaps in knowledge and understanding (Geels, 2002; Leeuwis and Aarts, 2011). Similarly, even at the individual level, social-psychological research demonstrates that knowledge is only one of the drivers of human behaviour (Ajzen, 1985). Thus, the focus of researchers and professionals on issues pertaining to research, knowledge exchange, and knowledge demand is a rather artificial insertion into reality, and arguably rather myopic.

Case 4: Privatised extension delivery on environmental issues: a voucher system to stimulate demand

Animal production systems in the Netherlands are very intensive, and rely on the massive import of animal feed from countries such as Brazil and Thailand. This has resulted in the overuse of animal manure and serious environmental degradation in rural areas. In the 1990s, the Dutch government took several measures to reduce emissions from animal production, including a compulsory bookkeeping system through which farmers had to register incoming and outgoing flows of nutrients such as nitrogen and phosphorus, and to pay fines in case of serious losses. The government also withdrew animal production rights after a major crisis with swine fever.

While the bookkeeping system was seen as highly complicated and bureaucratic, the latter measure was regarded by most farmers as 'theft' and a 'stab in the back.' In short, the relation between public authorities and farmers was far from optimal. In this context, the government started an experiment with a form of privatised extension (Klerkx et al., 2006). The Ministry of Agriculture had noted that farmers were not very active in seeking advice on how to reduce their nutrient use, and it wanted to support farmers in doing so through a sophisticated voucher system. In essence, all farmers in the Netherlands received a voucher of 250 euros, which they could spend at a private service provider to get advice and support on nutrient management. Before spending their voucher, they could participate in facilitated group sessions that would help them to discover their needs, and a website with certified advisory products was supposed to help them choose an appropriate service. The government investment was legitimised with reference to the idea that caring for the environment would not yield immediate economic benefit for farmers. The vouchers were seen an instrument that would persuade farmers to become more active, and to discover how they might also benefit from improved nutrient management.

Our study on how farmers responded to this opportunity revealed several things. First of all, it showed that relatively few farmers were initially interested to spend the voucher even though it was free. Many farmers argued they did not have a nutrient management problem, and that they had sufficient knowledge and understanding already. Moreover, the large majority of those who eventually did spent the voucher (about one third of those eligible) were actually persuaded and pushed into its use by their regular private service providers; they regarded the voucher mainly as a discount from the price of services that they already had to pay for in relation to such things as nutrient bookkeeping (Klerkx et al., 2006).

Confusing political, economic, and substantive demand. This experience demonstrates, again, that demands come about in a negotiation space where different actors have different interests. Politicians and public administrators demanded that extension services provide farmers with content on nutrient management, which incentivised privatised service providers to push farmers in using opportunities for free advice and support services. However, farmers expressed that they were not interested in additional knowledge about nutrient management, indicating that they had no internalised substantive demand. Although such expressions were in part a form of resistance against the government (with whom relations had become seriously strained) it is indeed also questionable whether farmers lacked knowledge on the topic in the first place. If they had wanted to reduce nutrient use, most of them indicated that they knew how. The problem was that they did not aspire to reduce nutrient use in the context of strained relationships. The government tried to compensate the lack of substantive demand by creating an artificial demand in the economic sense (a voucher to buy a service). The example makes clear that the notion of 'demand' can have substantive, economic, and political connotations, and that the possibility of exerting an economic demand (buying a service) does not guarantee a substantive demand. Similarly, there are many situations in the world where clients may have a (latent or explicit) substantive demand, but do not have the financial resources or political space to exert that demand (Nederlof et al., 2008; Feder et al., 2011).

Case 5: Conflicting interests in conservation-induced resettlement: the sensitivity of meeting knowledge demand

In the beginning of this century, the government of Mozambique aimed to resettle communities who were living in Limpopo National Park, because the removal of fences separating neighbouring national parks in Zimbabwe and South Africa would lead to intensified tension between human inhabitants and wildlife. The inhabitants of the Park were far from happy about moving elsewhere and were involved in negotiations with the government about compensation and further conditions for their departure. Neither communities nor Park authorities had precise knowledge and information about the quantity and quality of natural resources (e.g. arable land, grazing land, water, trees, etc.) that people living in the Park were accessing, and how this compared to resources they would be able to use in their projected area of resettlement. A PhD candidate who lived in the first community that was to be resettled started to make an inventory of such natural resources (Milgroom, 2012). She measured fields with a GPS device and gathered additional information through in-depth interviews and focus group discussions. Through her data collection efforts she became a valuable resource of information for both the communities and the Park authorities. The latter learned that they had under-estimated the resources that inhabitants in the Park used, and through the data collection efforts the communities became more aware that they were likely to lose out on resources. As a result, communities started to make stronger demands for compensation and the negotiations between inhabitants and Park authorities heated up considerably. Meanwhile, the researcher was kicked out of the Park as the authorities felt that her presence and data collection activities were delaying the resettlement process as well as becoming a political threat.

Knowledge as a weapon in the struggle. This example indicates that the creation and sharing of knowledge and information can be highly sensitive, especially when it fulfils a demand and strengthens the position of parties in a negotiation process (Giller et al., 2008). Knowledge and information can be used to support arguments for or against certain courses of action, and in some sense can be seen as a 'weapon' that stakeholders can use in their struggle. Thus, meeting demands for knowledge can—at least temporarily—lead to increased tension and conflict (Milgroom, 2012).

The research process can have societal impact before the results are clear. While knowledge is often regarded as insights that are formulated at the end of a research trajectory, this example shows that the research process also matters considerably. In the case described above, it was the process of data collection (measuring fields, conducting interviews) that awakened the communities' awareness and which led them to become more assertive in their negotiations with the Park. Well-articulated research findings and conclusions about the quantity and quality of resources were formulated only at a much later stage, long after the negotiations were over. Thus, it was the research process that had societal impact, and not the research findings (Milgroom, 2012). In line with this, the research methods used also had a performative dimension. Had the researcher used satellite images and algorithms to determine the quantity and quality of resources available, then it is very unlikely that there would have been an impact on the negotiation process.

Making demand-articulation work: embedding knowledge provision in the ongoing dynamic

The above experiences and lessons make clear that demand-articulation is not an easy and straightforward process, and that it is too simplistic to assume that identification of knowledge demands in society seamlessly results in more relevant knowledge production and greater utilisation. We have seen that societal demands for knowledge and technology are interactional; that is, they arise and emerge in a specific context where people engage with others (including allies, adversaries, and knowledge providers) to negotiate and realise specific ambitions. Thus, demands are not neutral and are part and parcel of politically laden views and strategies regarding desired futures. The small case-studies also suggest that the discovery, specification, and verification of demands can benefit greatly from intensive interaction with potential knowledge and technology providers over a period of time. In other words: the articulation of societal demand for knowledge and technology requires a high-quality process of interaction between the 'demand' and 'supply' side (Bentley et al., 2007; Klerkx et al., 2008). Below, I will outline some further thoughts related to what a 'high quality' process may look like and how those who are seen to be at the knowledge providing end may contribute to this.

Engaging with ongoing initiatives for change. Real demands emerge when societal stakeholders want to achieve something and bring about change. Thus, it may be wise for knowledge providers (e.g. research and extension staff) who want to be societally relevant to link up with 'where the action is' and connect to already ongoing initiatives and existing coalitions for change in society, rather than to start 'from scratch.' This simultaneously implies a commitment to the values that are pursued, and a willingness to address value-laden questions while maintaining scientific and/or professional integrity. Preferably, such engagement and commitment last for a prolonged period, as it may take time to discover and address demands. Moreover, relevant demands evolve over time as change processes—which tend to be slow—progress. In essence, the suggestion is to place knowledge provision and research 'in development,' rather than to do them from an outsider position 'for development' (Leeuwis et al., 2017).

From 'demand' and 'supply' to iterative dialogue. Notions like 'demand' and 'supply' have linear connotations as they tend to reinforce the misleading idea that there is a clear separation between those at the sending and the receiving end (Leeuwis, 2000). In a process of mutual engagement all parties involved have something to offer and something to ask for, and indeed formulating what the relevant questions are is equally (if not more) important to knowledge production than devising strategies to answering them. Overcoming the significant differences in taken-for-granted life-worlds between societal stakeholders with tacit contextual experience and those with scientific training requires an in-depth and iterative process of exchange and dialogue, whereby observation and listening to what is said and what is treated with silence is of critical importance (Aarts, 2015; Verouden et al., 2016). Thus, careful attention must be paid to how and where such dialogue is facilitated, since it is important to consider that engagement with the everyday bio-physical realities of stakeholders (e.g. agricultural fields, irrigation canals, processing plants, hospitals) can solicit highly relevant conversations (Chambers, 1994).

Maintaining cross-disciplinary conversations along the entire research process. As many societal challenges are multi-faceted, relevant demands are likely to exist vis-à-vis several bodies of knowledge. Thus, several disciplines and sources of expertise may need to take part in a dialogue. In cases where new knowledge needs to be created through research activity, it is important to recall that the research process itself can have meaningful impact upon society even before results are ready. Collaborative research with several stakeholders may contribute to changes in relationships, awareness of interdependencies, and the formation of discourse coalitions (Hajer and Laws, 2006) that already contribute to addressing societal challenges. To optimise the impact of the process and create continued opportunities for demand-articulation and knowledge integration (see Ludwig and Boogaard, this volume), it can be important to organise interaction and involvement along multiple stages of research processes, ranging from research design, choice of methods and location, data collection, data analysis, evaluation, and reporting activities (Jalbert and Kinchy, 2016). It is through such joint activities that newly created knowledge enters the societal conversation and can contribute to shifting these as an integral component of achieving societal change (Leeuwis and Aarts, 2011).

Finally, we need to end this discussion of the conundrum of demand-articulation with a caveat. Embedding knowledge provision in a high-quality process along the lines suggested above is easier said than done. It requires considerable skills and capacities on the side of both societal stakeholders and professional knowledge providers (Kibwika et al., 2009). Even more importantly, it requires an institutional environment in research and extension that encourages and incentivises these kinds of engagement and is able to accommodate them organisationally and financially. Evidence suggests that dominant ways of financing, staffing, planning, and controlling research and extension activities are often not thus conducive (Leeuwis, 2000; Leeuwis et al., 2017; Sumberg et al., 2017). Changing our own institutional realities is a challenge that we need to address with urgency.

References

Aarts, M. N. C. (2015). *The art of dialogue*. Inaugural lecture upon taking up the post of Personal Professor of Communication and Change in Life Science Contexts at Wageningen University on 3 September 2015.

Adjei-Nsiah, S., Leeuwis, C., Giller, K. E. and Kuyper, T. W. (2008). Action research on alternative land tenure arrangements in Wenchi, Ghana: Learning from ambiguous social dynamics and self-organized institutional innovation. *Agriculture and Human Values*, 25, 389–403.

Ajzen, I. (1985). From intentions to actions: A theory of planned behavior. In: Kuhl, J. and Beckmann, J. (eds.). *Action control: From cognition to behavior*. Dordrecht: Springer, 11–39.

Almekinders, C. J. M. (2011). The joint development of JM-12.7: A technographic description of the making of a bean variety. *NJAS - Wageningen Journal of Life Sciences*, 57(34), 207–216.

Chambers, R. (1994). Participatory Rural Appraisal (PRA): Analysis of experience. *World Development*, 22, 1253–1268.

Bentley, J., Velasco, C., Rodríguez, F., Oros, R., Botello, R., Webb, M., Devaux, A. and Thiele, G. (2007). Unspoken demands for farm technology. *International Journal of Agricultural Sustainability*, 5(1), 70–84.

Birner, R. and Anderson, J. (2007). How to make agricultural extension demand-driven. The case of India's agricultural extension policy. IFPRI discussion paper 00729. IFPRI.

Birner, R. and Byerlee, D. (2016). *Synthesis and lessons learned from 15 CRP evaluations*. Independent Evaluation Arrangement (IEA) of CGIAR. http://iea.cgiar.org/

Boon, W. and Edler, J. (2018). Demand, challenges, and innovation. Making sense of new trends in innovation policy. *Science and Public Policy*, 45, 435–447.

Bukenya, C. (2010). *Meeting farmer demand? An assessment of extension reform in Uganda*. Unpublished PhD dissertation, Wageningen University.

Damtew, E., Mierlo, Van, B., Lie, R., Struik, P., Leeuwis, C., Lemaga, B. and Smart, C. (2020). Governing a collective bad: Social learning in the management of crop diseases. *Systemic Practice and Action Research*, 33, 111–134.

De Graaf, B. A., Kan, R. and Molenaar, H. (eds.) (2017). *The Dutch National Research Agenda in Perspective. A reflection on research and science policy in practice*. Amsterdam: Amsterdam University Press.

Feder, G., Birner, R. and Anderson, J. R. (2011). The private sector's role in agricultural extension systems: Potential and limitations. *Journal of Agribusiness in Developing and Emerging Economies*, 1(1), 31–54.

Geels, F. W. (2002). Technological transitions as evolutionary reconfiguration processes: A multi-level perspective and a case-study. *Research Policy*, 31(8–9), 1257–1274.

Giller, K. E., Leeuwis, C., Andersson, J. A., Andriesse, W., Brouwer, A., Frost, P., ... and Windmeijer, P. (2008). Competing claims on natural resources: What role for science? *Ecology and Society*, 13(2). https://www.ecologyandsociety.org/vol13/iss2/art34/

Hajer, M. A. and Laws, D. (2006). Ordering through discourse. In: Moran, M., Rein and Goodin, R. E. (eds.). *The Oxford handbook of public policy*. Oxford: Oxford University Press, 249–266.

Jalbert, K. and Kinchy, A. J. (2016). Sense and influence: Environmental monitoring tools and the power of citizen science. *Journal of Environmental Policy and Planning*, 18(3), 379–397.

Kibwika, P., Wals, A. E. J. and Nassuna-Musoke, M. G. (2009). Competence challenges of demand-led agricultural research and extension in Uganda. *The Journal of Agricultural Education and Extension*, 150(1), 5–19.

Kilelu, C. W., Klerkx, L. and Leeuwis, C. (2014). How dynamics of learning are linked to innovation support services: Insights from a smallholder commercialization project in Kenya. *The Journal of Agricultural Education and Extension*, 20, 213–232.

Klerkx, L., Grip, K. de and Leeuwis, C. (2006). Hands off but strings attached: the contradictions of policy-induced demand-driven agricultural extension. *Agriculture and Human Values*, 23(2), 189–204.

Klerkx, L. W. A. and Leeuwis, C. (2008). Institutionalizing end-user demand steering in agricultural RandD: Farmer levy funding of RandD in The Netherlands. *Research Policy*, 37(3), 460–472.

Laborde, D., Porciello, J. and Smaller, C. (2020). Ceres2030: Sustainable solutions to end hunger. *Ceres2030*. https://ceres2030.org/

Leeuwis, C. and Arkesteyn, M. (1991). Planned technology development and local initiative: Computer supported enterprise-comparisons among Dutch horticulturists. *Sociologia Ruralis*, 31(2/3), 140–161.

Leeuwis, C. (2000). Learning to be sustainable. Does the Dutch agrarian knowledge market fail? *The Journal of Agricultural Education and Extension*, 7, 79–92.

Leeuwis, C. and Aarts, N. (2011). Rethinking communication in innovation processes: Creating space for change in complex systems. *Journal of Agricultural Education and Extension*, 17(1), 21–36.

Leeuwis, C., Schut, M. and Klerkx, L. (2017). Systems research in the CGIAR as an arena of struggle: Competing discourses on the embedding of research in development. In: Sumberg, J., Andersson, J. and Thompson, J. (eds.). *Agronomy for development: The politics of knowledge in agricultural research*. Milton Park: Routledge, 59–78.

Milgroom, J. (2012). *Elephants of democracy. An unfolding process of resettlement in the Limpopo National Park*. Unpublished PhD dissertation, Wageningen University.

Nederlof, E. S., Wennink, B. and Heemskerk, W. (2008). Access to agricultural services. *Background paper for the IFAD Rural Poverty Report 2011*. Amsterdam: Royal Tropical Institute.

Sartas, M., Schut, M., Thiele, G., Proietti, C. and Leeuwis, C. (2020). Scaling Readiness: Science and practice of an approach to enhance impact or research for development. *Agricultural Systems*, 183.

Schutz, A. and Luckmann, T. (1974). *The structures of the life-world*. Portsmouth: Heinemann Educational Books.

Sumberg, J. (ed.) (2017). *Agronomy for development: The politics of knowledge in agricultural research*. Milton Park: Routledge.

Tafesse, S., Damtew, E., Mierlo, B. van; Lie, R., Lemaga, B., Sharma, K., Leeuwis, C. and Struik, P. C. (2018). Farmers' knowledge and practices of potato disease management in Ethiopia. *NJAS - Wageningen Journal of Life Sciences*, 86–87, 25–38.

Tafesse, S., Lie, R., van Mierlo, B., Struik, P. C., Lemaga, B. and Leeuwis, C. (2020). Analysis of a monitoring system for bacterial wilt management by seed potato cooperatives in Ethiopia: Challenges and future directions. *Sustainability*, 12(9), 3580–3580.

Verouden, N. W., Van der Sanden, M. C. A. and Aarts, N. (2016). Silence in interdisciplinary research collaboration: Not everything said is relevant, not everything relevant is said. *Science as Culture*, 25(2), 264–288.

Vonk, R. (1990). *Prototyping: The effective use of CASE technology*. Hoboken: Prentice-Hall.

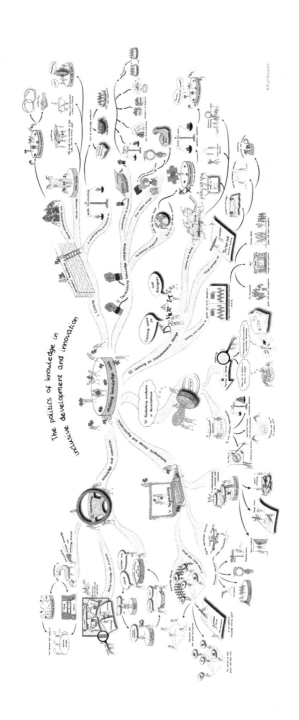

The politics of knowledge in inclusive development and innovation

INDEX

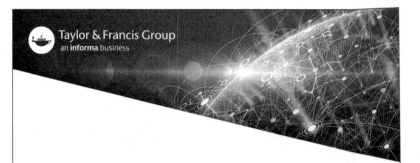